Lecture Notes in Computer Science

Lecture Notes in Artificial Intelligence **16685**

Founding Editor

Jörg Siekmann

The series Lecture Notes in Artificial Intelligence (LNAI) was established in 1988 as a topical subseries of LNCS devoted to artificial intelligence.

The series publishes state-of-the-art research results at a high level. As with the LNCS mother series, the mission of the series is to serve the international R & D community by providing an invaluable service, mainly focused on the publication of conference and workshop proceedings and postproceedings.

Giuseppina Andresini · Guy De Tré ·
Engelbert Mephu Nguifo · Mohand-Said Hacid ·
Annalisa Appice · Zbigniew W. Ras
Editors

Foundations of Intelligent Systems

28th International Symposium, ISMIS 2026 Lyon, France, July 22–24, 2026 Proceedings

Springer

Editors
Giuseppina Andresini
University of Bari Aldo Moro
Bari, Italy

Engelbert Mephu Nguifo
Université Clermont Auvergne
Aubière Cedex, France

Annalisa Appice
University of Bari Aldo Moro
Bari, Italy

Guy De Tré
Ghent University
Ghent, Belgium

Mohand-Said Hacid
Université Claude Bernard Lyon 1
Villeurbanne, France

Zbigniew W. Ras
University of North Carolina at Charlotte
Charlotte, NC, USA

ISSN 0302-9743 ISSN 1611-3349 (electronic)
Lecture Notes in Artificial Intelligence
ISBN 978-3-032-32642-3 ISBN 978-3-032-32643-0 (eBook)
https://doi.org/10.1007/978-3-032-32643-0

LNCS Sublibrary: SL7 – Artificial Intelligence

This Springer imprint is published by the registered company Springer Nature Switzerland AG
The registered company address is: Gewerbestrasse 11, 6330 Cham, Switzerland

Preface

This volume collects the papers selected for presentation at the 28th International Symposium on Methodologies for Intelligent Systems (ISMIS 2026), which took place in Lyon, France, during July 22–24, 2026. The symposium was organized by the Laboratoire d'InfoRmatique en Image et Systèmes d'information (LIRIS) of the Université Claude Bernard Lyon 1 & CNRS Lyon (France), in cooperation with the Computer Science Department of the University of Bari Aldo Moro, Bari (Italy), the department of Telecommunications and Information Processing (TELIN) of Ghent University (Belgium) and the Laboratoire d'Informatique, de Modélisation et d'Optimisation des Systèmes (LIMOS) of the Université Clermont Auvergne & CNRS (France).

ISMIS is a symposium series that started in 1986. Held twice every three years, ISMIS continues its tradition of being a unique venue for exchanging and discussing recent scientific advances in the development and analysis of methods for building intelligent systems. This year's symposium covered several main topics concerning "knowledge representation and formal reasoning", "generative models and representation learning", "reliability, safety and explainable AI", "time series and stream learning" and "AI for urban and environmental systems." More specifically, the first topic addresses neuro-symbolic models, temporal reasoning over hierarchical knowledge graphs, weighted argumentation frameworks, and the formalization of event-driven timelines. The second topic addresses deep generative models for multi-label machine learning, diffusion-based models, ensemble deep learning, and pattern discovery through dimensionality reduction. The third topic addresses adversarial approaches to malware detection, hallucination diagnosis in retrieval-augmented generation systems, and explanation techniques for predictions under missing data and for business process deviance management. The fourth topic addresses forecasting methods for additive manufacturing components, zero-shot learning for energy load forecasting, deep online learning for predictive process monitoring, and multi-timepoint data aggregation for quality-of-life deterioration in cancer immunotherapy. The fifth topic addresses indoor cellular coverage mapping using mobile robots, digital twins for adaptive smart-city simulation, and bioacoustic whale monitoring with distributed sensing systems. In addition, the 2026 edition of ISMIS also included a dedicated "Industry Session" offering a forum for exchanging ideas between leading researchers and industry practitioners, and encouraging industrial collaborations to build effective applications of various intelligent methods, algorithms, and tools related to Artificial Intelligence, covering several application areas, such as aviation incident report mining, intelligent agricultural decision support, carbon footprint assessment, and oncology rehabilitation.

With this broad vision, ISMIS 2026 aimed to contribute to the development of a new generation of intelligent systems capable of reasoning over complex knowledge structures, continuously learning from heterogeneous data streams, explaining their decisions transparently, and deploying responsibly in sensitive real-world sectors, including medicine, manufacturing, education, environmental monitoring, and smart cities.

ISMIS 2026 received 44 international paper submissions. After pre-screening by the program chairs 38 papers were sent to reviewers, applying a single-blind peer review process where each paper was carefully reviewed by at least three Program Committee (PC) members or external reviewers. Papers submitted to the "Industry Session" were subject to the same reviewing procedure as those submitted to the regular session. When a PC Chair was co-author of a paper, the other chairs managed its review process. After a rigorous reviewing process, 19 regular papers and 5 industrial papers were accepted for presentation at the conference and publication in this ISMIS 2026 proceedings volume.

The conference program included two invited keynote talks. João Gama, Professor Emeritus of the University of Porto (Portugal) gave a talk entitled "Data Streams: Learning and Forgetting". Sihem Amer-Yahia, of the Laboratoire d'Informatique de Grenoble (LIG), Université Grenoble Alpes (UGA,France), contributed with a talk entitled "From Dialogue to Decision: Orchestrating Agents for Conversational Data Exploration and Multi-Objective Optimization".

We would like to sincerely thank all the people who helped with the organization of this conference and made ISMIS 2026 a successful and exciting event. In particular, we would like to express our appreciation for the work of the ISMIS 2026 Program Committee members and external reviewers who helped to assure the high standard of accepted papers. We would like to thank all authors who contributed to ISMIS 2026. Without their high-quality submissions, the organization of the conference would not have been possible. We are grateful to the Steering Committee Chairs, Zbigniew Ras and Annalisa Appice, and the whole Steering Committee for their support in critical decisions concerning the organization of the event. We wish to express our thanks to the Local Organizing Committee Chair, Juba Agoun, and the whole organization team for their support and incredible work. We would like to express our gratitude to the organizers of the "Industry Session" at ISMIS 2026: Vincent Lemonde and Allel Hadjali and to our keynote speakers João Gama and Sihem Amer-Yahia for their valuable contribution to the conference program.

We believe that the proceedings of ISMIS 2026 will become a valuable source of references for your ongoing and future research activities.

May 2026

Giuseppina Andresini
Guy De Tré
Engelbert Mephu Nguifo
Mohand-Saïd Hacid
Annalisa Appice
Zbigniew Ras

Organization

General Chair

Mohand-Saïd Hacid	LIRIS, Université Claude Bernard Lyon 1, CNRS, France

Program Committee Chairs

Giuseppina Andresini	University of Bari Aldo Moro, Italy
Guy De Tré	Ghent University, Belgium
Engelbert Mephu Nguifo	Université Clermont Auvergne, France

Steering Committee

Annalisa Appice (Co-chair)	University of Bari Aldo Moro, Italy
Zbigniew Ras (Co-chair)	University of North Carolina at Charlotte, USA & Polish-Japanese Academy of Information Technology, Poland
Hanane Azzag	Sorbonne Paris Nord University, France
Michelangelo Ceci	University of Bari Aldo Moro, Italy
Alexander Felfernig	Graz University of Technology, Austria
Sergio Flesca	Università degli Studi della Calabria, Italy
Mohand-Said Hacid	Lyon 1 Université Claude Bernard, France
Allel Hadjali	ISAE-ENSMA - Poitiers, France
Denis Helic	Graz University of Technology, Austria
Nathalie Japkowicz	American University, USA
Janusz Kacprzyk	Polish Academy of Sciences, Poland
Gerhard Leitner	University of Klagenfurt, Austria
Jiming Liu	Hong Kong Baptist University, Hong Kong
Giuseppe Manco	ICAR-CNR, Italy
Elio Masciari	Università Federico II di Napoli, Italy
Martin Stettinger	Graz University of Technology, Austria

Program Committee

Fabrizio Angiulli	University of Calabria, Italy
Violaine Antoine	LIMOS, Université Clermont Auvergne, France
Annalisa Appice	University of Bari Aldo Moro, Italy
Hanane Azzag	Université Sorbonne Paris Nord, France
Sadok Ben Yahia	University of Southern Denmark, Denmark
Petr Berka	Prague University of Economics and Business, Czech Republic
Marenglen Biba	University of New York in Tirana, Albania
Jose Borges	University of Porto, Portugal
Gabriella Casalino	Università degli Studi di Bari Aldo Moro, Italy
Brice Chardin	ISAE-ENSMA, LIAS, France
Jianhua Chen	Louisiana State University, USA
Henning Christiansen	Roskilde University, Denmark
Roberto Corizzo	American University, USA
Annunziata D'Aversa	University of Bari Aldo Moro, Italy
Sarah Jane Delany	Technological University Dublin, Ireland
Wajdi Dhifli	University of Lille, France
Francesco M. Donini	Università della Tuscia, Italy
Issam Falih	LIMOS CNRS UMR 6158, France
Philippe Fournier-Viger	Shenzhen University, China
Naoki Fukuta	Shizuoka University, Japan
Paolo Garza	Politecnico di Torino, Italy
Martin Gebser	University of Klagenfurt, Austria
Mirsad Hadzikadic	University of North Carolina at Charlotte, USA
Allel Hadjali	LIAS/ENSMA, France
Sk. Imran Hossain	Khulna University of Engineering & Technology, Bangladesh
Dino Ienco	IRSTEA, France
Angelo Impedovo	NSA Italia s.r.l., Italy
Roberto Interdonato	CIRAD – UMR TETIS, France
Stéphane Jean	LISI/ENSMA and University of Poitiers, France
Matthias Klusch	DFKI, Germany
Mieczysław Kłopotek	Institute of Computer Science, Polish Academy of Sciences, Poland
Gerhard Leitner	University of Klagenfurt, Austria
Antoni Ligeza	AGH University of Science and Technology, Poland
Angelica Liguori	ICAR-CNR, Italy
Jerry Lonlac	IMT Nord Europe, France
Donato Malerba	University of Bari Aldo Moro, Italy

Giuseppe Manco	ICAR-CNR, Italy
Małgorzata Marciniak	Institute of Computer Science PAS, Poland
Elio Masciari	University of Naples Federico II, Italy
Amin Mesmoudi	Université de Poitiers, France
Mikhail Moshkov	King Abdullah University of Science and Technology, Saudi Arabia
Agnieszka Mykowiecka	Institute of Computer Science PAS & Polish-Japanese Academy of IT, Poland
Amedeo Napoli	LORIA Nancy, Université de Lorraine, France
Vincenzo Pasquadibisceglie	University of Bari Aldo Moro, Italy
Antonio Pellicani	University of Bari Aldo Moro, Italy
Ruggero G. Pensa	University of Turin, Italy
Jean-Marc Petit	INSA Lyon, France
Fabien Picarougne	LINA, University of Nantes, France
Gianvito Pio	University of Bari Aldo Moro, Italy
Giorgio Piras	University of Cagliari, Italy
Luca Piovesan	Università del Piemonte Orientale, Italy
Stefano Polimena	University of Bari Aldo Moro, Italy
Luigi Portinale	Università del Piemonte Orientale, Italy
Henryk Rybiński	Warsaw University of Technology, Poland
Hiroshi Sakai	Kyushu Institute of Technology, Japan
Abderrazak Sebaa	Université de Bejaia, Algeria
Monika Seisenberger	Swansea University, UK
Giancarlo Sperlì	University of Naples Federico II, Italy
Norbert Tsopze	Université de Yaoundé I, Cameroon
Herna Viktor	University of Ottawa, Canada
Alicja Wieczorkowska	Polish-Japanese Academy of Information Technology, Poland
David Wilson	University of North Carolina at Charlotte, USA
Yiyu Yao	University of Regina, Canada
Marcos Zampieri	George Mason University, USA
Gianluca Zaza	University of Bari Aldo Moro, Italy
Beata Zielosko	University of Silesia in Katowice, Poland
Tommaso Zoppi	University of Trento, Italy

Additional Reviewers

Jamie Duell
Nicolas Gutowski
Vito Nicola Losavio
Antonio Macaluso
Jay Paul Morgan
Simone Mungari
M. Saqib Nawaz

Invited Talks

Data Streams: Learning and Forgetting

João Gama
FEP – University of Porto and INESC TEC
jgama@fep.up.pt

Abstract. The increasing deployment of sensors, connected devices, and cyber-physical systems is generating continuous, high-speed data streams in dynamic, evolving environments. In such settings, learning systems must move beyond static models trained once on finite datasets, toward adaptive models that learn continuously, detect change, and forget outdated information.

This talk explores the role of learning and forgetting in data stream mining, with emphasis on real-time decision-making under limited computational resources. The first part presents a case study on interconnect bypass fraud detection in telecommunications. Traditional blacklist-based approaches are limited in their ability to detect new fraud patterns and adapt to behavioural changes. We discuss a data-driven online approach based on streaming algorithms, including Heavy Hitters and Hierarchical Heavy Hitters, and introduce a fast-forgetting extension of the Lossy Counting algorithm. Experimental results on large-scale call datasets show that forgetting improves the detection of recent abnormal activity while reducing memory usage and execution time.

The second part addresses rare-event explanation in industrial sensor streams. We present a neuro-symbolic architecture for real-time fault detection and explanation in air compressor units. The detection layer uses an LSTM autoencoder trained on normal behaviour, while the explanation layer learns online regression rules that map sensor inputs to reconstruction error. A Chebyshev-based sampling strategy focuses learning on rare, high-error observations. This architecture provides both global explanations through learned rule sets and local explanations through the rules triggered by individual anomalies.

Together, these examples illustrate how online learning, adaptive forgetting, and interpretable modelling can support robust, efficient, and explainable intelligence over data streams.

From Dialogue to Decision: Orchestrating Agents for Conversational Data Exploration and Multi-objective Optimization

Sihem Amer-Yahia
CNRS, Universitè Grenoble Alpes, Laboratoire d'Informatique de Grenoble (LIG)
Sihem.Amer-Yahia@univ-grenoble-alpes.fr

Abstract. Modern scientific discovery and decision-making necessitate agents capable of navigating both complex datasets and multifaceted, often conflicting, goal landscapes. This talk explores the intersection of conversational data exploration, an incremental process where agents help users articulate needs through data interaction, and multi-objective sequential decision making.

While traditional Reinforcement Learning (RL) has advanced task-specific agent training, we are witnessing a paradigm shift toward zero-shot orchestration. By leveraging a spectrum of techniques, from specialized RL policies to general-purpose Large Language Models (LLMs), we can reuse existing single-objective policies to solve complex multi-objective problems without training from scratch.

We will discuss empirical evidence from the field of Education showing that this orchestrated approach can achieve competitive Pareto quality while reducing computational cost. The talk concludes by examining open research questions regarding how LLM context richness and reflective foresight enable agents to bridge the gap between incremental data-driven insights and optimal sequential actions.

Contents

Reliability, Safety and Explainable AI

Industry Session

Time Series and Stream Data

AI for Urban and Environmental Systems

Knowledge Representation and Formal Reasoning

A Sub-Symbolic Model for the Geometric Intruder Task

Sara Damonte[2], Valentina Gliozzi[1](✉), Gian Luca Pozzato[1], and Alberto Valese[3]

[1] Dipartimento di Informatica, Università di Torino, Turin, Italy
{valentina.gliozzi,gianluca.pozzato}@unito.it
[2] IRCCS Azienda Ospedaliera Metropolitana, San Martino, Genova, Italy
[3] Dipartimento di Matematica, Università di Padova, Padua, Italy
alberto.valese@math.unipd.it

Abstract. Humans possess a unique ability to recognize and categorize geometric patterns. Cognitive neuroscience suggests this sensitivity may reflect a structured symbolic "Language of Thought." Recent findings challenge this symbolic-only account: similar sensitivity can emerge in large neural networks trained on massive visual data.

We propose a neuro-symbolic model showing that human sensitivity to geometric regularity can be explained by a small set of grounded geometric primitives, without invoking either a full symbolic grammar or large-scale statistical learning.

In a series of three simulations, we show that our model allows to explore which set of fundamental geometric features best explains the patterns of human behavior in a Geometric Intruder Task.

Keywords: Geometric reasoning · Neuro-Symbolic · Psychologically Plausible Neural Networks

1 Introduction

In Cognitive Science, a long-standing debate concerns the nature of mental representations implied in cognitive tasks. On one side are theories that posit a symbolic "Language of Thought" [8,17], consisting of symbolic primitives governed by combinatorial and recursive rules. These symbolic theories have been formalized in computational models and applied to domains such as spatial reasoning, numerical cognition, and concept learning [12,14,16,25]. On the other side are proposals that explain and model the same abilities without symbolic tools, emphasizing perceptual, distributed, or sub-symbolic representations [2,13,20,24].

This tension between symbolic and non-symbolic representations in human cognition overlaps with the debate in Artificial Intelligence about whether human-like knowledge and reasoning are best modeled by symbolic systems or by large-scale neural networks relying on statistical learning. Symbolic AI offers

G. Andresini et al. (Eds.): ISMIS 2026, LNAI 16685, pp. 3–12, 2027.
https://doi.org/10.1007/978-3-032-32643-0_1

explicit structure, compositionality and interpretability, whereas deep neural networks offer flexibility and powerful learning capabilities, often at the cost of transparency. Understanding whether higher-order intelligent behavior requires explicit symbolic representations, can emerge from statistical learning, or arises from structured representations grounded in neural processing remains a central question across both fields.

This debate has recently resurfaced in geometry, particularly in the Geometric Intruder Task [23], where symbolic explanations have been contrasted with large-scale neural models [5].

In this paper, we propose a third path and present a neuro-symbolic model showing that human sensitivity to geometric regularity can be explained by a small set of grounded geometric primitives—such as angles or parallel lines—without invoking a full symbolic Language of Thought. The proposed architecture is neuro-symbolic in that it combines a neural component for perceptual primitive detection with an explicit, structured representation of geometric features. While primitive extraction is performed by a neural network, the resulting features are encoded as discrete geometric properties that support structured comparison and intruder detection. The symbolic aspect of the model therefore resides in its representational layer rather than in a full combinatorial grammar.

Our approach is more parsimonious than symbolic grammars and more interpretable than large-scale deep networks.

The paper introduces a feature-based model of geometric regularity detection and shows that a small set of perceptual primitives can approximate human error patterns in the Geometric Intruder Task.

2 Theoretical Background

Humans exhibit sensitivity to geometric features that emerges early in life and is largely independent of formal education. Developmental and cross-cultural studies show that core geometric properties such as angles, symmetry, parallelism, and perpendicularity are available early and independently of formal schooling [1,4,6,7,9,10,15,21]. These findings suggest that geometric representations rely on early-emerging cognitive capacities rather than solely on formal instruction.

A recent study [23] tested adults (both mathematically educated French participants and Himba adults from a rural Namibian population with limited or no access to formal schooling), preschool children, and baboons in a Geometric Intruder Task requiring identification of an intruder shape among six quadrilaterals. Although the intruder was always defined by an identical amount of displacement of a single vertex, the results revealed a geometric regularity effect: detection was considerably easier when either the base shape or the intruder was a regular figure comprising right angles, parallelism, or symmetry rather than amore irregular shape. All human groups more easily detect intruders among regular shapes (e.g., squares, rectangles, parallelograms) than among irregular ones: this is the Geometric Regularity Effect. For French adults with a mathematical education the effect is shown in Fig. 1 taken from [23], where it can be observed that the error rate is lower for regular shapes and increases for irregular ones.

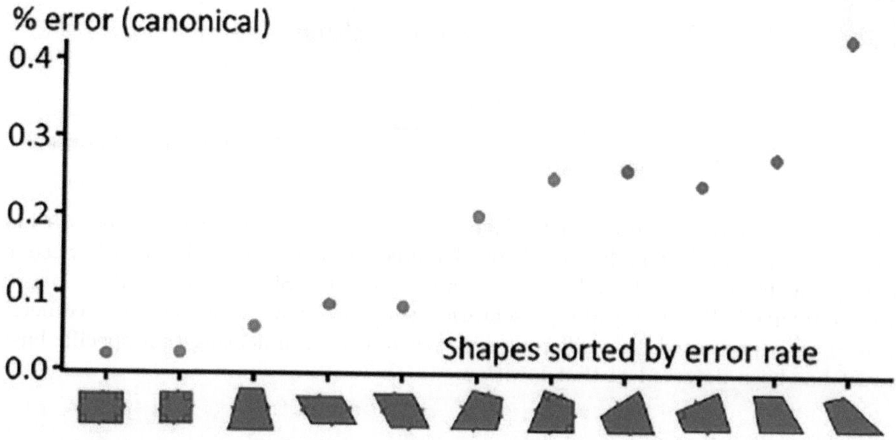

Fig. 1. Figure taken from [23] that displays adult human error (on the Y-axis) for the different shapes: rectangle, square, isoscele Trapezoid, parallelogram, losange, kite, right Kite, rusted Hinge, hinge, trapezoid, random quadrilater.

Baboons in contrast do not show the Geometric Regularity Effect, even after training, suggesting a qualitative difference in representational capacities.

Symbolic accounts interpret human performance as evidence for a Language of Thought for geometry, positing explicit representations of discrete geometric properties [22,23].

In contrast, recent work shows that very large pretrained neural networks can replicate the Geometric Regularity Effect through feature extraction [5], although their internal representations remain difficult to interpret.

The present work proposes an intermediate account. Rather than invoking a full combinatorial symbolic grammar or relying on massive end-to-end statistical learning, we test whether a small, explicitly represented set of geometric features (known to be salient from very early in human development [3,11,18]) suffices to approximate human error patterns in the task. The model proposed in the next section has therefore a double objective. First, it shows that the Geometric Regularity Effect can be simply explained by postulating an extreme sensitivity to some basic geometric features that are grounded and can be detected by a neural component in the input. Second, it shows that deep neural networks equipped with some basic filters built in might learn faster (e.g. with respect to [5]) to mimic human behavior in this task.

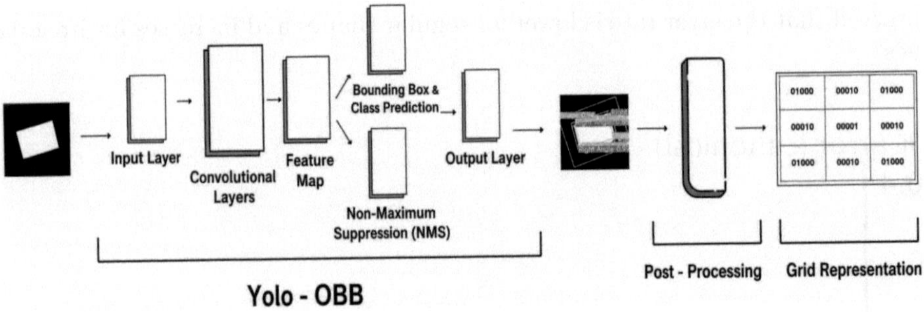

Fig. 2. Overall model. From Left to Right: First, geometric primitives (Angles- right, acute or obtuse- and Straight Lines) are detected by YOLO neural network. Second, more global features, as Parallelism, Symmetry and (in Simulation 3 only) Congruence are inferred. Third, a grid representation is formed, where the detected geometric features are represented by a different *perceptual symbol*, indicating that specific basic feature has been detected at that location.

3 The Model

The overall architecture is shown in Fig. 2. It follows a neuro-symbolic design: the neural component detects basic features in the input images, which are then mapped onto a grid representation that preserves their spatial arrangement. The detected features correspond to the features that previous experimental work has identified as salient in human geometric cognition, namely angles, straight lines, parallelism, symmetry, and congruence. This representation (the symbolic component of the model) is used to compute distances between geometric configurations and thereby identify the intruder.

The architecture consists of three stages.

3.1 Step 1: Local Primitive Detection

The input image is processed by a YOLOv8m-OBB network [19,26], pre-trained on COCO dataset and fine-tuned for 80 epochs on 300 geometric images (including the 11 quadrilaterals from [23]). YOLO is chosen for its efficiency and the OBB variant's ability to localize precisely rotated geometric shapes. It is used to identify within the input image *local* primitives (Angles: right, acute, obtuse; Straight Lines).

3.2 Step 2: Global Feature Inference

From the detected primitives, the model infers global features. Parallelism is computed by comparing the slopes of opposite sides; symmetry by testing candidate axes derived from pairs of parallel segments; and congruence by comparing the lengths of adjacent and opposite sides.

3.3 Step 3: Grid Representation

Detected features (both local and global) are mapped onto a 3×3 grid representation. Each cell encodes the presence or absence of detected features in that position, as shown in Figs. 3 and 4. This mapping reduces dimensionality while preserving spatial organization, producing a compact representation suitable for intruder detection.

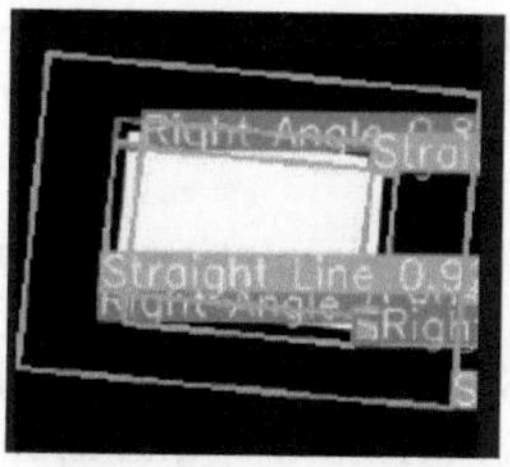

Fig. 3. Rectangle input image where basic features are detected by the YOLO component of the overall model (Step 1 and 2).

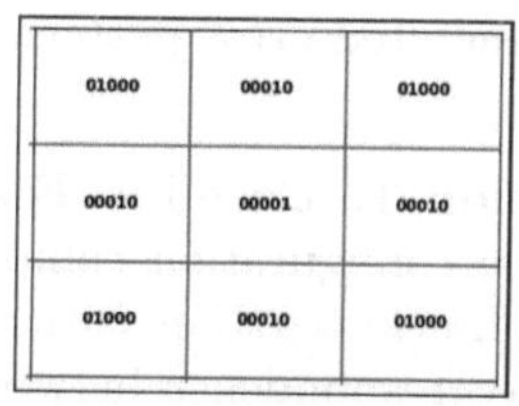

Fig. 4. Grid representation of the input figure out of detected basic features: right angles (01000) parallel lines (00010) vertical and horizontal. Symmetry (0001).

3.4 The Geometric Intruder Task

The Geometric Intruder Task is implemented by presenting the model with six figures: five are examples of a given shape, while one is an outlier, generated from a reference shape by modifying the position of the bottom-right vertex either along the bottom side or along a circle centered at the bottom-left vertex.

Following the steps outlined above, the model constructs a grid representation for each of the six figures. It then identifies the outlier as the figure that differs the most from the others—i.e., the one whose grid representation has the highest total Euclidean distance from all the others. For each grid G, the model computes its total Euclidean distance from the other five grids:

$$D(G) = \sum_i d(G, G_i).$$

where $d(G, G_i)$ denotes the Euclidean distance between the feature vectors associated with the two grids. The intruder is identified as the figure with the largest value of $D(G)$.

Overall, the model transforms each visual stimulus into a compact grid of experimentally grounded geometric features and identifies the intruder through comparison of these feature representations.

4 Experimental Results

Across three simulations, we progressively refined the feature set to determine which fundamental geometric properties best account for human performance in the intruder detection task.

In each simulation, the task was repeated for 100 iterations per each geometric class, and the mean error rate was computed for every class under consideration. The input figures presented to the model coincide with the figures used for humans by [23] (Fig. 1). This procedure allowed us to directly compare model-generated error patterns with those observed in human participants.

Simulation 1: Baseline Feature Set. In the first simulation, we adopted a baseline configuration composed of all local geometric features (Angles and Straight Lines) together with the global features Symmetry and Parallelism.

The correspondence between model and human errors was quantified using Pearson's correlation coefficient, yielding $r = 0.82$ and $r^2 = 0.67$.

As shown in Fig. 5, the model slightly overestimates errors while preserving their ordering.

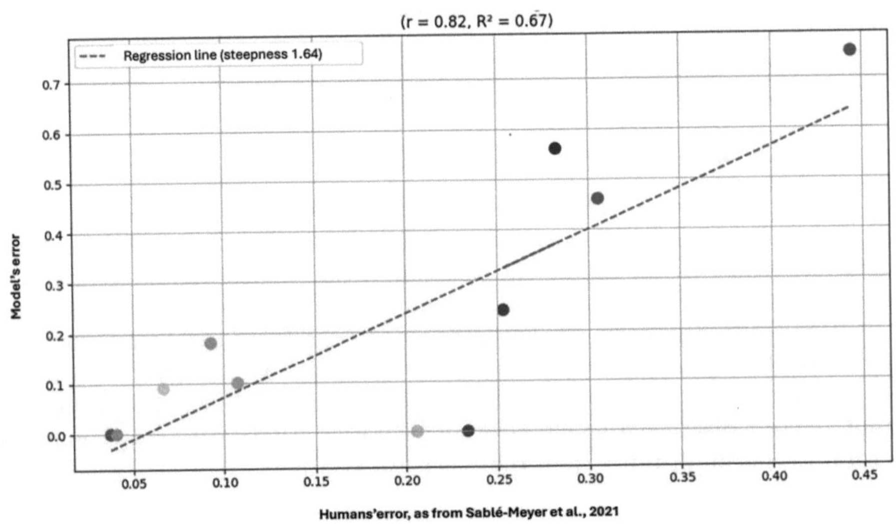

Fig. 5. Correlation between human and model error for the baseline configuration including Angles (right, obtuse, or acute), Symmetry, and Parallelism. The red line represents the fitted linear regression. Colors for different shapes as in Fig. 1. (Color figure online)

Simulation 2: Feature Weighting. We introduced feature-specific weights to examine the relative contribution of each geometric property.

Within this weighted framework, the optimal configuration assigned a weight of 3 to Symmetry, 1 to Parallelism, and 2 to Angles.

This configuration yielded $r = 0.84$ and $r^2 = 0.70$, slightly improving over Simulation 1.

This suggests that Symmetry and Angles contribute more strongly to human-like performance. Taken together, these findings indicate that differential weighting of geometric features contributes to a more precise representation of human error structure (Fig. 6).

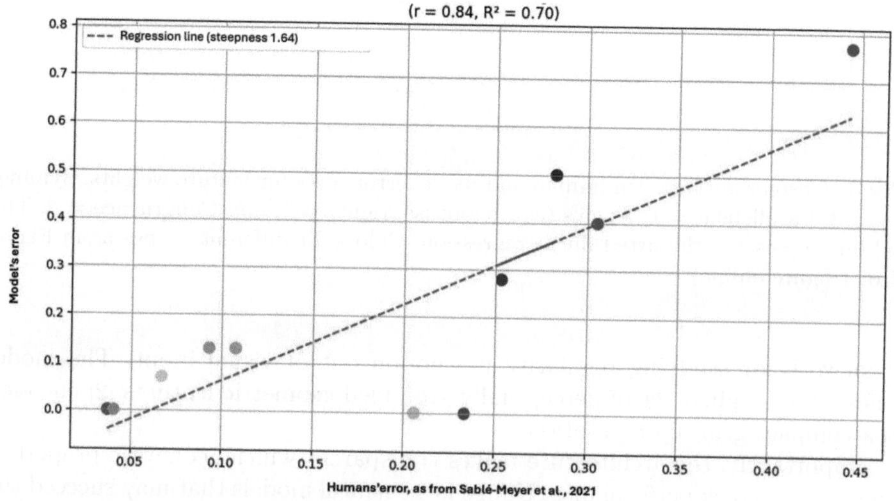

Fig. 6. Correlation between human and model error rates with feature weights: Symmetry = 3, Parallelism = 1, and Angles = 2. The red line represents the fitted linear regression. Colors for different shapes as in Fig. 1. (Color figure online)

Simulation 3: Feature Expansion. In the third simulation, we added Congruence, evaluated for adjacent and opposite edges.

The best configuration assigned weights: Symmetry = 3, Parallelism = 1, Angles = 1, and Congruence = 2.

This led to $r = 0.96$ and $r^2 = 0.92$, the best fit across simulations.

As shown in Fig. 7, the model slightly overestimates errors but preserves their ordering.

5 Discussion

We presented a simple and interpretable neuro-symbolic model designed to replicate human behavior in a Geometric Intruder Task [23], providing a concrete

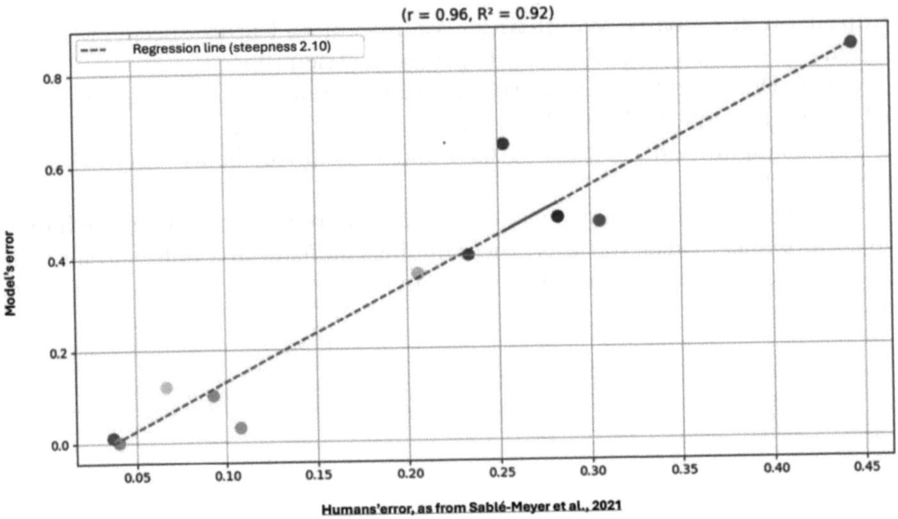

Fig. 7. Correlation between human and model error rates for feature weights: Symmetry = 3, Parallelism = 1, Angles (acute, obtuse, right) = 1, and Congruence = 2. The red line represents the fitted linear regression. Colors for different shapes as in Fig. 1. (Color figure online)

framework for studying regularity perception out of visual input. The model relies on an explicit set of perceptually grounded geometric features [2] encoded in a compact grid representation.

Importantly, the architecture makes transparent which geometric properties contribute to task performance. Unlike large neural models that may succeed the task without interpretability, the present framework enables controlled manipulation and systematic evaluation of specific features. This allows us to address questions such as which feature combinations best capture the error patterns of different populations (e.g., mathematically educated adults, preschool children, or uneducated groups).

Across the three simulations, results suggest that all basic features considered (Angle, Parallelism, Symmetry, and Congruence) may play a role in explaining human performance. These findings are consistent with the idea that humans are sensitive to these basic geometric properties from an early age: angles are categorized rapidly [11], parallelism and symmetry efficiently detected [3,18]. Our results suggest that some features may carry more weight than others, reflecting a hierarchy of perceptual salience that could be rooted in innate biases or shaped through early learning experiences—and that this hierarchy may differ across populations. In particular, Simulation 3, which provides the best fit with the performance of mathematically educated adults, indicates that Symmetry and Congruence are especially salient in supporting regularity detection for this group. This suggests that mathematically trained individuals may develop an enhanced sensitivity to forms of structural organization that involve global pattern coherence, potentially due to educational reinforcement or domain-specific expertise. On the contrary, other populations might use other geometric features.

6 Conclusions and Future Work

In this paper, we introduced a simple model of possible perceptual mechanisms underlying human sensitivity to geometric regularity, with an emphasis on feature-based transparency. The model isolates candidate geometric features that may drive this sensitivity and provides a bridge between neural perceptual encoding and explicit feature-level representation. Simulations 2 and 3 introduced feature-specific weights, which were manually specified; future work should test the robustness of the results across a range of values and explore ways of determining these weights automatically. Future work will also explore alternative perturbation strategies for generating intruders, in order to test whether the model–human correspondence generalizes beyond the specific vertex displacements used in the original task.

Future work will extend the framework in several directions:

1. Introducing graded (analog) feature representations to capture degrees of regularity (e.g., how close an angle approaches 90°, how parallel two lines are).
2. Expanding the feature set to more complex (potentially 3D) geometric shapes.
3. Systematically manipulating feature saliency to simulate different populations reported in [23].

A Appendix A: Code Availability

To ensure full reproducibility of our model, all the code used for training and testing, along with the complete dataset, are made available at the following public repository: https://osf.io/q76uy/?view_only=72e6765f0a0f44e1bb1c39635f7e2c4a The dataset used for both training and validation is included in the repository and organized to facilitate easy reproduction of our results.

References

1. Amalric, M., Dehaene, S.: Language and core knowledge in geometry. Trends Cogn. Sci. **21**(10), 703–715 (2017)
2. Barsalou, L.W.: Perceptual symbol systems. Behav. Brain Sci. **22**(4), 577–660 (1999)
3. Bertamini, M., Silvanto, J., Norcia, A.M., Makin, A.D.J., Wagemans, J.: The neural basis of visual symmetry and its role in mid- and high-level visual processing. Ann. N. Y. Acad. Sci. **1382**(1), 118–131 (2016)
4. Butterworth, B., Reeve, R., Reynolds, F., Lloyd, D.: Numerical thought with and without words. Oxford University Press (2008)

5. Campbell, D., Kumar, S., Giallanza, T., Griffiths, T.L., Cohen, J.D.: Human-like geometric abstraction in large pre-trained neural networks. arXiv preprint arXiv:2402.04203 (2024)
6. Dehaene, S., Izard, V., Pica, P., Spelke, E.: Core knowledge of geometry in an amazonian indigene group. Science **311**(5759), 381–384 (2006)
7. Dillon, M.R., Huang, Y., Spelke, E.S.: Young children's use of geometry to reorient in an open environment. Dev. Sci. **22**(4), e12831 (2019)
8. Fodor, J.: The Language of Thought. Harvard University Press (1975)
9. Izard, V., Pica, P., Spelke, E., Dehaene, S.: Development of intuitions about geometry: the case of parallelism. Dev. Sci. **14**(6), 1090–1098 (2011)
10. Izard, V., Pica, P., Spelke, E.S., Dehaene, S.: Flexible intuitions of euclidean geometry in an amazonian indigene group. Proc. Natl. Acad. Sci. **105**(25), 9136–9141 (2008)
11. Kim, I., Spelke, E.S.: Infants' sensitivity to effects of gravity on visible object motion. J. Exp. Psychol. Hum. Percept. Perform. **18**(2), 385–393 (1992)
12. Lake, B.M., Salakhutdinov, R., Tenenbaum, J.B.: Human-level concept learning through probabilistic program induction. Science **350**(6266), 1332–1338 (2015)
13. LeCun, Y., Bengio, Y., Hinton, G.: Deep learning. Nature **521**, 436–444 (2015)
14. Newell, A., Simon, H.A.: Computer science as empirical inquiry: symbols and search. Commun. ACM **19**(3), 113–126 (1976)
15. Pica, P., Lemer, C., Izard, V., Dehaene, S.: Exact and approximate arithmetic in an amazonian indigene group. Science **306**(5695), 499–503 (2004)
16. Pylyshyn, Z.W.: Computation and Cognition: Toward a Foundation for Cognitive Science. MIT Press (1984)
17. Quilty-Dunn, J., Porot, N., Mandelbaum, E.: The best game in town: the reemergence of the language-of thought hypothesis across the cognitive sciences. Behav. Brain Sci. **46** (2023)
18. Quinn, P.C.: Category representation in young infants. Curr. Dir. Psychol. Sci. **11**(2), 66–70 (2002)
19. Redmon, J., Divvala, S., Girshick, R., Farhadi, A.: You only look once: unified, real-time object detection. In: Proceedings of the IEEE Conference on Computer Vision and Pattern Recognition, pp. 779–788 (2016)
20. Rumelhart, D.E., McClelland, J.L., Group, P.R.: Parallel Distributed Processing: Explorations in the Microstructure of Cognition. MIT Press (1986)
21. Sablé-Meyer, M., Amalric, M., Dehaene, S.: Geometric intuition in an amazonian indigenous group. Cognition **210**, 104592 (2021)
22. Sablé-Meyer, M., Ellis, K., Tenenbaum, J., Dehaene, S.: A language of thought for the mental representation of geometric shapes. Cogn. Psychol. **139** (2022)
23. Sablé-Meyer, M., Fagot, J., Caparos, S., van Kerkoerle, T., Amalric, M., Dehaene, S.: Sensitivity to geometric shape regularity in humans and baboons: a putative signature of human singularity. Proc. Natl. Acad. Sci. **118**(16) (2021)
24. Smolensky, P.: On the proper treatment of connectionism. Behav. Brain Sci. **11**(1), 1–23 (1988)
25. Tenenbaum, J.B., Kemp, C., Griffiths, T.L., Goodman, N.D.: How to grow a mind: statistics, structure, and abstraction. Science **331**(6022), 1279–1285 (2011)
26. Terven, J., Córdova-Esparza, D.M., Romero-González, J.A.: A comprehensive review of yolo architectures in computer vision: from yolov1 to yolov8 and yolo-nas. Mach. Learn. Knowl. Extract. **5**(4), 1680–1716 (2023)

T-HiGra: Temporal Reasoning over Hierarchical Knowledge Graphs for Time-Constrained Open-Domain QA

Bao Le[1,2], Anh Nguyen[1,2], Hung Luu[1,2], and Tho Quan[1,2](✉)

[1] URA Research Group, Ho Chi Minh University of Technology (HCMUT), Ho Chi Minh City, Vietnam
{bao.lequoc1010,anh.nguyenkhmtk22,lchung.sdh231,qttho}@hcmut.edu.vn

[2] Vietnam National University Ho Chi Minh City, Ho Chi Minh City, Vietnam

Abstract. Temporal information is pivotal to real-world events, where events, roles, and relationships are inherently dynamic over time. Neglecting temporal structures in retrieval-augmented systems leads to chronological misalignment of evidence, ultimately compromising the accuracy of fact-checking for time-sensitive data. We present **T-HiGra**, a temporal graph RAG framework that treats time as a first-class signal across hierarchical knowledge graphs and the retrieval pipeline for open-domain, multi-hop question answering. T-HiGra **(i)** attaches structured temporal information data and provenance to entities, relations, passages and edges; **(ii)** preserves historical fidelity via alias validity windows during entity merging; and **(iii)** applies an adaptive time-aware ranking method that jointly combines temporal proximity and semantic similarity. We evaluate T-HiGra on a benchmark for time-sensitive questions, and report multi-facet RAG diagnostics using LLM-as-judge evaluators alongside traditional QA metrics. Against strong baselines (BM25, HippoRAG,...), we achieve the highest correctness (76.21%) while producing competitive retrieval relevance (77.04%) and improved temporal consistency, demonstrating that explicit temporal modeling reduces time-misalignment errors without degrading atemporal performance.

Keywords: Graph RAG · Temporal-Aware · Multi-hop QA

1 Introduction

Open-domain multi-hop question answering (QA) requires systems to locate, aggregate, and reason over evidence from multiple documents to answer compositional questions. While benchmark datasets and methods have driven progress in document retrieval, ranking, and answer composition [8]. However, many real-world facts are time-dependent, so semantically relevant evidence may still be chronologically invalid for temporally constrained queries. Recent graph-based

G. Andresini et al. (Eds.): ISMIS 2026, LNAI 16685, pp. 13–23, 2027.
https://doi.org/10.1007/978-3-032-32643-0_2

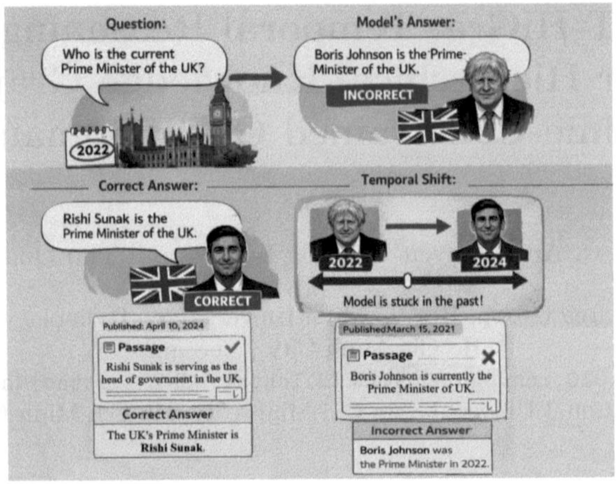

Fig. 1. Illustration of Temporal Misalignment in Time-related Question Answering.

retrieval methods [3] improve multi-step evidence discovery by exploiting entity-relation structure, but most Graph-RAG implementations and iterative reasoning methods still treat time too coarsely, which can cause temporal misalignment and miss valid historical evidence or evolving aliases (Fig. 1).

These limitations motivate a framework that treats time as a first-class property of graph elements and incorporates temporal relevance into structural and semantic ranking. T-HiGra[1] addresses this by **(i)** constructing a temporal hierarchical knowledge graph with interval annotations, **(ii)** using a dual-stage temporal-aware retriever with time filtering, misalignment pruning, and adaptive fusion, and **(iii)** evaluating the system on TimeQA to show improved correctness and groundedness over strong baselines.

2 Related Works

2.1 Temporal Information Extraction and Retrieval

Time-aware QA requires understanding temporal information in text and queries. Prior surveys highlight methods for identifying timestamps, intervals, and event order, as well as approaches that integrate symbolic reasoning to construct coherent event timelines, while noting limitations in jointly modeling diverse temporal cues [10,12]. In a temporal information retrieval study [1], the importance of incorporating time into both queries and documents is emphasized to improve relevance, while addressing challenges such as temporal ambiguity and alignment with query constraints. Together, these works underscore the need for models that distinguish facts by validity periods and handle evolving information.

---

[1] Code and data are available at: https://github.com/10baole/T-HiGra-Temporal-Hierarchical-Knowledge-Graphs.

2.2 Graph-Augmented QA

Retrieval-Augmented Generation (RAG) has become a key paradigm for open-domain QA, where a retriever fetches relevant evidence from external data to improve large language models (LLMs) answers [5]. Graph-based extensions (GraphRAG) frameworks extend RAG by leveraging the relational structure of graphs to capture entity relationships that embedding-based search misses [15]. In practice, Traditional KG construction often relies on entity–relation extraction. Early systems like HippoRAG [9] utilized OpenIE-style methods to populate relational structures; NodeRAG [16] and HiRAG [7] have transitioned to leveraging LLMs to generate more descriptive and structured graphs from textual data. Approaches like RAPTOR [14] manage large corpora by building hierarchical structures through passage clustering.

2.3 Graph RAG Retrieval

Current retrieval methodologies generally bifurcate into similarity-based and graph-based strategies. A critical limitation of purely structural algorithms or similarity-embedding systems is their inability to capture fine-grained semantic cues, often struggling with high-degree nodes that function as high-centrality hubs. Conversely, triplet-driven retrieval like T2RAG [4] can reduce context noise but risks omitting broader evidence necessary for multi-hop reasoning. MoDeGraph [13] addresses this challenge by generating a multi-hop dependency graph from the question to guide an LLM, decomposing complex queries into entities and relations to enable coherent reasoning and improve multi-hop QA accuracy.

2.4 Temporal Graph RAG

Temporal GraphRAG methods improve retrieval consistency by adding time awareness to the knowledge graph. T-GRAG [11] uses a multi-stage retrieval pipeline by assigned timestamps to facts (each edge) and splits the KG into temporal "slices" (temporal subgraphs) to answer time-anchored queries. Similarly, TG-RAG [6] explicitly models time by representing the corpus as a bi-level graph: a knowledge graph with timestamped relations and a hierarchical time graph of periods. For each time node, it generates multi-granularity summaries and retrieves period-specific information. In general, these methods constrain retrieval to time-valid evidence to improve factual and temporal accuracy.

3 Temporal Knowledge Graph Construction

We propose **T-HiGra**, a bi-layer hierarchical knowledge graph that embeds temporal dimensions into both graph schema and retrieval pipeline. Unlike standard HKGs focused on semantic structure, T-HiGra supports time-aware reasoning to reduce misalignment and improve retrieval precision in dynamic settings (Fig. 2).

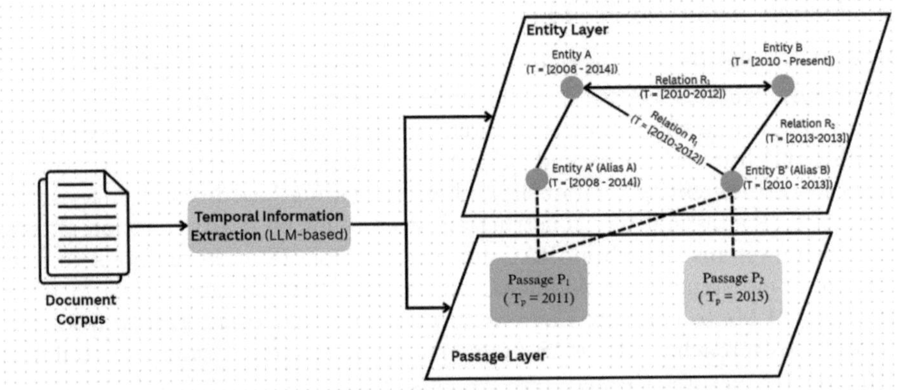

Fig. 2. Construction Pipeline of Temporal Hierarchical Knowledge Graph (T-HiGra)

3.1 Graph Construction and Temporal Fields

Extraction and Coreference Resolution. Given a corpus of passages P, we first apply coreference resolution to obtain a refined corpus P'. For each passage $p_i \in P'$, we perform entity and relation extraction using a Large Language Model (LLM), yielding a tuple (E_i, R_i), where E_i is the set of entities and R_i is the set of relations identified in p_i. These sets are aggregated across all passages to construct the global entity and relation sets: $\mathcal{E} = \bigcup_{p_i \in P'} E_i$ and $\mathcal{R} = \bigcup_{p_i \in P'} R_i$

Temporal Entity–Relation Schema. Each entity e in the set of all entities E is represented by a tuple: $e = (id_e, N_e, A_e, D_e, T_e, V_e)$, where: id_e is a unique identifier, N_e is the canonical name, A_e is the set of aliases, D_e is a textual description, T_e is the set of types, V_e is the temporal validity interval $V_e = (t_{\text{start}}, t_{\text{end}})$, which specifies the time span during which the entity (or a particular alias) is valid. Similarly, each relation $r \in R$ is defined as: $r = (id_s, N_r, id_t, V_r)$, where id_s and id_t denote the source and target entities, N_r is the relation label, and V_r is the validity interval of the relation. This schema preserves aliases and temporal scopes, which are essential for downstream alignment and retrieval.

3.2 Entity Merging and Linking

Entity Merging. The entity alignment phase performs a dual-stage deduplication process to resolve disparate references to the same real-world entity. Initially, exact-match merging is performed, where two entities $e_i, e_j \in E$ are merged if they share a common name or alias within their nomenclature set $S_e = \{N_e\} \cup A_e$ with the merging condition $S_{e_i} \cap S_{e_j} \neq \emptyset$. To address non-identical aliases (e.g., abbreviated names) or ambiguous mentions, we perform embedding-based clustering: $C = \text{Cluster}(E, \phi, \tau)$, where ϕ is the embedding function and τ is the similarity threshold. Each cluster is then reviewed by a Large Language Model (LLM) using names, aliases, types, and descriptions to determine final merges.

Entity Linking. To enhance graph connectivity and coverage, we perform iterative linking at both entity and passage levels. For Entity-level Linking, we infer missing relations between semantically similar but structurally disconnected entities. By using a process similar to semantic merging, we first cluster the refined entities and use Large Language Model (LLM) to predict new, high-confidence relations. Simultaneously, with Entity-Passage Linking, for each passage $p \in P$, we establish a link (e, p) only if that entity is not among top-K common words and its frequency is below threshold θ. Each passage is assigned a primary timestamp t_p inferred from its content, which enables time-aware retrieval by supporting both point-in-time (year 2010) and interval annotations (from 2008 to 2014).

3.3 Temporal Information Extraction

Time to Entities and Relations. We implement automated temporal expression detection, normalize them into standardized intervals, and attach them to the corresponding entities and relations using a combination of NLP-based normalization and LLM-assisted annotation. For each extracted entity/relation in passage p, we assign a validity interval either from the passage-level or proximal temporal expressions. When explicit temporal indicators are missing, we preserves graph integrity by imputing the passage's document-level default time.

Temporal-Aware Validity Tracking. During semantic clustering and entity merging, each alias a is assigned a validation interval $V_a = (t_a^{\text{start}}, t_a^{\text{end}})$. Aliases are merged only when their validity intervals overlap or when the LLM identifies strong co-reference evidence. If multiple aliases correspond to different time periods of the same real-world entity, we represent both aliases on the same entity while preserving their individual validity intervals.

4 Temporal-Aware Retrieval

Our retrieval algorithm ranks the most relevant graph relations and passages for a given query q in a sequential pipeline. It combines structural connectivity, semantic relevance, and temporal modeling as shown in Fig. 3.

4.1 Query Intent Detection

To regulate the influence of temporal signals, we introduce a query intent detection module that estimates how strongly a query depends on time. Rather than treating all queries uniformly, we adjust the weight of temporal evidence based on user intent. Queries are classified into 4 mutually exclusive intent categories:

1. **Explicit temporal queries:** contain specific time expressions (years, dates, or intervals). These are assigned a high signal, retrieval and ranking should prioritize evidence with validity intervals matching the specified time.

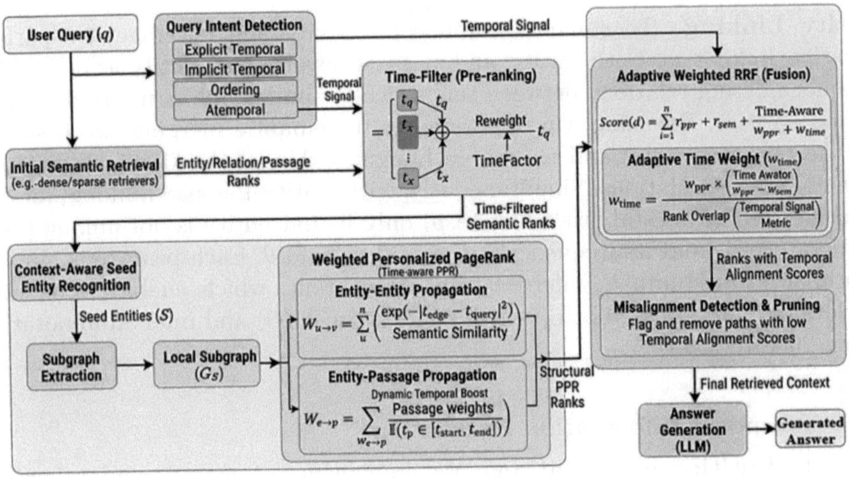

Fig. 3. Overview of Temporal-Aware Retrieval and Adaptive Fusion Framework.

2. **Implicit temporal queries:** refer to time through events or periods. These receive a moderate signal, reflecting the need for temporal alignment while accounting for potential ambiguity in temporal boundaries.
3. **Ordering/Sequence queries:** seek a temporal ordering between entities or events. These treated as high signal, emphasizing relative consistency.
4. **Atemporal queries.** Queries involve general facts or timeless knowledge. These receive a low signal to avoid overemphasizing time information.

4.2 Time-Filtering (Pre-ranking)

When a query q carries temporal constraints (explicit year, relative time reference, or a temporal intent detected by the Query Intent classifier), we apply a Time-Filter that prunes graph components before similarity ranking. If q specifies an explicit point t_q or interval $[t_q^{\text{start}}, t_q^{\text{end}}]$, we use a Gaussian kernel to compute a temporal relevance factor for each passage/edge/node element (x):

$$\text{TimeFactor}(x) = \exp\left(-\frac{(t_{\text{center}}(x) - t_q)^2}{2\sigma^2}\right), \tag{1}$$

where σ controls acceptable time spread and $t_{\text{center}}(x)$ is the midpoint of element's validity interval $(t_q^{\text{start}}, t_q^{\text{end}})$. If x has no explicit time, we assign a default fallback $\gamma \in (0, 1]$ to ensure permissive retrieval rather than hard pruning. For elements lacking a t_{end} (ongoing events or open intervals), we treat the interval as extending to the current year. For interval queries, TimeFactor(x) is taken as the overlap fraction between the query interval and x's validity interval.

4.3 Time-Weighted Personalized PageRank

We adapt Personalized PageRank (PPR) to integrate temporal edge relevance and semantic relation similarity. For unweighted adjacency transition probability, we use a normalized edge weight $w_{u\to v}$ that combines temporal proximity and semantic similarity:

$$\widetilde{w}_{u\to v} = \alpha \cdot \exp\left(-\frac{(t_{\text{edge}} - t_q)^2}{2\sigma^2}\right) + (1-\alpha)\cdot \text{CosineSimilarity}\big(e_{\text{rel}}, q\big), \quad (2)$$

where t_{edge} is the temporal center of the edge's validity interval, e_{rel} is a learned embedding for the relation/triplet context, q and t_q is the query embedding and time, and $\alpha \in [0,1]$ balances time with semantic similarity. Row-normalize $\widetilde{w}$ to obtain w and form the transition matrix M. The PPR iteration becomes:

$$\mathbf{p}_t = \alpha_{\text{PPR}} M^\top \mathbf{p}_{t-1} + (1-\alpha_{\text{PPR}})\,\boldsymbol{\pi}, \quad (3)$$

where the personalization vector $\boldsymbol{\pi}$ is initialized over seed entities and optionally time-weighted by TimeFactor. This weighted PPR favors nodes connected through temporally relevant edges and semantically similar relations.

4.4 Entity-to-Passage Weighting: Dynamic Temporal Boost

We assign dynamic weights to entity–passage links to favor passages whose timestamps lie within the query window:

$$w_{e\to p} = \text{TF}-\text{IDF}(e,p)\cdot\big(1+\beta_{boost}\cdot \mathbf{1}_{t_p\in[t_q^{\text{start}},t_q^{\text{end}}]}\big), \quad (4)$$

where $\mathbf{1}.$ is the indicator that passage time t_p lies within the query window; TF-IDF(e, p) represents the specificity of entity e within passage p relative to its frequency across the entire corpus. The parameter $\beta_{boost} > 0$ to control temporal boost and $\beta = 0$ when the query time is absent.

4.5 Misalignment Detection and Pruning

We introduce a misalignment detector that flags subgraphs and paths whose dominant temporal mass conflicts with the query time. For a candidate path P (set of elements $x \in P$), we define the average alignment score and paths with $\text{Align}(P) < \tau_{\text{align}}$ are demoted or pruned to avoid hallucinations.

$$\text{Align}(P) = \frac{1}{|P|}\sum_{x\in P}\text{TimeFactor}(x). \quad (5)$$

4.6 Adaptive Weighted Reciprocal Rank Fusion (RRF)

We fuse three complementary ranked lists: **(i)** structural PPR ranking (r_{ppr}), **(ii)** semantic ranking (r_{sem}), and **(iii)** time-aware ranking (r_{time}), using an adaptive weighted Reciprocal Rank Fusion that accounts for the query's temporal intent and rank overlap between components. For a candidate document d, we define the fused score as a weighted sum of reciprocal-rank terms:

$$\text{Score}(d) = w_{\text{ppr}} \cdot \frac{1}{k + r_{\text{ppr}}(d)} + w_{\text{sem}} \cdot \frac{1}{k + r_{\text{sem}}(d)} + w_{\text{time}} \cdot \frac{1}{k + r_{\text{time}}(d)}, \quad (6)$$

where $r_{\cdot}(d)$ is the 1-based rank of d in the corresponding list, $k > 0$ is a stabilizing constant (prevents domination by rank-1 documents), and the weights $w_{\text{ppr}}, w_{\text{sem}}, w_{\text{time}}$ are normalized so that $w_{\text{ppr}} + w_{\text{sem}} + w_{\text{time}} = 1$.

Adaptive Time Weight. Rather than using a fixed time weight, we compute a query-specific weight to strengthen time influence when the query is temporally grounded, and reduce redundancy when temporal and structural signals overlap:

$$w_{\text{time}} = \alpha_f \cdot \text{TemporalSignal}(q) + \beta_f \cdot (1 - \text{OverlapMetric}(r_{\text{ppr}}, r_{\text{time}})), \quad (7)$$

- TemporalSignal$(q) \in [0, 1]$ is the scalar output of the Query Intent Detector.
- OverlapMetric $\in [0, 1]$ is a normalized rank-similarity metric (use Kendall-τ distance scaled to $[0, 1]$) measuring how similar PPR and time rankings; high overlap reduces the second term to avoid double-counting the same signal.
- α_f and β_f are fusion hyperparameters tuned on a held-out validation set to balance explicit intent versus the redundancy of structural signals.

Before fusion we normalize each component's ranking to ensure consistent ordering and assign a large rank to missing documents. The adaptive RRF then balances structural, semantic, and temporal evidence according to the query.

5 Experimental Setup and Evaluation

5.1 Datasets

We evaluate *T-HiGra* on ***TimeQA: Time-Sensitive Question Answering*** [2] benchmark, a time-sensitive QA dataset designed to test sensitivity to chronological shifts and temporal reasoning. The dataset contains 20,000 question–answer pairs covering about 5,500 time-evolving facts across 70 relations. It is built following a multi-stage pipeline through fact mining from Wikidata, alignment to Wikipedia passages using hyperlink matching and TF–IDF scoring, and human verification to refine noisy matches and temporal boundaries.

5.2 Metrics

We adopt an *LLM-as-a-judge* evaluation protocol following the ***LangChain RAG***[2] guideline for a more robust assessment. The evaluation decomposes RAG behavior into four complementary evaluation axes that measure the relationship between the question, the retrieved context, and the generated response.

1. **Correctness (Response vs. Reference).** Measures factual accuracy of the generated answer relative to the ground-truth (reference) answer.
2. **Relevance (Response vs. Input).** Assesses how effectively the generated response addresses user's query (regardless of matching a gold reference).
3. **Groundedness (Response vs. Retrieved).** Measures how responses aligns with retrieved documents, ensuring faithfulness and detecting hallucinations.
4. **Retrieval Relevance (Retrieved vs. Input).** Quantifies the quality of the retrieval phase by judging whether the retrieved documents contain relevant semantic content or keywords for the question.

5.3 Baselines

We compare our method to the following systems, all implemented are tuned with identical generator models and prompt templates to return the same number of candidate passages per query to isolate the effect of ranker or temporal modeling:

1. **Simple Methods:** *Parametric* (only LLM without retrieved context), *BM25* (sparse lexical retriever), *Dense Retriever* (embedding similarity), and *Hybrid Retriever* (BM25 and Dense combined) as basic approaches.
2. **Single-Step Reasoning Graph Methods:** *HippoRAG* [9], and *T-GRAG* [11], as recent graph-based retrieval and time-aware variants methods.

5.4 Experimental Results

Overall Performance. Table 1 summarizes the performance of our model and baselines across the evaluation suite. As shown, **T-HiGra** achieves the best overall performance on correctness, relevance, and groundedness, with 76.25% correctness, 74.81% relevance, and 60.14% groundedness. These results indicate that explicit temporal modeling improves answer accuracy, better addresses the query, and reduces unsupported outputs. For retrieval relevance, T-HiGra reaches 86.02%, which is lower than Hybrid (90.74%) and BM25 (89.96%), but remains competitive while offering stronger temporal consistency. Overall, the results suggest that T-HiGra provides a better trade-off between retrieval quality and temporal alignment for time-constrained QA.

[2] Evaluate a RAG application. Available: https://docs.langchain.com/langsmith/evaluate-rag-tutorial.

Table 1. Performance comparison between T-HiGra and baseline methods.

Model	Correctness	Relevance	Groundedness	Retrieval Relevance
Ours	**76.25%**	**74.81%**	**60.14%**	86.02%
Parametric	33.74%	37.04%	0.00%	0.00%
BM25	70.00%	70.97%	43.85%	89.96%
Dense	61.67%	72.22%	42.14%	84.95%
Hybrid	65.69%	71.11%	46.59%	**90.74%**
HippoRAG2	63.84%	74.04%	35.00%	76.32%
T-GRAG	75.88%	73.52%	56.85%	82.18%

6 Conclusion

We presented **T-HiGra**, a temporal hierarchical knowledge graph framework for time-constrained open-domain multi-hop QA. By propagating temporal validity through graph construction and retrieval, T-HiGra reduces chronological misalignment and improves answer reliability. Experiments on TimeQA show the best correctness and groundedness among strong baselines, while maintaining competitive retrieval relevance. Future work will focus on more robust temporal extraction and iterative reasoning for conflict resolution.

Acknowledgments. This research is conducted under Contract No. 71/2024/HĐ-QKHCN and is funded by the Department of Science and Technology of Ho Chi Minh City. We also acknowledge Ho Chi Minh City University of Technology (HCMUT), VNU-HCM, for supporting this study.

References

1. Campos, R., Dias, G., Jorge, A.M., Jatowt, A.: Survey of temporal information retrieval and related applications. ACM Comput. Surv. **47**(2) (2014)
2. Chen, W., Wang, X., Wang, W.Y.: A dataset for answering time-sensitive questions. In: Thirty-fifth Conference on Neural Information Processing Systems Datasets and Benchmarks Track (2021)
3. Edge, D., Trinh, H., Cheng, N., Bradley: from local to global: a graph rag approach to query-focused summarization. arXiv preprint arXiv:2404.16130 (2024)
4. Gong, S., Tang, X., Yang, C.: Beyond chunks and graphs: retrieval-augmented generation through triplet-driven thinking. CoRR arxiv:2508.02435 (2025)
5. Han, H., Wang, Y., Shomer, H., Guo, K., Ding, J.: Lei: Retrieval-augmented generation with graphs. arXiv preprint arXiv:2501.00309 (2024)
6. Han, J., Cheung, A., Wei: Rag meets temporal graphs: time-sensitive modeling and retrieval for evolving knowledge. arXiv preprint arXiv:2510.13590 (2025)
7. Huang, H., et al.: Retrieval-augmented generation with hierarchical knowledge. In: Findings of the Association for Computational Linguistics: EMNLP 2025, pp. 6044–6060. Association for Computational Linguistics, Suzhou (2025)

8. Izacard, G., Grave, E.: Leveraging passage retrieval with generative models for open domain question answering. In: 16th Conference of the European Chapter of the Association for Computational Linguistics: Main Volume, pp. 874–880 (2021)
9. Jimenez Gutierrez, B., Shu, Y., Gu, Y., Yasunaga, M., Su, Y.: Hipporag: neurobiologically inspired long-term memory for large language models. Adv. Neural. Inf. Process. Syst. **37**, 59532–59569 (2024)
10. Leeuwenberg, A., Moens, M.F.: A survey on temporal reasoning for temporal information extraction from text (extended abstract). In: Proceedings of the Twenty-Ninth International Joint Conference on Artificial Intelligence (2021)
11. Li, D., Niu, Y., Ai, Y.: Zou: T-grag: a dynamic graphrag framework for resolving temporal conflicts and redundancy in knowledge retrieval. In: Proceedings of the 33rd ACM International Conference on Multimedia, pp. 11880–11889 (2025)
12. Lim, C., Jeong, Y., Choi, H.: Survey of temporal information extraction. J. Inf. Process. Syst. **15**, 931–956 (2019)
13. Oruche, R., Dmonte, A., Seth, V., Zeng: disentangling complex questions in LLMs via multi-hop dependency graphs. In: Proceedings of the 34th ACM International Conference on Information and Knowledge Management, pp. 2243–2252 (2025)
14. Sarthi, P., Abdullah, S., Tuli, A., Khanna, S., Goldie, A., Manning, C.D.: Raptor: recursive abstractive processing for tree-organized retrieval. In: The Twelfth International Conference on Learning Representations (2024)
15. Xiang, Z., Wu, C., Zhang, Q., Chen, S., Hong, Z.: When to use graphs in RAG: a comprehensive analysis for graph retrieval-augmented generation. In: The Fourteenth International Conference on Learning Representations (2026)
16. Xu, T., Zheng, H., Li, C., Chen, H., Liu, Y.: Noderag: structuring graph-based rag with heterogeneous nodes. arXiv preprint arXiv:2504.11544 (2025)

An Attack/Support-Aware Weight Composition Strategy for Bipolar Weighted Argumentation Frameworks

Stefano Ferilli(✉)

University of Bari, 70125 Bari, BA, Italy
stefano.ferilli@uniba.it

Abstract. Argumentation is the inferential strategy aimed at coping with inconsistent knowledge, e.g. in order to justify or dismiss contrasting positions in a discussion. Abstract Argumentation, specifically, is based on a graph model where nodes are claims and arcs denote relationships between pair of claims. In some extensions of the original, basic framework, relationships may denote attacks or supports, and may be weighted. A characterizing feature of this setting is how the weights are composed along chains of arcs, so that the resulting indirect effect, and the final outcome of the argumentation, are intuitive and effective. Previous approaches adopted the same composition strategy for both attacks and supports. However, their meaning is different, and should result in different composition behaviors. In this paper we propose a new approach that distinguishes the two cases. We motivate it, provide computational procedures and show sample use cases demonstrating its effect on practical situations.

Keywords: Abstract Argumentation · Bipolar Weighted Argumentation Frameworks · Automated Reasoning

1 Introduction

Argumentation is the inferential strategy for practical and uncertain reasoning aimed at coping with inconsistent knowledge, in order to assign a justification value to the different contrasting positions in a discussion [13]. A typical case is a debate, in which each participant tries to support one position with suitable claims (the *arguments*), also attacking the arguments put forward by others to support competing positions, and defending his position from the attacks of the others. Since different forms of disputes (or anyway situations with contrasting evidence) are ubiquitous in real life, the availability of automated techniques for carrying out argumentation would be extremely useful. Hence, the motivation for research in a specific branch of Artificial Intelligence aimed at developing models, approaches, techniques and systems for dealing with different aspects of argumentative reasoning.

Abstract argumentation, in particular, focuses only on 'external' information about the arguments, neglecting their internal structure or interpretation. Traditional Abstract Argumentation Frameworks (AFs for short) [7] can express only

G. Andresini et al. (Eds.): ISMIS 2026, LNAI 16685, pp. 24–34, 2027.
https://doi.org/10.1007/978-3-032-32643-0_3

attacks among arguments. While capturing the core of a debate, this obviously limits expressiveness. So, several lines of research expanded this basic framework in different directions. Of interest here are the possibility of expressing supports between arguments (in addition to attacks), or the 'strength' of attacks (in the form of a number). These extensions were usually developed independently of each other, so that they cannot be straightforwardly combined into a more powerful framework encompassing all of them. *Generalized Argumentation Framework*, or GAFs [9], can simulate many such frameworks, also bringing to a cooperation their features, yielding a much more powerful model to carry out abstract argumentation. It additionally provides the possibility of assigning a degree of 'strength' also to the arguments, not just to their relationships.

A relevant question is how the arguments directly and indirectly affect each other along the paths in the graph, i.e., how the weights in the graph are combined to determine the degree of justification of the arguments. [9] proposed to apply an approach based on a progressive decay of the weights to both attack and support relationships. While fit for sequences of attacks, that are expected to progressively weaken the justification degree of the arguments, it may be counterintuitive for sequences of supports, that are expected to progressively increase such degree. In this paper we propose a novel approach for sequences of arguments that aligns with intuition and still fulfils the constraints of the framework, this way giving GAFs a more balanced behavior.

The paper is organized as follows. After recalling basic concepts of abstract AFs in general, and of GAFs in particular, in the next section, in Sect. 3 we define the new combination strategy. Then, in Sect. 4 we show some practical examples of application of the new approach, demonstrating its intuitiveness and ability to provide sensible outcomes to the argumentation problem, before concluding the paper in Sect. 5.

2 Basics and Related Work

In abstract argumentation, a *semantics* is the formal definition of a strategy for the argument evaluation process, that results in the final outcome of argumentation. There are different approaches to semantics. Extension-based semantics determine which subset(s) of arguments in an AF, called *extensions*, can stand together and possibly be considered as the 'winners' of the dispute expressed by the AF. The basic, mandatory requirement is *conflict-freeness* [7], on which several additional constraints have been imposed in the literature to define different semantics. Instead of sets of arguments, ranking-based semantics [1] individually evaluate single arguments, and determine a ranking thereof in the form of a pre-order (reflexive and transitive relation). For obvious reasons, the latter are more directly connected to weighted frameworks, of interest in this paper.

The original Abstract Argumentation setting [7] expresses only the attack relationship between pairs of arguments. While capturing the core of disagreement, this does not allow us to express explicit agreement between arguments: only indirect agreement can be derived based on the notion of *defense* (attacking an attacker). Several works tried to overcome the limitations of this setting, and improve its expressive power, by introducing additional components. Two research directions are of interest in this paper. *Bipolar* AFs (or *BAF*s) [6] can express two kinds of interactions between arguments: the *attack* relation and the *support* relation. Traditional assumptions for the bipolar case are the following:

1. attacking the attacker of an argument amounts to defending (i.e., somehow supporting) that argument (known as *reinstatement*);
2. attacking the supporter of an argument amounts to attacking that argument;
3. supporting the attacker of an argument amounts to attacking that argument;
4. supporting the supporter of an argument amounts to supporting that argument.

Weighted AFs (or *WAF*s) [8] allow to specify numeric weights for attacks (only), expressing their relative strength. The bias toward attacks of the weighted setting, that this paper aims at solving, is already apparent. Exactly for this reason, BAFs and WAFs cannot be immediately combined: the computational procedures for WAFs are not straighforwardly applicable to supports. To solve this problem, [4] extended a previous work on graph-based computational strategies for unipolar AFs, while [11] proposed a new framework (the *Bipolar Weighted Argumentation Framework*, or BWAF) and a gradual evaluation strategy for it. Here we will focus on BWAFs, since they guarantee a representationaly symmetry between attacks and supports by embedding such notions into the weights, through their sign.

Definition 1. *A* BWAF *is a triplet* $F = \langle \mathcal{A}, \hat{\mathcal{R}}, w_{\hat{\mathcal{R}}} \rangle$, *where* $\mathcal{A}$ *is a finite set of arguments,* $\hat{\mathcal{R}} \subseteq \mathcal{A} \times \mathcal{A}$ *and* $w_{\hat{\mathcal{R}}} \colon \hat{\mathcal{R}} \mapsto [-1, 0[\,\cup\,]0, 1]$ *assigns a weight to each relation instance. Within* $\hat{\mathcal{R}}$, *the attack sub-relation is defined as* $\hat{\mathcal{R}}_{att} = \{\langle \alpha, \beta \rangle \in \hat{\mathcal{R}} \mid w_{\hat{\mathcal{R}}}(\langle \alpha, \beta \rangle) \in [-1, 0[\, \}$, *while the support sub-relation is defined as* $\hat{\mathcal{R}}_{sup} = \{\langle \alpha, \beta \rangle \in \hat{\mathcal{R}} \mid w_{\hat{\mathcal{R}}}(\langle \alpha, \beta \rangle) \in \,]0, 1]\}$.

Weight 0 is not considered, since it would mean the absence of an attack or support relation. Note that this sign-based weighting scheme allows to smoothly combine supports and attacks in the same mathematical formula.

An additional useful feature in a weighted setting is the possibility of specifying a degree of 'strength' or 'reliability' also for the arguments by themselves (not only for the relationships among them). E.g., according to [2], the *intrinsic strength* of an argument may come from different sources: the certainty degree of its reason [3], the importance of the value it promotes if any [5], the reliability of its source [10]. In this perspective, the *Trust-affected Bipolar Weighted Argumentation Framework* (or T-BWAF) [12] further extended the BWAF framework by determining their *intrinsic strength* as the result of several factors, internal to the argument (the authority of the source of the argument and its own confidence in the validity of the argument) or external to it (the trust of a community in the source of the argument).

Generalized Argumentation Frameworks [9] encompass all these works, and many more, further extending them with additional features and providing a uniform environment in which carrying out our research. For this reason, from now on we will refer to GAFs.

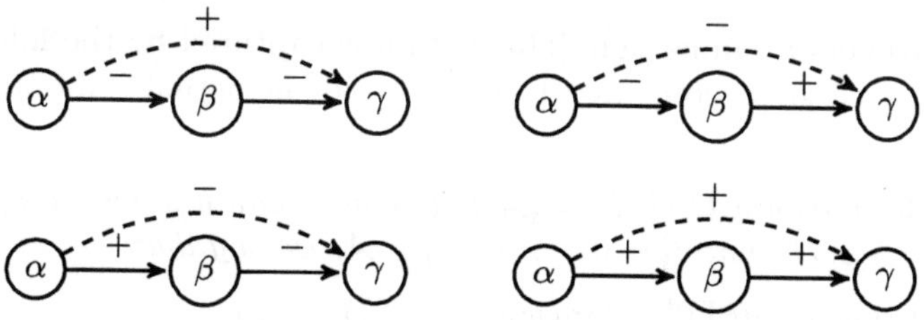

Fig. 1. Sign rule for attacks and supports

Definition 2. *A* Generalized Argumentation Framework *(**GAF**) is a tuple* $F = \langle \mathcal{A}, \mathcal{S}, w_{\mathcal{A}}, w_{\mathcal{R}} \rangle$*, where:*

- $\mathcal{A}$ *is a finite set of arguments,*
- $\mathcal{S}$ *is a system providing external information on the arguments in* $\mathcal{A}$*,*
- $w_{\mathcal{A}} \colon \mathcal{A} \mapsto [0, 1]$ *assigns a weight to each argument, to be considered as its intrinsic strength, also based on* $\mathcal{S}$*, and*
- $w_{\mathcal{R}} \colon \mathcal{A} \times \mathcal{A} \mapsto [-1, 1]$ *assigns a weight to each pair of arguments, also based on* $\mathcal{S}$*.*

It is up to the knowledge engineer defining, case by case, what $\mathcal{S}$ is, and how it affects the assessment of the 'intrinsic' reliability of arguments or of their attack/support relationships. For the purposes of this paper, we may ignore $\mathcal{S}$.

Weight 0 for $w_{\mathcal{R}}$ can be interpreted as the absence of any (attack or support) relationship, and ignored when drawing the argumentation graph. The bipolar relationship considered in BWAFs can be easily extracted as

$$\hat{\mathcal{R}} = \{(\alpha, \beta) \in \mathcal{A} \times \mathcal{A} \mid w_{\mathcal{R}}(\alpha, \beta) \neq 0\}$$

Using negative weights for attacks and positive weights for supports is comfortable (the kind of relationship can be immediately distinguished by its sign), intuitive (attacking an argument subtracts to its credibility, supporting an argument adds to its credibility), and also enables a straighforward translation of the traditional assumptions for the bipolar case into the sign rule used in mathematics:

followed by	Support	Attack
Support	Support	Attack
Attack	Attack	Support

$\equiv$

$\times$	+	−
+	+	−
−	−	+

(see Fig. 1 for a graphical representation). More in general, it allows us to immediately turn the notions of indirect attacks and defenses into mathematical operations. Indeed, just like a path of relationships including an even number of attacks amounts to a defense, so the product of an even number of minus signs gets a plus sign; *vice versa*, just like a path of relationships including an odd number of attacks still amounts to an attack, so the product of an odd number of minus signs gets a minus sign. This notion is captured by the following definition (slightly changed compared to [9] to avoid the actual computation of the weight):

Definition 3. *Given a GAF* $F = \langle \mathcal{A}, \mathcal{S}, w_\mathcal{A}, w_\mathcal{R} \rangle$ *and a sequence of arguments* $\langle x_0, x_1, \ldots, x_n \rangle$ *such that* $\forall i = 0, \ldots, n : x_i \in \mathcal{A}$*, we say that:*

- x_0 g-defends x_n *iff* $\prod_{i=1}^{n} \text{sign}(w_\mathcal{R}(x_{i-1}, x_i)) = +1$
- x_0 g-attacks x_n *iff* $\prod_{i=1}^{n} \text{sign}(w_\mathcal{R}(x_{i-1}, x_i)) = -1$

Compared to traditional weighted frameworks (WAFs), where the weight of an attack could be any number, bounding the absolute weights within fixed minimum and maximum values determines a level of strength at which the attacking argument 'fully' defeats the attacked one (or the supporting argument 'fully' supports the supported one). The specific $[0, 1]$ range helps intuition (due to its wide use in probability and fuzzy theories) and computation (because it preserves the justification value in a multiplication).

As said, GAFs encompass, combine and extend less expressive models. When the additional information provided by GAFs is not needed for the current purposes, a GAF can be reduced to each those models, by stripping the information they cannot convey and keeping only the portion that they can express.

3 Weight Spreading Computation and Combination

We now introduce and discuss our proposal for combining the weights. Our approach is based on the following concepts:

Definition 4. *Given an argument* α *in an argumentation graph* G*:*

- *The* linear justification multiplier *for* α *through a linear path* P *converging on* α *in* G *is the value* $\text{ljm}(\alpha, P) \in [0, 1]$ *representing the composition of attack/support strengths associated to arcs in* P*.*
- *The* justification multiplier *for* α *is the value* $\text{jm}(\alpha) \in [0, 1]$ *representing the composition of the linear justification multipliers associated to all paths in* G *that converge on* α*.*
- *The* justification value *for* α *is obtained by multiplying its justification multiplier for the intrinsic strength of the argument.*

In the following we will focus on the linear justification multiplier. Due to space limitations, discussing the strategies for computing the justification multiplier is out of the scope of this paper. For the purposes of this paper, it can be computed as the average of the linear justification multipliers associated to all the paths converging in that argument. For the sake of simplicity, in the following we will assume all arguments to have intrinsic strength 1.0, so the justification value of an argument coincides with its justification multiplier.

Since the assessment of justification in the argumentation graph must not depend on the order in which its single elements are processed, we want our composition strategy to fulfil the following properties:

1. staying within the upper bound allowed for activation values (to avoid the unfair behavior due to regularization, that may cause loss of information);
2. being commutative (and associative), i.e., its final result must not depend on the order in which the partial values were combined (because the algorithm has no control over the order in which the nodes and arcs are processed, but the final result must be deterministic);
3. being compliant with the intuition that, while attacks should reduce the justification of the target arguments, supports should increase it. Based on this consideration, we propose two different formulas for the two cases.

Consider a sequence of nodes, starting from an initial node n_0 with associated justification value $p_0 \in [0,1]$, and ending in a final node n_k through a sequence of arcs $P = \langle a_1, \ldots, a_k \rangle$ with their associated weights $\forall i = 1, 2, \ldots, k : p_i = w_{\mathcal{R}}(x_{i-1}, x_i) \in [-1, 0[\cup]0, +1]$. Any such sequence can be split into a number of alternating subsequences involving only arcs of the same type (attack or support).

Given a sequence P of arcs of the same type (attacks or supports), i.e.:

$$\forall i = 1, 2, \ldots, k : \text{sign}(p_i) = +1 \vee \forall i = 1, 2, \ldots, k : \text{sign}(p_i) = -1$$

we define a corresponding sequence of functions $\text{ljm}_i(P)$ as follows. For a (sequence of) attack(s):

$$\forall i = 1, 2, \cdots : \text{ljm}_i(P) = \begin{cases} 1 - |p_1| & \text{if } i = 1 \\ 1 - \text{ljm}_{i-1}(P) \cdot |p_i| & \text{if } i > 1 \end{cases}$$

For a (sequence of) support(s):

$$\forall i = 0, 1, 2, \cdots : \text{ljm}_i(P) = \begin{cases} p_0 & \text{if } i = 0 \\ \text{ljm}_{i-1}(P) + (1 - \text{ljm}_{i-1}(P)) \cdot p_i & \text{if } i > 0 \end{cases}$$

In both cases, we define the linear justification multiplier for the target node n_k through sequence P as

$$\text{ljm}(P) = \text{ljm}_k(P)$$

Note that we need to distinguish and treat homogeneous sequences because our strategy provides for a cumulative 'reinforcement' in both cases, but the reinforcement formula is different. So, it is not sufficient to define the combination effect only at the single edge's level.

4 Sample Use Cases

We will now show the proposed approach in action with a few sample use cases. In all these cases only a linear path is considered, and thus the linear justification multiplier coincides with the justification multiplier for all involved nodes. Also recall that, since all claims have intrinsic strengh equal to 1.0, only attack and supports affect the overall reliability of a claim after computing the argumentation, and the justification value coincides with the justification multiplier.

Let's start with two abstract cases of sequences of attacks and supports, respectively. Figures 2 and 3 show two generic paths in the graph, with the same sequence of weights, but in the former case they are attacks, while in the latter they are supports.

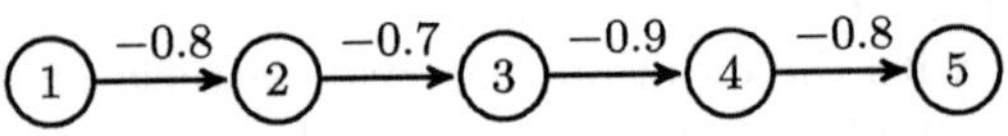

Fig. 2. Sample sequence of attacks

In Fig. 2, we have the following situation for each node:

1. is the initial argument, having no attacks, so it is justified (+) with value 1.0;
2. is attacked by argument 1 with strength 0.8, so it is not justified $(+ \times - = -)$ and gets justification multiplier $1.0 - 0.8 = 0.2$;
3. is attacked by argument 2 with strength 0.7, so it is justified $(- \times - = +)$ and gets justification multiplier $1.0 - (0.7 \cdot 0.2) = 1.0 - 0.14 = 0.86$;
4. is attacked by argument 3 with strength 0.9, so it is not justified $(+ \times - = -)$ and gets justification multiplier $1.0 - (0.9 \cdot 0.86) = 1.0 - 0.774 = 0.226$;
5. is attacked by argument 4 with strength 0.8, so it is justified $(- \times - = +)$ and gets justification multiplier $1.0 - (0.8 \cdot 0.226) = 1.0 - 0.1808 = 0.8192$.

Note that, as intuitive, all justified nodes get high justification multiplier, while all non-justified ones get low values.

Fig. 3. Sample sequence of supports

In Fig. 3, we have the following situation for each node:

1. is the initial argument, having no attacks, so it is justified (+) with value 1.0 (as a consequence, all other arguments in the sequence are justified as well, since the sequence involves only supports);
2. is supported by argument 1 with strength 0.8, which is the initial support in the sequence, so it gets justification multiplier 0.8;
3. is supported by argument 2 with strength 0.7, so it gets justification multiplier $0.8 + (1 - 0.8) \cdot 0.7 = 0.8 + 0.2 \cdot 0.7 = 0.8 + 0.4 = 0.94$;
4. is supported by argument 3 with strength 0.9, so it gets justification multiplier $0.94 + (1 - 0.94) \cdot 0.9 = 0.94 + 0.06 \cdot 0.9 = 0.94 + 0.054 = 0.994$;
5. is supported by argument 4 with strength 0.8, so it gets justification multiplier $0.994 + (1 - 0.994) \cdot 0.8 = 0.994 + 0.006 \cdot 0.8 = 0.994 + 0.0048 = 0.9988$.

Note that, as intuitive, the justification multiplier is increased as long as we advance in the sequence.

Let us now show a case of mixed attacks and supports, using a hypothetical real-world case. Consider the following sequence of claims (arguments):

1. Yesterday was a bank holiday
2. Yesterday was a working day for John, a high school teacher
3. Yesterday John was at home, sleeping all day
4. Yesterday morning John was hit by a bicycle
5. Yesterday John fell to the ground
6. Yesterday John's glasses hit the ground
7. Yesterday John's glasses got broken
8. Yesterday afternoon John was wearing his glasses
9. John is nearsighted
10. John enjoyed the fireworks
11. Yesterday there were fireworks
12. Yesterday there were flashes in the sky

Figure 4 shows a chain of relationships among these claims, with solid arrows representing attacks, and dashed arrows representing supports, whose strength is reported as a weight in [0, 1]. Note that other relationships may hold among these claims (e.g., 2 attacks 1, 8 would support 10, etc.), but for our purposes we will only consider this chain. The sequence can be split in subsequences involving only relationships of the same type, and specifically: $\langle a_1, a_2, a_3 \rangle$ (attacks), $\langle a_4, a_5, a_6 \rangle$ (supports), $\langle a_7, a_8, a_9 \rangle$ (attacks), $\langle a_{10}, a_{11} \rangle$ (supports).

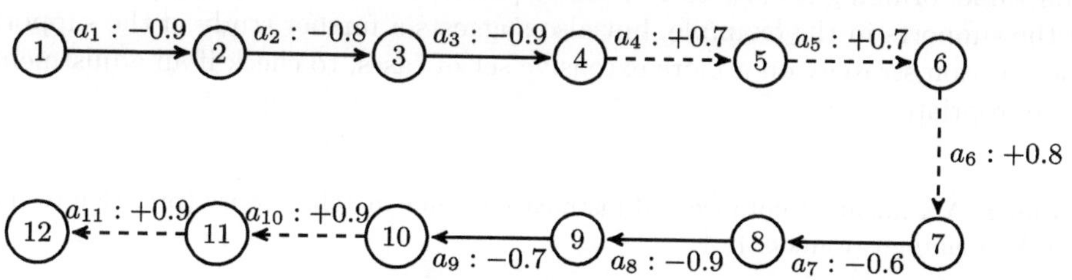

Fig. 4. Relationships for John's story arguments

Table 1 shows, for each argument in the previous list, if it is accepted or not and the corresponding justification value. Let's analyze them.

1. initial argument in the chain, no attack, so it is accepted (+) and preserves its justification value 1.0.
2. attacked by 1, not accepted ($+ \times - = -$), gets justification value $1.0 - 0.9 = 0.1$.
3. attacked by 2, accepted ($- \times - = +$), gets justification value $1.0 - 0.8 \cdot 0.1 = 0.92$.

4. attacked by 3, not accepted $(+ \times - = -)$, gets justification value $1.0 - 0.9 \cdot 0.92 = 0.172$.
5. supported by 4, not accepted $(- \times + = -)$, gets justification value $0.172 + (1.0 - 0.172) \cdot 0.7 = 0.7516$.
6. supported by 5, not accepted $(- \times + = -)$, gets justification value $0.7516 + (1.0 - 0.7516) \cdot 0.7 = 0.92548$.
7. supported by 6, not accepted $(- \times + = -)$, gets justification value $0.92548 + (1.0 - 0.92548) \cdot 0.8 = 0.985096$.
8. attacked by 7, accepted $(- \times - = +)$, gets justification value $1 - 0.985096 \cdot 0.6 = 0.4089424$.
9. attacked by 8, not accepted $(+ \times - = -)$, gets justification value $1 - 0.4089424 \cdot 0.9 = 0.63195184$.
10. attacked by 9, accepted $(- \times - = +)$, gets justification value $1 - 0.63195184 \cdot 0.7 = 0.557633712$.
11. supported by 10, accepted $(+ \times + = +)$, gets justification value $0.557633712 + (1.0 - 0.557633712) \cdot 0.9 = 0.9557633712$.
12. supported by 11, accepted $(+ \times + = +)$, gets justification value $0.9557633712 + (1.0 - 0.9557633712) \cdot 0.9 = 0.99557633712$.

So, in the end the winning position is $\{1, 3, 8, 10, 11, 12\}$: yesterday was a bank holiday and John enjoyed the fireworks. The other position is also internally consistent, but defeated. The high justification value for arguments $\{5, 6, 7, 9\}$, in spite of their being defeated, can be explained by considering that the justification value of the arguments expresses how strong they are within the position they are consistent with. We note that the supports quickly raise the justification value, bringing it close to 1.0: this is partly due to the high support weights of the supports in the example, but also suggests a further study of the support composition strategy on a more extensive set of cases, to check if an adjustment is appropriate.

Table 1. Argument acceptance and justification value in John's story (precision to the 3rd decimal digit, rounded)

Argument	1	2	3	4	5	6	7	8	9	10	11	12
Subpath type	—	attacks			supports			attacks			supports	
Acceptance	+	–	+	–	–	–	–	+	–	+	+	+
Justification	1.0	0.100	0.920	0.172	0.752	0.926	0.985	0.409	0.632	0.558	0.956	0.996

5 Conclusion

Bipolar Weighted Abstract Argumentation Frameworks can express weighted attacks and supports between pairs of arguments. Based on the strength and topology of such attacks and supports, they aim at identifying the subsets of arguments that consistently support the same position in a dispute or debate, and possibly determine the winning position. This raises the need to define composition strategies for the attack/support weights, that determine the final justification value of each argument based on the full set of relationships directly or indirectly affecting it. In the GAF framework, we proposed a strategy that fulfils desirable properties, including intuitiveness, and demonstrated its application in the case of chains of relationships.

In future work, we will further study the behavior of the proposed approach, and refine it accordingly. We will also expand the approach to the non-linear case, and test it on more extensive and/or real-world use cases.

Disclosure of Interests. The authors have no competing interests to declare that are relevant to the content of this article.

References

1. Amgoud, L., Ben-Naim, J.: Ranking-based semantics for argumentation frameworks. In: SUM, pp. 134–147. Springer, Heidelberg (2013). https://doi.org/10.1007/978-3-642-40381-1_11
2. Amgoud, L., Ben-Naim, J.: Axiomatic foundations of acceptability semantics. In: Proceedings of the International Conference on Principles of Knowledge Representation and Reasoning, KR, vol. 16 (2016)
3. Amgoud, L., Cayrol, C.: A reasoning model based on the production of acceptable arguments. Ann. Math. Artif. Intell. **34**(1–3), 197–215 (2002)
4. Amgoud, L., en Naim, J.: Weighted bipolar argumentation graphs: axioms and semantics. In: IJCAI'18: Proceedings of the 27th International Joint Conference on Artificial Intelligence (2018)
5. Bench-Capon, T.J.M.: Persuasion in practical argument using value-based argumentation frameworks. J. Log. Comput. **13**(3), 429–448 (2003)
6. Cayrol, C., Lagasquie-Schiex, M.: On the acceptability of arguments in bipolar argumentation frameworks. In: ECSQARU, vol. 3571, pp. 378–389 (2005)
7. Dung, P.M.: On the acceptability of arguments and its fundamental role in nonmonotonic reasoning, logic programming and n-person games. Artif. Intell. **77**(2), 321–357 (1995)
8. Dunne, P.E., Hunter, A., McBurney, P., Parsons, S., Wooldridge, M.: Weighted argument systems: basic definitions, algorithms, and complexity results. Artif. Intell. **175**(2), 457–486 (2011)
9. Ferilli, S.: Introducing general argumentation frameworks and their use. In: Baldoni, M., Bandini, S. (eds.) AIxIA 2020. LNCS (LNAI), vol. 12414, pp. 136–153. Springer, Cham (2021). https://doi.org/10.1007/978-3-030-77091-4_9
10. Parsons, S., Tang, Y., Sklar, E., McBurney, P., Cai, K.: Argumentation-based reasoning in agents with varying degrees of trust. In: The 10th International Conference on Autonomous Agents and Multiagent Systems, vol. 2, pp. 879–886. International Foundation for Autonomous Agents and Multiagent Systems (2011)
11. Pazienza, A., Ferilli, S., Esposito, F.: Constructing and evaluating bipolar weighted argumentation frameworks for online debating systems. In: Proceedings of the 1st Workshop on Advances In Argumentation In Artificial Intelligence, AI^3 2017 @ AI*IA 2017, pp. 111–125 (2017)

12. Pazienza, A., Ferilli, S., Esposito, F.: On the gradual acceptability of arguments in bipolar weighted argumentation frameworks with degrees of trust. In: Foundations of Intelligent Systems - 23rd International Symposium, ISMIS, pp. 195–204 (2017)
13. Toulmin, S.E.: The Uses of Argument. University Press (1958). https://books.google.it/books?id=WffWAAAAMAAJ

Timeline Generation from Event Logs Under Evolving Properties

Rikayan Chaki(✉) and Diego Calvanese

Free University of Bozen-Bolzano, 39100 Bolzano, Italy
{rchaki,diego.calvanese}@unibz.it

Abstract. When building a process model from an event log, behavioural process querying methods often focus on analysing an execution's control flow. This is because event logs typically do not encode data flow through a process explicitly. Domain knowledge about the effects of activities on objects and relations between objects can be modelled using condition-effect rules, and exploiting path querying in such rules enables us to determine the values of dynamic object attributes that are indirectly related to events. This allows us to leverage temporally local knowledge of a system's evolving data state to generate timelines from process instances. Within this setting, our main contribution is two-fold: *(i)* We enrich previous models with a new form of rules that allows for dynamic attribute value changes to be computed and recorded as part of the timeline. *(ii)* We provide a formalization of rule semantics using a transition system, in which states represent data configurations, and transitions represent the updates to those configurations resulting from the rules' effects. Finally, we provide a formal construction that generates a timeline that is correct with respect to the aforementioned rule semantics.

Keywords: Event Knowledge Graphs · Regular Path Queries · Condition-Effect Rules · Temporal Property Graphs

1 Introduction

Traditional process mining techniques rely on the implicit or explicit presence of a single *case notion*, which results in process executions being modelled as *flat* event logs. However, flattening logs in which objects and their relations interact leads to problems like *data convergence* and *divergence* [4]. Such flattening may also result in severely underspecified models with misleading process mining results [1]. To avoid this, *Object-Centric Process Mining* techniques instead model event logs using graph schemas, such as *Event Knowledge Graphs* (EKGs) [8].

However, such schemas provide only a *static* view of the data involved in processes. A timeline that shows how the data in a system is affected by the

G. Andresini et al. (Eds.): ISMIS 2026, LNAI 16685, pp. 35–45, 2027.
https://doi.org/10.1007/978-3-032-32643-0_4

events can serve as actionable information for domain experts managing a system. For example, a mismatch between the data state evolution expected according to domain knowledge, and the one actually recorded, indicates a possible bug. In [7], using an EKG as input, as well as a set of condition-effect rules to encode such domain knowledge, a timeline-generation algorithm was devised. We extend this approach with the ability to compute modifications of object attribute values and to record the modification times. The importance of modifiable attribute values is recognized by the OCEL v2.0 standard [3], which regards them as "dynamic attributes". Importantly, we provide a formal semantics for the timeline-generation, and revise the algorithm in [7] to fit such semantics.

Our primary assumption is that the evolution of system data occurs solely as a result of event execution. For each event we consider a set of objects participating in it. Given the types of an event and of a participating object, the *role* of the object in the event is fixed and known a priori. Additionally, given the data state before the execution of an event, the way in which the data state evolves can be determined with First-Order logic formulae. Finally, it assumes that for an event and a set of objects correlated to it *(i)* only objects correlated to the event, and relations with at least one object correlated to the event, are affected by it, and *(ii)* attribute values are only changed for objects that can be reached following paths along known relation types from objects correlated to the event.

2 Preliminaries

This section includes some fundamental concepts and terms that are used in the rest of the paper. In the following, let $\mathbb{N}$ be the set of all non-negative integers and, given $k \in \mathbb{N}$ and a set $\mathcal{S}$, we use $\mathcal{S}^k$ to denote the set of all k-tuples over $\mathcal{S}$.

As noted earlier, timeline generation requires an *object-centric event log.* Each event in such a log has an activity describing the performed action and a timestamp indicating *when* it occurred. Let $\mathbb{A}$ denote the set of all activities and $\mathbb{T}$ the set of all timestamps.

For an event e, let $corr_e$ denote the set of *objects* participating in it. These objects are drawn from a set $\mathbb{O}$. For an object $a \in \mathbb{O}$, let $\mathsf{type}(a)$ denote its type. The collection of all such types is denoted by $\mathbb{E}$. A subset $\mathbb{E}_S \subseteq \mathbb{E}$ contains *static types*, whose objects do not evolve over time, and are assumed to be present in the initial data state before any process execution. Objects may have attributes from a set $\mathbb{K}$, with values in $\mathbb{V}$, which may change over time. To set attribute values dynamically, we model *external services* as functions $f\colon 2^{\mathbb{V}^k} \times \mathbb{T} \to \mathbb{V}$, where $k \in \mathbb{N}$. The collection of such f forms a heterogeneously-typed family $\mathbb{F}$ of functions. We assume that functions are computable for every possible input. Object types belong to a *conceptual model* describing possible relations having types in a set $\mathbb{R}$. For $X, Y \in \mathbb{E}$ and $R \in \mathbb{R}$, we use $\mathsf{R_X}(R) = \langle X, Y\rangle$ to denote that R-relations are binary relations that connect objects of type X to objects of type Y.

Finally, let $\mathbb{I} \subseteq (\mathbb{R} \times \mathbb{O} \times \mathbb{O}) \cup (\mathbb{K} \times \mathbb{O} \times \mathbb{V})$ represent a set of assertions denoting relations and attribute value assignments involving static-typed objects. For each process execution, the static-typed objects in it, along with a subset of $\mathbb{I}$ determines its *initial data configuration.*

The sets $\mathbb{O}$, $\mathbb{E}$, $\mathbb{R}$, $\mathbb{K}$, $\mathbb{V}$, $\mathbb{A}$, and $\mathbb{T}$ are assumed *countably infinite and mutually disjoint,* and disjoint from the set $\{\mathsf{ts}, \mathsf{act}\}$ of special attributes (see later).

As common graph structure, we use *Labeled Property Graphs* (LPGs). Formally, an LPG over finite sets $\mathcal{L}$ of labels, $\mathcal{K}$ of property keys, and $\mathcal{V}$ of property values, is a tuple $G = \langle V, E, \mathsf{label}, \mathsf{prop}\rangle$, where V is a finite set of vertices, $E \subseteq V^2$ is a set of edges, $\mathsf{label}\colon V \cup E \to 2^{\mathcal{L}}$ is a labelling function, and $\mathsf{prop}\colon (V \cup E) \times \mathcal{K} \nrightarrow \mathcal{V}$ is a partial function that sets vertex/edge properties.

Definition 1. *An* Event Knowledge Graph *(EKG) $G = \langle V, E, \mathsf{label}, \mathsf{prop}\rangle$ is an LPG over labels $\mathcal{L} \subseteq \mathbb{R}$, property keys $\mathcal{K} \subseteq \mathbb{K} \cup \{\mathsf{ts}, \mathsf{act}\}$, and values $\mathcal{V} \subseteq \mathbb{V} \cup \mathbb{T} \cup \mathbb{A}$. The set V is partitioned into sets V^E of events and $V^O \subseteq \mathbb{O}$ of objects. If $a, b \in V^O$, $\langle a, b\rangle \in E$ is possible only if both $\mathsf{type}(a)$ and $\mathsf{type}(b)$ are in $\mathbb{E}_S$. The type(s) of relations from a to b form the labeling $\mathsf{label}(\langle a, b\rangle)$. Additionally, an object a can have value $u \in \mathbb{V}$ for some $K \in \mathbb{K}$ only if a is static-typed, formally, $\mathsf{prop}(a, K) = u$ only if $\mathsf{type}(a) \in \mathbb{E}_S$.*

Suppose that $\mathbb{I}_G$ contains (i) relation assertions $\langle R, a_0, a_1\rangle$, where $a_0, a_1 \in V^O$, $\langle a_0, a_1\rangle \in E$ and $R \in \mathsf{label}(\langle a_0, a_1\rangle)$ and (ii) attribute assertions $\langle K, a, u\rangle$, where $a \in V^O, u \in \mathbb{V}$, and $\mathsf{prop}(a, K) = u$. We assume that the above assertions denote the relations and attribute assignments in G, and thus require $\mathbb{I}_G \subseteq \mathbb{I}$.

Events are assumed to be atomic *and have properties* ts *(for timestamp) and* act *(for activity). Edges connect an event $e \in V^E$ to objects in V^O such that $o \in corr_e$. Formally, we have that $\langle e, o\rangle \in E$ only if $o \in corr_e$.*

Definition 2. *A* Temporal Property Graph *(TPG) $D = \langle V, E, \mathsf{label}, \mathsf{prop}\rangle$ is an LPG over labels $\mathcal{L} \subseteq \mathbb{R} \cup \mathbb{E}$, property keys $\{\mathsf{createTimes}, \mathsf{deleteTimes}\}$, and values $\mathcal{V} \subseteq \bigcup_{k \in \mathbb{N}} \mathbb{T}^k$. V is partitioned into a set of objects and a set of attribute key-value pairs drawn from $\mathbb{K} \times \mathbb{V}$. Attribute assignments are represented as edges from objects to attribute key-value pairs, while edges between objects denote relations. Given an object $x \in V \cap \mathbb{O}$, we define (i) the type T of x as its label, formally, $\mathsf{label}(x) = \{T\}$, and (ii) $\mathsf{prop}(x, \mathsf{createTimes})$ and $\mathsf{prop}(x, \mathsf{deleteTimes})$ as tuples of timestamps representing the creation and deletion times of x. Similarly, attribute and relation edges store creation/deletion times, and relation edges encode their types in labels.*

Regular path queries [5,6] allow events to also affect attributes that are (possibly indirectly) connected to its participating objects when the event occurred. They are defined as follows. Let Σ be an alphabet, and $\Sigma^- = \{a^- \mid a \in \Sigma\}$. We consider here *two-way single-source regular path queries* (2SSRPQs) [2] (over Σ), which syntactically are just regular expressions over $\Sigma \cup \Sigma^-$. The evaluation semantics of such queries is defined over an edge-labelled graph G, where edges are labelled by subsets of Σ. Formally, $G = \langle V, E, \lambda\rangle$, where $E \subseteq V^2$ and $\lambda : E \to 2^{\Sigma}$. For some $n \in \mathbb{N}$, let $v_0, \ldots, v_n$ be vertices in V, and $b_1, \ldots, b_n$ symbols in $\Sigma \cup \Sigma^-$. Then, a *two-way path* in G from v_0 to v_n is defined as a sequence $\rho = \langle v_0, b_1, v_1, \ldots, v_{n-1}, b_n, v_n\rangle$, where for each $1 \leq i \leq n$, either $\langle v_{i-1}, v_i\rangle \in E$

and $b_i \in \lambda(\langle v_{i-1}, v_i\rangle)$, or $\langle v_i, v_{i-1}\rangle \in E$, $b_i = a^-$, and $a \in \lambda(\langle v_i, v_{i-1}\rangle)$. For such two-way path ρ, we define $\mathsf{word}(\rho)$ as the string $b_1 \cdots b_n$ over $\Sigma \cup \Sigma^-$.

Definition 3. *Given a graph G and a vertex $v_s \in V$, the* answer of a 2SSRPQ Q in G from v_s *is* $[\![Q]\!]_{G,v_s} = \{v \in V \mid \exists$ *a two-way path ρ in G from v_s to v with* $\mathsf{word}(\rho) \in \mathcal{L}(Q)\}$, *where $\mathcal{L}(Q)$ is the language of the regular expression Q.*

3 Rules to Evolve the System State

We illustrate our approach on the following example.

Example 1 (Order Management). Consider a system where customers can order *Items*. We model it using types *Item*, *Product*, and *Order*. We also have *HasItem* relations from *Product* to *Item*, and *Contains* relations from *Order* to *Item*. *Item* and *Product* are static types (i.e., in $\mathbb{E}_S$). Each *Product* has attributes `lUpd` and `price`. Every process execution defines initial attribute values for the available *Products*, and *HasItem* relations. Via a PLACEORDER-event, a customer may then create an *Order* and connect it to the *Items* in it (at least one) via *Contains*. Via a SHIPORDER-event, an *Order* is shipped and gets deleted. The attribute `lUpd` stores the last time the `price` of a product changed. During SHIPORDER, the `price` of products connected to items in the shipped *Order* is increased at a fixed rate of 5% per year, if at least one year has passed since the last update. We define an EKG $G_{ex} = \{V_{ex}, E_{ex}, \mathsf{label}_{ex}, \mathsf{prop}_{ex}\}$ for this system, where $V^E_{ex} = \{\mathtt{e}^1, \mathtt{e}^2\}$ and $V^O_{ex} = \{\mathtt{o}, \mathtt{i}_1, \mathtt{i}_2, \mathtt{p}\}$. Further, let $\mathsf{prop}(\mathtt{e}^1, \mathsf{ts}) = 1$, $\mathsf{prop}(\mathtt{e}^2, \mathsf{ts}) = 2$, $\mathsf{prop}(\mathtt{e}^1, \mathsf{act}) = \mathit{PlaceOrder}$, $\mathsf{prop}(\mathtt{e}^2, \mathsf{act}) = \mathit{ShipOrder}$, $\mathsf{prop}(\mathtt{p}, \mathtt{price}) = 100$ and $\mathsf{prop}(\mathtt{p}, \mathtt{lUpd}) = 0$. Finally, let $\{\langle \mathtt{p}, \mathtt{i}_1\rangle, \langle \mathtt{p}, \mathtt{i}_2\rangle\} \subseteq E_{ex}$, $corr_{\mathtt{e}^1} = \{\mathtt{o}, \mathtt{i}_1, \mathtt{i}_2\}$, $corr_{\mathtt{e}^2} = \{\mathtt{o}\}$ and $\mathsf{label}_{ex}(\langle \mathtt{p}, \mathtt{i}_1\rangle) = \mathsf{label}_{ex}(\langle \mathtt{p}, \mathtt{i}_2\rangle) = \{\mathit{HasItem}\}$. ◁

3.1 Rule Syntax

In this section, we describe the syntax of rules. To do so, we define:

1. A set of atomic propositions (APs) denoting objects, their types, relations, and attribute value assignments, given by

$$\mathbb{AP} = \{\mathtt{Obj}(a) \mid a \in \mathbb{O}\} \cup \{\mathtt{hasType}(a, X) \mid a \in \mathbb{O} \wedge X \in \mathbb{E}\} \cup \{P(a, a') \mid P \in \mathbb{R} \wedge a, a' \in \mathbb{O}\} \cup \{P(a, v) \mid P \in \mathbb{K} \wedge a \in \mathbb{O} \wedge v \in \mathbb{V}\}.$$

2. A first order (FO) theory $\mathcal{T}$ over sorts $\mathbb{V}$ and $\mathbb{O}$, whose predicates belong to those in $\mathbb{AP}$ union $\{\mathtt{Corr}\}$, where $\mathtt{Corr}$ is a *unary* predicate over the sort $\mathbb{O}$.

   Given these, each rule r has the form

$$\langle Q;\ Act^{\ell}_{t}, \varphi \rightsquigarrow \eta\rangle \tag{1}$$

where Q is a 2SSRPQ over $\mathbb{R}$, and $Act^{\ell}_{t}, \varphi \rightsquigarrow \eta$ is a condition-effect rule in which: $Act \in \mathbb{A}$; $\ell \in \{o, r, a\}$ specifies whether the *target* of the rule (i.e., the element mentioned in the Effect η) is an object, attribute, or relation; $t \in \{\perp, \mathtt{int}, \mathtt{ext}\}$; φ is a $\mathcal{T}$-formula; and the form of the effect η is specified in the conditions below, where we make use of $\mathbb{O}$-sorted free variables x, x_0, and x_1 in $\mathcal{T}$.

- When $\ell = o$: $Q = \varepsilon$ (i.e., the empty string); $t = \bot$; $\eta = \mathtt{Obj}(x)$ (i.e., object creation) or $\eta = \neg\mathtt{Obj}(x)$ (i.e., object deletion), and x is the free variable of φ.
- When $\ell = r$: $Q = \varepsilon$; $t \in \{\mathtt{int}, \mathtt{ext}\}$; and $\eta = R(x_0, x_1)$ (i.e., relation creation) or $\eta = \neg R(x_0, x_1)$ (i.e., relation deletion), where $R \in \mathbb{R}$ and x_0, x_1 are the free variables of φ.
- When $\ell = a$: $t = \bot$; and $\eta = \langle K, f, \Psi\rangle$, where $K \in \mathbb{K}$, $f \in \mathbb{F}$, and Ψ is a $\mathcal{T}$-formula having x as its only $\mathbb{O}$-sorted free variable. If for some $k \in \mathbb{N}$, Ψ also has k $\mathbb{V}$-sorted free variables, then the domain of f must be $2^{\mathbb{V}^k} \times \mathbb{T}$, i.e., $f : 2^{\mathbb{V}^k} \times \mathbb{T} \to \mathbb{V}$.

We use $\mathbb{C}$ to denote the set of rules that have the above form.

Example 2. For the scenario presented in Example 1, the rule that creates the *Order* connected to an event observing the PLACEORDER activity is: $\langle \varepsilon; \text{PLACEORDER}^o_\bot, \mathtt{hasType}(x, \mathit{Order}) \rightsquigarrow \mathtt{Obj}(x)\rangle$. Events observing the SHIPORDER activity update the attributes of a *Product* indirectly connected to the *Order* participating in it. The rule affecting the `price` attribute is:

$$\begin{aligned}\langle \mathit{Contains} \cdot \mathit{HasItem}^-;\, \mathit{ShipOrder}^a_\bot,&\\ \mathtt{true} \rightsquigarrow \langle \mathtt{price}, f, \mathtt{lUpd}(x, \mathit{dt}) \wedge \mathtt{price}(x, \mathit{pr})\rangle\rangle&\end{aligned} \tag{2}$$

where $f \in \mathbb{F}$ is defined as follows. Given a set $\{(\mathtt{dt}_0, \mathtt{p}_0)\}$ where $\mathtt{dt}_0$ is a timestamp and $\mathtt{p}_0$ a floating-point value, we define $y = f(\{(\mathtt{dt}_0, \mathtt{p}_0)\}, \tau)$ as follows. Let Δ be the amount of fractional years by which $\mathtt{dt}_0$ precedes τ. Then, $y = \mathtt{p}_0$ if $\Delta < 1$, else $y = (1 + (0.05\Delta))\mathtt{p}_0$. Let $\mathcal{C}_{ex}$ be the set of rules obtained by continuing to encode the data evolution semantics of the order management domain like this. ◁

3.2 Rule Semantics

To describe the semantics of rules, we introduce some auxiliary concepts. We represent a data state s through a set of APs, where *(i)* $\mathtt{Obj}(a)$ indicates that an object a is in s, *(ii)* $\mathtt{hasType}(a, X)$ denotes that a has type X, *(iii)* atom $R(a, b)$ denotes that a relation of type $R \in \mathbb{R}$ exists from $a \in \mathbb{O}$ to $b \in \mathbb{O}$, and *(iv)* atom $K(a, u)$ denotes that an attribute $K \in \mathbb{K}$ of $a \in \mathbb{O}$ has the value $u \in \mathbb{V}$.

Definition 4 (Data State). *A data state s is a finite set of APs in $\mathbb{AP}$ such that, for each $a \in \mathbb{O}$, the conditions below hold. We denote by $\mathbb{S}$ the set of all such data states.*

$$\begin{aligned}\mathtt{Obj}(a) \in s &\implies \mathtt{hasType}(a, \mathsf{type}(a)) \in s,\\ \forall b \in \mathbb{O}, R \in \mathbb{R}.\, R(a, b) \in s &\implies \{\mathtt{Obj}(a), \mathtt{Obj}(b)\} \subseteq s \wedge \mathsf{R}_\mathsf{X}(R) = \langle \mathsf{type}(a), \mathsf{type}(b)\rangle,\\ \forall u \in \mathbb{V}, K \in \mathbb{K}.\, K(a, u) \in s &\implies \mathtt{Obj}(a) \in s \wedge \nexists u' \in \mathbb{V}.\, u \neq u' \wedge K(a, u') \in s.\end{aligned} \tag{3}$$

Example 3 The initial data state $s_0^{ex} \in \mathbb{S}$ of G_{ex} (of Example 1) is as follows

$$\{\ \texttt{Obj}(\texttt{i}_1), \texttt{Obj}(\texttt{i}_2), \texttt{Obj}(\texttt{p}), \texttt{Obj}(\texttt{o}), \texttt{hasType}(\texttt{i}_1, \mathit{Item}), \\ \texttt{hasType}(\texttt{i}_2, \mathit{Item}), \texttt{hasType}(\texttt{p}, \mathit{Product}), \texttt{hasType}(\texttt{o}, \mathit{Order}), \\ \mathit{HasItem}(\texttt{p}, \texttt{i}_1), \mathit{HasItem}(\texttt{p}, \texttt{i}_2), \texttt{price}(\texttt{p}, 100), \texttt{lUpd}(\texttt{p}, 0)\ \}. \tag{4}$$

◁

We can now define the semantics of formulae in the FO-theory $\mathcal{T}$ introduced earlier. Given a *model* $\mathcal{M} = \langle s, \mathcal{O}\rangle$, where $s \in \mathbb{S}$ and $\mathcal{O}$ is a finite subset of $\mathbb{O}$, we evaluate each AP p in a $\mathcal{T}$-formula over $\mathcal{M}$ as follows. If p is $\texttt{Corr}(x)$, it holds if and only if $x \in \mathcal{O}$. Otherwise, $p \in \mathbb{AP}$ is evaluated against s. Evaluation of complex formulae follows standard FO semantics. For a formula ϕ with k free variables $x_1, \ldots, x_k$, let $\phi[x_1/c_1, \ldots, x_k/c_k]$ be the closed formula obtained by substituting $c_i \in \mathbb{O} \cup \mathbb{V}$ for x_i, for $i \in \{1, \ldots, k\}$.

Definition 5 (Restricted Answer Set). *The* restricted answer set *of a FO-formula ϕ with exactly one free variable x of sort $\mathbb{O}$ and k free variables $y_1, \ldots, y_k$ of sort $\mathbb{V}$, given $s \in \mathbb{S}$, a finite set $\mathcal{O} \subseteq \mathbb{O}$, and some object $\texttt{a} \in \mathbb{O}$ is defined as the set $\mathcal{RA}_\phi^{s,\mathcal{O},\texttt{a}} = \{\langle b_1, \ldots, b_k\rangle \mid \phi[x/a, y_1/b_1, \ldots, y_k/b_k]$ is true in $\langle s, \mathcal{O}\rangle\}$.*

We define from a data state a graph over which the 2SSRPQs rules are to be evaluated.

Definition 6 (Graph Interpretation). *For a data state $s \in \mathbb{S}$, we define the* graph interpretation *s_G of s to be a labelled graph where (i) each $\texttt{Obj}(a) \in s$ has a corresponding vertex $\texttt{v}_a$, and (ii) for each $a_0, a_1 \in \mathbb{O}$ such that $R(a_0, a_1) \in s$ holds for some $R \in \mathbb{R}$, there is an edge $\langle \texttt{v}_{a_0}, \texttt{v}_{a_1}\rangle$ with $R \in \lambda(\langle \texttt{v}_{a_0}, \texttt{v}_{a_1}\rangle)$.*

We describe now how a data state evolves. To ensure that constraint 3 is maintained as a data state is updated, we define an *update set* to be a set $\mathcal{U}$ of literals over $\mathbb{AP} \setminus \{\texttt{hasType}(a, X) \mid \texttt{hasType}(a, X) \in \mathbb{AP}\}$ such that, for each $a \in \mathbb{O}, K \in \mathbb{K}$ *(i)* there is at most one $u \in \mathbb{V}$ such that $K(a, u)$ is in $\mathcal{U}$, and *(ii)* for all $u' \in \mathbb{V}$, $\neg K(a, u') \notin \mathcal{U}$.

Definition 7 (Composition Operator). *We define the composition operator '$\circ$' for $s \in \mathbb{S}$ and an update set $\mathcal{U}$, as the set:*

$$\begin{aligned} s' = s'' \setminus \big(&\{R(a,b) \in s'' \mid R \in \mathbb{R} \wedge \neg(\{\texttt{Obj}(a), \texttt{Obj}(b)\} \subseteq s'')\} \\ &\cup \{K(a,u) \in s'' \mid K \in \mathbb{K} \wedge \texttt{Obj}(a) \notin s''\} \\ &\cup \{K(a,u) \in s \mid K \in \mathbb{K} \wedge \exists_{u' \in \mathbb{V}, u' \neq u} K(a,u') \in \mathcal{U}\}\big) \end{aligned}$$

where $s'' = s \cup \mathcal{U}^+ \setminus \mathcal{U}^-$, and where $\mathcal{U}^+$ and $\mathcal{U}^-$ are disjoint *sets of APs, defined as $\mathcal{U}^+ = \{p \mid p \in \mathcal{U} \wedge \neg p \notin \mathcal{U}\}$ and $\mathcal{U}^- = \{p \mid p \notin \mathcal{U} \wedge \neg p \in \mathcal{U}\}$.*

The above mechanism ensures that the resulting set s' obtained by applying the composition operator to a data state s and an update set $\mathcal{U}$ satisfies the constraints for being a data state. It does so by removing relations/attributes from s if the object(s) in them are removed by $\mathcal{U}$. Also, an existing attribute predicate is deleted if a new one is introduced for the same object-attribute pair. Finally, if $\mathcal{U}$ contains both an atom p and its negation $\neg p$, the data state is not modified with respect to p.

Definition 8 (Instantiation Domain). *An* instantiation domain *is a tuple* $\langle s, \tau, Act, \mathcal{O}\rangle$ *where* $s \in \mathbb{S}$, $\tau \in \mathbb{T}$, $Act \in \mathbb{A}$, *and* $\mathcal{O}$ *is a* finite *subset of* $\mathbb{O}$ *representing a set of objects providing a context. We denote by* $\mathbb{D}$ *the set of all instantiation domains.*

Let $id = \langle s, \tau, A, \mathcal{O}\rangle \in \mathbb{D}$, let r be a rule of the form 1, and let $\mathsf{a} \in \mathbb{O} \cup \mathbb{O}^2$.

For attribute rules, if $\mathsf{a} \notin \mathcal{O}$, the evaluation stops and yields no effect. Otherwise, let $\mathsf{a} = \mathtt{a}$. Q is evaluated over s_G (see Definition 6) and the starting vertex $v_\mathtt{a}$, to obtain the set of vertices $[\![Q]\!]_{s_G, v_\mathtt{a}}$. The condition-effect rule r^1 is applied to each object $\mathtt{b}$ that corresponds to this set of vertices. For object/relation rules, the condition-effect rule applies directly to a.

The semantics of condition-effect rules viz. r^1 are as follows. The applicability of r^1 to b over id is captured by a predicate $\mathtt{Eval}(r^1, \mathsf{b})$ over id, which is true if $Act = A$ and one of the following holds.

- When $\ell = o$: $\mathsf{b} = \mathtt{b} \in \mathcal{O}$ and $\varphi[x/\mathtt{b}]$ is true in $\langle s, \mathcal{O}\rangle$.
- When $\ell = a$: $\mathsf{b} = \mathtt{b} \in \mathbb{O}$ and $\varphi[x/\mathtt{b}]$ is true in $\langle s, \mathcal{O}\rangle$.
- When $\ell = r$: $\mathsf{b} = \langle \mathtt{b}_0, \mathtt{b}_1\rangle$, $\varphi[x_0/\mathtt{b}_0, x_1/\mathtt{b}_1]$ is true in $\langle s, \mathcal{O}\rangle$, and either
  (*i*) r affects relations within objects in $\mathcal{O}$, that is, $t = \mathtt{int} \wedge \mathsf{b} \in \mathcal{O}^2$, or
  (*ii*) r affects relations between an object in $\mathcal{O}$ and an object not in $\mathcal{O}$, that is, $t = \mathtt{ext} \wedge \mathsf{b} \in (\mathcal{O} \times (\mathbb{O} \setminus \mathcal{O})) \cup ((\mathbb{O} \setminus \mathcal{O}) \times \mathcal{O})$.
  Also, $\mathsf{R}_\mathsf{X}(R) = \langle \mathsf{type}(\mathtt{b}_0), \mathsf{type}(\mathtt{b}_1)\rangle$, where $R \in \mathbb{R}$ is the relation type r affects.

If $\mathtt{Eval}(r^1, \mathsf{b})$ holds over id, for rules affecting objects and relations, the effect of the rule is simply the literal in η, grounded by b. For rules affecting attributes, the literal containing the new attribute assignment for an effect $\langle K, f, \Psi\rangle$ is determined by applying the function f to the restricted answer set for Ψ over s, $\mathcal{O}$ and $\mathtt{b}$, and the timestamp τ, formally, this is the literal $K(\mathtt{b}, f(\mathcal{RA}_\Psi^{s,\mathcal{O},\mathtt{b}}, \tau))$.

Let $\mathsf{Effs}\colon \mathbb{S} \times (\mathbb{O} \cup \mathbb{O}^2) \times \mathbb{D} \to 2^{\mathbb{AP}}$ map a rule, an object/object pair, and an instantiation domain to its *combined effects* set, which is a subset of $\mathbb{AP}$. Given r, id, and a as defined above, we define $\mathsf{Effs}(r, \mathsf{a}, id)$ to be $\emptyset$ when $\ell = o$ or $\ell = a$ and $\mathsf{a} \notin \mathbb{O}$, or $\ell = r$ and $\mathsf{a} \notin \mathbb{O}^2$: $\emptyset$. Otherwise:

- When $\ell = o$: $\{\eta[x/\mathtt{a}] \mid \mathtt{Eval}(r^1, \mathtt{a}) \text{ holds in } id\}$, where $\mathsf{a} = \mathtt{a} \in \mathbb{O}$,
- When $\ell = r$: $\{\eta[x_0/\mathtt{a}_0, x_1/\mathtt{a}_1] \mid \mathtt{Eval}(r^1, \langle \mathtt{a}_0, \mathtt{a}_1\rangle) \text{ holds in } id\}$, where $\mathsf{a} = \langle \mathtt{a}_0, \mathtt{a}_1\rangle \in \mathbb{O}^2$, and
- When $\ell = a$: $\{K(\mathtt{b}, f(\mathcal{RA}_\Psi^{s,\mathcal{O},\mathtt{b}}, \tau)) \mid v_\mathtt{b} \in [\![r^0]\!]_{s_G, v_\mathtt{a}} \wedge \mathtt{Eval}(r^1, \mathtt{b}) \text{ holds in } id\}$, where $\mathsf{a} = \mathtt{a} \in \mathbb{O}$.

Example 4 (Rule Evaluation Sample). Consider the EKG G_{ex} and the set $\mathcal{C}_{ex}$ of rules given in Examples 1 and 2, respectively, as well as the initial data state s_0^{ex} of G_{ex}, as given in Formula 4. Since e^1 observes *PlaceOrder*, it adds $\mathtt{Obj}(\mathtt{o})$, *Contains*$(\mathtt{o}, \mathtt{i}_1)$, and *Contains*$(\mathtt{o}, \mathtt{i}_2)$ to s_0^{ex}, following rules in $\mathcal{C}_{ex}$. We denote the resulting state as s_1^{ex}. The evaluation of the $\mathtt{price}$ update rule $r \in \mathcal{C}_{ex}$ (see rule 2), over the instantiation domain $id = \langle s_1^{ex}, 2, ShipOrder, \{\mathtt{o}\}\rangle$ and the object $\mathtt{o} \in \{\mathtt{o}\}$ proceeds as follows. First, the 2SSRPQ *Contains* $\cdot$ *HasItem*$^-$

is evaluated over $\langle s_1^{ex}{}_G, v_o\rangle$. It yields a singleton set containing a vertex that corresponds to the *Product* p.

For p, we evaluate the condition-effect rule. Since the activity *ShipOrder* matches the expectation of the rule, and the FO-formula in the condition is simply `true`, the effect of this rule is applied. The FO-formula in the effect of r produces the restricted answer set $\{\langle 0, 100\rangle\}$ on evaluation. Then, $f(\{\langle \mathtt{0}, \mathtt{100}\rangle\}, 2)$ is computed, yielding $(1 + 2 \cdot 0.05) \cdot 100 = 110$. Thus, we have $\mathsf{Effs}(r, \mathtt{o}, id) = \{\mathtt{price}(\mathtt{p}, 110)\}$. ◁

Theorem 1. *Given a rule $r \in \mathbb{C}$, data state $s \in \mathbb{S}$, and an instantiation domain $id = \langle s, \tau, A, \mathcal{O}\rangle \in \mathbb{D}$, the set $\mathcal{U} = \bigcup_{\mathtt{a} \in \mathbb{O} \cup \mathbb{O}^2} \mathsf{Effs}(r, \mathtt{a}, id)$ is an* update set *and it can be effectively computed.*

Proof. By definition, s, and therefore s_G is finite. Thus, the set $[\![Q]\!]_{s_G, v_\mathtt{a}}$ is finite. Additionally, the evaluation $\mathtt{Eval}(r^1, \mathtt{b})$ can be effectively computed for every $r \in \mathbb{C}$, $\langle s, \tau, Act', \mathcal{O}\rangle \in \mathbb{D}$, and $\mathtt{b} \in \mathcal{O}$, since the set $\mathcal{O}$ and the state s over which the FO and path formulae are evaluated are finite. Finally, it is known that for all $f \in \mathbb{F}$ and any input arguments, f can be effectively computed on such input. □

4 Execution Semantics

In this section, we describe how rule application to evolve the data leads to a finite transition system. We define a *finite restriction* to be a tuple $\mathcal{W} = \langle \mathcal{D}, \mathcal{C}, \mathcal{T}, \mathcal{A}, \mathcal{I}, n\rangle$, where the set $\mathcal{D} \subseteq \mathbb{O}$ of domain objects, $\mathcal{C} \subseteq \mathbb{C}$ of rules, $\mathcal{T} \subseteq \mathbb{T}$ of timestamps, $\mathcal{A} \subseteq \mathbb{A}$ of activities, and $\mathcal{I} \subseteq \mathbb{I}$ of assertions are finite sets, and $n \in \mathbb{N}$ represents an upper bound on the process size considered for timeline construction. We partition the set $\mathcal{C}$ of rules by type, and denote the resulting subsets by $\mathcal{C}_{tp}$, where $tp \in \{\mathtt{co}, \mathtt{do}, \mathtt{cr}, \mathtt{dr}, \mathtt{ua}\}$ indicates whether the rules create objects, delete objects, create relations, delete relations, or update attribute values, respectively. To avoid ambiguity in computing attribute values, we assume that for each attribute of type $K \in \mathbb{K}$ and each activity $Act \in \mathcal{A}$, there is at most one rule in $\mathcal{C}_{\mathtt{ua}}$ that affects attributes of type K and has Act among its conditions.

The transition system $TS_{\mathcal{W}} = \langle \mathcal{S}, \mathsf{s}_0, \Rightarrow\rangle$ with respect to $\mathcal{W}$ is defined as follows:

- $\mathcal{S} \subseteq \mathbb{S}$ is a *finite* set of states, defined inductively below (together with $\Rightarrow$).
- $\mathsf{s}_0 \in \mathcal{S}$ is the initial state, consisting of all objects in $\mathcal{D}$ that have static types, their types, and the initial relations and attributes in $\mathcal{I}$. Formally $\mathsf{s}_0 = \{\mathtt{Obj}(a) \mid a \in \mathcal{D} \wedge a_{\mathsf{type}} \in \mathbb{E}_S\} \cup \{\mathtt{hasType}(a, \mathsf{type}(a)) \mid a \in \mathcal{D}\} \cup \{P(x_0, x_1) \mid (P, x_0, x_1) \in \mathcal{I}\}$.
- $\Rightarrow \subseteq \mathcal{S} \times \mathcal{T} \times \mathcal{A} \times (2^{\mathcal{D}} \setminus \emptyset) \times \mathcal{S}$ is the transition relation between states, where each transition is labelled with a timestamp in $\mathcal{T}$, an activity in $\mathcal{A}$, and a non-empty set of objects in $\mathcal{D}$. We denote the components of a transition $t = \langle s, \tau, Act, \mathcal{O}, s'\rangle \in \Rightarrow$ as follows: $s = \mathsf{s}(t)$, $s' = \mathsf{t}(t)$, and $\langle \tau, Act, \mathcal{O}\rangle = \mathbb{L}(t)$.

For each $0 \leq k \leq 2n$, suppose that $\mathit{Reaches}_k$ is the set of states reachable from the initial state s_0 by traversing exactly k $\Rightarrow$-relations. The transition relation $\Rightarrow$ and the $\mathit{Reaches}_k$ family of sets are defined by mutual induction over k as follows.

For the base case, $k = 0$, we define $\mathit{Reaches}_0 = \{\mathsf{s}_0\}$. For the induction step, assume that $s \in \mathit{Reaches}_k$ where k is even and $0 \leq k < 2n$. Then, for each tuple $\langle \tau, \mathit{Act}, \mathcal{O}\rangle \in \mathcal{T} \times \mathcal{A} \times (2^{\mathcal{D}} \setminus \emptyset)$, we define:

1. An instantiation domain $id = \langle s, \tau, \mathit{Act}, \mathcal{O}\rangle \in \mathbb{D}$ and a state s_1 constructed by applying the effects of all pairs $\langle r, a\rangle \in \mathcal{C}_{\mathsf{co}} \times \mathcal{O}$ where the conditions of r hold for the argument a, formally $s_1 = s \circ \bigcup_{\langle r,a\rangle \in \mathcal{C}_{\mathsf{co}} \times \mathcal{O}} \mathsf{Effs}(r, a, id)$.
2. A transition $\langle s, \tau, \mathit{Act}, \mathcal{O}, s_1\rangle \in \Rightarrow$.
3. An instantiation domain $id = \langle s_1, \tau, \mathit{Act}, \mathcal{O}\rangle \in \mathbb{D}$ and a state s_2 that is constructed by taking the union of the effects from each pair $\langle r, a\rangle$ that is either *(i)* in $(\mathcal{C}_{\mathsf{cr}} \cup \mathcal{C}_{\mathsf{dr}}) \times (\mathcal{D} \times \mathcal{D})$ or in $\mathcal{C}_{\mathsf{do}} \times \mathcal{O}$, or *(ii)* is drawn from $\langle r, a\rangle \in \mathcal{C}_{\mathsf{ua}} \times \mathcal{O}$. Formally, if $\mathcal{F} = \{\langle r, a\rangle \mid \big((r \in \mathcal{C}_{\mathsf{cr}} \cup \mathcal{C}_{\mathsf{dr}} \wedge a \in \mathcal{D}^2\big) \vee (r \in \mathcal{C}_{\mathsf{do}} \wedge a \in \mathcal{O})\big)\}$ then the resulting state is $s_2 = s_1 \circ \bigcup_{\langle r,a\rangle \in \mathcal{F} \cup \mathcal{C}_{\mathsf{ua}} \times \mathcal{O}} \mathsf{Effs}(r, a, id)$.
4. A transition $\langle s_1, \mathit{Act}, \mathcal{O}, s_2\rangle \in \Rightarrow$.

Observe that Theorem 1 ensures that both s_1 and s_2 above are states, and that they can be effectively computed. Each state s_1 constructed from s is directly connected to a state in $\mathit{Reaches}_k$, hence it belongs to $\mathit{Reaches}_{k+1}$. Following a similar logic, s_2 is in $\mathit{Reaches}_{k+2}$. Continuing in this manner, $\mathit{Reaches}_{2n}$ is constructed, which contains all objects that can be reached from s_0 in $2n$ steps. The set of all relations defined above forms the transition relation $\Rightarrow$, while $\mathcal{S}$ is defined as the set $\bigcup_{k=0}^{2n} \mathit{Reaches}_k$, which contains all states reachable from s_0 in at most $2n$ steps. Observe that, given a data state and an instantiation domain, we apply the rules in $\mathcal{C}$ in two stages. First, all object creation rules are applied, and then the remaining ones. This allows the domain expert to encode with rules an activity that both creates an object and associates it to relations/attributes, as, for instance, is the case with the *PlaceOrder* activity.

5 Timeline Construction

We construct a TPG $D = \langle V_D, E_D, \mathsf{label}_D, \mathsf{prop}_D\rangle$ with respect to a set $\mathcal{C} \subseteq \mathbb{C}$ of rules, for an input EKG $G = \langle V, E, \mathsf{label}, \mathsf{prop}\rangle$ as follows. Let $\mathcal{W} = \langle V^O, \mathcal{C}, \mathcal{T}, \mathcal{A}, \mathbb{I}_G, n\rangle$, where $\mathcal{T}$ and $\mathcal{A}$ are the sets of timestamp and activity values of the events in V^E, and n is the size of V^E, be a finite restriction as defined in Sect. 4, and let $\mathcal{E} = \langle e^0, \ldots, e^{n-1}\rangle$ be an ordering of V^E based on event timestamps. We define a path π of length $2n$ inductively as follows: $\pi^0 = \langle \mathsf{s}_0\rangle$ and for all $i \in \{0, \ldots n-1\}$, π^{i+1} is obtained from π^i by appending $\langle t^{2i} s^{2i+1} t^{2i+1} s^{2i+2}\rangle$, where *(i)* $\mathit{lab}^i = \langle \mathsf{prop}(e^i, \mathsf{ts}), \mathsf{prop}(e^i, \mathsf{act}), \mathit{corr}_{e^i}\rangle$ is the label of e^i, *(ii)* $s^{2i+1} \in \mathit{Reaches}_{2i+1}$ and $s^{2i+2} \in \mathit{Reaches}_{2i+2}$ are the states resulting from the two-stage application of lab^i starting from the end of π^i (i.e., s^{2i}), and *(iii)* $t^{2i} = \langle s^{2i}, \mathit{lab}^i, s^{2i+1}\rangle$ and $t^{2i+1} = \langle s^{2i+1}, \mathit{lab}^i, s^{2i+2}\rangle$ are transitions in $\Rightarrow$. The path π is then defined as π^n.

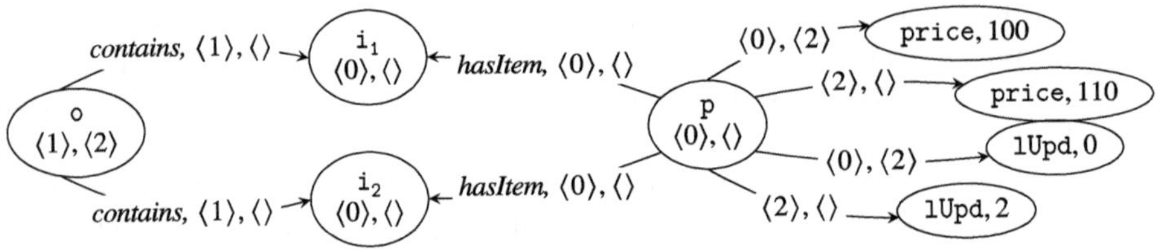

Fig. 1. Timeline obtained for the Order-Management domain with the EKG G_{ex}

We begin constructing D by adding, for each object (resp., relation/attribute value assignment) in s_0, a vertex (resp., edge) to it, and by setting the $\mathsf{createTimes}$ attribute of this vertex (resp., edge) to $\langle \mathsf{prop}(e^0, \mathsf{ts})\rangle$ and the $\mathsf{deleteTimes}$ attribute to $\langle\rangle$. Then, for each $0 \leq i < n$, if $\tau = \mathsf{prop}(e^i, \mathsf{ts})$, D is constructed iteratively as follows.

1. For $a \in V^O$ and $\tau \in \mathcal{T}$, τ is added to $\mathsf{prop}_D(a, \mathsf{createTimes})$ (adding a to V_D if necessary) if $\mathtt{Obj}(a) \in s^{2i+2} \backslash s^{2i}$. Similarly, τ is added to $\mathsf{prop}_D(a, \mathsf{deleteTimes})$ if $\mathtt{Obj}(a) \in s^{2i} \setminus s^{2i+2}$.
2. Object-object relations in D, along with their $\mathsf{createTimes}$ and $\mathsf{deleteTimes}$, are constructed analogously.
3. For $a \in V^O$, $u \in \mathbb{V}$, $K \in \mathbb{K}$, we add τ to $\mathsf{prop}_D(\langle a, \langle u, K\rangle\rangle, \mathsf{createTimes})$ if $K(a,u) \in s^{2i+2} \backslash s^{2i}$. The vertices a, u and edge $\langle a, \langle K, u\rangle\rangle$ are created if absent. Similarly, τ is added to $\mathsf{prop}_D(\langle a, \langle K, u\rangle\rangle, \mathsf{deleteTimes})$ if $K(a,u) \in s^{2i} \setminus s^{2i+2}$.

The path π provides provenance for every timestamp in D, ensuring that each timestamp in it can be traced back to the execution semantics provided by $\mathcal{C}$, captured by $TS_{\mathcal{W}}$. Therefore, we claim that D constructed as above is consistent and complete with respect to the semantics of $\mathcal{C}$ for the input EKG G

Example 5 (Timeline Generation). Consider the EKG G_{ex} and the set $\mathcal{C}_{ex}$ of rules described in Examples 1 and 4 respectively.

The finite restriction induced by G_{ex} and $\mathcal{C}_{ex}$ is given by $\mathcal{W} = \langle V^O_{ex}, \mathcal{C}_{ex}, \{1, 2\}, \{PlaceOrder, ShipOrder\}, \mathbb{I}_{G_{ex}}, 2\rangle$. We note that the state s_0^{ex} described in Example 3 is the initial state of $TS_{\mathcal{W}}$. Figure 1 is a visualization of the TPG constructed as above for the input G_{ex}, given the semantics provided by $\mathcal{C}_{ex}$. Vertices are labelled by object identifiers/attribute-attribute value pairs. Edges between objects are labelled by their relation types. Following this, all vertices and edges also have their $\mathsf{createTimes}$ and $\mathsf{deleteTimes}$ sequences presented as tuples. ◁

6 Conclusions

In this paper, we have provided a formal basis for using a combination of 2SSR-PQs and condition-effect rules for the purpose of timeline generation. We defined a transition system where each state corresponds to a data state, and transitions between states are governed by the effects of rules. Given an event log and a set of rules, we have shown how such a transition system can produce a timeline that is consistent and complete with the rules' semantics when applied to the input log. We are currently working on an effective and efficient implementation of the algorithm that follows the proposed consistent and complete timeline construction. We also plan to develop a tool that leverages log schemas commonly used in the OCPM community for both its input and output, to ensure interoperability with already existing tools.

Acknowledgments. This research has been partially supported by the HEU project CyclOps (GA n. 101135513), by the Province of Bolzano and FWF through project OnTeGra (DOI 10.55776/PIN8884924), by the Province of Bolzano and EU through projects ERDF-FESR 1078 CRIMA, and ERDF-FESR 1047 AI-Lab, and by MUR through the PRIN project 2022XERWK9 S-PIC4CHU.

References

1. Aalst, W.M.P.: Object-centric process mining: dealing with divergence and convergence in event data. In: Ölveczky, P.C., Salaün, G. (eds.) SEFM 2019. LNCS, vol. 11724, pp. 3–25. Springer, Cham (2019). https://doi.org/10.1007/978-3-030-30446-1_1
2. Belyanin, G., Grigoriev, S., Suvorov, R.: Single-source regular path querying in terms of linear algebra. CoRR Technical Report arXiv:2412.10287. arXiv org e-Print archive (2025), also published in the Proc. of the Workshop on Large-Scale Graph Data Analytics (LSGDA)
3. Berti, A., et al.: OCEL (Object-Centric Event Log) 2.0 specification. CoRR Technical Report arXiv:2403.01975. arXiv org e-Print archive (2024)
4. Berti, A., Montali, M., van der Aalst, W.M.P.: Advancements and challenges in object-centric process mining: a systematic literature review. CoRR Technical Report arXiv:2311.08795. arXiv org e-Print archive (2023)
5. Buneman, P.: Semistructured data. In: Proceedings of PODS, pp. 117–121 (1997)
6. Calvanese, D., De Giacomo, G., Lenzerini, M., Vardi, M.Y.: Reasoning on regular path queries. SIGMOD Rec. **32**(4), 83–92 (2003). https://doi.org/10.1145/959060.959076
7. Chaki, R., Calvanese, D., Montali, M.: Generation of timelines from event knowledge graphs using domain knowledge. In: Proceedings of the 24th International Conference on Computer Information Systems and Industrial Management Applications (CISIM). LNCS, vol. 15927, pp. 275–289. Springer, Heidelberg (2025). https://doi.org/10.1007/978-3-032-02406-0_20
8. Fahland, D.: Process mining over multiple behavioral dimensions with Event Knowledge Graphs. In: van der Aalst, W.M.P., Carmona, J. (eds.) Process Mining Handbook, LNBIP, vol. 448, pp. 274–319. Springer, Heidelberg (2022). https://doi.org/10.1007/978-3-031-08848-3_9

Generative and Representation Learning

ReMemDiff: Multi-label Lifelong Machine Learning Using Deep Generative Replay

Mohammed Awal Kassim[1], Herna Viktor[1(✉)], and Wojtek Michalowski[2]

[1] School of Electrical Engineering and Computer Science, University of Ottawa, Ottawa, ON, Canada
{mkass005,hviktor}@uottawa.ca

[2] Telfer School of Management, University of Ottawa, Ottawa, ON, Canada
wojtek@telfer.uottawa.ca

Abstract. Lifelong machine learning systems continuously learn in dynamic environments, using experience from previous tasks to improve future learning and prediction. In multi-label lifelong learning, the model assigns multiple labels to each instance and updates its knowledge progressively as new tasks arrive. The aim is to maintain accurate predictions for earlier tasks while integrating new ones. However, combining lifelong learning with multi-label prediction presents a particular challenge in retaining past knowledge due to the high diversity and overlap in label semantics. To address this, we introduce **Memory-based Diffusion Replay (ReMemDiff)**, a framework that learns from multi-label image tasks while reducing catastrophic forgetting. Our approach uses stable diffusion, a generative model that synthesises high-quality images via a progressive denoising process. It also incorporates variational autoencoders (VAEs) for efficient latent space operations, as well as a U-Net for precise denoising in the reverse diffusion process. This is guided by textual embeddings that are generated using the bootstrapping language image pre-training (BLIP) model. The ReMemDiff framework uses a convolutional neural network (CNN) to assign multiple labels to images. Selected image samples are converted into textual representations and stored in a buffer. These are then used to generate synthetic images interleaved with real images from the current task. This ensures that the generated samples reflect past tasks and reinforce knowledge retention. Experimental evaluations on two multi-task, multi-label image datasets validate the effectiveness of our approach.

Keywords: Lifelong learning · generative replay · multi-label learning

1 Introduction

The ability to accumulate knowledge across a sequence of distinct tasks, while retaining competence on earlier ones, is key to developing truly intelligent systems that can operate in dynamic and complex environments [1]. In such lifelong

G. Andresini et al. (Eds.): ISMIS 2026, LNAI 16685, pp. 49–59, 2027.
https://doi.org/10.1007/978-3-032-32643-0_5

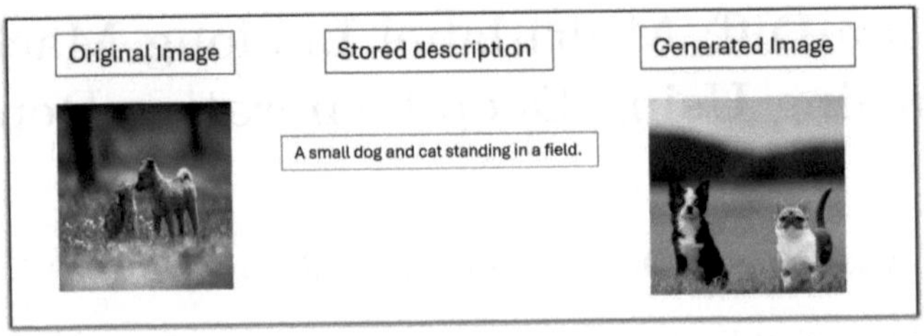

Fig. 1. Sample image, stored textual descriptions, and generated image.

learning settings, the model must integrate new knowledge without degrading performance on previously learned tasks. The data encountered in these settings are often multi-label, meaning that each data point can belong to multiple classes simultaneously. Unlike traditional multi-label learning, where a model predicts several labels from a fixed dataset, multi-label lifelong learning requires the model to adapt to newly introduced tasks and label sets sequentially while preserving performance on labels learned in earlier tasks.

A widely used technique in lifelong machine learning is to reuse previously encountered examples to refresh the model's memory and prevent the forgetting of previously learned information while continuously learning new tasks. This process is known as 'exemplar rehearsal' or 'experience replay'. However, although this technique is effective in reducing forgetting, it demands a considerable amount of working memory [2]. This can be a significant drawback, especially when computational resources are limited. Deep generative replay addresses this limitation by training a generative model to approximate the distribution of past tasks and synthesising representative samples on demand, thereby avoiding the need to store original data [3].

In this paper, we propose Memory-based Diffusion Replay (ReMemDiff), a generative replay framework for continual multi-label learning that mitigates catastrophic forgetting without storing past data. As illustrated in Fig. 1, ReMemDiff synthesizes representative images of previous tasks, removing the need for explicit data retention. The method leverages a Stable Diffusion model to generate diverse replay samples, while an image-to-text module explicitly recovers all labels present in generated images, preventing the label loss which limits existing multi-label continual learning approaches. We empirically demonstrate the effectiveness of ReMemDiff through comparisons with state-of-the-art baselines, showing improved multi-label performance and stronger retention of previously learned knowledge.

The remainder of this paper is organised as follows. Section 2 details our ReMemDiff framework. This is followed by our experimental evaluation in Sect. 3. Finally, Sect. 4 concludes our paper and highlights future work.

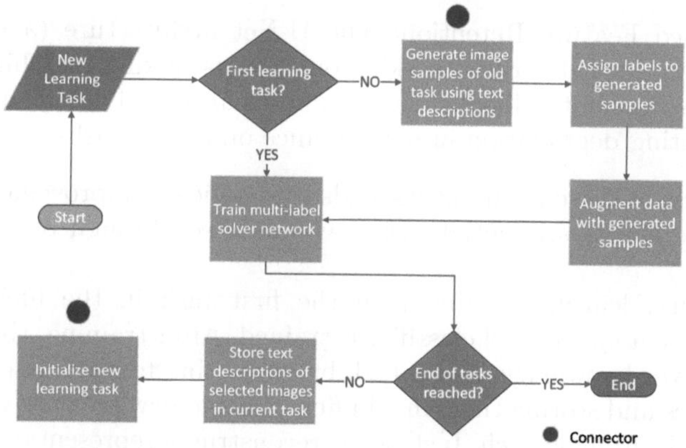

Fig. 2. Workflow of the ReMemDiff framework.

2 ReMemDiff Framework

Our ReMemDiff framework includes a solver designed to learn from multiple labels and a generator tasked with deriving text descriptions from input images during training. In the course of learning a new task, the model uses the textual descriptions from preceding tasks to generate synthetic image samples, which are seamlessly interleaved with the data pertaining to the current task. This interleaved training approach is aimed at enhancing the model's ability to adapt to new tasks while retaining the knowledge gained from prior learning experiences. The workflow for our ReMemDiff framework is shown in Fig. 2.

Stable diffusion excels in synthesizing high-quality images through a progressive denoising process. In this study, it is enhanced with VAEs to enable efficient operations in the latent space and a U-Net architecture for precise denoising, all guided by textual embeddings generated using the BLIP model. As such, the key techniques used to mitigate forgetting during multi-label lifelong learning are as follows:

1. Synthetic Data Generation: Stored textual descriptions from previous tasks are used as prompts to generate synthetic images that approximate the distribution of past data, allowing the model to rehearse prior knowledge while maintaining consistency with multi-label annotations.
2. Text-Guided Conditioning: BLIP-based textual descriptions (image captions automatically extracted from images) encode the semantic content and label relationships present in each sample, enabling the model to reconstruct correct label co-occurrences across tasks.
3. Continuous Representation Learning: The VAE architecture (a probabilistic encoder–decoder model that maps images to a compact latent representation and reconstructs them from it) compresses visual features into a low-dimensional latent space and reconstructs them during replay, reducing storage and computational requirements.

4. Fine-Grained Feature Retention: The U-Net architecture (a convolutional encoder–decoder network with skip connections linking matching resolution layers) preserves both global structure and local spatial details during denoising, preventing degradation in performance on earlier tasks.

The integration of these components leads to significant improvements in retaining knowledge across sequential tasks, as validated through our experimental evaluation.

In summary, learning begins with the first task in the lifelong learning sequence, where a multi-label classifier is trained. After training, the ReMemDiff system preserves knowledge of this task by extracting textual descriptions from selected images and storing them in a buffer. When a new task arrives, the model does not retrain from scratch. Instead, it reconstructs representative samples of previous tasks by generating images from the stored textual descriptions and assigning the corresponding labels. These synthetic samples are combined with the new task data to form an augmented training set. By repeatedly replaying generated samples while learning new tasks, the model reinforces previously acquired knowledge and reduces forgetting. This cycle continues sequentially until all tasks have been learned.

2.1 Multi-label Solver

We employ a convolutional neural network (CNN) because of its ability to learn salient visual features and maintain translation invariance, allowing objects to be recognised regardless of their position in the image. The solver is built on MobileNetV2 [4], a lightweight CNN architecture known for its computational efficiency and fast training.

At the output layer, a sigmoid activation function is applied and the model is trained using binary cross-entropy (BCE) loss. This choice naturally supports multi-label classification, where each output neuron independently predicts the presence or absence of a class. BCE measures the discrepancy between predicted probabilities and true labels; for a dataset of N samples, it is defined as

$$\text{BCE} = -\frac{1}{N}\sum_{i=1}^{N}\left(y_i \log(p_i) + (1-y_i)\log(1-p_i)\right) \tag{1}$$

where y_i is the actual label and p_i is the predicted probability for class membership. While this learning framework enables effective multi-label prediction, it does not inherently address catastrophic forgetting, where learning new tasks degrades performance on earlier ones. To mitigate this, we next introduce the generator component and describe how it interacts with the solver.

2.2 Image Generator

ReMemDiff's generator produces samples resembling data from previous tasks by maximizing their likelihood under the real data distribution [3]. We implement this using a stable diffusion model, which learns the underlying data distribution rather than decision boundaries, enabling the synthesis of realistic new samples. To support this process, the diffusion model operates in a latent space provided by a Variational Autoencoder (VAE). The VAE encoder maps inputs to a probabilistic latent representation, and the decoder reconstructs the data from latent samples [5]. This allows for efficient compression while preserving the structure necessary for generation. Generation itself follows the diffusion paradigm: a forwards process progressively adds noise to the data [6], and the model learns the reverse denoising process to reconstruct the original structure. Together, the VAE latent representation and the reverse diffusion process yield a flexible, high-fidelity generative model of the data distribution. In this work, samples are selected for storage using a simple random strategy; more sophisticated buffer management policies (e.g., class-balanced selection or capacity-aware sampling) are left for future investigation.

Algorithm 1. Multi-Label Deep Generative Replay (MLDGR) With Diffusion and BLIP

Input: Sequence of tasks $T_1, T_2, \ldots, T_N$ with datasets $D_1, D_2, \ldots, D_N$
Output: Trained model
Initialise a model $\mathcal{M}$ for the first task T_1
Initialise a buffer $\mathcal{B}$ for storing image captions
for each task T_i in $T_1, T_2, \ldots, T_N$ **do**
  Train $\mathcal{M}$ on D_i using gradient descent and backpropagation
  if $T_i == T_N$ **then**
    End learning process
  else
    for each epoch **do**
      for each minibatch b in D_i **do**
        Randomly select an image x from b
        Generate a caption c for x using the BLIP model
        Store (c) in the buffer $\mathcal{B}$
      end for
    end for
    Initialise a new model $\mathcal{M}_{\text{new}}$ for task T_{i+1}
    Initialise a generator $\mathcal{G}$
    Load content from the buffer $\mathcal{B}$
    for each minibatch b in D_{i+1} **do**
      Use $\mathcal{G}$ and text from $\mathcal{B}$ to generate samples $\tilde{x}$ representing previous tasks
      Augment b with $\tilde{x}$ to create an augmented batch $\hat{b}$
      Train $\mathcal{M}_{\text{new}}$ on the augmented batch $\hat{b}$
    end for
    $\mathcal{M} \leftarrow \mathcal{M}_{\text{new}}$
  end if
end for

In the iterative forwards diffusion pass, we start with an image and then add a small amount of noise. This noising process is repeated many times [7].

Mathematically, this can be represented as

$$x_t = \sqrt{1-\beta_t}\,x_{t-1} + \sqrt{\beta_t}\epsilon \tag{2}$$

where x_t represents the data at step t (the image, in this case), β_t is a small noise scale at step t, and ϵ is random noise from a normal distribution. After many steps, the data are transformed into pure noise. The model then learns to reverse the noising process to reconstruct the original data. This is done by training a neural network to predict the noise that was added at each step during the forwards process [7]. Then, this predicted noise is subtracted from the noisy data. The reverse process can be represented as

$$x_{t-1} = \frac{1}{\sqrt{1-\beta_t}}\left(x_t - \frac{\beta_t}{\sqrt{1-\beta_t}}\epsilon_\theta(x_t, t)\right) \tag{3}$$

Here, x_{t-1} represents the reconstructed data at step $t-1$, and $\epsilon_\theta(x_t, t)$ is the noise predicted by the neural network at step t. During training, the model is shown pairs of noisy images and the corresponding noise. Its job is to learn to predict the noise that was added to the data. This is typically done using a loss function that measures the difference between the predicted noise and the actual noise. These equations briefly represent the core of how diffusion probabilistic models operate, transitioning data from a noisy state back to its original form through learned denoising steps.

In our implementation, we leverage the open-source stable diffusion model proposed by Rombach et al. [8]. This sophisticated framework operates by gradually transforming random noise into detailed images through controlled denoising. The model starts with a canvas of pure noise and, step by step, refines it into a coherent image, guided by the input text. This technique ensures that each phase of noise reduction is not only a move towards clarity but also a step towards realising an image dictated by the text prompt. ReMemDiff stores knowledge of past tasks in the form of text, which is then used to guide the generation of samples to be interleaved with data from the current task. Recall that, to identify labels in images with minimal error, we use a pre-trained model, BLIP [9], which excels at understanding and generating content. Employing this methodology achieves state-of-the-art results in learning from sequential tasks with minimal catastrophic forgetting.

3 Experimental Evaluation

We use two widely used multi-label image datasets, namely MSCOCO [10] and NUS-WIDE [11]. Details of the datasets and tasks are provided in Tables 1 and 2. For each dataset, we defined five distinct tasks, each grouping semantically different labels to evaluate the model under varied learning conditions. The tasks span diverse object and scene categories (Table 2), ensuring that the model must adapt to new visual concepts while retaining previously learned ones, and thereby providing a comprehensive test of continual multi-label learning and resistance

Table 1. Overview of the MSCOCO and NUS-WIDE Datasets

Characteristics	MSCOCO	NUS-WIDE
Total Dataset Size (images)	328,000	269,648
Number of Annotated Images	205,000	67,412
Number of Unannotated Images	123,000	202,236
Number of Object Categories	80	81
Average Captions per Image	5	2

Table 2. Description of Learning Tasks and Label Sets for Datasets

MSCOCO labels	NUS-WIDE labels
Person, Bicycle, Car, Motorcycle	Animal, Beach, Buildings
Airplane, Bus, Train, Truck	Clouds, Flowers, Grass
Light, Bench, Bird, Cat	Lake, Mountain, Ocean
Dog, Backpack, Umbrella, Handbag	Person, Plants, Reflection
Tie, Ball, Skateboard, Surfboard	Road, Rocks, Sky

to forgetting. All images were resized to 256 × 256 pixels to ensure consistent CNN input for batch processing. Unlike cropping, resizing preserves the full image content, which is important in multi-label settings where multiple objects may appear in a single image. We note that this resizing may reduce fine-grained details for small objects in multi-label scenes, potentially affecting the generator's ability to reconstruct subtle label-specific features.

3.1 Experimental Setup

We conducted five iterations, each with a distinct seed to mitigate the influence of random initialization on the outcomes. In each run, we recorded several key performance metrics: the mean average precision (mAP), overall F_1 score (OF_1), class-wise F_1 score (CF_1), and the forgetting metric [12]. F_1 scores combine precision and recall, allowing detection of forgetting (low recall) and misclassification (low precision). Mean average precision (mAP) summarizes performance across all tasks, reflecting how well the model preserves past knowledge while adapting to new tasks. Forgetting quantifies how much performance on earlier tasks degrades after learning new tasks. For a given task t, the forgetting is calculated as:

$$F_t = \max_{k \leq t} \left(a_{t,k} - a_{t,t} \right) \tag{4}$$

where $a_{t,k}$ is the accuracy on task t after learning task k, while $a_{t,t}$ is the accuracy on task t immediately after it was learned. This metric captures the worst decline in performance on a task, indicating how much the model has forgotten since the task was initially learned [12]. These metrics collectively provide a comprehensive insight into the model's performance, capturing its precision, recall, and ability to retain knowledge over time.

We compared ReMemDiff with a naive baseline and three state-of-the-art continual learning methods (Table 3). All results reported in Tables 3 and 4 were obtained through our own experimental implementation and evaluation of these methods under a consistent setup. The naive baseline uses the same architecture but no mechanism to prevent forgetting; it is trained sequentially, leading to performance degradation on earlier tasks. The comparison methods are Learning Without Forgetting (LWF), Elastic Weight Consolidation (EWC), and Synaptic Intelligence (SI) [13,14]. LWF preserves prior knowledge through knowledge distillation across shared and task-specific parameters [15]. EWC limits changes to parameters important for previous tasks via a quadratic penalty [16]. Similarly, SI constrains updates to important synapses by estimating their task relevance [14]. Next, we present the experimental results.

Table 3. Experimental Results against Datasets

MSCOCO	mAP	OF_1	CF_1
Naive Baseline	62.26	6.83	7.14
EWC	77.54	62.90	61.32
LWF	76.71	60.88	58.74
ReMemDiff (Ours)	**89.05**	**78.69**	**78.11**
SI	79.34	67.67	66.44
NUS-WIDE	**mAP**	**OF_1**	**CF_1**
Naive Baseline	65.81	5.21	5.08
EWC	79.25	66.23	64.59
LWF	77.26	61.92	59.64
ReMemDiff (Ours)	**87.93**	**77.19**	**77.13**
SI	79.91	68.44	67.05

Table 4. Forgetting Metrics for MSCOCO and NUS-WIDE Datasets

Dataset	Naive Baseline	EWC	LWF	ReMemDiff	SI
MSCOCO	0.07853	0.03745	0.03988	**0.00058**	0.03228
NUS-WIDE	0.11260	0.05725	0.05398	**0.02145**	0.05153

3.2 Experimental Results and Discussion

We first examine performance as tasks accumulate, as illustrated in Fig. 3, where each point corresponds to the model's performance after sequentially learning up

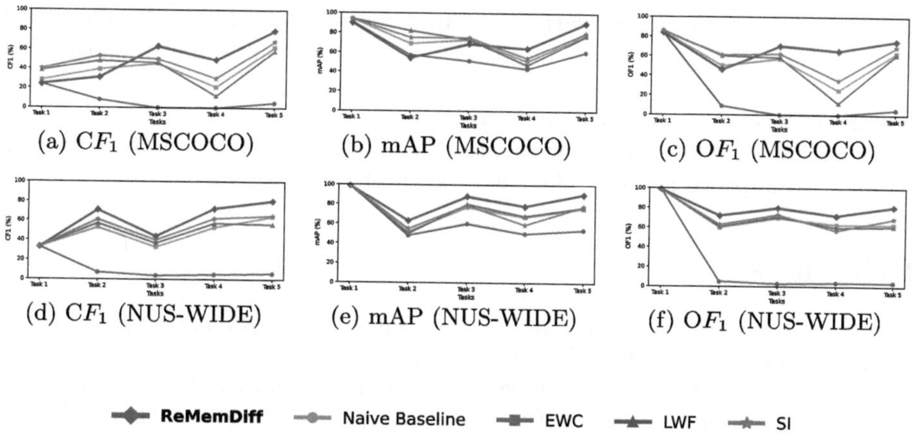

Fig. 3. Performance across sequential tasks on MSCOCO and NUS-WIDE. ReMemDiff is highlighted in the shared legend.

to the given task. The naive baseline consistently performs worst, as expected. EWC and SI maintain strong, stable mAP across tasks, while LWF performs well overall, peaking on task 2 and dropping on task 4. ReMemDiff initially declines when learning the second task, like the others, but improves as more tasks are added, achieving the best mAP, OF_1, and CF_1 by the fifth task, indicating effective cumulative learning.

We further analyse the results in Table 3. ReMemDiff achieves the highest mAP, OF_1, and CF_1 across both datasets, indicating accurate and consistent multi-label predictions. Again, the naive baseline performs poorly, while EWC, LWF, and SI improve performance, with SI showing stronger CF_1 scores, suggesting robustness to class imbalance. Across all methods, mAP values exceed OF_1 and CF_1 because mAP rewards correct ranking of labels (whereas F_1 more strictly penalises both false positives and false negatives), offering a more accurate assessment of the model's performance. The forgetting metric ranges from -1 (positive transfer) to 1 (complete forgetting), with 0 indicating no forgetting, as indicated in Table 4. Promisingly, ReMemDiff shows the lowest forgetting on both datasets, nearly zero on MSCOCO and still significantly better than other methods on NUS-WIDE. The naive baseline forgets the most, while EWC, LWF, and SI provide partial mitigation but remain less effective than ReMemDiff, confirming its strong knowledge retention across tasks.

4 Conclusion and Future Work

We have presented the ReMemDiff framework for continual multi-label learning that reduces forgetting without storing past data. By generating replay samples using stable diffusion guided by textual descriptions, the model preserves previously learned knowledge while adapting to new tasks. Experiments show that combining synthetic replay with structured representations enables consistent performance across tasks and improves retention in multi-label settings. Our future work will focus on selecting more informative samples that better represent the complete label distribution, including the design of principled buffer management strategies (e.g., class-balanced selection and explicit capacity constraints) to improve memory efficiency and replay quality.

References

1. Chen, Z., Liu, B.: Lifelong Machine Learning, vol. 1. Springer, Cham (2018). https://doi.org/10.1007/978-3-031-01581-6
2. Mocanu, D.C., Vega, M.T., Eaton, E., Stone, P., Liotta, A.: "Online contrastive divergence with generative replay: experience replay without storing data," 2016. arXiv:1610.05555
3. Shin, H., Lee, J.K., Kim, J., Kim, J.: Continual learning with deep generative replay. Adv. Neural Inf. Process. Syst. **30** (2017)
4. Sandler, M., Howard, A., Zhu, M., Zhmoginov, A., Chen, L.-C.: MobileNetV2: inverted residuals and linear bottlenecks. In: Proceedings of the IEEE Conference on Computer Vision and Pattern Recognition, pp. 4510–4520, 2018
5. Kingma, D.P., Welling, M.: Auto-encoding variational Bayes. In: Proceedings of the 2nd International Conference on Learning Representations (ICLR), 2014
6. Sohl-Dickstein, J., Weiss, E., Maheswaranathan, N., Ganguli, S.: Deep unsupervised learning using nonequilibrium thermodynamics. In: International Conference on Machine Learning. PMLR, pp. 2256–2265, 2015
7. Luo, C.: Understanding diffusion models: a unified perspective, 2022. arXiv:2208.11970
8. Rombach, R., Blattmann, A., Lorenz, D., Esser, P., Ommer, B.: High-resolution image synthesis with latent diffusion models. In: Proceedings of the IEEE/CVF Conference on Computer Vision and Pattern Recognition, pp. 10 684–10 695, 2022
9. Li, J., Li, D., Xiong, C., Hoi, S.: BLIP: bootstrapping language-image pre-training for unified vision-language understanding and generation. In: International Conference on Machine Learning, PMLR, pp. 12 888–12 900, 2022
10. Lin, T.-Y., et al.: Microsoft COCO: common objects in context. In: Fleet, D., Pajdla, T., Schiele, B., Tuytelaars, T. (eds.) Computer Vision – ECCV 2014. ECCV 2014. LNCS, vol. 8693, pp. 740–755. Springer, Cham (2014). https://doi.org/10.1007/978-3-319-10602-1_48
11. Chua, T.S., Tang, J., Hong, R., Li, H., Luo, Z., Zheng, Y.: NUS-WIDE: a real-world web image database from National University of Singapore. In: Proceedings of the ACM International Conference on Image and Video Retrieval, pp. 1–9, 2009
12. Chaudhry, A., Ranzato, M.A., Rohrbach, M., Elhoseiny, M.: Efficient lifelong learning with A-GEM. In: Proceedings of the 7th International Conference on Learning Representations (ICLR), 2019
13. Du, K.: AGCN: augmented graph convolutional network for lifelong multi-label image recognition. In: 2022 IEEE International Conference on Multimedia and Expo (ICME). IEEE 2022, pp. 01–06 (2022)

14. Zenke, F., Poole, B., Ganguli, S.: Continual learning through synaptic intelligence. In: International Conference on Machine Learning. PMLR, pp. 3987–3995, 2017
15. Li, Z., Hoiem, D.: Learning without forgetting. IEEE Trans. Pattern Anal. Mach. Intell. **40**(12), 2935–2947 (2017)
16. Kirkpatrick, J., et al.: Overcoming catastrophic forgetting in neural networks. Proc. Natl. Acad. Sci. U.S.A. **114**(13), 3521–3526 (2017)

Guided Conditional Diffusion for Correction of Weather Radar Beam Blockage Artefacts

Assaad Zeghina[1,2](✉), Victor Enescu[1,2], Nicolas Viltard[1], Laurent Barthes[1,2], and Cécile Mallet[1,2]

[1] LATMOS/IPSL, UVSQ Université Paris-Saclay, Sorbonne Université, CNRS, Guyancourt, France
{assaad.zeghina,victor.enescu,nicolas.viltard,laurent.barthes, cecile.mallet}@latmos.ipsl.fr
[2] ARCHES Team, Inria, Paris, France

Abstract. Weather radar mosaics provide high-resolution precipitation estimates but are often degraded by beam-blockage artefacts caused by terrain or infrastructure. These artefacts introduce systematic attenuation of radar reflectivity and distort precipitation patterns, particularly in complex topographic environments. Traditional correction approaches typically rely on geometric modeling or multi-radar fusion and often treat detection and correction as separate problems. In this work, we propose a guided conditional diffusion framework for correcting radar beam-blockage artefacts. The model reconstructs the precipitation field through a conditional reverse diffusion process guided by the corrupted radar observation and its associated quality map. During training, beam-blockage patterns are simulated on clean radar sectors to generate corrupted observations while preserving the original precipitation fields as references. This enables the model to learn both the spatial characteristics of blockage and the structure of precipitation fields. The method is evaluated on real radar mosaics containing both simulated and naturally occurring beam-blockage effects. Quantitative results show that the proposed approach reduces reconstruction errors within blocked regions while preserving precipitation values in unaffected areas. Qualitative analysis further demonstrates the recovery of coherent precipitation structures in degraded regions.

Keywords: Generative models · Deep learning · Remote sensing · Diffusion models

1 Introduction

Ground-based weather radars provide high temporal and spatial resolution precipitation measurements that are essential for hydrological modelling, flood forecasting, and climate research. Accurate quantitative precipitation estimation (QPE) is therefore crucial for understanding climate variability and hydrological responses [2]. However, radar observations are often affected by measurement

G. Andresini et al. (Eds.): ISMIS 2026, LNAI 16685, pp. 60–69, 2027.
https://doi.org/10.1007/978-3-032-32643-0_6

artefacts and systematic biases. In particular, terrain or infrastructure may partially block the radar beam, attenuating the returned signal and distorting precipitation patterns. Additional gaps may also arise from scanning strategies, blind zones, or temporary outages [9]. Traditional correction methods rely on geometric modelling, climatological adjustments, or multi-radar fusion. While physically grounded, these approaches often depend on auxiliary data and can be difficult to generalize across radar systems [10]. Deep learning approaches have recently been proposed to address these limitations by treating radar correction as an image restoration or inpainting problem. CNN and GAN-based methods have shown promising results in reconstructing precipitation fields [13], but they typically rely on masking corrupted regions and attempting to recreate the missing data from scratch, which may introduce unrealistic textures or excessive smoothing. In this work, we propose a guided conditional diffusion framework for correcting radar beam-blockage artefacts. Instead of masking regions and performing pure inpainting, the proposed approach leverages the information already present in degraded radar observations, enabling automatic correction of the affected sectors. We note that the proposed method operates on radar mosaics, where traditional reflectivity-based geometric and fusion correction methods cannot be directly applied. The model uses a conditional reverse diffusion process guided by both the precipitation field and its associated quality map to identify and remove attenuation artefacts while preserving valid measurements. Although the quality map provides a reliability prior, the model must still learn to reconstruct precipitation structures from degraded observations rather than directly using the map as a correction mask.

2 Related Works

Deep learning methods for radar correction generally formulate the problem as image restoration or inpainting, where corrupted radar observations are mapped to reconstructed precipitation fields. Early approaches used convolutional encoder–decoder networks such as U-Net architectures to fill blocked radar sectors [7,14]. Later works introduced conditional GANs trained on artificially masked radar regions to improve spatial consistency across sector boundaries [13]. Subsequent studies extended these models to polarimetric radar data and incorporated global spatial context [8,11,12]. Radar observations may also contain irregular gaps caused by blind zones or system outages. Studies comparing interpolation and generative models show that GAN-based methods better reproduce spatial variability, although they may generate unrealistic textures [3]. Architectures such as EFNet [15] and DSA-UNet [4] address these limitations through specialized loss functions and attention mechanisms. More recently, diffusion models have been explored for radar restoration due to their improved stability and ability to capture fine-scale structures. Noise-guided diffusion models [17] and conditional diffusion approaches [16] have shown promising results. However, the previously mentioned methods rely on explicitly masked regions and attempt to inpaint them, typically treating naturally occurring artefacts as missing areas. To the best of our knowledge, there are no approaches specifically designed to automatically detect beam-blockage sectors and directly correct the resulting attenuation artefacts.

3 Background

Raw weather radar observations acquire reflectivity Z, representing the backscattered power from hydrometeors within a resolution volume. Reflectivity is mathematically linked to the targeted rainfall rate R via an empirical power-law relationship: $Z = \alpha R^{\beta}$ where α and β are empirical coefficients dependent on precipitation type and drop-size distribution [1]. Rainfall rate R is typically expressed in millimeters per hour (mm/h), representing the depth of accumulated precipitation that would fall over one hour if the observed rainfall intensity remained constant. Because reflectivity increases nonlinearly with rain intensity, measurement degradations severely impact downstream estimation. When the radar beam encounters terrain or infrastructure, it experiences blockage, creating wedge-shaped sectors of artificially low or missing data.

3.1 Diffusion Probabilistic Models

Denoising Diffusion Probabilistic Models (DDPM) [5], are generative models that learn to synthesize data by reversing a gradual noising process. Let $\mathbf{x}_0 \sim q(\mathbf{x}_0)$ denote a data sample (e.g., an image). The forward diffusion process progressively adds Gaussian noise over T timesteps according to a fixed Markov chain:

$$q(\mathbf{x}_t \mid \mathbf{x}_{t-1}) = \mathcal{N}\left(\mathbf{x}_t; \sqrt{1-\beta_t}\mathbf{x}_{t-1}, \beta_t \mathbf{I}\right), \tag{1}$$

where $\{\beta_t\}_{t=1}^{T}$ is a predefined variance schedule. This process admits a closed-form expression:

$$q(\mathbf{x}_t \mid \mathbf{x}_0) = \mathcal{N}\left(\mathbf{x}_t; \sqrt{\bar{\alpha}_t}\mathbf{x}_0, (1-\bar{\alpha}_t)\mathbf{I}\right), \tag{2}$$

with $\alpha_t = 1 - \beta_t$ and $\bar{\alpha}_t = \prod_{s=1}^{t} \alpha_s$.

The reverse process is parameterized by a neural network (typically a U-Net) trained to predict the noise ϵ added at timestep t. In the conditional setting, the model is guided by an additional input $\mathbf{c}$ representing auxiliary information. In our case, $\mathbf{c}$ corresponds to the corrupted precipitation observation and its associated quality map. The reverse process is therefore defined as:

$$p_\theta(\mathbf{x}_{t-1} \mid \mathbf{x}_t, \mathbf{c}) = \mathcal{N}\left(\mathbf{x}_{t-1}; \mu_\theta(\mathbf{x}_t, t, \mathbf{c}), \sigma_t^2 \mathbf{I}\right). \tag{3}$$

Accordingly, the network predicts the noise term conditioned on this information: $\epsilon_\theta(\mathbf{x}_t, t, \mathbf{c})$. The training objective remains the minimization of the noise prediction error, now conditioned on $\mathbf{c}$:

$$\mathcal{L} = \mathbf{E}_{\mathbf{x}_0, \epsilon, t}\left[\|\epsilon - \epsilon_\theta(\mathbf{x}_t, t, \mathbf{c})\|^2\right]. \tag{4}$$

After training, generation starts from pure Gaussian noise $\mathbf{x}_T \sim \mathcal{N}(0, \mathbf{I})$ and iteratively applies the learned conditional reverse transitions to obtain $\mathbf{x}_0$.

4 Methodology

The proposed methodology follows a structured pipeline, which integrates radar data preprocessing, artifact modeling, and a dual-conditioned diffusion model for precipitation reconstruction. The following sections describe the different stages of this pipeline and the data used at each step.

4.1 Data Characteristics and Preprocessing

The data used in this study consist of radar precipitation mosaics generated through the fusion of multiple radar sensors, providing spatially continuous estimates of precipitation over large regions. Each mosaic contains two types of information: the precipitation intensity field and an associated quality map (as illustrated in Fig. 1).

Precipitation Intensity Maps. Rainfall information is represented as two-dimensional spatial grids encoding the rain rate R. Each grid corresponds to a snapshot of the precipitation field acquired at 5-min intervals and expressed in mm/h. Each pixel represents precipitation over a 1×1 km area.

Quality Maps (Q). Each precipitation mosaic is accompanied by a Quality Map (Q). For every pixel (i, j), $Q_{i,j} \in [0, 100]$ provides a quantitative index of the measurement's reliability. A score of 100 indicates optimal conditions, while lower scores signal potential degradations. We observe that Q maps exhibit a high spatial correlation with physical artifacts, making them an ideal auxiliary signal for guiding the correction process.

Region Sampling and Selection. For training, it is necessary to distinguish between clean precipitation observations and regions affected by beam-blockage artefacts. Wedge-shaped sectors associated with low values in the quality map Q are first identified as corrupted regions and reserved for qualitative evaluation during inference. Training samples are extracted from clean areas of the radar mosaics where Q indicates no artefacts. From these regions, patches are cropped and used as ground-truth precipitation fields. Synthetic beam-blockage masks are then applied to generate corrupted observations, forming training triplets composed of the clean precipitation field (x_0), the corrupted observation (x_{beam}), and the corresponding simulated quality map (Q_{sim}).

Synthetic Beam-Blockage Generation. To simulate realistic beam-blockage artefacts during training, we generate attenuation patterns that reproduce the radial geometry of weather radar measurements. Beam blockage appears as sectors originating from the radar location; in our formulation, the number of beams controls the number of blocked directions, while the beam width defines the angular size of each sector. A precipitation patch in Cartesian coordinates is first transformed into a polar representation centered at the radar location. Beam blockage is then simulated by attenuating precipitation values along selected beam directions. The resulting mask produces a corrupted observation and an associated quality map following the same beam pattern. Both are finally transformed back to Cartesian coordinates to create realistic training samples.

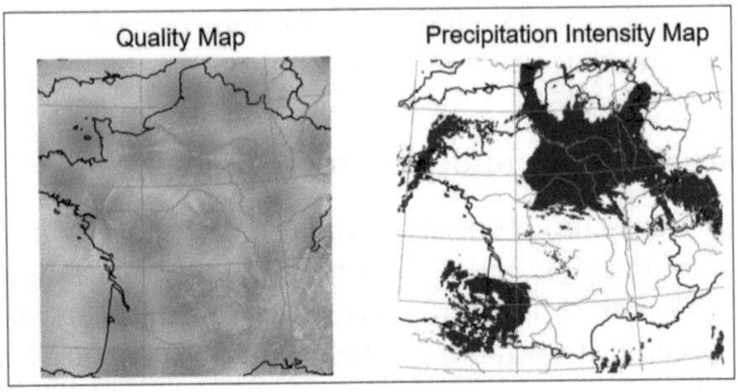

Fig. 1. Example of a radar precipitation mosaic (rain rate R in mm/h) and its associated quality map Q.

4.2 Dual-Conditioned Diffusion Architecture

The core of our approach is a DDPM adapted for conditional image restoration, illustrated in Fig. 2. Unlike deterministic regression models, this framework treats the recovery of blocked precipitation as a stochastic process, allowing for the generation of high-frequency details that are physically consistent with the surrounding meteorological context.

Training Phase: Artifact-Aware Learning. The training dataset is constructed from "clean" precipitation sectors. For each clean sample x_0, we generate a corresponding conditioned input, denoted as x_{cond}. This input is a composite tensor $x_{cond} = \{x_{beam}, Q_{sim}\}$, where x_{beam} is the precipitation field after the application of the parametric polar blockage filter, and Q_{sim} is the simulated quality map. During training, we employ a joint training strategy to enable Classifier-Free Guidance (CFG) [6]. The conditional U-Net, $\epsilon_\theta(x_t, t, x_{cond})$, is trained such that the conditioning x_{cond} is randomly replaced by a null token $\emptyset$ (e.g., a zero tensor) with a fixed probability $p_{uncond} = 10\%$. This allows the single model to learn both the conditional score $\nabla \log p(x_t|x_{cond})$ and the unconditional score $\nabla \log p(x_t)$ simultaneously. The training follows the same noise prediction objective defined in Eq. 4, where $\mathbf{c} \in \{x_{cond}, \emptyset\}$ is the conditioning variable.

Inference Phase: Guided Reconstruction. At inference time, the model is applied to real radar mosaics x_{real} where the ground truth precipitation field is unknown. The conditioning variable x_{cond} consists of the observed precipitation field x_{obs} together with its operational quality map Q. Reconstruction is performed through the reverse diffusion process starting from Gaussian noise

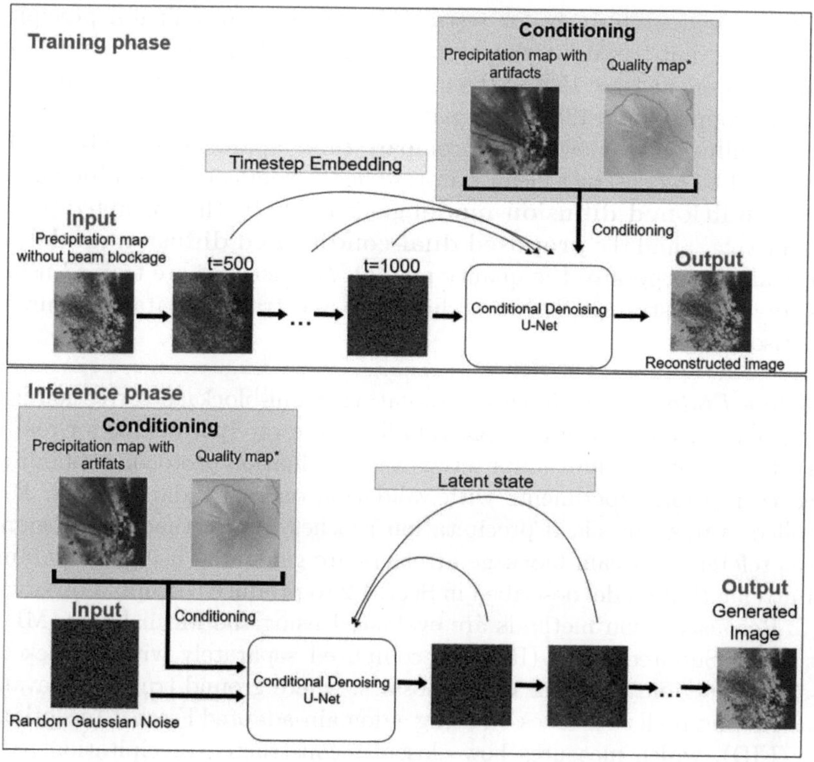

Fig. 2. Overview of the proposed beam-blockage correction framework.

$x_T \sim \mathcal{N}(\mathbf{0}, \mathbf{I})$ and iteratively denoising the latent variable. At each timestep t, the network receives the current latent state x_t and the conditioning information $x_{cond} = \{x_{obs}, Q\}$ to predict the noise component $\epsilon_\theta(x_t, t, x_{cond})$. The quality map guides the reconstruction by acting as a spatial reliability indicator: regions with high Q preserve the observed precipitation values, while regions with low quality are progressively reconstructed by the generative process. Through this guided sampling procedure, the model replaces beam-blockage artefacts with precipitation patterns that remain consistent with the surrounding meteorological structures, producing a reconstructed field $\hat{x}_0$.

5 Experiments

5.1 Dataset and Training Protocol

We use operational radar mosaics provided by *Météo-France*[1]. To evaluate the generalization capability of the model, the dataset is split temporally and spatially. Radar observations from 2015–2019 are used for training, while the year

[1] https://donneespubliques.meteofrance.fr.

2020 is reserved exclusively for testing. To focus on meaningful precipitation patterns, an event-based filtering step is applied: only radar patches where precipitation covers at least 15% of the map area are retained. The selected mosaics are then cropped into 128 × 128 patches used for training. To evaluate the proposed diffusion framework, we compare three approaches: a **U-Net baseline** trained to reconstruct clean rain-rate fields from corrupted observations, a **single-conditioned diffusion model** guided only by the corrupted precipitation field x_{beam}, and the **proposed dual-conditioned diffusion model**, which additionally incorporates the quality map Q. All methods are trained using the same corruption strategy, U-Net architecture and training data to ensure a fair comparison.

Evaluation Protocol and Metrics. Evaluating beam-blockage correction is challenging since ground-truth precipitation fields are rarely available for real radar observations. We therefore adopt a two-stage evaluation protocol combining controlled corruption experiments with validation on real radar mosaics. For the controlled evaluation, clean precipitation patches from artifact-free regions are used as references. Beam-blockage artefacts are generated using the parametric polar attenuation model described in Sect. 4.2 to produce corrupted observations x_{beam}. Reconstruction methods are evaluated using the Mean Error (ME) and Root Mean Squared Error (RMSE), computed separately within blocked and non-artifact regions. For real radar mosaics, where ground truth is unavailable, reconstruction realism is assessed using a domain-adapted Fréchet Inception Distance (FID), which measures how closely reconstructed precipitation patterns match the statistics of artifact-free radar observations.

5.2 Quantitative Results on Synthetic Data

Table 1 reports reconstruction errors evaluated separately in artifact and non-artifact regions and for two precipitation regimes ($R < 10$ and $R \geq 10$ mm/h). In artifact regions, the U-Net baseline strongly underestimates precipitation, with ME $= -3.98$ and RMSE $= 5.11$ for $R < 10$, and ME $= -14.73$ with RMSE $= 21.20$ for $R \geq 10$. The single-conditioned diffusion model reduces this error (RMSE $= 2.87$ and 11.20), while the dual-conditioned model achieves the lowest errors (RMSE $= 1.60$ and 5.80) and compensates the attenuation with small positive ME values. In non-artifact regions, the U-Net baseline performs reasonably for low precipitation (RMSE $= 2.38$), but introduces large errors for higher values (RMSE $= 15.30$), indicating over-smoothing of strong rainfall. The diffusion models maintain lower errors overall, with the dual-conditioned model achieving the best results (RMSE $= 1.61$ and 4.58).

5.3 Qualitative and Distributional Evaluation

Figure 3 illustrates visual examples of precipitation fields reconstructed from real radar mosaics affected by beam-blockage artefacts. The diffusion model conditioned only on the corrupted precipitation field is able to recover the overall

Table 1. Quantitative evaluation on synthetic beam-blockage data using Mean Error (ME) and RMSE (mm/h). Errors are reported separately for artifact and non-artifact regions.

Method	Artifact Regions				Non-Artifact Regions			
	$R < 10$		$R \geq 10$		$R < 10$		$R \geq 10$	
	ME	RMSE	ME	RMSE	ME	RMSE	ME	RMSE
U-Net Baseline	−3.98	5.11	−14.73	21.20	−1.29	2.38	−13.68	15.30
Diffusion (1 cond)	−1.57	2.87	−7.08	11.20	−1.72	2.85	−7.33	10.43
Diffusion (2 cond)	**1.02**	**1.60**	**3.35**	**5.80**	**0.98**	**1.61**	**3.03**	**4.58**

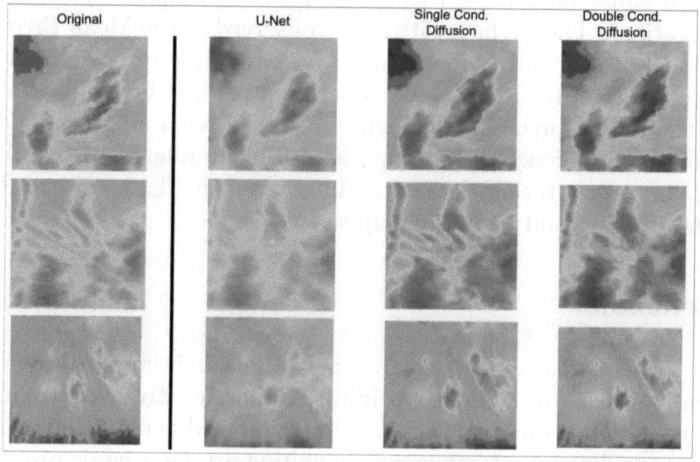

Fig. 3. Qualitative examples (upscaled) of beam-blockage correction using different models.

rainfall structure within blocked sectors, although inconsistencies may remain near sector boundaries. In contrast, the proposed dual-conditioned diffusion model produces more spatially coherent reconstructions and better preserves surrounding precipitation patterns by leveraging the quality map as an additional reliability signal.

Table 2 reports the FID scores for several reference distributions and reconstruction methods. The reference distributions show that natural clean radar observations have the lowest FID, while naturally blocked sectors already deviate significantly from this distribution. Artificial beam-blockage observations remain close to the natural blocked distribution, indicating the robustness of our beam-blockage generation approach. After reconstruction, the U-Net baseline fails to recover realistic precipitation statistics, producing high FID values for both natural and artificially corrupted samples. The diffusion model conditioned only on the corrupted observation improves the distributional consistency for artificially corrupted data, but does not reduce the FID for natural beam-blockage arte-

Table 2. Domain-adapted FID evaluation (lower is better).

Method	Artifact-free	Natural Artifact	Artificial Artifacts
Reference Data	8.4	42.7	48.9
U-Net Correction	–	69.3	35.8
Diffusion (1 cond) Correction	–	46.4	30.7
Diffusion (2 cond) Correction	–	**21.6**	**22.9**

facts. The best results are obtained with the proposed dual-conditioned diffusion model, which substantially reduces the distribution gap for naturally blocked radar observations. The slight positive bias observed in the Mean Error suggests that the model occasionally compensates too strongly for attenuation in highly degraded regions, likely because the generative process favors spatial continuity with surrounding precipitation structures. The remaining discrepancy with the clean natural reference distribution is also likely related to the difficulty of preserving fine precipitation details, as illustrated in Fig. 3, and to differences between the training and testing precipitation regimes.

6 Conclusion

This paper presented a guided conditional diffusion framework for correcting radar beam-blockage artefacts in precipitation mosaics. By conditioning the diffusion process on both the corrupted precipitation field and its associated quality map, the proposed approach removes attenuation artefacts while preserving reliable radar observations. Experiments show that the dual-conditioned diffusion model improves reconstruction accuracy in degraded regions while maintaining realistic precipitation patterns. Future work will focus on incorporating temporal information from radar sequences in order to better preserve precipitation dynamics and improve reconstruction consistency over time. Additional analyses regarding statistical significance and hyperparameter ablation studies will also be investigated to better characterize the robustness of the proposed framework. Future developments will also explore more efficient diffusion sampling strategies such as transformer-based generative backbones.

References

1. Doviak, R.J., Zrnic, D.S.: Doppler Radar and Weather Observations. Dover Publication Inc., New York (2006)
2. Fabry, F.: Radar Meteorology: Principles and Practice. Cambridge University Press, Cambridge (2015)
3. Geiss, A., Hardin, J.C.: Inpainting radar missing data regions with deep learning. Atmos. Meas. Tech. **14**, 7729–7747 (2021)
4. Gong, A., Chen, H., Ni, G.: Improving the completion of weather radar missing data with deep learning. Remote Sens. (Basel) **15**(18), 4568 (2023)

5. Ho, J., Jain, A., Abbeel, P.: Denoising diffusion probabilistic models (2020). https://arxiv.org/abs/2006.11239
6. Ho, J., Salimans, T.: Classifier-free diffusion guidance (2022). https://arxiv.org/abs/2207.12598
7. Lepetit, P., et al.: Using deep learning for restoration of precipitation echoes in radar data. IEEE Trans. Geoscience Remote Sens. **PP**, 1–14 (2021)
8. Liu, Q., Sun, J., Zhang, Y., Liu, X.: DenMerD: a feature enhanced approach to radar beam blockage correction with edge-cloud computing. J. Cloud Comput. Adv. Syst. Appl. **13**(1) (2024)
9. McRoberts, D.B., Nielsen-Gammon, J.W.: Detecting beam blockage in radar-based precipitation estimates. J. Atmos. Oceanic Tech. **34**(7), 1407–1422 (2017)
10. Ryzhkov, A., Diederich, M., Zhang, P., Simmer, C.: Potential utilization of specific attenuation for rainfall estimation, mitigation of partial beam blockage, and radar networking. J. Atmos. Oceanic Tech. **31**(3), 599–619 (2014)
11. Tan, S., Chen, H.: A conditional generative adversarial network for weather radar beam blockage correction. IEEE Trans. Geosci. Remote Sens. **61**, 1–14 (2023)
12. Tan, S., Chen, H., Lee, W.C.: Deep learning for weather radar beam blockage correction: potential impacts on qpe over complex terrain in northern California. Artif. Intell. Earth Syst. **4**(4), 240111 (2025). https://journals.ametsoc.org/view/journals/aies/4/4/AIES-D-24-0111.1.xml
13. Tan, S., Chen, H., Yao, S., Chandrasekar, V.: Weather radar beam blockage correction using deep learning. In: 2023 United States National Committee of URSI National Radio Science Meeting (USNC-URSI NRSM), pp. 296–297 (2023)
14. Wu, H., Liu, Q., Liu, X., Zhang, Y., Xu, X., Bilal, M.: A fcn approach to blockage correction in radars. In: 2021 IEEE International Conference on Dependable, Autonomic and Secure Computing, Intl Conf on Pervasive Intelligence and Computing, International Conference on Cloud and Big Data Computing, International Conference on Cyber Science and Technology Congress (DASC/PiCom/CBDCom/CyberSciTech), pp. 482–487 (2021)
15. Yin, X., Hu, Z., Zheng, J., Li, B., Zuo, Y.: Study on radar echo-filling in an occlusion area by a deep learning algorithm. Remote Sensing **13**(9), 1779 (2021)
16. Zhang, W., Zhang, X., Dong, J., Song, X., Pang, R.: Cidm: a comprehensive inpainting diffusion model for missing weather radar data with knowledge guidance. ISPRS J. Photogramm. Remote Sens. (2025). https://api.semanticscholar.org/CorpusID:276436254
17. Zhang, W., Zhang, X., Jin, Z., Wen, Y., Liu, J.: Inpainting radar missing data via denoising iterative restoration. IEEE J. Sel. Top. Appl. Earth Obs. Remote Sens. **17**, 10715–10725 (2024)

Boosting SSVEP Multi-subject Classification Through Mixture of ResNet-Based Experts

Francesco Capria, Franco Cicirelli, Alberto Falcone, Massimo Guarascio(✉), and Antonio Guerrieri

Institute for High Performance Computing and Networking, National Research Council of Italy, Via P. Bucci 8/9C, 87036 Rende, CS, Italy
{francesco.capria,franco.cicirelli,alberto.falcone,massimo.guarascio, antonio.guerrieri}@icar.cnr.it

Abstract. Accurate classification of electroencephalographic (EEG) signals in multi-subject Brain–Computer Interfaces (BCIs) is challenged by high inter-subject variability. When data from different individuals are aggregated, distribution shifts and subject-specific patterns may introduce noise and reduce the ability of machine learning models to learn robust representations. This issue is particularly critical in Steady-State Visually Evoked Potential (SSVEP)-based BCIs, where precise frequency-specific responses must be reliably detected. In this work, we propose a Mixture-of-Experts (MoE) framework for SSVEP classification. Each expert is a Multi-Level ResNet trained on one or multiple subjects, while a gating network learns to combine experts' predictions. The framework is evaluated on a real-world multi-subject SSVEP dataset acquired using a Bitbrain Diadem IoT device. Results show improved classification performance and computational efficiency compatible with real-time deployment on devices with limited processing capabilities.

Keywords: Brain-Computer Interfaces · Steady-State Visually Evoked Potentials · Deep Ensemble Learning · SSVEP Classification

1 Introduction

Steady-State Visually Evoked Potential (SSVEP)-based Brain-Computer Interfaces (BCIs) represent a well-established paradigm for human–machine interaction, including robotic control and assistive technologies for motor-impaired users, owing to their robustness and classification accuracies often exceeding 90% [1,2]. SSVEP responses consist of neural oscillations phase-locked to periodic visual stimuli at specific frequencies (e.g., 8–12 Hz). However, reliable decoding of multichannel EEG signals remains challenging due to low signal-to-noise ratio, temporal non-stationarity, and inter-subject variability, which significantly hinder model generalization in multi-subject settings.

Traditional SSVEP decoding approaches are largely based on signal processing techniques such as Canonical Correlation Analysis (CCA), Filter-Bank CCA

G. Andresini et al. (Eds.): ISMIS 2026, LNAI 16685, pp. 70–80, 2027.
https://doi.org/10.1007/978-3-032-32643-0_7

(FBCCA), and Task-Related Component Analysis (TRCA), as well as shallow machine learning (ML) classifiers including Support Vector Machines (SVM), Linear Discriminant Analysis (LDA), and k-Nearest Neighbors (k-NN) [7,13]. These methods are widely adopted as baselines due to their interpretability, modest data requirements, and suitability for real-time execution on standard or consumer-grade hardware. Frequency-domain techniques, in particular, have demonstrated effectiveness in low-latency applications (e.g., drone navigation).

More recently, deep learning (DL) models have proven to outperform standard approaches through end-to-end feature learning directly from raw EEG or spectral representations [8,14]. These approaches reduce the need for handcrafted feature extraction and can operate effectively even with a limited number of channels. Nevertheless, their practical deployment remains challenging: deep models typically require large training datasets, are prone to overfitting in subject-dependent evaluations, and often rely on GPU acceleration or edge-cloud offloading [12,15]. Ensemble-based strategies can improve robustness, yet their adoption in SSVEP scenarios remains relatively limited.

Despite these advances, several open issues persist. First, many studies rely on small datasets (often fewer than 10 subjects) and subject-dependent validation protocols, limiting conclusions about cross-subject generalization. Second, global deep neural networks (DNN) often degrade in performance as the number of subjects increases, whereas subject-specific models lack scalability and require retraining when new subjects are introduced. Finally, deployment constraints must be considered for computational efficiency in designing DNN architecture.

To address these limitations, we propose a subject-specific Mixture-of-Experts (MoE) framework for SSVEP classification. Each expert consists of a specific lightweight ResNet model, named Multi-Level ResNet aRchitecture (MLR^2-SSVEP), trained on data from individual subjects, while a gating network combines expert predictions without requiring explicit subject identity information. The architecture also supports incremental expansion through a buffer mechanism that stores newly acquired subject data; once filled, a new expert is trained and integrated into the MoE, requiring only the gating network to be updated. This design enables progressive aggregation of subject-specific knowledge, increasing representational capacity while maintaining computational scalability and controlled growth in parameters. Notably, if the buffer capacity is 1, a subject-specific expert is trained; otherwise, a multi-subject expert is learned, reducing the spatial cost of the overall model.

The proposed approach is evaluated on a 27-subject dataset acquired using the Bitbrain Diadem device. Experimental results demonstrate improvements over traditional ML and DL baselines. Furthermore, the framework is assessed in a real-time mobile robot navigation scenario, highlighting its suitability for edge-compatible, latency-constrained BCI applications.

The remainder of this paper is organized as follows. Section 2 presents the proposed framework based on MoE. Section 3 describes the experimental setup and evaluation protocols. Section 4 reports and discusses the results. Finally, Sect. 5 concludes the paper and outlines future research directions.

2 Solution Approach

In this section, we define the deep learning-based solution adopted for multi-subject signal classification. Specifically, in Sect. 2.1, we formalize the addressed problem, while in Sect. 2.2, we illustrate the framework and the incremental strategy used to learn the neural ensemble model.

2.1 Problem Definition

Our aim is to investigate the decoding of neural signals from BCIs to identify the user's intended action by identifying the visual stimulus to which they have paid attention from multichannel sensor data. This task is essential for SSVEP-based BCIs, in which users focus on one of several visual targets on the screen that flash at different frequencies (e.g., 8.57 Hz, 10 Hz, 12 Hz), allowing for real-time identification of the attended stimulus.

Let $\mathbf{X}_n \in \mathbb{R}^T$ denote the time series recorded from the n-th EEG sensor ($n = 1, \ldots, N$), comprising T time samples, expressed as $\mathbf{X}_n = [x_n^1, x_n^2, \ldots, x_n^T]^\top$.

The set of C visual targets is denoted as $\mathcal{C} = \{1, \ldots, C\}$, with $C = 4$ in our experiments. Specifically, $\mathcal{C}$ comprises three flickering visual stimuli presented at distinct frequencies, together with an additional class corresponding to a no-blink (idle) condition. The flickering stimuli are simultaneously displayed during EEG acquisition using platforms such as OpenViBE [11].

The objective is to learn a mapping function $f : \mathbb{R}^{N \times T} \to \mathcal{C}$ that, given a multichannel EEG segment $X \in \mathbb{R}^{N \times T}$, predicts the attended target $c \in \mathcal{C}$. The EEG matrix is defined as:

$$X = \begin{bmatrix} x_1^1 & x_1^2 & \cdots & x_1^T \\ x_2^1 & x_2^2 & \cdots & x_2^T \\ \vdots & \vdots & \ddots & \vdots \\ x_N^1 & x_N^2 & \cdots & x_N^T \end{bmatrix}, \tag{1}$$

where x_i^j represents the i-th channel value at time step j. This formulation constitutes a multi-class time-series classification problem, challenged by the low signal-to-noise ratio and inter-subject variability inherent in EEG signals.

2.2 MoE-Based Framework

This section introduces the proposed Mixture of Experts Framework, designed with a modular architecture that enables an end-to-end system for translating raw EEG signals into control commands for real-time mobile robot navigation. As shown in Fig. 1, the incoming EEG stream is initially processed by the *Data Gathering and Preprocessing* module, which structures the data into a format suitable for the subsequent *MoE MLR*^{2}*-SSVEP* component. This module identifies four distinct commands, which are subsequently mapped by the *Command Translation and Actuation* module into the robot's motion primitives: `forward`, `stop`, `left turn`, and `right turn`.

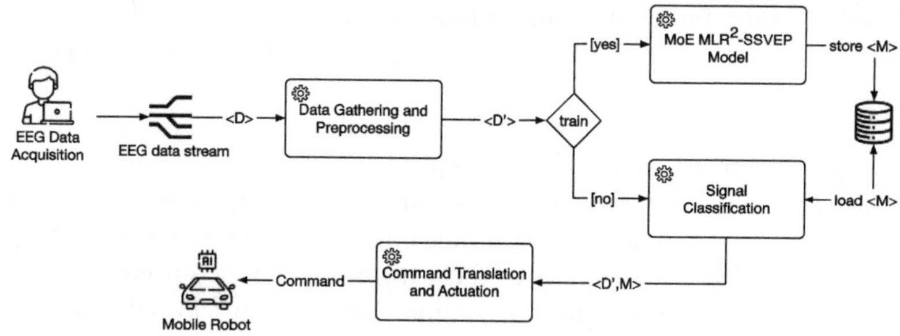

Fig. 1. Architecture of the subject-specific Mixture-of-Experts framework.

The Deep Neural Network (DNN) ensemble underlying the proposed framework features a feed-forward configuration enriched with multiple skip connections. This design follows the principles of Residual Networks (ResNets) [3], effectively mitigating the degradation problem encountered as network depth increases, while maintaining a favorable trade-off between convergence speed and model expressiveness. Such advantages stem from the ensemble-like behavior of ResNets, where the final output aggregates contributions from parallel processing paths of varying lengths, creating a composite ensemble representation.

Each base learner in the ensemble adopts a fully connected architecture employing ReLU activations [10], batch normalization for stable training [6], and dropout for regularization [5]. These components constitute the core *Building Block*, which is replicated twice per Residual Block with skip connections and repeated q times. This structural pattern emulates the ResNet design [3], balancing network depth, convergence efficiency, and expressiveness, while fostering ensemble behavior through multiple computational pathways [4]. The final layer consists of a number of neurons equal to the number of signals to classify, and it uses a softmax activation function.

Our framework is designed to support two local model training strategies. In the first case, a subject-specific expert is trained exclusively on data collected from a single individual, learning decision boundaries that capture the characteristics of individual brain signals. Although this approach can maximize subject-level specialization, it scales linearly with the number of subjects, increasing both total parameter count and computational overhead. To address this limitation, we introduced a second strategy aggregating data from a batch of k subjects to train a single shared expert and allowing to limit the total number of experts to $K = \lceil N/k \rceil$ and memory consumption.

In more detail, to boost the classification robustness and make our approach incremental, our solution adopts a MoE mechanism [9], which leverages the complementary strengths of the specific local models. The MoE framework dynamically weights the predictions of individual experts, ensuring that the final decision for a given input x is predominantly influenced by the most specialized experts for that input region. A dedicated trainable Gating Network, implemented as a Multi-Layer Perceptron (MLP) with k outputs, computes the weighting coefficients $(z_1, \ldots, z_k) = \text{MLP}^k(x)$. The aggregated output score y is then obtained as a convex combination of the per-expert predictions $(y^{(1)}, \ldots, y^{(k)})$, defined as $y = \sum_{i=1}^{k} z_i \cdot y^{(i)}$.

During training, only the Gate parameters are updated, while the base experts remain frozen. The MoE training follows an incremental strategy based on a buffer B of size b, which stores data from b newly acquired subjects. Once the buffer is filled, a new expert is trained on the aggregated data and integrated into the MoE, after which only the gating network is updated. When $b = 1$, the architecture reduces to a fully subject-specific configuration with one expert per subject; increasing k groups multiple subjects per expert, reducing the total number of parameters and improving efficiency at the possible cost of a moderate performance trade-off (Fig. 2).

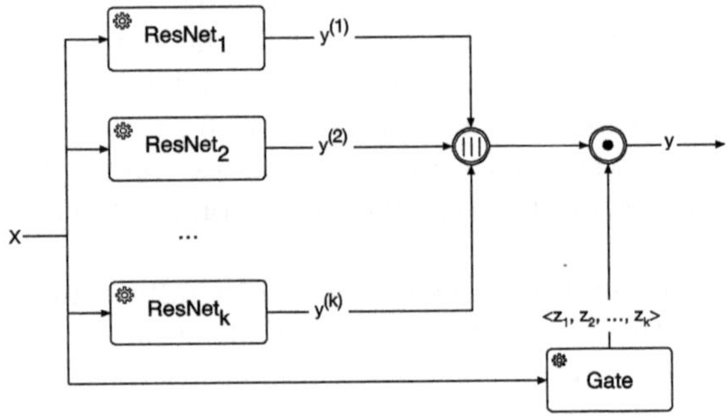

Fig. 2. MoE-Based Architecture.

3 Experimental Setup

This section details the dataset acquisition, preprocessing, evaluation protocols, and implementation settings used to assess the proposed framework.

3.1 Dataset and Preprocessing

EEG data were collected at the Institute for High Performance Computing and Networking (ICAR-CNR), Rende, Italy, from 27 healthy subjects (aged 19–53, normal or corrected vision, no contraindications like epilepsy). Sessions occurred in a dimly lit room, with subjects seated 0.85 m from a monitor displaying three flickering squares at 8.57 Hz, 10 Hz, and 12 Hz. Each trial featured a 1 s cue, 7 s stimulation, and 4 s rest, randomized across ≈6.25 min sessions. Data were acquired using the IoT Bitbrain Diadem dry-EEG device (a 12-channel EEG device, of which we focused on the parieto-occipital/occipital channels: PO7,

PO8, O1, O2). Raw streams were segmented into 2 s windows ($W = 2$, overlap $S = 0.25$), bandpass-filtered (4th-order Butterworth, 6–30 Hz), and notch-filtered (5th-order, 50 Hz). PSD features were extracted at 50 frequencies per channel, yielding 202 features per record (plus `EventId`, `SubjectId`), for 1,536 records per subject. Although data were collected from only 27 subjects, signal processing yielded approximately 41,472 records, unevenly distributed across the four stimulation classes. Specifically, the records are distributed as follows: the classes `forward`, `left turn`, and `right turn` comprise 14.6% of the dataset, respectively, while the remaining records are associated with the `stop` class (56.2%).

3.2 Parameters, Evaluation Protocol and Metrics

Experiments employ subject-stratified splits per subject (70% train, 10% validation, 20% test), pooled across subjects for multi-subject scenarios. The MoE framework follows a two-stage training protocol. In Stage 1, individual experts are pre-trained and frozen on subject-specific (or group-specific) data. In Stage 2, the gating MLP (128–64–ReLU–Softmax) is optimized on pooled features, without subject identifiers.

Performances are evaluated using accuracy (Acc), precision (Prec), recall (Rec), and F1-score, prioritizing F1-score for robustness to class imbalance and recall for BCI sensitivity. Baselines include Random Forest (RF) and AdaBoost (AB), implemented using the `scikit-learn` library, whereas XGBoost has been implemented using the `dmlc/XGBoost`[1] library, all with default parameters. These are compared against the proposed MLR^2-SSVEP model and its extended variant, MoE MLR^2-SSVEP, which incorporates a Mixture of Experts architecture. Specifically, each expert adopts the MLR^2-SSVEP architecture ($K = 1$ residual block, 256-ReLU dense layer, Softmax output), trained using the Adam optimizer ($lr = 1 \times 10^{-3}$, 50–100 epochs, cross-entropy loss), with expert weights frozen during gating training. The gating network is a fully-connected MLP with two hidden layers of 128 and 64 neurons, respectively, both using ReLU activations, followed by a Softmax layer to produce normalized combination weights.

Implementation uses Python 3.10 with Keras/TensorFlow. Configurations scale subjects (10/15/20/27) and experts (K = 3–7). Results averaged over multiple seeds ensure reproducibility[2].

4 Numerical Results

This section describes the experimental evaluation of the proposed framework. The analysis evaluates the effectiveness, robustness, and practical use of MoE MLR^2-SSVEP across diverse operating conditions.

---

[1] https://xgboost.readthedocs.io/en/latest/index.html.

[2] Code available at https://github.com/francescocapria1998/Mixture-of-Expert.git.

4.1 Comparison with Baseline Methods

In this section, we compare our solution with some standard supervised ensemble models, including RF, AB, and XGBoost. We consider the architecture of a single expert composing the MoE as a baseline.

Table 1 reports the results for each evaluated model, along with the corresponding percentage improvement or reduction relative to the baseline. The results reveal the inherent limitations of conventional ML in handling inter-subject EEG heterogeneity, thereby underscoring the rationale for our subject-specific MoE paradigm. In particular, although RF achieves the highest precision (+17.84%), this improvement comes at the cost of a substantial decrease in recall (–11.47%). XGBoost exhibits a more balanced but overall degraded performance across all metrics. AdaBoost shows a dramatic performance collapse, with reductions exceeding 50% across all metrics. In contrast, our approach achieves the best overall accuracy (0.779) and F1-score (0.771), improving the baseline by +2.91% and +1.18%, respectively.

Table 1. Performance of ML ensembles across different numbers of subjects. Percentage variations (Δ%) w.r.t. MLR^2-SSVEP baseline.

Model	Acc	Prec	Rec	F1	ΔAcc	ΔPrec	ΔRec	ΔF1
MLR^2-SSVEP	0.757	0.751	**0.776**	0.762	–	–	–	–
RF	0.762	**0.885**	0.687	0.752	0.66	17.84	–11.47	-1.31
AB	0.356	0.351	0.380	0.354	–52.97	–53.26	–51.03	–53.54
XGboost	0.680	0.671	0.655	0.662	–10.17	–10.65	–15.59	–13.12
MoE MLR^2-SSVEP	**0.779**	0.805	0.745	**0.771**	2.91	7.19	–3.99	1.18

4.2 MoE with One-Expert-per-Subject

Also in this test, a distinct expert is trained for each subject (hereafter we refer to this strategy as *MoE-OES*). The goal is to evaluate whether SSVEP classification benefits from modeling subject-dependent data distributions instead of learning a single global decision function that neglects inter-individual variability.

For each subject i, the dataset D_i (acquired via the Bitbrain Diadem device) is split into training (70%), validation (10%), and test (20%) sets using class-stratified sampling across SSVEP frequencies. The training procedure consists of two stages. In Stage 1, each expert E_i is trained independently on its subject-specific training set and validated on the corresponding validation set. This enforces subject-specialized decision boundaries capturing individual physiological and signal characteristics. After convergence, expert parameters are frozen. In Stage 2, the gating network G is trained on the union of the selected subjects' training sets and validated on the union of their validation sets. The gate

Table 2. Performance of subject-specific MoE across increasing numbers of subjects.

#Subjects	Acc	Prec	Rec	F1
10	0.848	0.868	0.833	0.849
15	0.828	0.853	0.805	0.826
20	0.842	0.853	0.830	0.841
ALL	0.779	0.805	0.745	0.771

operates exclusively on frequency-domain representations, learning to dynamically weight the experts $\{E_i\}$ based on EEG content without access to subject identity, thereby simulating subject-agnostic deployment.

The MoE model is evaluated on the union of all subjects' test sets, reflecting a realistic BCI scenario in which the system selects the most appropriate expert for incoming samples. Experiments are conducted on progressively larger subsets of subjects (10, 15, 20, and 27, denoted as "ALL"), resulting in a proportional number of experts.

This experiment highlights the performance gains achieved through per-subject specialization, confirms the robustness of the approach under varying numbers of subjects, and provides a baseline for subsequent evaluations (Table 2).

4.3 MoE with Grouped-Subjects-per-Expert

While the *MoE-OES* configuration achieves strong performance, it requires up to 27 experts, limiting scalability. To improve parameter efficiency, we adopt a grouped-subjects-per-expert strategy (hereafter *MoE-GES*), where multiple subjects are assigned to the same expert through a buffer-based incremental procedure. Let $S = \{1, \ldots, N\}$ with $N = 27$ denote the subject set. Each dataset D_i is split into 70/10/20 training, validation, and test sets, as in the previous experiment. Subjects are first randomly ordered to simulate progressive acquisition and then accumulated in a buffer B of size k. Once the buffer is full, the corresponding subjects form a group $G_j \subset S$, and a single expert is trained on the aggregated training data of that group. Repeating this process yields $K = \lceil N/k \rceil$ experts. We consider buffer sizes inducing $K \in \{3, 4, 5, 6, 7\}$ experts, corresponding to approximately N/K subjects per expert ($\sim$ 9–4).

Also, in this case, the experiment is configured in two stages. In the first stage, each expert E_k is trained on the combined training data $\cup_{i \in G_k} D_i^{\text{train}}$, and validated on $\cup_{i \in G_k} D_i^{\text{val}}$. This yields shared expert models per group, trading subject-specific specialization for enhanced data diversity and generalization. The expert weights are frozen once convergence is reached. In the second stage, the gating network G is then trained on the pooled training data $\cup_k(\cup_{i \in G_k} D_i^{\text{train}})$, with validation performed on the corresponding pooled validation sets. The gate learns to route inputs to the most suitable expert E_k based on the input features.

Table 3. Performance of grouped-specific MoE across increasing numbers of experts.

# Experts (K)	Acc	Prec	Rec	F1
3	0.804	0.834	0.775	0.800
4	0.857	0.869	0.847	0.857
5	0.826	0.842	0.809	0.824
6	0.840	0.854	0.830	0.841
7	0.834	0.852	0.819	0.834

The final evaluation is performed on the test set comprising all subjects. Table 3 reports the resulting performance metrics. Notably, in this setting, we achieve better results than the MoE one-expert-per-subject test.

From a model complexity perspective, by reducing the number of experts and increasing the amount of training data per expert, the total number of MoE parameters decreases from over 3.3 million in *MoE-OES* to approximately 894,000 in *MoE-GES*. The resulting spatial improvement stems directly from the reduced expert multiplicity, yielding a lower memory footprint and improved deployability on resource-constrained platforms. As a result, the model continues to achieve good performance while maintaining a reduced parameter footprint.

In addition, the architecture supports incremental deployment: When data from new subject data are made available, only the corresponding expert E_{new} is trained on the new data, followed by refinement of the gating network with existing experts kept frozen. This avoids full retraining of the entire model and ensures temporal scalability as new subjects are introduced. Table 4 reports the number of parameters required for expert construction, showing that the MoE-GES configuration is more parameter-efficient than the MoE-OES one.

Table 4. Differences in terms of network parameters between MoE-OES and MoE-GES configurations.

Configuration	Sum of Experts	Gate	MoE Full
MoE-OES (ALL experts)	3.28M	45.7k	3.33M
MoE-GES (7 experts)	851k	43.1k	894k

The average inference time per batch was 6.567 ± 1.28 ms (MoE-OES) and 2.699 ± 0.29 ms (MoE-GES), evaluated on a 3.80 GHz Intel Core Ultra 7 155H CPU with 16 GB of RAM running CPU-only, demonstrating that the compressed MoE-GES variant achieves a lower latency than MoE-OES with significantly fewer trainable parameters.

5 Conclusions

In this work, we introduced a MoE framework for SSVEP classification with Multi-Level ResNet experts and a lightweight gate. Experiments on real-world dry-EEG data collected with the IoT Bitbrain Diadem show consistent improvements over classical ML methods and single multi-subject DNNs. The framework shows robust scaling across subject populations through both *one-expert-per-subject* and *grouped-subjects-per-expert* configurations, achieving peak F1-scores of 0.857 while reducing parametric complexity by $\sim$73% (894k vs 3.33M parameters) to enable real-time edge deployment.

The proposed solution effectively mitigates inter-subject variability while maintaining computational efficiency suitable for mobile robotic BCIs. Future work will explore online adaptation mechanisms, integration with hybrid EEG paradigms (e.g., hybrid P300-SSVEP), and real-world validation on assistive robotic platforms.

References

1. Chai, X., et al.: A hybrid bci-controlled smart home system combining ssvep and emg for individuals with paralysis. Biomed. Signal Process. Control **56**, 101687 (2020)
2. Chiuzbaian, A., Jakobsen, J., Puthusserypady, S.: Mind controlled drone: an innovative multiclass ssvep based brain computer interface. In: 2019 7th International Winter Conference on Brain-Computer Interface (BCI), pp. 1–5 (2019)
3. He, K., Zhang, X., Ren, S., Sun, J.: Deep residual learning for image recognition. In: Proceedings of the IEEE Conference on Computer Vision and Pattern Recognition, pp. 770–778 (2016)
4. Hinton, G., Srivastava, N., Krizhevsky, A., Sutskever, I., Salakhutdinov, R.: Improving Neural Networks by Preventing Co-adaptation of Feature Detectors. arXiv preprint arXiv:1207.0580 (2012)
5. Hinton, G., Srivastava, N., Krizhevsky, A., Sutskever, I., Salakhutdinov, R.: Dropout: a simple way to prevent neural networks from overfitting. J. Mach. Learn. Res. **15**, 1929–1958 (2014)
6. Ioffe, S., Szegedy, C.: Batch normalization: accelerating deep network training by reducing internal covariate shift. In: Proceedings of the 32Nd International Conference on International Conference on Machine Learning, pp. 448–456 (2015)
7. Kanagaluru, V.M.S.: Artificial intelligence based bci using ssvep signals with single channel eeg. Technol. Health Care **33**(4), 1905–1916 (2025)
8. Li, X., Yang, S., Fei, N., Wang, J., Huang, W., Hu, Y.: A convolutional neural network for ssvep identification by using a few-channel eeg. Bioengineering **11**(6) (2024)
9. Masoudnia, S., Ebrahimpour, R.: Mixture of experts: a literature survey. Artif. Intell. Rev. **42**(2), 275–293 (2014)
10. Nair, V., Hinton, G.: Rectified linear units improve restricted Boltzmann machines. In: Proceedings of the 27th International Conference on International Conference on Machine Learning, pp. 807–814 (2010)
11. Renard, Y., et al.: OpenViBE: an open-source software platform to design, test, and use brain-computer interfaces in real and virtual environments. Presence **19**(1), 35–53 (2010)

12. Rizzo, L., et al.: Modeling the edge-cloud continuum: a brain-computer interface case study. In: 2025 IEEE 5th International Conference on Human-Machine Systems (ICHMS), pp. 362–368 (2025)
13. Rizzo, L., Zicari, P., Cicirelli, F., Guerrieri, A., Micieli, M., Vinci, A.: A study on consumer-grade eeg headsets in bci applications. In: 2024 IEEE Conference on Pervasive and Intelligent Computing (PICom), pp. 67–74 (2024)
14. Wei, Q., Li, C., Wang, Y., Gao, X.: Enhancing the performance of ssvep-based bcis by combining task-related component analysis and deep neural network. Sci. Rep. **15**, 365 (2025)
15. Zhu, F., Jiang, L., Dong, G., Gao, X., Wang, Y.: An open dataset for wearable ssvep-based brain-computer interfaces. Sensors **21**(4) (2021)

Accelerating Frequent Gradual Pattern Discovery Through Dimensionality Reduction

Herman Tcheneghon Motcheyo[1(✉)], Issam Falih[1], Lauraine Tiogning-Djiogue[2], and Engelbert Mephu Nguifo[1]

[1] Université Clermont Auvergne, Clermont Auvergne INP, ENSMSE, CNRS, LIMOS, 63000 Clermont–Ferrand, France
herman.tcheneghon_motcheyo@etu.uca.fr, {issam.falih,engelbert.mephu_nguifo}@uca.fr

[2] National Advanced School of Engineering, University of Yaoundé 1, Yaounde, Cameroon
lauraine.djiogue@univ-yaounde1.cm

Abstract. With the rapid advancement of modern technologies, exponential data growth has become an unavoidable reality, which presents major obstacles to knowledge extraction. Gradual patterns enable the discovery of meaningful relationships within such data, expressed in the form "more/less X, more/less Y," where X and Y denote data attributes. These patterns play a crucial role in supporting data-driven decision-making processes. Although several approaches for gradual pattern discovery have been proposed in the literature, the computational cost, particularly in terms of execution time and memory consumption, remains a major challenge, even with the availability of parallel solutions. In this paper, we propose the use of Principal Component Analysis (PCA) as a preprocessing technique to accelerate gradual pattern discovery by reducing data dimensionality. The proposed approach is evaluated on multiple datasets from diverse application domains and compared against the GRAANK and GRAANK-based metaheuristic algorithms (PSO, GA, PRS). Experimental results demonstrate a substantial reduction in both execution time and memory usage.

Keywords: Dimensionality reduction · Gradual pattern mining · Data mining

1 Introduction

In recent years, the exponential growth of data volumes has driven the development of numerous data mining algorithms to extract meaningful knowledge from large datasets. Among the pioneering approaches, [1] introduced Apriori for mining association rules of the form X → Y from transactional databases, later improved by FP-Growth [5]. However, these methods fail to capture gradual dependencies within datasets [3], especially at large scale. To address this

G. Andresini et al. (Eds.): ISMIS 2026, LNAI 16685, pp. 81–90, 2027.
https://doi.org/10.1007/978-3-032-32643-0_8

limitation, several algorithms for gradual pattern discovery have been proposed [2,3,6–9,12,17].

Gradual patterns identify progressive covariations between attributes, where systematic changes in one attribute correspond to similar or inverse changes in others. They have been applied in domains such as e-commerce [9] and paleontology [10,11], where co-evolutionary patterns among indicators are of particular interest. For example, in Table 1, one can extract the pattern *"the more Poaceae increases, the more Secale.t decreases"*.

However, these approaches all face major challenges in terms of execution time and memory consumption, which grow with the number of transactions and attributes [6]. Existing methods [6–8,17] rely on support computation, pruning criteria, and antimonotonicity to reduce the search space, but the problem persists.

In this paper, we propose not to rely on the method of computing the support of each pattern but to reduce the initial database before extracting frequent gradual patterns in order to retain those that are important for pattern extraction. To do this, we propose integrating principal component analysis (PCA) as a preprocessing step to improve the efficiency of gradual pattern exploration using GRAANK [8]. The rest of this article is organized as follows: Sect. 2 presents the state of the art on the exploration and acceleration of the generation of frequent gradual patterns; Sect. 3 presents the proposed method; Sect. 4 presents the experiments and results.

2 Related Work

Gradual pattern extraction has attracted growing interest in recent years, focusing on the identification of co-variation relationships between variables, particularly in temporal or ordered contexts [2].

2.1 Gradual Patterns

The search for gradual patterns involves discovering covariances between numerical attributes in a dataset, generally expressed in the form: *more/less of X, more/less of Y* [3,12]. Let $X \in \mathbb{R}^{N \times n}$ be a numerical database containing a set of observations N, each described by a set of attributes $\mathcal{I}$ where $x_p[i]$ denotes the value of the attribute $i \in \mathcal{I}$ for observation $p \in \{1, \ldots, N\}$. Table 1 is a sample of paleoecological data [11]; its columns are labeled with scientific names of different indicators.

Definition 1 (Gradual item). *A gradual item is denoted i^*, where $i \in \mathcal{I}$ and $* \in \{\uparrow, \downarrow\}$ which indicates the direction of variation of the pattern. The domain of the values of i is provided with a total order relation. When $*$ is $'\uparrow'$ respectively $'\downarrow'$, this means that the value i increases (or decreases, respectively).*

Definition 2 (Gradual itemset). *A gradual itemset is a non-empty set of gradual items: $g = (i_1^{*_1}, i_2^{*_2}, \ldots, i_k^{*_k})$. It expresses a combination of trends for several attributes. A k-itemset is an itemset containing k gradual items.*

For illustration, Table 1 is considered as a database [11] containing a set of objects (from p_1 to p_7) described by a set of attributes $\mathcal{I}$. Taking the feature Poaceae (i_1), we observe that its values for objects p_2, p_4, and p_6 are strictly increasing: $x_{p_2}[i_1] = 116 < x_{p_4}[i_1] = 124 < x_{p_6}[i_1] = 136$. This trend can therefore be encoded as the gradual item $g = \texttt{Poaceae}^{\uparrow}$ (which can be interpreted as "Poaceae increases").

Table 1. Example of paleontological database [11]

ID	Poaceae	Secale.t	Rumex.ace	Equisetum
p_1	84	61	7	0
p_2	116	36	4	1
p_3	90	52	2	3
p_4	124	34	1	5
p_5	102	49	0	6
p_6	136	17	0	1
p_7	106	40	3	1

Support of Gradual Patterns. The quality of a gradual pattern or item is measured by its frequency support. This support is defined as the proportion of object couples that respect the gradual variations given collectively by all the items in the pattern [3,8,14]. Gradual patterns are frequent if their support is greater than or equal to a minimum threshold set by the user. The extraction of frequent gradual patterns consists of finding the set of all the frequent gradual patterns in a numerical database, according to a minimum frequency threshold. Formally, given a gradual pattern $P = \{g_1, \ldots, g_k\}$, its support is:

$$\sigma_P = \frac{|\{(p_i, p_j) \in \mathcal{D}^2 : \forall g_l = a^{*_l} \in P,\ x_{p_i}[a] \diamond_l x_{p_j}[a]\}|}{N(N-1)/2},$$

where $\diamond_l$ is "<" if $*_l = \uparrow$ and ">" otherwise. For example, taking $g = \texttt{Poaceae}^{\uparrow}$, the values of Poaceae can be totally ordered as $84 < 90 < 102 < 106 < 116 < 124 < 136$, so all $\binom{7}{2} = 21$ object pairs are concordant. Therefore, $\sigma_g = 21/21 = 1$.

Referring to the database, $\{\texttt{Poaceae}^{\uparrow}, \texttt{Secale.t}^{\downarrow}\}$ is a gradual itemset, which indicates that *the more the indicator Poaceae increases, the more the indicator Secale.t decreases*. In this case, the complete set of concordant pairs is obtained by performing the AND operation between the ranking matrices of $\texttt{Poaceae}^{\uparrow}$ and $\texttt{Secale.t}^{\downarrow}$: $\mathcal{C}_P = \{(p_1, p_3), (p_1, p_5), (p_1, p_7), (p_1, p_2), (p_1, p_4), (p_1, p_6), (p_3, p_5), (p_3, p_7), (p_3, p_2), (p_3, p_4), (p_3, p_6), (p_5, p_7), (p_5, p_2), (p_5, p_4), (p_5, p_6), (p_7, p_2), (p_7, p_4), (p_7, p_6), (p_2, p_4), (p_2, p_6), (p_4, p_6)\}$. For instance, comparing p_2 and p_4: Poaceae increases ($116 < 124$) while Secale.t decreases ($36 > 34$), confirming the trend. The support of P thus reaches its maximum: $\sigma_P = 21/21 = 1$.

2.2 Techniques for Frequent Gradual Patterns Discovery

Existing methods mainly differ in the support computation and the type of data considered.

Precedence Graph-Based Approach. Data is modeled as a graph whose nodes are objects and edges encode the precedence relation induced by the items. GRITE [3], the first such method, leverages anti-monotonicity to prune unpromising candidates, but remains costly in time and memory. SGrite [17] refines this pruning via the support equality lemma, improving efficiency. MsGriteMiner [7] traverses the search space in lexicographic order but was not evaluated on large datasets. More recently, [6] extended GRITE and ParaMiner [13] with new pruning criteria, significantly reducing non-informative candidates, although performance still depends on the data distribution.

Rank Correlation-Based Approach. GRAANK [8] mines gradual patterns using the Kendall rank correlation and follows an Apriori-like principle adapted to ordered variables. As datasets grow, such exhaustive mining becomes highly time and memory-consuming. To alleviate this, [14,15] proposed metaheuristic variants of GRAANK that prune many irrelevant candidates, although their complexity can reach $(n \times n)!$ depending on the number of iterations [14]. Where n is the number of objects in the dataset. From a different angle related to the type of data, [12] introduced a constraint-based SAT framework extensible to temporal constraints. Since gradual pattern mining shares similarities with association rule mining, reducing explanatory variables prior to extraction is a natural direction to limit search-space complexity.

2.3 Acceleration of Association Rule Discovery

Principal Component Analysis (PCA) has been successfully used as a preprocessing step to accelerate association rule mining. [4] first proposed projecting the data into a reduced space preserving most of the variance, and [18] later applied this idea to sports data with significant quality gains. [16] combined PCA with FP-Growth [5] to further optimize pattern search and memory usage. These results motivate extending such a preprocessing strategy to gradual pattern mining, where dimensionality growth causes an exponential increase in computational cost. We hypothesize that reducing redundant features can improve gradual pattern discovery. The next section details our approach.

3 Proposed Method

PCA reduces the data by selecting a limited number of principal components that preserve most of the variance. Then, correlations between the original variables and the retained components are used to identify the variables most relevant for gradual pattern extraction (Algorithm 1, line 2). A key concern is to preserve monotonic relationships between variables, e.g., an increase in Poaceae associated with a decrease in Secale.t, so that such relationships remain detectable after reduction.

Definition 3 (Reduction function). *A reduction function is a continuous mapping $F : \mathcal{X} \to \mathcal{Y}$ where $\mathcal{X} \subseteq \mathbb{R}^n$ and $\mathcal{Y} \subseteq \mathbb{R}^k$ with $k < n$ that transforms data from the original space to a lower-dimensional space, satisfying:*

$$\forall (x_1, x_2) \in X^2, \exists \alpha > 0 \text{ such that } \|F(x_1) - F(x_2)\| \geq \alpha \|x_1 - x_2\|$$

This ensures that distances, and therefore relationships, are proportionally preserved.

Proposition 1. *For all $x \in X$, if F preserves monotonic relations, then $J_F(x)^\top J_F(x)$ is positive definite, where J_F denotes the Jacobian matrix of F.*

Proof. Let $x \in X$ and $v \in \mathbb{R}^n$, $v \neq 0$. Setting $M = J_F(x)^\top J_F(x)$, we have $\|J_F(x)v\|^2 = v^\top M v$. Since F preserves monotonic relations, $\|J_F(x)v\| > 0$ for every $v \neq 0$, hence $v^\top M v > 0$. Therefore, $J_F(x)^\top J_F(x)$ is positive definite.

Lemma 1 (Local preservation). *For every $x \in \mathcal{X}$, there exists a neighborhood $U(x)$ of x on which the monotonic relations of F are preserved.*

Proof. Let $J_F(x)$ be the Jacobian matrix of F at x. $M = J_F(x)^\top J_F(x)$. By Proposition 1, M is symmetric and positive definite, so its smallest eigenvalue $\lambda_{\min}(x) > 0$ satisfies $h^\top M h \geq \lambda_{\min}(x)\, \|h\|^2$ for all $h \in \mathbb{R}^n$. By the differentiability of F,

$$\|F(x+h) - F(x)\|^2 = h^\top M h + o(\|h\|^2).$$

Setting $r = \dfrac{\lambda_{\min}(x)}{2\|J_F(x)\|}$ and $U(x) = B(x, r)$, we obtain $\|F(x+h) - F(x)\| \geq \sqrt{\lambda_{\min}(x)}\, \|h\|$ for every h with $\|h\| < r$, which ensures that monotonic relations are preserved on $U(x)$.

Algorithm 1 PCA with feature selection for gradual patterns

Require: Data $X \in \mathbb{R}^{n \times p}$, variance threshold $\gamma \in [0.85, 0.95]$, correlation threshold $\omega \in [0, 1]$
Ensure: Reduced dataset X_{S_ω}, set of selected attributes S_ω
1: Z = Run PCA and retain principal components with cumulative variance $> \gamma$
2: Compute the loadings $L_{ji} = \text{corr}(X_j, Z_i)$ and select $S_\omega = \{j \in \mathcal{I} \mid \max_i |L_{ji}| \geq \omega\}$
3: Build the reduced matrix X_{S_ω} from S_ω and apply GRAANK to X_{S_ω}

This local preservation property motivates Algorithm 1: by selecting the original variables most correlated with the principal components which themselves preserve variance and, locally, monotonic relations by Lemma 1; We identify a subset S_ω on which gradual order relations are likely to be preserved after reduction. The reduction applied to the data in our context is the canonical projection $F_\omega : \mathcal{X} \to \mathbb{R}^{|S_\omega|}$ that restricts X to the columns indexed by S_ω; Where S_ω is determined from PCA loadings with the correlation threshold ω (Algorithm, line 2). To preserve the interpretability of the original variables, we applied GRAANK, an exhaustive approach, to the selected initial variables after reduction, instead of applying it to the principal components.

4 Experiments

We evaluated the proposed method on four datasets from the medical, environmental, transportation, and zoonoses domains, originally introduced by [14]. Table 2 summarizes their characteristics. Missing values were imputed using the mean, which preserves sample size without significant bias for non-skewed numerical data. For Cargo 2000, variables with more than 50% missing values were removed, and non-numerical variables were discarded from Air Quality. The GRAANK algorithm was used for gradual pattern discovery, and its performance was evaluated both with and without dimensionality reduction. The experiments were conducted on a server equipped with 640 GB of RAM and 192 CPU cores. Performance was assessed in terms of execution time, memory consumption, and the number of candidate patterns generated. The source code used for the experiments is available at[1].

Table 2. Characteristics of the datasets

Datasets	Domain	#Objects	#Attributes(A)	# Preprocessed(A)
Hepatitis C (HCV)	Medical	615	11	11
Air Quality	Environment	9358	15	13
Chickenpox	Zoonosis	521	20	20
Cargo 2000	Transport	3942	98	38

4.1 Database

Figure 1 illustrates preprocessing applied before pattern discovery. A cumulative variance threshold of 85% was retained for each dataset (Fig. 1a), balancing information preservation and dimensionality reduction. Figure 1b shows variables retained after loading analysis (Fig. 1c). The correlation threshold was set to $\omega = 0.5$ for all datasets, guided by the distribution of loading coefficients: higher ω retains fewer variables, while lower ω tends to retain all original variables.

4.2 Results and Discussion

Performance Analysis: Execution Time, Memory, Number of Candidate Patterns. We compared the proposed approach with *GRAANK* and three metaheuristic-based variants: *GA-GRAANK*, *PSO-GRAANK*, and *RS-GRAANK* [14]. Metrics were evaluated for minimum support thresholds from 0.3 to 1. Figure 2 presents the results related to frequent pattern, evaluated according to three criteria. The experimental results show a significant reduction in

[1] https://github.com/Herman-Motcheyo/Gradual-Pattern-Discovery-through-PCA#.

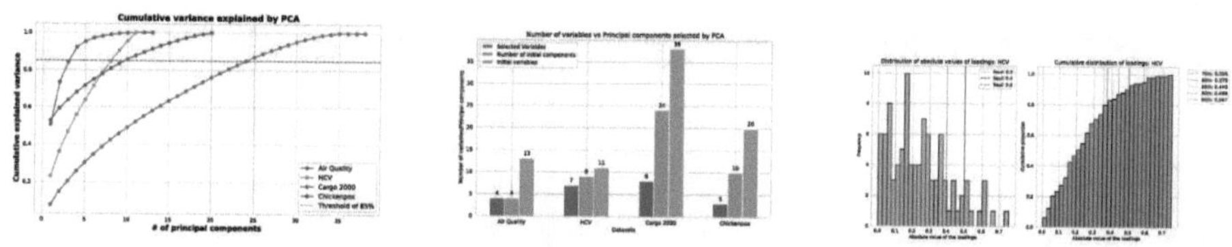

(a) Cumulative variance vs number of principal components (b) Number of variables and components retained (c) Distribution of loadings for HCV

Fig. 1. Preprocessing of the different datasets

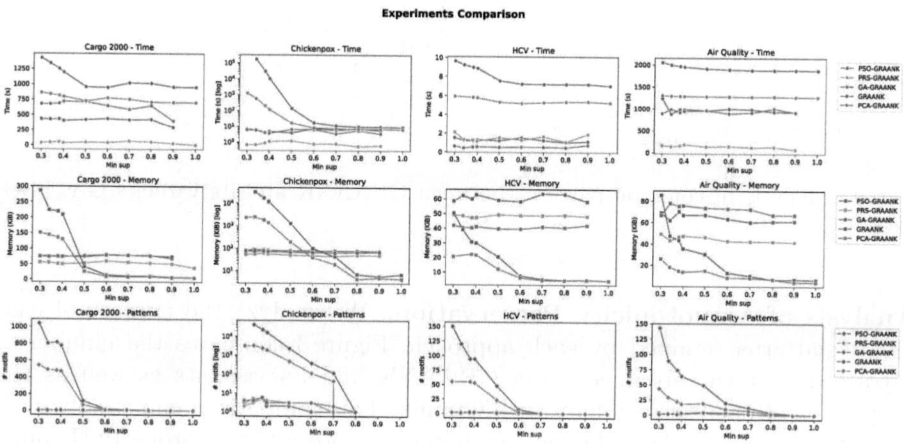

Fig. 2. Performance analysis: execution time, memory, and number of patterns meeting the minimum support

both execution time and memory consumption, reflecting a notable decrease in the explored search space. It should also be noted that, regardless of whether PCA is applied, the performance of the *GRAANK* algorithm tends to stabilize for all evaluation criteria starting from a support threshold of 0.8. This stabilization occurs because the number of generated candidates becomes extremely small, or even zero. Furthermore, in terms of memory consumption, the PCA-GRAANK approach consistently shows lower values across support thresholds compared with the other methods. In contrast, *RS-GRAANK*, *PSO-GRAANK*, and *GA-GRAANK* maintain an almost constant execution time. This behavior can be explained by their exploration strategies, which rely on heuristic search rather than exhaustive candidate generation. Regarding the number of candidates generated, our approach produces a larger number of patterns. However, the non-exhaustive methods generate very few patterns often fewer than ten. We therefore hypothesize that these approaches may miss some valid patterns during the search process.

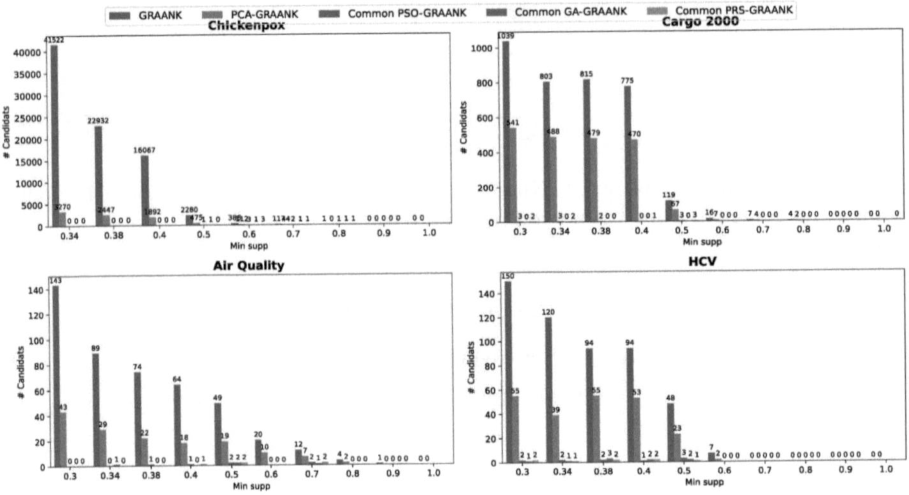

Fig. 3. Analysis of common patterns between GRAANK and its variants GA, PSO, PRS, PCA

Analysis of Monotonicity Preservation. We analyze the number of candidate patterns retained by each approach. Figure 3 compares the number of extracted patterns obtained using GRAANK and its variants as well as the proportion of patterns common with Graank. This comparison empirically evaluates the extent to which the local monotonicity preservation property (Lemma 1) translates into the preservation of gradual patterns. If F_ω preserved order relations globally on the variables in S_ω, then all patterns involving only these variables would be recovered by GRAANK applied on new dataset.

For the HCV dataset, PCA significantly reduces the number of candidates. For example, at a minimum support threshold of 0.3, GRAANK generates 150 candidates, whereas PCA-GRAANK produces only 55. In contrast, the metaheuristic approaches (PSO-GRAANK, GA-GRAANK, and PRS-GRAANK) extract a very small number of patterns fewer than five in most cases. Specifically, only 2, 1, and 2 patterns, respectively, are common with those obtained by GRAANK. However, PCA-GRAANK retains a notable portion of common patterns (around 20% at support 0.3). This indicates that although PCA removes many patterns, it still preserves a representative subset of the original rules. Consequently, the information loss remains moderate and acceptable.

For the Cargo 2000 dataset, the situation is even more favorable. A substantial reduction in the number of candidates is observed, decreasing from 1039 with GRAANK to 541 with PCA-GRAANK at a support threshold of 0.3. Despite this reduction, the proportion of common patterns remains relatively high (approximately 40%).

In the Air Quality dataset, the gap becomes more pronounced. At a support threshold of 0.3, GRAANK produces 143 candidates compared to only 43 with PCA-GRAANK. However, the number of common patterns is relatively small (around ten patterns, approximately 7%). This indicates that PCA significantly modifies the structure of the extracted frequent patterns. We also remark that the patterns discovered by the metaheuristic approaches are substantially different from those obtained by the exhaustive approach. In this case, the information loss becomes more substantial and may affect the representativeness of the resulting patterns.

For Chickenpox (support 0.34), candidates drop from 41000 to $\sim$3270, but only 1% of patterns are common. This loss of information may be explained by the correlation threshold of $\omega = 0.5$ applied during the preprocessing step, which removes a large portion of the explanatory variables before dimensionality reduction.

5 Conclusion

This work explored the integration of Principal Component Analysis (PCA) as a preprocessing method to improve frequent gradual pattern discovery, addressing computational challenges on large datasets. Experiments on real datasets demonstrated notable improvements in execution time and memory. The trade-off between acceleration and pattern completeness depends critically on threshold calibration: PCA may exclude low-variance attributes that carry significant order relationships, as illustrated by the Air Quality and Chickenpox cases. This finding indicates that, while PCA optimizes the overall representation of the data, particular attention must be paid to calibrating the selection threshold to ensure the preservation of gradual patterns, which depend on more local relationships. Future works will explore feature selection strategies that better preserve attributes with low variance but strong order relationships, and assess patterns in terms of domain relevance and interpretability.

Acknowledgements. The authors would like to thank CNRS for funding the DSCA project FDMI-AMG (https://fdmi.limos.fr/), the providers of datasets, and the authors of GRAANK and its variants. We also thank the anonymous reviewers for their valuable comments, the members of the FDMI-AMG project for their fruitful discussions, and William Guyot from LIMOS for his assistance with the computational resources used during the experiments.

References

1. Agrawal, R., Imieliński, T., Swami, A.: Mining association rules between sets of items in large databases. In: Proceedings of the 1993 ACM SIGMOD International Conference on Management of Data, pp. 207–216 (1993)
2. Boujike, M.C., Lonlac, J., Tsopze, N., Mephu Nguifo, E., Fotso, L.P.: Grapgt: gradual patterns with gradualness threshold. Int. J. Gen. Syst. **52**(5), 525–545 (2023)

3. Di-Jorio, L., Laurent, A., Teisseire, M.: Mining frequent gradual itemsets from large databases. In: IDA, pp. 297–308 (2009)
4. Gerardo, B.D., Lee, J., Ra, I., Byun, S.: Association rule discovery in data mining by implementing principal component analysis. In: Kim, T.G. (ed.) Artificial Intelligence and Simulation. AIS 2004. LNCS, vol 3397, pp. 50–60. Springer, Berlin, Heidelberg (2005). https://doi.org/10.1007/978-3-540-30583-5_6
5. Han, J., Pei, J., Yin, Y., Mao, R.: Mining frequent patterns without candidate generation: a frequent-pattern tree approach. Data Min. Knowl. Disc. **8**(1), 53–87 (2004)
6. Kamga Nguifo, D., Lonlac, J., Fleury, A., Mephu Nguifo, E.: Mining faster, not harder: a new criterion for gradual pattern mining. In: IEEE International Conference on Fuzzy Systems (FUZZ-IEEE 2025, Reims, France (2025)
7. Kenmogne, E.B., Tabueu Fotso, L.C., Tayou Djamegni, C.: A novel algorithm for mining maximal frequent gradual patterns. Eng. Appl. Artif. Intell. **120**, 105939 (2023)
8. Laurent, A., Lesot, M.J., Rifqi, M.: GRAANK: exploiting rank correlations for extracting gradual itemsets. In: Andreasen, T., Yager, R.R., Bulskov, H., Christiansen, H., Larsen, H.L. (eds.) Flexible Query Answering Systems. FQAS 2009. LNCS, vol. 5822, pp. 382–393. Springer, Berlin, Heidelberg (2009). https://doi.org/10.1007/978-3-642-04957-6_33
9. Lonlac, J., Doniec, A., Lujak, M., Lecoeuche, S.: Mining frequent seasonal gradual patterns. In: Song, M., Song, I.Y., Kotsis, G., Tjoa, A.M., Khalil, I. (eds.) Big Data Analytics and Knowledge Discovery. DaWaK 2020. LNCS, vol. 12393, pp. 197–207. Springer, Cham (2020). https://doi.org/10.1007/978-3-030-59065-9_16
10. Lonlac, J., Mephu Nguifo, E.: A novel algorithm for searching frequent gradual patterns from an ordered data set. Intell. Data Anal. **24**(5), 1029–1042 (2020)
11. Lonlac, J., Miras, Y., Beauger, A., Mazenod, V., Peiry, J.L., Nguifo, E.M.: An approach for extracting frequent (closed) gradual patterns under temporal constraint. In: 2018 IEEE International Conference on Fuzzy Systems (FUZZ-IEEE), pp. 1–8. IEEE Press (2018). https://doi.org/10.1109/FUZZ-IEEE.2018.8491665
12. Lonlac, J., Ouled Dlala, I., Jabbour, S., Mephu Nguifo, E., Raddaoui, B., Saïs, L.: On the discovery of frequent gradual patterns: a symbolic ai-based framework. SN Comput. Sci. **5**(7), 944 (2024)
13. Négrevergne, B., Termier, A., Rousset, M., Méhaut, J.: Para miner: a generic pattern mining algorithm for multi-core architectures. DMKD **28**(3), 593–633 (2014)
14. Owuor, D.O., Runkler, T., Laurent, A.: A metaheuristic approach for mining gradual patterns. Swarm Evol. Comput. **75**, 101205 (2022)
15. Owuor, D.O., Runkler, T., Laurent, A., Bonyo, L.: Clustering-based gradual pattern mining. Int. J. Mach. Learn. Cybern. **15**(6), 2263–2281 (2024)
16. Taha, T.M.F., Shomo, E., Oweis, N.E., Snasel, V.: In: Abraham, A., Kovalev, S., Tarassov, V., Snášel, V. (eds.) Proceedings of the First International Scientific Conference "Intelligent Information Technologies for Industry" (IITI'16), pp. 99–109. Springer, Cham (2016). https://doi.org/10.1007/978-3-319-33609-1
17. Tayou Djamegni, C., Tabueu Fotso, L.C., Kenmogne, E.B.: A novel algorithm for extracting frequent gradual patterns. Mach. Learn. Appl. **5**, 100068 (2021)
18. UmaMaheswari, P., Rajaram, M.: A novel approach for mining association rules on sports data using principal component analysis: for cricket match perspective. In: 2009 IEEE International Advance Computing Conference, pp. 1074–1080 (2009)

Reliability, Safety and Explainable AI

MalARN: An Adversarial Reconstruction Network for Improving Detection of Evolving Malware

Francesco Pasqualatto[1], Luca Caviglione[2], Massimo Guarascio[3](✉), Angelica Liguori[3], Giuseppe Manco[3], Ettore Ritacco[1], and Antonino Rullo[3]

[1] University of Udine, Udine, Italy
pasqualatto.francesco@spes.uniud.it, ettore.ritacco@uniud.it
[2] Institute for Applied Mathematics and Information Technologies - National Research Council (IMATI-CNR), Genova, Italy
luca.caviglione@ge.imati.cnr.it
[3] Institute for High Performance Computing and Networking - National Research Council (ICAR-CNR), Rende, Italy
{massimo.guarascio,angelica.liguori,giuseppe.manco, antonino.rullo}@icar.cnr.it

Abstract. Evolving a malware into a family is an effective technique to hinder detection mechanisms. A recent trend exploits generative models to support threat actors in the creation of "mutations" for rapidly preparing malware families. However, artificial intelligence can also be used to develop effective countermeasures. To this end, we propose MalARN, a deep learning-based solution for creating synthetic representations of malware variants to make detectors more robust and facilitate spotting never-seen threats. MalARN takes advantage of a pre-trained large language model to map both malicious and benign binary samples into embeddings. To bypass the requirement for executable binaries, an adversarial reconstruction network is used to operate directly in the embedding space. Evaluated against four real malware families, MalARN outperforms the baseline solution in terms of specific metrics for unbalanced scenarios.

Keywords: malware detection · synthetic malware generation · adversarial learning

1 Introduction

The proliferation of malware requires new solutions for detecting 0-day attacks or variants prepared to hinder signature-based mechanisms [12]. As an example, threat actors regularly use metamorphic engines for reordering instructions or swapping CPU registers to produce binary artifacts with new signatures [5]. A recent trend exploits Large Language Models (LLMs) for automatizing the creation of malicious payloads or attack routines. For instance, LLMs can be

G. Andresini et al. (Eds.): ISMIS 2026, LNAI 16685, pp. 93–103, 2027.
https://doi.org/10.1007/978-3-032-32643-0_9

employed for preparing programs and scripts with dead code, reordered instructions, or unconventional patterns of functions [14]. Therefore, countermeasures against malicious software require a partial rethink. First, distilling suitable signatures could not scale when in presence of rapidly-evolving or large malware families [2]. Second, the performance of classifiers endowed with some form of Artificial Intelligence (AI) may degrade over time due to "drifts", which could be either natural or accelerated by well-planned elusive campaigns [7]. Despite many works focus on whether LLMs can produce malicious code (see, e.g., [17]), a growing corpus of research explores how to "enrich" the training data with artificial malware samples for making deep learning-based classifiers more accurate and robust [4]. As a paradigmatic example, the work in [6] introduces a mechanism for generating synthetic malware samples to devise better datasets and improve the training phases. A similar idea can help to prevent concept drifts in detectors for Android OS or to mitigate 0-day attacks [7,19]. Unfortunately, the generation of binary artifacts that correctly run is still the major open issue towards the creation of better countermeasures [1].

To fill this gap, we introduce `MalARN`, a deep learning-based solution that leverages a pre-trained LLM to map both malicious and benign Windows Portable Executable (PE) samples into high-quality embeddings [3]. To bypass the need for generating functional PE binaries, our method synthesizes realistic malware variants directly in the embedding space via an Adversarial Reconstruction Network (ARN) [10]. Despite using a limited number of malware samples per family, `MalARN` turned out to be suitable for improving detection in few-shot and highly imbalanced scenarios.

Compared to our previous work [3], this paper has the following improvements: the generation framework uses ARN for creating synthetic malware variants and learning a discriminative function to distinguish between goodware and malware samples, and the performance evaluation campaign has been expanded by also considering the Seduploader malware family.

The rest of the paper is organized as follows. Section 2 introduces the problem considered, Sect. 3 showcases the architecture for generating malware and the detection model, and Sect. 4 presents numerical results. Lastly, Sect. 5 concludes the paper and outlines future research directions.

2 Problem Statement

In general, detectors using Machine Learning (ML) to distinguish between malicious and legitimate software (i.e., goodware) rely upon highly-imbalanced datasets, thus leading to poor minority-class performance [13]. This issue is exacerbated by the rapid release of new threats that may outpace updates. Figure 1 depicts the major approaches for improving the detection of evolving malware. Without loss of generality, we focus on the *.text* section of Windows PE files, which is the main container of executable code. To evade detection, a threat actor may evolve a malware into one or more variants (i.e., a family). For instance, if the original code directly sets the register `eax` to 1 via a `mov` instruction, a

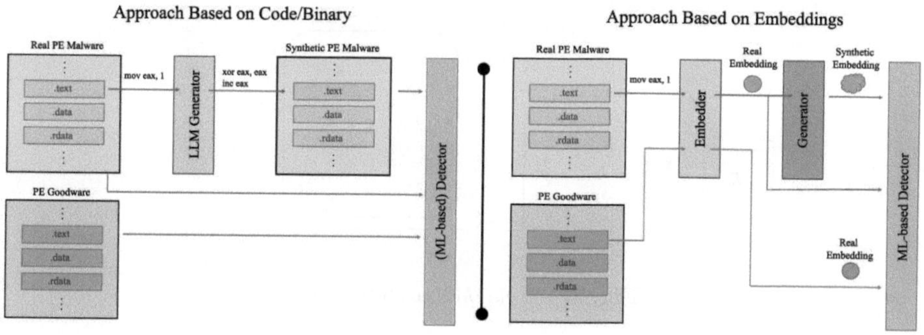

Fig. 1. Main approaches for generating malware variants to improve detection.

new-but-equivalent PE can be prepared by `xor`-ing and incrementing the `eax` register by 1. The idea is to design better detectors by "anticipating" mutations via the creation of suitable training datasets. To this aim, an LLM can be used to generate synthetic variants to improve the training phase by also considering goodware examples. Since generating runnable PE files is a hard problem, we propose to use an embedder to map the original *.text* section into a learned feature space. Accordingly, the new malware is not generated anymore by varying the "`mov eax, 1`" statement. Rather, the ML detector is only fed with representations in the embedding space of malware and goodware samples, thus preventing the need of any running malicious assembly prose. This approach also prevents the need of testing malicious PE files via sandboxes or other resource-consuming procedures.

The generation approach via embeddings in Fig. 1 can be formalized as follows. We denote as $\mathcal{D}_G = \{x_i^G\}_{i=1}^n$ and $\mathcal{D}_M = \{x_i^M\}_{i=1}^m$ the goodware and malware sets respectively, where $m \ll n$. Our dataset is $\mathcal{D} = \mathcal{D}_G \cup \mathcal{D}_M$, where each $x \in D$ represents a *.text* section. We address a twofold problem:

1. Define an embedding function $h : x \to \mathbb{R}^d$ to map the *.text* section to a numerical representation $e_x = h(x)$.
2. Define an adversarial learning framework composed of a generative function $f_\varphi : \mathbb{R}^d \to \mathbb{R}^d$ that produces realistic malware variants in the embedding space, and a discriminative function $p_\theta : \mathbb{R}^d \to \{0, 1\}$ that distinguishes between goodware and malware. The goal is to jointly learn φ and θ so that f_φ synthesizes realistic malware variants, while p_θ learns how to separate malware samples from goodware.

3 Proposed Approach

Figure 2 depicts the `MalARN` neural architecture leveraging a pre-trained LLM to map both malicious and benign code samples into semantic representations. To mitigate generalization issues caused by the limited availability of emerging malware samples, `MalARN` employs an adversarial generation strategy based on the

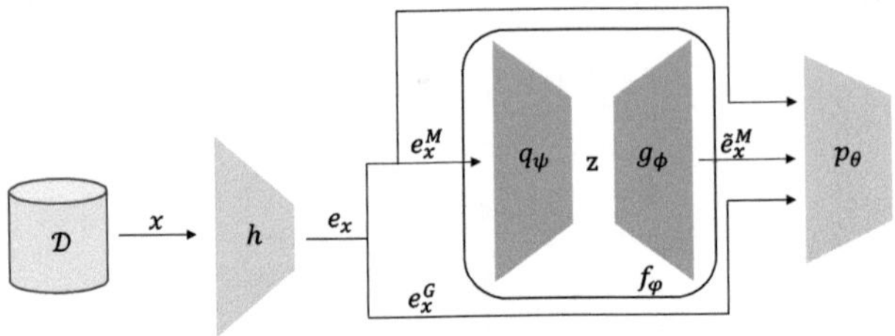

Fig. 2. the `MalARN` architecture.

ARN framework [10]. Formally, given a sample $x \in \mathcal{D}$, the LLM-based embedding function h maps x to a latent representation e_x, which is then used to train the ARN architecture. For a malware embedding e_x^M, the generative function f_φ indicated with the encoder-decoder pair (q_ψ, g_ϕ) generates a minimally perturbed version, denoted $\tilde{e}_x^M$. The discriminator p_θ is trained to correctly classify both original and generated malware embeddings, as well as goodware embeddings. The function h that maps each sample x to a fixed-size representation $e_x \in \mathbb{R}^d$ takes the form of an LLM. As proposed in [3], `MalARN` computes the embeddings using a pre-trained CodeT5 language model, i.e., a transformer-based architecture designed for code understanding and generation tasks [18]. The ARN framework processes the embeddings to generate realistic malware variants, while jointly learning a classifier to discriminate between malware and goodware. Since ARN operates on the embeddings $e_x = h(x)$, we simply denote e_x as x in the following.

The generator used by ARN is a Variational Autoencoder (VAE) [9], composed of a probabilistic encoder q_ψ and a decoder g_ϕ, while the discriminative function p_θ is a multi-layer perceptron acting as a binary detector. The probabilistic encoder $q_\psi(z|x)$ maps the embedding x into a latent representation $z \in \mathbb{R}^k$. The generator g_ϕ produces minimally-perturbed variants starting from z, i.e., $\tilde{x} = g_\phi(z)$. Unlike ARN, `MalARN` learns to synthesize realistic malware variants from a limited number of available malware samples. In more detail, the discriminator of `MalARN` leverages both original and generated malware embeddings, as well as goodware ones, and is trained with the following objective function:

$$\max_{\theta} \min_{\phi,\psi} \underbrace{\mathbb{E}_{x,y\sim\mathbb{P}_\mathcal{D}}\Big[\log p_\theta(y|x)\Big]}_{\text{Label real instances①}} + \underbrace{\mathbb{E}_{\substack{x,y\sim\mathbb{P}_\mathcal{M}\\ z\sim q_\psi(\cdot|x)\\ \tilde{x}\sim g_\phi(z)}}\Big[\log p_\theta(y|\tilde{x})\Big]}_{\text{Flag synthetic variants②}}$$
$$+ \underbrace{\mathbb{E}_{\substack{x\sim\mathbb{P}_\mathcal{M}\\ z\sim q_\psi(\cdot|x)\\ \tilde{x}\sim g_\phi(z)}}\Big[\log p(x|\tilde{x})\Big]}_{\text{Maximize reconstruction likelihood③}} + \underbrace{\mathbb{KL}\left[q_\psi(z|x)\|p(z)\right]}_{\text{Latent space regularization④}} \quad (1)$$

where $\mathbb{P}_{\mathcal{D}}$ is the unknown distribution generating codes, while $\mathbb{P}_{\mathcal{M}}$ is the distribution generating malware.

Specifically, Eq. 1 defines an adversarial min-max game between the discriminator p_θ and the VAE-based generator (q_ψ, g_ϕ). The objective is to improve the detection capability of the discriminator by generating diverse and realistic (unseen) malware samples that are correctly classified as malware. The discriminator is then trained to accurately distinguish between goodware ($y = 0$) and malware ($y = 1$) samples drawn from the real data (term ①), while simultaneously classifying the synthetic variants $\tilde{x}$ produced by the generator as malware (term ②). The generated samples $\tilde{x} = g_\phi(q_\psi(x))$ enhance the ability of recognizing general malware embeddings, while the reconstruction constraint (term ③) prevents indiscriminate exploration of the embedding space by forcing generated samples to remain close, while still distinct, from the original malware representations. Finally, regularization of the latent variable $z = q_\psi(x)$ is enforced through the Kullback-Leibler (KL) divergence, promoting a structured and well-behaved latent space (term ④). To effectively instantiate `MalARN` and prevent training instability such as mode collapse or vanishing gradients, we incorporate specific architectural refinements. The discriminator p_θ is equipped with spectral normalization [11] across its linear layers to strictly bound the Lipschitz constant, further aided by dropout mechanisms to prevent the network from overfitting. The generator g_ϕ leverages residual connections and layer normalization rather than batch normalization. This ensures stable gradient flows and consistent normalization statistics, even when operating with extremely small and variable batch sizes typical of the few-shot learning environment.

Finally, to address the extreme scarcity of malicious instances ($m \ll n$), our generation phase incorporates a dynamic latent resampling mechanism. During the training loop, the few available input malware embeddings are expanded by a factor of k (multiple unique latent vectors are sampled from the posterior distribution $q_\psi(z|x)$ for each single input). This forces the decoder to map a single real malware sample into a diverse, localized cluster of synthetic variants within the latent manifold. In this way, the framework can efficiently explore the boundaries of the malware distribution without yielding executable artifacts. It also forces the discriminator to build a highly robust classification boundary for improving its ability to identify evasive mutations or 0-days [4].

4 Experiments

This section presents the experimental evaluation of `MalARN`. Specifically, Sect. 4.1 presents the datasets, the evaluation protocol, and the metrics, while Sect. 4.2 introduces the model parameters and main implementation details. Finally, Sect. 4.3 showcases numerical results.

4.1 Datasets, Evaluation Protocol and Metrics

In our experimentation, we considered the MOTIF collection of disarmed Windows PE malware samples labeled with ground-truth information [8], which is a de-facto standard dataset for assessing malware detection tasks. Specifically, we focused on four ransomware families: IcedID, Phorpiex, Trickbot, and Seduploader, including respectively 142, 54, 41, and 40 samples after a preprocessing and cleaning phase. These families were selected to assess whether `MalARN` can generalize across diverse behavioral patterns and elusive techniques (e.g., Base64-encoded strings). The goodware was extracted from MalConv[1] collection composed of 1,000 benign samples. In more detail, we shortlisted 648 samples to have an heterogeneous snapshot of legitimate applications [16].

To evaluate the effectiveness of our approach, we adopt a hold-out protocol designed to simulate a few-shot learning scenario. Specifically, the training set consists of only 5 malware samples from a given family and 200 goodware samples, while the test set includes the remaining malware instances for each family together with additional goodware samples (i.e., 448 benign applications).

We consider two strategies for selecting the 5 malware samples used for training, namely Temporal Split (TS) and Random Split (RS). The TS approximates a forward-in-time evaluation setting, where training is performed on the earliest available samples of a malware family and testing is conducted on subsequent variants. In this case, malware samples are chronologically sorted according to their creation and first submission dates reported by VirusTotal[2]. Conversely, the RS removes the chronological constraint and selects the 5 training samples uniformly at random from the available malware samples. This allows to evaluate the performance of the detector independently of temporal ordering, assuming that samples are collected "in the wild" without a strict timing structure.

Given the extreme class imbalance established during the training phase and the inherent nature of anomaly detection, standard decision thresholds may yield a suboptimal recall. We then set a strict decision threshold of $\tau = 0.025$ for all binary classification evaluations, which has been chosen as an approximation of the prior probability of the malicious class within the training distribution, i.e., $\frac{5}{205} \approx 0.025$.

To assess the performance of `MalARN`, we employ standard metrics including F1-Score, the Area Under the Precision-Recall Curve (AUPRC) and Accuracy [15]. In particular, we consider the F1-score as our main metric, as it provides a reliable estimate of model performance in scenarios where a validation set is unavailable and additional fine-tuning may be needed.

4.2 Model Parameters and Implementation

The volume of synthetic data generated to "augment" each real malware sample is the key hyperparameter ruling the behavior of the proposed approach. To understand to what extent the number of generated synthetic variants influences the performance of `MalARN`, we considered three configurations denoted as $\texttt{MalARN}_3$, $\texttt{MalARN}_{15}$, and $\texttt{MalARN}_{30}$. In $\texttt{MalARN}_3$, the generator produces 3 synthetic variants for every real malware sample. Similarly, in $\texttt{MalARN}_{15}$ and

[1] MalConv Malware Classification Dataset: https://github.com/0x13enny/MalConv.

[2] VirusTotal: https://www.virustotal.com/.

$\texttt{MalARN}_{30}$, the generator produces 15 and 30 synthetic variants per real sample, respectively. This test allows to assess whether higher augmentation ratios facilitate a broader and more robust exploration of the latent manifold.

Regarding the specific parameters of MalARN, the generator is a VAE working in the embedding space. The encoder progressively reduces the dimensionality of the input embeddings (dimension $d = 768$) through fully connected layers ($768 \rightarrow 256 \rightarrow 64$), followed by Layer Normalization and LeakyReLU activations. The latent representation is composed of two linear layers producing the mean and variance of a latent vector of size $z = 16$, sampled using the reparameterization trick. The decoder mirrors the encoder structure and reconstructs the embedding through fully connected layers ($64 \rightarrow 256 \rightarrow 768$) using ReLU activations, while the final layer uses a tanh activation. Skip connections are introduced within both encoder and decoder stages to stabilize training and accelerate convergence.

The discriminator takes the form of an MLP composed of fully connected layers with decreasing dimensionality ($768 \rightarrow 512 \rightarrow 256 \rightarrow 128 \rightarrow 1$). The final output layer uses a sigmoid activation to estimate the probability that a given embedding corresponds to a malicious sample. The Adam optimizer is used with a learning rate of 10^{-3} and 10^{-4} for the generator and discriminator, respectively. The loss functions used to jointly train the generator and the discriminator follow the formulation introduced in Eq. 1.

To conduct tests, we used a prototypical implementation of MalARN based on the PyTorch framework, which has been made publicly available[3]. Experiments have been conducted on a machine with an Intel Core i5-10300H CPU @ 2.50 GHz 24 GB of RAM and a NVIDIA GeForce RTX 3060 with 6 GB of VRAM, running Ubuntu 20.04.6 LTS.

4.3 Results and Discussion

Table 1 presents the performance of MalARN across different data-splitting strategies and malware families. For the sake of comparison, it also reports results for the baseline used in [3]. In more detail, when handling malware samples with the TS strategy, MalARN exhibits improvements over the baseline for all the metrics across the different malware families. For the case of the Seduploader ransomware, the AUPRC increases from 0.843 for the baseline to 0.994 when using $\texttt{MalARN}_{3}$. Similar behaviors can be observed for the Phorpiex and Trickbot families, where higher volumes of generated samples improve both Accuracy and F1 scores, e.g., $\texttt{MalARN}_{15}$ and $\texttt{MalARN}_{30}$ lead to perfect metrics when detecting the Trickbot ransomware. Our approach can also improve the detection of the IcedID malware family. In this case, both baseline and $\texttt{MalARN}_{15}$ models achieve an Accuracy of 0.772, but our approach further optimizes the precision-recall trade-off by boosting the AUPRC from 0.780 to 0.807 with $\texttt{MalARN}_{3}$. This could be ascribed to a "reactive" capability of MalARN against mechanisms for impairing the PE analysis. For instance, IcedID tries to hinder feature-based detectors by avoiding clear strings or XOR-cyphering API names in the *.text* section. Hence,

[3] Code of MalARN: https://anonymous.4open.science/r/MalARN-C14C/.

Table 1. Comparison between MalARN and the baseline under TS and RS strategies and percentage improvements over the baseline.

Split	Family	Model	F1	AUPRC	Acc	ΔF1%	ΔAUPRC%	ΔAcc%
TS	Phorpiex	Baseline	0.953	0.918	0.983	–	–	–
		$\texttt{MalARN}_3$	0.965	**0.952**	0.987	+1.26	+3.70	+0.41
		$\texttt{MalARN}_{15}$	**0.977**	0.947	**0.992**	+2.52	+3.16	+0.92
		$\texttt{MalARN}_{30}$	**0.977**	**0.952**	**0.992**	+2.52	+3.70	+0.92
	Trickbot	Baseline	0.913	1.000	0.979	–	–	–
		$\texttt{MalARN}_3$	0.992	1.000	0.997	+8.66	0.00	+1.84
		$\texttt{MalARN}_{15}$	**1.000**	1.000	**1.000**	+9.53	0.00	+2.14
		$\texttt{MalARN}_{30}$	**1.000**	1.000	**1.000**	+9.53	0.00	+2.14
	IcedID	Baseline	**0.463**	0.780	**0.772**	–	–	–
		$\texttt{MalARN}_3$	**0.463**	**0.807**	0.770	0.00	+3.46	–0.26
		$\texttt{MalARN}_{15}$	**0.463**	0.788	**0.772**	0.00	+1.03	0.00
		$\texttt{MalARN}_{30}$	**0.463**	0.806	0.770	0.00	+3.33	–0.26
	Seduploader	Baseline	0.900	0.843	0.977	–	–	–
		$\texttt{MalARN}_3$	**0.921**	**0.994**	**0.981**	+2.33	+17.91	+0.41
		$\texttt{MalARN}_{15}$	**0.921**	0.992	**0.981**	+2.33	+17.67	+0.41
		$\texttt{MalARN}_{30}$	**0.921**	0.992	**0.981**	+2.33	+17.67	+0.41
RS	Phorpiex	Baseline	0.958	0.969	0.985	–	–	–
		$\texttt{MalARN}_3$	0.971	0.977	0.989	+1.36	+0.83	+0.41
		$\texttt{MalARN}_{15}$	**0.977**	**0.978**	**0.992**	+1.98	+0.93	+0.71
		$\texttt{MalARN}_{30}$	**0.977**	**0.978**	**0.992**	+1.98	+0.93	+0.71
	Trickbot	Baseline	**0.984**	**1.000**	**0.995**	–	–	–
		$\texttt{MalARN}_3$	**0.984**	**1.000**	**0.995**	0.00	0.00	0.00
		$\texttt{MalARN}_{15}$	**0.984**	**1.000**	**0.995**	0.00	0.00	0.00
		$\texttt{MalARN}_{30}$	**0.984**	0.999	**0.995**	0.00	–0.10	0.00
	IcedID	Baseline	0.933	**0.997**	0.955	–	–	–
		$\texttt{MalARN}_3$	**0.963**	**0.997**	**0.974**	+3.21	0.00	+1.99
		$\texttt{MalARN}_{15}$	0.955	0.996	0.969	+2.36	–0.10	+1.47
		$\texttt{MalARN}_{30}$	0.950	**0.997**	0.965	+1.82	0.00	+1.05
	Seduploader	Baseline	**1.000**	**1.000**	**1.000**	–	–	–
		$\texttt{MalARN}_3$	0.992	**1.000**	0.997	–0.80	0.00	–0.30
		$\texttt{MalARN}_{15}$	**1.000**	**1.000**	**1.000**	0.00	0.00	0.00
		$\texttt{MalARN}_{30}$	**1.000**	**1.000**	**1.000**	0.00	0.00	00.00

MalARN proven to be more effective than the baseline in distilling meaningful features from the binary code of the various PEs. Our approach exhibits a similar robustness also when facing families handled via the RS strategy. For the case of Phorpiex, $\texttt{MalARN}_{30}$ achieves the highest scores, i.e., it achieves 0.992, 0.977, and 0.978, for the Accuracy, F1, and AUPRC, respectively. For IcedID, $\texttt{MalARN}_{3}$ boosts the Accuracy from 0.955 to 0.974 and the F1 from 0.933 to 0.963, whereas for Seduploader and Trickbot the baseline already exhibits saturated or near-perfect performance. Here, the augmentation enforced by `MalARN` safely matches these optimal levels without degrading the decision boundary. As shown, `MalARN` consistently improves or maintains the detection capabilities of the baseline model, especially in highly restrictive few-shot scenarios. The overall trend then confirms its ability to distinguish the minority malicious class within severely imbalanced data.

To assess the quality of `MalARN`, we also conduct a qualitative analysis by visualizing the t-SNE projection of the embeddings of goodware and both real and generated malware, from the training and test sets. For the sake of brevity, we limit our analysis to the Phorpiex family. As shown in Fig. 3, generated malware "samples" lie close to real threats, highlighting the effectiveness of our representation.

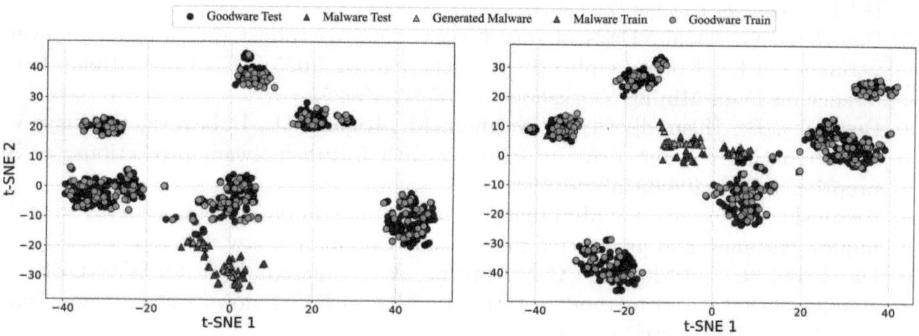

Fig. 3. t-SNE visualization of goodware and Phorpiex data.

5 Conclusions

This work presented a framework for the mitigation of malware avoiding detection by evolving into a family. Named `MalARN`, it combines the mapping capabilities of LLMs with synthetic embeddings generated via ARN to train detectors that can effectively generalize beyond known samples. By operating entirely within the latent space, our approach prevents the need of PE binaries that correctly run. Results demonstrated that `MalARN` achieves a F1-Score above 90% except for IcedID, which deploys mechanisms to hinder the detection.

Future work aims at extending the experimental campaign to broader malware families and to consider threat actors using generative AI for automatically producing offensive variants. Morever, we plan to compare our solution with other approaches based on data augmentation strategies. Part of our ongoing research is devoted to assessing the explainability of the detector by using the same LLM-based embedder. Finally, we want to incorporate `MalARN` with few-shot active learning strategies within a human-in-the-loop setting.

Acknowledgments. This work was partially supported by project Security and Rights in the Cyberspace - SERICS (PE00000014) under the MUR National Recovery and Resilience Plan funded by the European Union - NextGenerationEU and by project PERUN (101225653) - Protecting Sensitive Cyber Ecosystems from Upcoming Next Generation and AI-generated Malware Threats under the Horizon Europe Program funded by the European Union.

References

1. Akil, M.A., et al.: LLMalMorph: On The Feasibility of Generating Variant Malware Using Large-Language-Models. arXiv (2025)
2. Aslan, Ö.A., Samet, R.: A comprehensive review on malware detection approaches. IEEE Access **8**, 6249–6271 (2020)
3. Benedetti, G., et al.: Days of future past: towards robust detection of malware variants via LLM-based embedding generation. In: 2025 IEEE International Conference on Data Mining Workshops, ICDMW (2025)
4. Bosansky, B., Hospodkova, L., Najman, M., Rigaki, M., Babayeva, E., Lisy, V.: Counteracting concept drift by learning with future malware predictions. arXiv preprint arXiv:2404.09352 (2024)
5. Brezinski, K., Ferens, K.: Metamorphic malware and obfuscation: a survey of techniques, variants, and generation kits. Secur. Commun. Netw. **2023**(1) (2023)
6. De Rose, L., Andresini, G., Appice, A., Malerba, D.: OLIVANDER: a counterfactual-based method to generate adversarial windows PE malware. Data Min. Knowl. Disc. **39**(46) (2025)
7. He, Y., Lei, J., Qin, Z., Ren, K., Chen, C.: Combating concept drift with explanatory detection and adaptation for android malware classification. In: Proceedings of the 2025 ACM SIGSAC Conference on Computer and Communications Security, pp. 978–992 (2025)
8. Joyce, R.J., Amlani, D., Nicholas, C., Raff, E.: MOTIF: a malware reference dataset with ground truth family labels. Comput. Secur. **124**, 102921 (2023)
9. Kingma, D.P., Welling, M.: Auto-encoding variational bayes. In: International Conference on Learning Representations (2014)
10. Liguori, A., Ritacco, E., Pisani, F.S., Manco, G.: Robust anomaly detection via adversarial counterfactual generation. Knowl. Inf. Syst. **66**(12), 7437–7468 (2024)
11. Miyato, T., Kataoka, T., Koyama, M., Yoshida, Y.: Spectral normalization for generative adversarial networks. In: International Conference on Learning Representations (2018)
12. Moreira, C.C., Moreira, D.C., Sales, C., Jr.: A comprehensive analysis combining structural features for detection of new ransomware families. J. Inf. Secur. Appl. **81**, 103716 (2024)
13. Oak, R., Du, M., Yan, D., Takawale, H., Amit, I.: Malware detection on highly imbalanced data through sequence modeling. In: Proceedings of the 12th ACM Workshop on Artificial Intelligence and Security, pp. 37–48 (2019)

14. Setak, M., Madani, P.: Fine-tuning LLMs for code mutation: a new era of cyber threats. In: 2024 IEEE 6th International Conference on Trust, Privacy and Security in Intelligent Systems, and Applications, pp. 313–321. IEEE (2024)
15. Sokolova, M., Lapalme, G.: A systematic analysis of performance measures for classification tasks. Inf. Process. Manag. **45**(4), 427–437 (2009)
16. Tuan, A.P., Phuong, A.T.H., Thanh, N.V., Van, T.N.: Malware Detection PE-Based Analysis Using Deep Learning Algorithm Dataset (2018)
17. Wang, G., Chen, D., Gu, X., Chen, Y., Shen, B.: Synthetic malware at scale: malicious code generation with code transplanting. IEEE Trans. Softw. Eng. **52**(1), 171–186 (2025)
18. Wang, Y., Wang, W., Joty, S.R., Hoi, S.C.H.: CodeT5: identifier-aware unified pre-trained encoder-decoder models for code understanding and generation. In: Empirical Methods in Natural Language Processing, pp. 8696–8708. Association for Computational Linguistics (2021)
19. Won, D.O., Jang, Y.N., Lee, S.W.: Plausmal-gan: plausible malware training based on generative adversarial networks for analogous zero-day malware detection. IEEE Trans. Emerg. Top. Comput. **11**(1), 82–94 (2022)

Diagnosing Hallucinations in RAG-Based Educational Recommendation Systems: A Controlled Comparative Study

Ichrak Ennaceur[1,2](✉), Haytham Elghazel[1], Alexandre Aussem[1], Guillaume Lefebvre[2], and Matthieu Sonnati[2]

[1] Université Claude Bernard Lyon 1, CNRS, INSA Lyon, LIRIS, UMR5205, Villeurbanne, France
ichraknaceurr@gmail.com
[2] Inokufu, Lyon, France

Abstract. When Retrieval-Augmented Generation (RAG) systems are used in educational settings, ensuring reliability and transparency becomes essential. However, these systems can sometimes generate information that is not properly grounded in the underlying knowledge sources, and the reasons behind these failures remain insufficiently understood. In this paper, we introduce a diagnostic framework designed to analyze hallucination phenomena in RAG-based educational recommendation systems. Our approach distinguishes between two main sources of errors: those originating from pipeline-level issues, such as generation artifacts or catalogue traceability problems, and those related to retrieval grounding. To better understand these behaviors, we evaluate system performance under different retrieval depths, which allows us to identify two distinct phenomena: structural hallucinations and depth-sensitive generalization. Experiments conducted on a real educational catalogue show that evaluation protocols and retrieval depth strongly influence how hallucinations are diagnosed. These results highlight the importance of careful evaluation when deploying RAG systems in educational environments. Our framework provides practical methodological guidelines for analyzing groundedness and improving the reliability of educational AI systems.

Keywords: Hallucination · Retrieval-Augmented Generation · Groundedness · Educational Recommendation · Evaluation Protocols

1 Introduction

Large language models (LLMs) have recently shown strong capabilities in natural language understanding and generation [1,11,17,18]. They are increasingly used in educational technologies, including intelligent tutoring systems, automated feedback tools, and conversational assistants that help learners navigate large

G. Andresini et al. (Eds.): ISMIS 2026, LNAI 16685, pp. 104–113, 2027.
https://doi.org/10.1007/978-3-032-32643-0_10

collections of educational resources. By enabling interactive explanations and personalized guidance, such systems can support more adaptive and accessible learning experiences.

At the same time, their deployment raises important reliability concerns. A well-known issue is *hallucination*, where models produce fluent but unsupported or incorrect information [9,10]. In educational settings, such errors can be especially harmful because inaccurate explanations may introduce misconceptions, reinforce incorrect reasoning, or mislead learners. Ensuring that generated responses remain grounded in trustworthy educational resources is therefore essential for responsible educational AI systems.

Retrieval-Augmented Generation (RAG) [12] has emerged as a practical way to address this challenge. By combining neural generation with external retrieval, RAG systems allow language models to access curated knowledge sources such as textbooks, course catalogues, and learning repositories. Conditioning generation on retrieved evidence can improve factual grounding while preserving the flexibility of large language models, making RAG a widely adopted paradigm for knowledge-grounded question answering and recommendation systems [6,19].

However, applying RAG to educational recommendation introduces additional difficulties. Student queries are often ambiguous or underspecified, and retrieved passages may be noisy or only partially relevant. Recent work has therefore explored the use of contextual signals to guide retrieval and reasoning. For example, RAMO [15] introduces contextual cues to better align user queries with educational content, while CLARE [5] incorporates semantic categories and in-context signals to improve learning object recommendation.

Still, the interaction between contextual enrichment, retrieval mechanisms, and generation processes in educational RAG systems remains insufficiently understood. In particular, it is often unclear whether incorrect recommendations come from genuine hallucinations, retrieval limitations, or artifacts introduced by the generation pipeline. Without controlled evaluation methodologies, diagnosing these behaviors remains difficult.

In this paper, retrieval depth denotes the number of catalogue items considered when evaluating whether a generated recommendation is supported by retrieval. A shallow depth (e.g., $K = 20$) reflects the evidence typically available to the generator, whereas a larger depth (e.g., $K = 100$) is used diagnostically to determine whether an apparently unsupported recommendation is absent from the retrieval space or simply appears beyond the shallow cutoff.

Research Question. How can we distinguish genuine hallucinated recommendations from retrieval-depth limitations and pipeline-level artifacts in RAG-based educational recommendation systems?

To answer this question, we propose a structured diagnostic framework for analyzing hallucination phenomena in RAG-based educational recommendation systems. Rather than introducing a new recommendation architecture, we focus on evaluation methodology and controlled analysis. More specifically, we introduce a pipeline-level traceability analysis that separates generation artifacts from retrieval grounding behavior, define two complementary evaluation protocols, *conditioned* and *penalized*, to distinguish retrieval performance from end-to-end system reliability, and propose a depth-aware diagnostic analysis that reveals distinct grounding regimes depending on retrieval depth.

Experiments on a real educational catalogue show that hallucination assessment in RAG-based recommendation systems is highly sensitive to evaluation protocol design and retrieval depth. These findings highlight the importance of careful and transparent evaluation strategies when deploying RAG systems in educational environments.

2 Related Work

Hallucinations are widely recognized as a major limitation of large language models (LLMs). They refer to outputs that appear fluent and coherent but are unsupported by the provided context or factually incorrect. Prior work distinguishes between *intrinsic hallucinations*, which contradict the source input, and *extrinsic hallucinations*, which introduce unverifiable information beyond the available evidence [9,10]. In educational settings, such errors are particularly concerning, since incorrect explanations may introduce persistent misconceptions for learners.

Retrieval-Augmented Generation (RAG) was introduced as an effective strategy to mitigate unsupported generation by grounding language models in external knowledge sources [12]. In a typical RAG pipeline, relevant documents are retrieved from an indexed corpus and incorporated into the generation process. Recent research shows that the effectiveness of RAG systems depends on several interacting components, including document chunking, embedding quality, retrieval strategies, reranking, and prompt design [6,16,19]. Despite these improvements, failures may still occur when retrieved documents are noisy, only partially relevant, or poorly integrated during generation. To improve reasoning over retrieved information, approaches such as Chain-of-Note structure how models read and evaluate retrieved evidence before generating answers [20]. More generally, retrieval-based reasoning pipelines have been explored as a way to improve factual grounding in LLM systems [7].

Another line of work focuses on evaluating groundedness in RAG systems. Several recent studies examine the reliability of LLM-based evaluators and highlight the sensitivity of evaluation results to prompt design, reference availability, and evaluation protocols [2,8,13]. Complementary research on model calibration suggests that consistency across multiple sampled generations can serve as an indicator of uncertainty and help identify unreliable outputs [14].

In the educational domain, RAG-based recommendation systems have been proposed to help learners navigate large course catalogues through conversational interfaces. RAMO applies a retrieval-augmented generation pipeline to recommend MOOCs, particularly addressing scenarios where user interaction history is limited [15]. Building on this idea, CLARE introduces a category-aware RAG framework that incorporates semantic categories and in-context examples to improve pedagogical alignment [5]. Although these systems report improved recommendation quality, systematic methodologies for diagnosing when recommendations become unsupported, whether due to retrieval truncation, generation artifacts, or pipeline design remain limited. Our work addresses this gap by proposing a diagnostic evaluation framework that separates pipeline traceability, evaluation protocol effects, and retrieval-depth sensitivity under a controlled infrastructure.

3 Studied Systems and Controlled Experimental Setup

This section introduces the two retrieval-augmented generation paradigms analyzed in this study and the controlled experimental setup used for their comparison. Rather than focusing solely on recommendation performance, our objective is to analyze how different RAG designs influence the groundedness of generated recommendations. To ensure a fair comparison, both paradigms are evaluated under an identical retrieval infrastructure so that observed differences originate from prompt design and contextual signals rather than from indexing or retrieval variations.

3.1 Two Representative RAG Paradigms

The first paradigm follows a category-aware design inspired by CLARE [5]. In this approach, structured learning categories are injected into the prompt and act as semantic anchors guiding the generation process. Predicted categories allow the model to interpret user queries within a pedagogically meaningful context. In addition, examples of learner trajectories may be included through in-context learning (ICL), illustrating typical learning progressions within the catalogue.

The second paradigm corresponds to a retrieval-conditioned design inspired by RAMO [15]. Here, generation relies primarily on the user query and retrieved course descriptions without explicit pedagogical scaffolding. The prompt therefore contains retrieved catalogue entries but does not incorporate category signals or learner trajectory information. As a result, generation is mainly driven by semantic similarity between the query and retrieved documents.

For comparability, the RAMO-style paradigm is implemented within the same infrastructure as the CLARE-style system so that differences reflect prompt design rather than system-level implementation choices.

3.2 Controlled Retrieval Infrastructure

Both paradigms operate on the same indexed catalogue and use identical embedding representations for course descriptions. The vector index is implemented using the FAISS library [4] with inner-product similarity applied to normalized embeddings.

The generation stage is also standardized across systems. Recommendations are produced using the same large language models, including Mistral [11] and LLaMA-2 [18]. This controlled configuration ensures that differences in groundedness behavior originate from prompt structure and contextual signals rather than from the retrieval backbone.

3.3 Dataset and Retrieval Setup

Experiments are conducted on a curated educational catalogue containing 3,416 courses annotated with titles, descriptions, categories, and difficulty levels. The dataset also includes interaction trajectories from 5,594 learners, which are used in the category-aware paradigm to provide in-context examples of learning progression.

All course descriptions are encoded into dense embeddings and indexed using the FAISS library [4]. Retrieval uses inner-product similarity over normalized vectors. Grounding support is evaluated across retrieval depths $K \in \{20, 40, 60, 80, 100\}$ by verifying whether recommended items appear among the Top-K retrieved documents.

4 Diagnostic Framework

We propose a diagnostic framework to analyze hallucination phenomena in retrieval-augmented educational recommendation systems. Instead of focusing only on recommendation accuracy, the framework examines how generation and retrieval interact within the pipeline.

Pipeline Traceability. Generated recommendations are first aligned with catalogue entries through a normalization step (lowercasing and title matching). Each recommendation can therefore be uniquely mapped, ambiguously mapped, or unmappable. Only uniquely mapped items can be evaluated for retrieval grounding.

Retrieval Groundedness. For a query q, groundedness is measured by verifying whether the catalogue item corresponding to a generated recommendation appears among the Top-K retrieved documents $D_K(q)$:

$$\text{Hit@}K(q) = \frac{|\{r \in R(q) \mid r \in D_K(q)\}|}{|R(q)|}.$$

Evaluation Protocols. Two complementary evaluation settings are considered. The *conditioned* protocol evaluates only uniquely mapped recommendations and therefore isolates retrieval behavior. The *penalized* protocol includes all generated outputs, treating unmappable recommendations as unsupported. Comparing these protocols allows us to distinguish retrieval limitations from pipeline-level artifacts.

Depth-Aware Diagnosis. Groundedness is evaluated across multiple retrieval depths $K \in \{20, 40, 60, 80, 100\}$ in order to analyze retrieval truncation effects. Based on the pair $(Hit@20, Hit@100)$ we identify four grounding regimes: stable grounding, depth-sensitive generalization, structural hallucination, and retrieval instability. This typology provides a compact view of how grounding behavior evolves with retrieval depth.

5 Experimental Diagnosis

This section applies the proposed diagnostic framework to the two RAG paradigms under a controlled experimental setup. Both systems are evaluated using the same indexed catalogue, embedding model, retrieval configuration, and generation models. This controlled infrastructure ensures that observed differences arise from the design of the recommendation pipeline rather than from implementation variations.

Rather than focusing solely on recommendation accuracy, our analysis examines how retrieval and generation interact under different evaluation protocols and retrieval depths. The objective is to identify grounding patterns and understand how contextual signals influence the reliability of generated recommendations.

5.1 Pipeline-Level Traceability

We first analyze whether generated recommendations can be reliably aligned with entries in the course catalogue before evaluating retrieval support. Figure 1 shows the proportion of uniquely mapped, ambiguous, and missing recommendations produced by each paradigm.

In both systems, the large majority of recommendations can be uniquely mapped to catalogue entries, indicating strong compatibility between generated titles and the indexed course catalogue. However, CLARE produces slightly fewer missing recommendations and a higher proportion of uniquely traceable outputs compared to RAMO.

This difference suggests that structured contextual signals such as semantic categories and in-context examples encourage the model to generate titles that remain closer to canonical catalogue entries. This step is important because retrieval groundedness can only be evaluated for recommendations that can be reliably aligned with catalogue items. Pipeline-level deviations therefore directly affect end-to-end evaluation, particularly under penalized protocols.

5.2 Retrieval Groundedness Analysis

We next evaluate retrieval groundedness using the conditioned protocol, which considers only uniquely mappable recommendations. This protocol isolates the behavior of the retrieval component independently from generation artifacts.

Table 1 reports Hit@K across different retrieval depths. Groundedness increases consistently as K grows, indicating that some recommendations appear beyond shallow retrieval thresholds and become supported when deeper retrieval is considered.

Using the same generation model, CLARE generally shows slightly stronger grounding at shallow depths. This suggests that contextual signals in the category-aware prompting strategy help align generated recommendations with relevant catalogue entries.

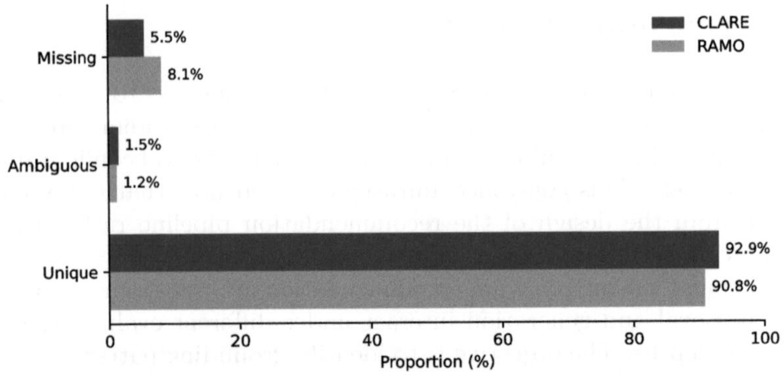

Fig. 1. Catalogue traceability comparison between CLARE and RAMO.

Table 1. Retrieval groundedness across retrieval depths (Conditioned protocol).

System	Model	K = 20	K = 40	K = 60	K = 80	K = 100
CLARE	Mistral	0.915	0.945	0.953	0.958	0.961
CLARE	LLaMA-2	0.893	0.911	0.923	0.931	0.944
RAMO	Mistral	0.832	0.898	0.902	0.910	0.912
RAMO	LLaMA-2	0.78	0.846	0.858	0.865	0.869

To obtain an end-to-end perspective, we also evaluate groundedness using the penalized protocol, where all generated recommendations are included in the evaluation and unmappable outputs are treated as unsupported. As expected, groundedness scores decrease under this stricter setting. For example, CLARE with LLaMA-2 decreases from Hit@20 = 0.915 to 0.893. Despite this reduction, CLARE maintains slightly stronger grounding across several depths, suggesting that contextual enrichment helps reduce both retrieval misalignment and generation artifacts.

5.3 Depth Sensitivity and Case Typology

Aggregate metrics provide a global view of groundedness but do not capture how recommendations behave across retrieval depths. To address this limitation, we analyze grounding patterns using the Depth-Aware Grounding Typology introduced earlier.

Figure 2 shows the distribution of recommendations across four grounding regimes defined by the pair (Hit@20, Hit@100).

In both paradigms, most recommendations fall into the stable grounding category, meaning they are already supported at shallow retrieval depth. A smaller proportion corresponds to depth-sensitive generalization cases, where support appears only when deeper retrieval is considered. Structural hallucinations recommendations unsupported even at $K = 100$ remain relatively limited. CLARE exhibits slightly fewer such cases than RAMO, suggesting that contextual signals help reduce unsupported generation.

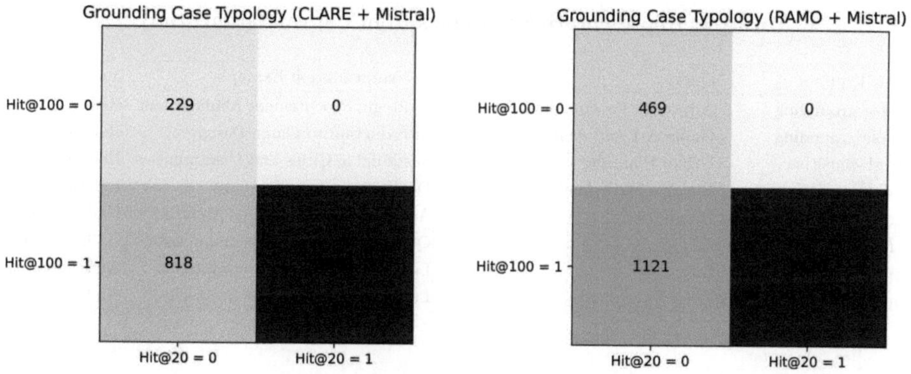

Fig. 2. Depth-aware grounding typology for CLARE (left) and RAMO (right).

5.4 Qualitative Error Analysis

Finally, we examine representative examples from each grounding regime. Structural hallucinations often arise from underspecified or ambiguous queries that cannot be reliably linked to catalogue entries. Depth-sensitive generalization cases correspond to recommendations that appear only at deeper retrieval levels. Pipeline mismatches occur when generated titles deviate from canonical catalogue formulations, preventing reliable mapping.

Overall, these observations suggest that hallucination phenomena in educational RAG systems often emerge from the interaction between query ambiguity, retrieval depth, and prompt design rather than from generation errors alone.

6 Validation of the Diagnostic Framework

To verify whether the grounding regimes identified by the diagnostic framework correspond to meaningful semantic behaviors, we conducted a complementary validation study on the CLARE paradigm.

A balanced set of 60 queries was constructed by sampling 15 queries from each grounding regime defined by the Depth-Aware Grounding Typology. For each query, the Top-3 generated recommendations were evaluated using two complementary signals: an LLM-as-a-Judge evaluation and a confidence score derived from the Trustworthy Language Model (TLM) framework [3].

The LLM judge evaluates whether recommendations are semantically aligned with the user query and assigns a relevance score between 1 and 5. Stable grounding cases consistently receive high relevance scores, while structural hallucination cases often associated with underspecified queries that are judged as semantically misaligned.

Depth-sensitive generalization cases exhibit intermediate behavior: although unsupported at shallow retrieval depth, many become supported at deeper levels and are judged relevant by the evaluator. These results confirm that shallow retrieval cutoffs may overestimate hallucination rates.

Table 2. Representative examples from the validation study.

Case Type	Query	Recommendation Example	Judge Verdict
Stable grounding	Advanced Procurement Strategies	Strategic Procurement Management	Relevant
Stable grounding	Game Art and Animation	Introduction to Game Design	Relevant
Depth-sensitive	Urban Planning	Sustainable Cities and Communities	Relevant
Depth-sensitive	Finance Data Analytics	Data Analysis for Business	Relevant
Structural hallucination	Hands	Advanced Cybersecurity Architecture	Hallucinated
Structural hallucination	IT	Quantum Computing Fundamentals	Hallucinated
Pipeline mismatch	Follow	Leadership Communication Skills	Ambiguous
Pipeline mismatch	Long	Long-Term Investment Strategies	Ambiguous

To complement semantic evaluation, we compute a confidence score inspired by the Trustworthy Language Model framework. The score combines generation consistency across multiple outputs and a self-verification signal reflecting whether the model considers its recommendation grounded in the retrieved context. Across the validation set, the average confidence score is approximately 0.82, indicating generally stable recommendations for well-defined queries and lower confidence for ambiguous inputs (Table 2).

Overall, the validation confirms that the hallucination patterns identified by the proposed framework correspond to meaningful semantic behaviors: stable grounding cases produce relevant and confident recommendations, while structurally unsupported cases are consistently detected through semantic evaluation and confidence estimation.

7 Conclusion

This work introduced a diagnostic framework for analyzing hallucination phenomena in retrieval-augmented educational recommendation systems. By separating pipeline traceability, retrieval grounding, and evaluation protocol design, the proposed framework provides a structured methodology for understanding how unsupported recommendations emerge in RAG pipelines.

Experiments conducted under a controlled infrastructure show that hallucination assessment is strongly influenced by retrieval depth and evaluation protocol. The results also suggest that contextual enrichment strategies can improve alignment between generated recommendations and catalogue resources.

Future work will explore the application of the proposed framework to additional RAG architectures and retrieval configurations. We also plan to investigate prompt refinement and query reformulation strategies, as well as the development of domain-specialized LLM-as-a-Judge models tailored to educational contexts.

References

1. Achiam, J., et al.: Gpt-4 technical report. arXiv preprint arXiv:2303.08774 (2023)
2. Brehme, L., Ströhle, T., Breu, R.: Can llms be trusted for evaluating rag systems? a survey of methods and datasets (2025)
3. Cleanlab: Trustworthy language model (tlm): A practical approach to more reliable LLM outputs (2024). https://cleanlab.ai/blog/trustworthy-language-model/
4. Douze, M., et al.: The faiss library. CoRR (2024)
5. Ennaceur, I., Elghazel, H., Aussem, A., Lefebvre, G., Sonnati, M.: Clare: a category-aware rag-based framework for recommending learning objects in education and professional training. In: Proceedings of the 26th International Conference on Web Information Systems Engineering. WISE 2025 Accepted for publication
6. Fan, W., et al.: A survey on rag meeting LLMs: towards retrieval-augmented large language models (2024)
7. Gao, Y., et al.: Retrieval-augmented generation for large language models: a survey. arXiv preprint arXiv:2312.10997 (2023)
8. Gu, J., et al.: A survey on llm-as-a-judge. The Innovation (2024)
9. Huang, L., et al.: A survey on hallucination in large language models: principles, taxonomy, challenges, and open questions. ACM Trans. Inf. Syst. (2025)
10. Ji, Z., et al.: Survey of hallucination in natural language generation. ACM Comput. Surv. (2023)
11. Jiang, A.Q., et al.: Mistral 7b. arXiv preprint arXiv:2310.06825 (2023)
12. Lewis, P., et al.: Retrieval-augmented generation for knowledge-intensive NLP tasks (2020)
13. Li, H., et al.: Llms-as-judges: a comprehensive survey on LLM-based evaluation methods. arXiv preprint arXiv:2412.05579 (2024)
14. Lyu, Q., et al.: Calibrating large language models with sample consistency (2025)
15. Rao, J., Lin, J.: RAMO: retrieval-augmented generation for enhancing moocs recommendations. In: CEUR Workshop Proceedings (2024)
16. Shi, Y., Pan, Y., Sun, K., Yu, D.: A survey on retrieval-augmented generation for large language models. arXiv preprint arXiv:2312.10997 (2023)
17. Touvron, H., et al.: Llama: open and efficient foundation language models. arXiv preprint arXiv:2302.13971 (2023)
18. Touvron, H., et al.: Llama 2: open foundation and fine-tuned chat models. arXiv preprint arXiv:2307.09288 (2023)
19. Wang, X., et al.: Searching for best practices in retrieval-augmented generation (2024)
20. Yu, W., et al.: Chain-of-note: enhancing robustness in retrieval-augmented language models (2024)

A Local Reliability Index for Trust-Aware Prediction Explanations Under Missing Data

Thanina Amirat[1(✉)], Ilhem Arroudj[1], Juba Agoun[2], Louenas Bounia[3], and Lamia Yessad[1]

[1] École Nationale Supérieure Informatique (ESI), Alger, Algeria
{lt_amirat,li_arroudj,l_yessad}@esi.dz
[2] Université Lumière Lyon 2, Université Claude Bernard Lyon 1, ERIC, 69007 Lyon, France
juba.agoun@univ-lyon2.fr
[3] LIPN – UMR CNRS 7030, Université Sorbonne Paris Nord, Villetaneuse, France
bounia@lipn.univ-paris13.fr

Abstract. One of the most enduring and difficult issues in data analysis and machine learning is missing data. A missing value corresponds to an unobserved entry in a dataset that would otherwise contain valuable information for statistical inference or predictive modeling. The presence of missing values in a dataset affects both the performance of machine learning models and the reliability of interpretation methods. In this work, we propose a Local Reliability Index (LRI) that measures the local reliability of model predictions by combining the SHAP importance of each feature with a confidence score on observed or imputed data. Missing values are imputed using missForest, a robust non-parametric method based on random forests. In its initial version, LRI uses a constant mask for imputed values, limiting interpretability. We then introduce an improved uncertainty-aware version, where the mask for imputed values is determined in a data-driven manner. While the uncertainty-aware approach does not necessarily increase the average LRI dramatically, it produces a score that is more robust, interpretable, and consistent with the actual uncertainty level, particularly for high missing rates. The proposed LRI offers a practical tool to guide the analysis and interpretation of machine learning models on incomplete datasets.

Keywords: Missing Data · Data Imputation · MissForest · Machine Learning · Explainable AI · Local Reliability Index

1 Introduction

Missing data remain one of the most persistent challenges in data analysis and machine learning. In real-world datasets, missing values frequently arise from sur-

This work was supported by the ANR JCJC project FORM-XAI of the French National Research Agency (ANR) and the European Union's Horizon Europe programme under the Marie Skłodowska-Curie Actions, Grant Agreement No. 101131117 (HarmonicAI).

G. Andresini et al. (Eds.): ISMIS 2026, LNAI 16685, pp. 114–123, 2027.
https://doi.org/10.1007/978-3-032-32643-0_11

vey non-response, sensor failures, data corruption, or privacy constraints. Their presence may reduce statistical power, introduce bias, and compromise predictive performance. The validity of inference depends strongly on the missingness mechanism, classically categorized as Missing Completely at Random (MCAR), Missing at Random (MAR), and Missing Not at Random (MNAR) [14,16].

To handle incomplete data, various imputation strategies have been proposed. Traditional statistical approaches include regression and Expectation–Maximization methods [14], while more recent techniques rely on machine learning algorithms to capture nonlinear dependencies. Among them, missForest [17] is a robust non-parametric imputation method based on random forests, capable of handling both numerical and categorical variables without distributional assumptions.

Although imputation methods aim to preserve predictive performance, their impact on model interpretability has received less attention. Post-hoc explanation techniques such as SHAP [15] provide local feature attributions grounded in cooperative game theory, enabling consistent interpretation of complex models. However, SHAP assumes that input features are reliable. When features are imputed, especially under high missing rates, explanations may rely on uncertain values, potentially leading to misleading interpretations.

To address this limitation, we introduce a Local Reliability Index (LRI) that quantifies the reliability of individual predictions in the presence of missing data. The LRI combines SHAP feature importance with a confidence score reflecting whether a feature is observed or imputed. While an initial version assigns a constant penalty to imputed values, this approach does not account for variability in imputation uncertainty. We therefore propose an improved uncertainty-aware formulation, where confidence scores are automatically derived from missForest through tree prediction dispersion for numerical variables and majority vote proportions for categorical variables.

By integrating imputation uncertainty into local explanation analysis, the proposed LRI provides a practical and interpretable measure of prediction reliability. Experimental results on numerical and mixed datasets under varying missingness rates demonstrate that the uncertainty-aware LRI yields more robust and consistent reliability estimates, particularly in high missing scenarios.

2 Related Work

Missing Data and Imputation Methods: The statistical treatment of missing data has been widely studied. According to Donald Rubin's framework, missingness mechanisms are classified as MCAR, MAR, and MNAR [16], a distinction that determines the validity of statistical inference [14]. Traditional statistical imputation methods, such as mean substitution, regression imputation, EM, and MICE [14,18], rely on explicit parametric and inferential assumptions. However, simple techniques may introduce bias and underestimate variability under MAR mechanisms, while incorrect specification of assumptions can weaken statistical power and lead to unreliable results [7]. Moreover, conventional statistical approaches are often inadequate for complex mechanisms such as MNAR, which require more sophisticated modeling strategies [7].

To address these challenges, learning-based methods have been proposed as more advanced alternatives for handling complex missingness patterns [7]. Machine learning and deep learning approaches are particularly recommended for high missingness ratios, nonlinear dependencies, and MNAR mechanisms, where traditional methods may fail to provide accurate estimates [7]. Among them, missForest [17] is a non-parametric method based on random forests that iteratively predicts missing values and effectively handles mixed-type and high-dimensional data. However, like most imputation techniques, it does not explicitly quantify how imputation uncertainty affects downstream interpretation.

Model Interpretability: The increasing deployment of complex machine learning systems has raised major concerns about transparency and trust. As emphasized by Adadi and Berrada, the black-box nature of modern AI models limits users' ability to understand the reasoning behind predictions, making explainability a critical requirement for trustworthy AI [6]. Explainable Artificial Intelligence (XAI) aims to provide accurate yet interpretable models [6]. Interpretability methods can be global or local. SHAP (SHapley Additive exPlanations) [15], based on Shapley values, offers theoretically grounded local explanations with properties such as consistency and additivity, and is widely used for explaining complex models. However, SHAP assumes reliable input features. When data are imputed, explanation methods do not explicitly account for imputation uncertainty, which may lead to overconfident interpretations.

Reliability and Uncertainty in Machine Learning: Quantifying uncertainty has become increasingly important in machine learning, especially for safety-critical applications. Common approaches include Bayesian modeling [9], Monte Carlo dropout [11], ensemble methods [13], and predictive variance estimation [12], which aim to provide model-level confidence in predictions. Measures such as predictive entropy or ensemble variance offer global or instance-level uncertainty estimates. However, these frameworks typically focus on predictive uncertainty, neglecting uncertainty originating from missing or imputed data [10]. Consequently, existing methods do not combine feature importance with imputation-specific confidence to assess the reliability of explanations.

To our knowledge, no prior work integrates local explanation importance with feature-level imputation confidence into a unified reliability metric. The proposed Local Reliability Index (LRI) addresses this gap by combining SHAP attributions [15] with data-driven confidence scores derived from the imputation process, providing a principled measure of explanation reliability under missing data.

3 Methodology

Notations: Let $X \in \mathbb{R}^{n \times p}$ be a dataset with n instances and p features. Each instance is $x_i = (x_{i1}, \ldots, x_{ip})$, where some entries may be missing.

After imputation, we obtain a completed dataset $\tilde{X}$. Let f be a trained predictive model. For instance x_i, SHAP provides feature attributions $\phi_i = (\phi_{i1}, \ldots, \phi_{ip})$, where $|\phi_{ik}|$ reflects the importance of feature k for the prediction.

To account for reliability of observed or imputed features, we introduce a confidence mask $M_i = (M_{i1}, \ldots, M_{ip})$, with $M_{ik} \in [0, 1]$. By definition, $M_{ik} = 1$ if feature k is observed, and $M_{ik} < 1$ if it is imputed. The exact computation of M_{ik} depends on the imputation method.

Local Reliability Index – Initial Version (Fixed M_k): The initial version of the Local Reliability Index (LRI) uses a fixed confidence value for all imputed features. For an instance x_i, the LRI is defined as:

$$\text{LRI}(i) = \frac{\sum_{k=1}^{p} |\phi_{ik}| \cdot M_{ik}}{\sum_{k=1}^{p} |\phi_{ik}|}, \tag{1}$$

with the confidence mask assigned as:

$$M_{ik} = \begin{cases} 1 & \text{if feature } k \text{ is observed,} \\ 0.5 & \text{if feature } k \text{ is imputed.} \end{cases} \tag{2}$$

The constant value 0.5 was chosen arbitrarily to downweight imputed features. While simple, this fixed-mask approach has important limitations: it is non-adaptive, assigning the same weight to all imputed features regardless of their type, actual uncertainty, or the missing rate; it is non-variable-specific, treating all features equally even when imputation quality differs; and it lacks probabilistic coherence, as two different imputations of the same feature yield identical contributions to the LRI, ignoring the true variability of the imputed values. These limitations motivate the uncertainty-aware extension described in the next section.

Local Reliability Index – Uncertainty-Aware Version: To address the limitations of the fixed-mask LRI, we define an uncertainty-aware mask M_k that reflects the confidence of each feature based on the imputation process. Let x_i be an instance and $\tilde{X}$ the imputed dataset using `missForest`. Then:

$$M_{ik} = \begin{cases} 1 & \text{if feature } k \text{ is observed,} \\ 1 - \dfrac{\sigma_{ik}}{\max(\sigma_k)} & \text{if feature } k \text{ is numerical and imputed,} \\ p_{\max,ik} & \text{if feature } k \text{ is categorical and imputed,} \end{cases} \tag{3}$$

where:

- σ_{ik} is the standard deviation of predictions across all trees of the random forest ensemble for the imputed value of feature k in instance i. A larger σ_{ik} indicates that the trees disagree strongly about the imputed value, reflecting high uncertainty; accordingly, $M_{ik} = 1 - \sigma_{ik}/\max(\sigma_k)$ maps high dispersion to low confidence and low dispersion to high confidence, with $\max(\sigma_k)$ denoting the maximum standard deviation across all instances for feature k, used for normalization into $[0, 1]$.

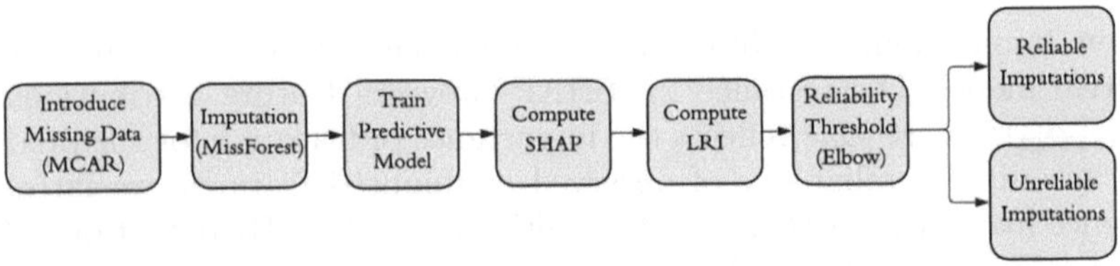

Fig. 1. Overview of the proposed LRI pipeline.

- $p_{\max,ik}$ is the proportion of trees in the random forest that voted for the majority class when predicting the imputed value of categorical feature k for instance i. Formally, if T trees cast votes $\{v_1, \ldots, v_T\}$ over the set of possible categories, then $p_{\max,ik} = \max_c(\#\{t : v_t = c\})/T$. A value close to 1 indicates near-unanimous agreement among trees, yielding high confidence; a value close to $1/|\mathcal{C}|$ (where $|\mathcal{C}|$ is the number of categories) indicates high uncertainty.

The full methodology is implemented as a straightforward end-to-end pipeline, illustrated in Fig. 1. Starting from an incomplete dataset, artificial missing values are introduced under a controlled mechanism. The data is then imputed using `missForest`, after which SHAP values are computed for each instance to derive local feature attributions. The uncertainty-aware confidence mask M_{ik} is subsequently applied to compute the LRI for every imputed value. Finally, the distribution of LRI scores is analyzed via the Elbow method to determine a data-driven reliability threshold, enabling a principled classification of imputations as reliable or unreliable.

4 Experiments

4.1 Experimental Protocol

Datasets: The experimental evaluation was conducted on five publicly available datasets covering both numerical and mixed-type data, and addressing classification as well as regression tasks. Their diversity in size, feature composition, and predictive objective ensures a comprehensive evaluation of the proposed LRI across heterogeneous settings. The datasets are summarised in Table 1.

Missing Data Generation: Missing values were artificially introduced under the Missing Completely at Random (MCAR) mechanism following the protocol of Fouad et al. [8]. Under this protocol, each cell (i, k) of the feature matrix is independently eligible to become missing, and missing entries are drawn uniformly at random across all feature columns (excluding the target variable) until the desired global missing rate is reached. Concretely, all $n \times p$ cells are first shuffled randomly, and cells are sequentially marked as missing until the cumulative count reaches the target fraction of the total number of cells. This cell-level, feature-agnostic procedure ensures that no single feature is systematically more

Table 1. Summary of datasets used in the experimental evaluation.

Dataset	Type	Instances	Features
Diabetes [4]	Numeric	442	10
Breast Cancer Wisconsin [1]	Numeric	569	30
Heart Disease [3]	Mixed	303	13
Titanic [5]	Mixed	891	12
Forest Fires [2]	Mixed	517	12

affected than others, and that the effective missing rate is controlled at the dataset level rather than per feature. Missing rates were varied from 5% to 50% in increments of 5%, yielding ten experimental scenarios per dataset. This progressive range allows a fine-grained analysis of reliability degradation as dataset incompleteness increases.

While MCAR is the least complex missingness mechanism, it constitutes the standard baseline for evaluating imputation and reliability methods, as it provides a controlled and reproducible setting in which the ground truth is fully known [14]. Extensions to more realistic mechanisms such as MAR and MNAR are discussed in the conclusion.

Implementation Environment: All experiments were implemented in Python 3.12.5 and executed in a Google Colab environment using NVIDIA T4 GPU instances with 12.7 GB of GPU memory and up to 25 GB of system RAM. Sessions were run using Colab's standard runtime with no persistent storage between runs; all intermediate artefacts were saved to Google Drive and reloaded at the start of each session.

The imputation pipeline is built on top of `scikit-learn`'s `IterativeImputer` backend, with custom Random Forest estimators used at each iteration following the MissForest strategy [17], namely `RandomForestRegressor` for numerical variables and `RandomForestClassifier` for categorical variables. SHAP values were computed via the `SHAP` library using `TreeExplainer`. Categorical variables were label-encoded prior to imputation and decoded afterward, while numerical variables were standardised using `StandardScaler`. The reliability threshold was determined per experiment via the Elbow method applied to the sorted LRI score distribution. Key package versions were: `scikit-learn` 1.3, `SHAP` 0.44, and `Numpy` 1.26.

All experiments were run with a fixed random seed (`random_state = 42`) for the random forest estimators, the `IterativeImputer`, and the missing-data generation procedure. This single seed was kept constant across all ten missing-rate scenarios and all five datasets, ensuring full reproducibility. Results were verified to be stable across alternative seed values (21, 123), with no qualitative change in the observed trends. The full source code is publicly available at: https://github.com/thanina-amrt/Local-Reliability-Index.

4.2 Results and Key Findings

Figure 2 summarizes imputation quality across datasets. Since MAE values vary strongly across datasets, they are min-max normalized to [0, 1] for fair comparison. The normalized MAE increases consistently with the missing rate, indicating a gradual degradation of imputation quality, with stronger effects on Forest Fires and Breast Cancer and more stability on Heart Disease.

For mixed datasets, MAE is computed for numerical variables, while the Proportion of Falsely Classified (PFC) is used for categorical variables. PFC is defined as:

$$\mathrm{PFC} = |\mathcal{M}_{\mathrm{cat}}|^{-1} \sum_{(i,k)\in\mathcal{M}_{\mathrm{cat}}} \mathbf{1}[\hat{x}_{ik} \neq x_{ik}], \tag{4}$$

which increases with missingness but remains below 30% even at high missing rates, confirming the robustness of missForest for categorical imputation.

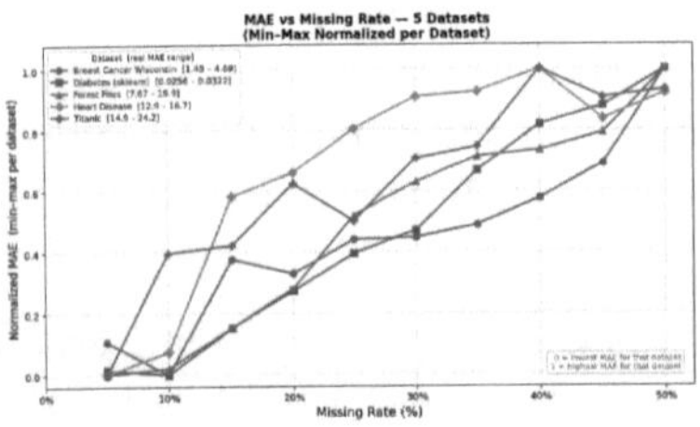

(a) Normalized MAE vs. missing rate across all five datasets

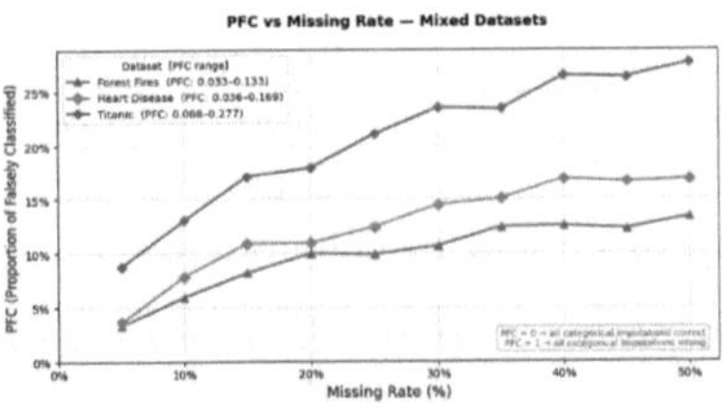

(b) Proportion of Falsely Classified (PFC) vs. missing rate

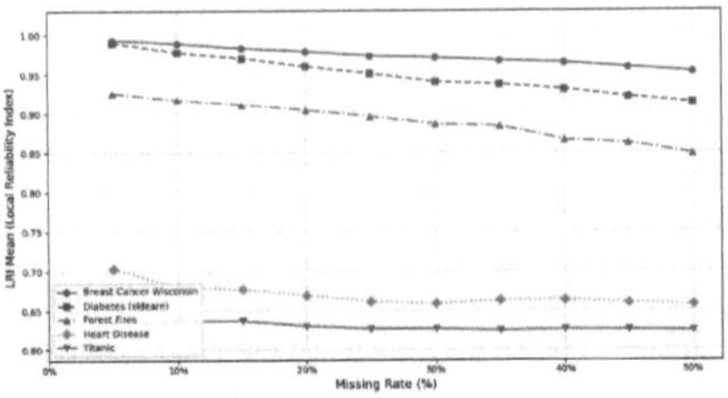

(c) Mean Local Reliability Index (LRI) as a function of the missing rate

Fig. 2. Comparison of normalized MAE, PFC, and LRI as functions of the missing rate

We evaluated the Local Reliability Index (LRI) as a function of missing rate on all five datasets. As expected, the mean LRI decreases as the missing rate increases, reflecting the growing uncertainty in the imputed features.

The absolute starting level of LRI differs between datasets. Datasets with many correlated numerical features, like Breast Cancer and Diabetes, start near 0.9 because missing values can be predicted with high confidence across trees. In contrast, datasets with fewer features, weaker correlations, or more categorical variables, such as Titanic and Heart Disease, start around 0.6–0.7. We think that for categorical features, tree predictions may be less consistent, which can lower the confidence mask M_i and reduce the initial LRI, while fully numerical datasets are less affected due to more stable predictions.

We illustrate the difference between fixed and adaptive masks using the Diabetes dataset (Fig. 3):

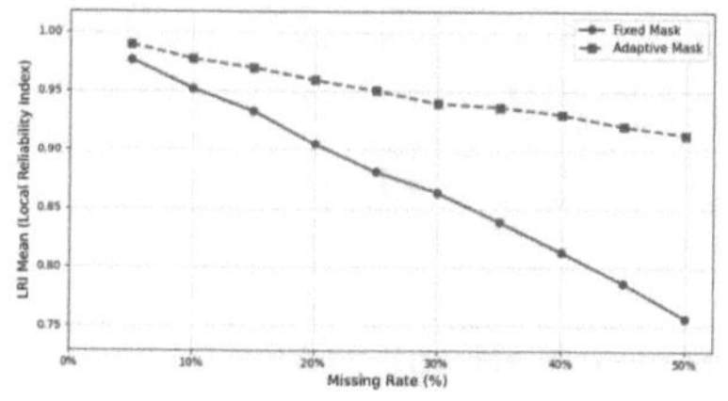

(a) Mean LRI: fixed vs. adaptive mask.

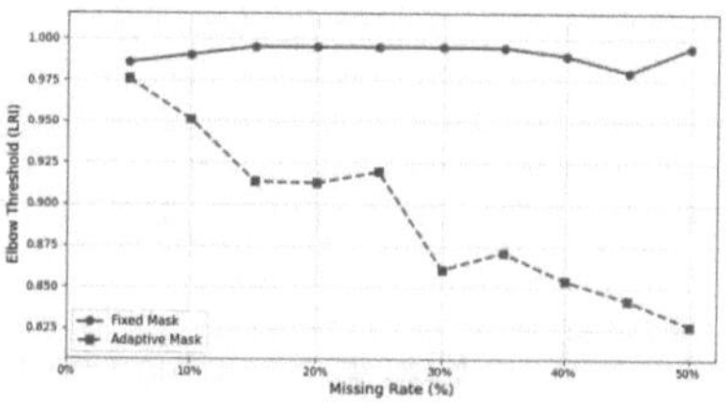

(b) Elbow threshold: fixed vs. adaptive mask.

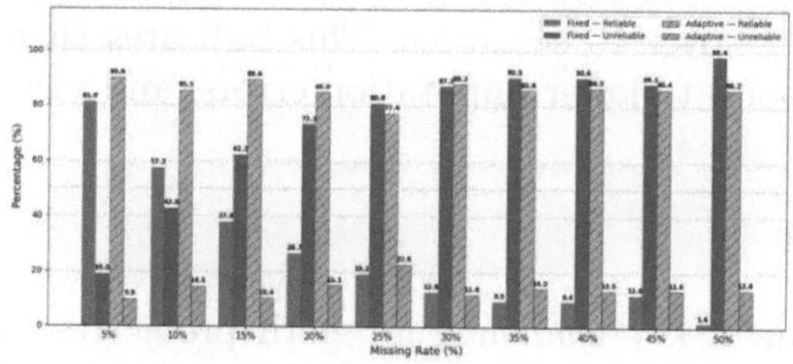

(c) Proportion of reliable vs. unreliable instances: fixed vs. adaptive mask.

Fig. 3. Comparison of fixed and adaptive mask strategies on the Diabetes dataset.

The LRI mean decreases with missing rate for both masks, as expected, but the adaptive mask consistently maintains higher values (∼0.91–0.99) compared to the fixed mask (∼0.76–0.98). The elbow threshold for the fixed mask stays almost constant (∼0.99), while the adaptive threshold decreases with increasing missingness (∼0.975 → ∼0.827), better reflecting growing uncertainty.

The reliable/unreliable proportions show that the fixed mask classifies most values as unreliable at high missing rates, whereas the adaptive mask keeps the reliable proportion stable (∼85–90%).

Overall, the adaptive mask better captures imputation uncertainty, producing higher LRI scores and a more realistic threshold, making it more robust and interpretable.

We assessed LRI as an imputation quality indicator by computing the Spearman correlation between mean LRI and MAE across missing rates (5–50%) for the Diabetes dataset (Fig. 4).

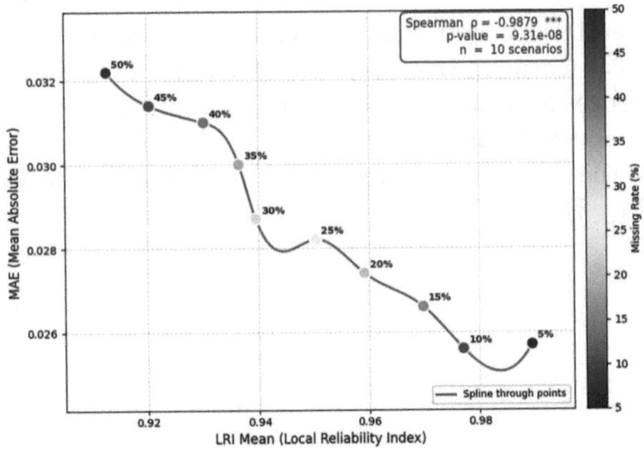

Fig. 4. Spearman correlation between mean LRI and MAE

The results show a very strong negative correlation: Spearman $\rho = -0.9879$ with $p = 9.31 \times 10^{-8}$ over 10 scenarios. This indicates that higher LRI values consistently correspond to lower imputation errors, and vice versa.

5 Conclusion

Missing data remain a key challenge for both predictive modeling and interpretability. In this work, we introduced the Local Reliability Index (LRI), which combines SHAP feature importance with confidence scores from imputed values to quantify prediction reliability under missingness. Our results show that the adaptive, uncertainty-aware LRI consistently outperforms a fixed-mask version, maintaining higher reliability scores, adapting thresholds to uncertainty, and preserving interpretability even at high missing rates. Spearman correlation analysis further confirms that LRI strongly reflects imputation error, supporting its use as a practical indicator of prediction quality.

Regarding missingness assumptions, MCAR was used as a standard baseline, as it provides a controlled and reproducible setting where the ground truth is known and the missingness process is independent of the data. This choice, commonly adopted in the literature, enables a clear validation of the method. However, real-world data often follow MAR or MNAR mechanisms, where missingness depends on observed or unobserved variables. Extending LRI to these more realistic settings is therefore an important next step, as reliability scores are expected to be more sensitive to the underlying missingness process.

Future work will also explore improved uncertainty quantification through Bayesian or probabilistic approaches, as well as more advanced handling of categorical features beyond majority voting, particularly for real-world and medical applications.

References

1. Breast cancer wisconsin. https://archive.ics.uci.edu/dataset/17/breast+cancer+wisconsin+diagnostic
2. Forest fires. https://archive.ics.uci.edu/dataset/162/forest+fires
3. Heart disease. https://archive.ics.uci.edu/dataset/45/heart+disease
4. Pima indians diabetes database. https://scikit-learn.org/stable/datasets/toy_dataset.html#diabetes-dataset
5. Titanic. https://www.kaggle.com/competitions/titanic/data
6. Adadi, A., Berrada, M.: Peeking inside the black-box: a survey on explainable artificial intelligence (XAI). IEEE Access **6**, 52138–52160 (2018)
7. Afkanpour, M., Tehrany Dehkordy, D., Momeni, M., Tabesh, H.: Conceptual framework as a guide to choose appropriate imputation method for missing values in a clinical structured dataset. BMC Med. Res. Methodol. **25**(1), 43 (2025)
8. Fouad, K.M., Ismail, M.M., Azar, A.T., Arafa, M.M.: Advanced methods for missing values imputation based on similarity learning. PeerJ Comput. Sci. **7**, e619 (2021). https://doi.org/10.7717/peerj-cs.619
9. Gal, Y., Ghahramani, Z.: Dropout as a Bayesian approximation: representing model uncertainty in deep learning. In: International Conference on Machine Learning, pp. 1050–1059. PMLR (2016)
10. Josse, J., Husson, F.: Handling missing values in exploratory multivariate data analysis methods. Journal de la société française de statistique **153**(2), 79–99 (2012)
11. Kendall, A., Gal, Y.: What uncertainties do we need in Bayesian deep learning for computer vision? In: Advances in Neural Information Processing Systems, p. 30 (2017)
12. Kuleshov, V., Fenner, N., Ermon, S.: Accurate uncertainties for deep learning using calibrated regression. In: International Conference on Machine Learning, pp. 2796–2804. PMLR (2018)
13. Lakshminarayanan, B., Pritzel, A., Blundell, C.: Simple and scalable predictive uncertainty estimation using deep ensembles. In: Advances in Neural Information Processing Systems, p. 30 (2017)
14. Little, R.J., Rubin, D.B.: Statistical Analysis with Missing Data. Wiley, Hoboken (2019)
15. Lundberg, S.M., Lee, S.I.: A unified approach to interpreting model predictions. In: Advances in Neural Information Processing Systems, p. 30 (2017)
16. Rubin, D.B.: Inference and missing data. Biometrika **63**(3), 581–592 (1976)
17. Stekhoven, D.J., Bühlmann, P.: Missforest–non-parametric missing value imputation for mixed-type data. Bioinformatics **28**(1), 112–118 (2012)
18. Van Buuren, S., Groothuis-Oudshoorn, K.: mice: Multivariate imputation by chained equations in R. J. Stat. Softw. **45**, 1–67 (2011)

Counterfactuals to Manage Ongoing Business Process Deviances

Vincenzo Pasquadibisceglie(✉), Rossella Anna Giansante, Annalisa Appice, and Donato Malerba

University of Bari Aldo Moro, Bari, Italy
{vincenzo.pasquadibisceglie,annalisa.appice,donato.malerba}@uniba.it, r.giansante@studenti.uniba.it

Abstract. Business Process Deviance (BPD) refers to the phenomenon of business process executions (traces) that deviate with respect to the desirable outcome. BPD detection is a Predictive Process Monitoring (PPM), which covers predictive methods designed to distinguish deviant traces from non-deviant traces. In this paper, we focus on the task of predicting BPD cases without waiting for the completion of process executions. To this purpose, we describe a PPM methodology, named FIREFOX, to monitor ongoing traces of a business process, to early identify process executions that are expected to deviate from the desirable outcome. FIREFOX equips BPD predictions with counterfactual recommendations of actions to perform in the near future, to avoid the detected deviance risk. A preliminary evaluation explores the effectiveness of the proposed methodology on traces recorded for some business processes.

Keywords: Predictive Process Monitoring · Business Process Deviance Detection · Counterfactual Analysis

1 Introduction

The digitization of business processes coupled with the recent amazing achievements of Process Mining (PM) [1] have led the ongoing worldwide transformation of public and private organizations that increasingly rely on Process-Aware Information Systems (PAISs) to gain both efficiency and quality in the management of operational processes. The springboard to use PM for improving business process management is the event data log collected by PAISs tracking the execution traces of business processes. PM serves to process event logs to extract process-related information. In particular, Predictive Process Monitoring (PPM) [2] is an important branch of PM, which uses decision models, commonly trained using machine learning algorithms, to predict the unfolding (e.g., outcome, next-activity or completion time) of a process execution based on the event data recorded in its ongoing trace. Each event recorded in a trace refers to an activity (i.e., a well-defined step in some process) and is associated

G. Andresini et al. (Eds.): ISMIS 2026, LNAI 16685, pp. 124–134, 2027.
https://doi.org/10.1007/978-3-032-32643-0_12

with a timestamp. The events recorded in a trace are ordered by the timestamp, to define the activity control-flow of the trace that is seen as a description of a "run" of a process.

Business Process Deviance (BPD) detection [6] is a PPM task to learn a decision model that determines execution traces that deviate from the standard ones. The input of a BPD approach is a collection of traces with each trace labelled as deviant or non-deviant. The output is a decision model to be used on any unseen trace to predict whether its activity control-flow deviates from the desirable outcome. Finally, the usual learning pipeline of a BPD approach resorts to a feature encoder of the activity control-flows of labelled traces to supervise the decision model development through a machine learning algorithm. Existing BPD detection methods [3–5] mainly consider complete traces for their learning pipeline, focusing on developing decision model to predict deviance of complete traces. Instead, the early detection of deviance risk in ongoing traces (i.e., incomplete traces) is a useful service to plan and execute prompt and proactive interventions to put deviant ongoing traces in a position to achieve the expected outcome at their completion. Notably, a few recent studies have also focused on developing BPD methods to perform the root cause analysis of deviant trace prediction [6], and explain reasons of deviations. The root cause analysis can be used to formulate guidelines to facilitate the execution in the future of non-deviant traces. However, it does not provide any guideline to proactively manage deviances of ongoing traces when actions can still be taken in the near future to avoid the deviance condition upon completion of the execution trace.

Based on the background described above, the paper investigates the effectiveness of a BPD pipeline, named FIREFOX (CounterFactuals-based devIance Risk managEment For Business prOcess eXecutions), designed to perform the predictive monitoring of the ongoing traces of a business process and predict the deviance risk as new events are recorded in the execution traces. In addition, this predictive facility is equipped with a counterfactual facility to suggest activities to perform in the near future to normalize the behaviour of ongoing traces that risk to be deviant at their completion. Specifically, counterfactuals [7] are eXplainable Artificial Intelligence (XAI) methods to provide "what-if" explanations of a predictions of a decision model in the form of minimal perturbation to an input sample that changes the original prediction. In PM, counterfactuals have been recently used as a sequential activity-to-resource assignment strategy [9]. In FIREFOX, counterfactuals are produced and interpreted to be transformed into appropriate activities to perform in near-future events.

The paper is organized as follows. Section 2 describes the background of this study, while Sect. 3 describes the proposed methodology. Section 4 presents the experimental study. Finally, Sect. 5 sketched the future work.

2 Background

This section gives the background concepts of this paper.

2.1 Process Mining and Predictive Monitoring Concepts

Event, Trace, Event Log and Activity Histogram Encoder. Let $\mathcal{P}$ be a business process so that $\mathcal{A}$ is the universe of activity names, $\mathcal{T}$ is the universe of timestamps, and $\mathcal{I}$ is the universe of process execution identifiers in $\mathcal{P}$. Let $\perp$ be the activity that is recorded at the completion of a trace. In various business processes (e.g., ticket resolution, hospitalization), the completion activity is declared coupled to a class label that notifies whether the process execution achieved a desirable outcome. In this study, we consider business processes for which process managers assess the desirable outcome at the completion of a process execution. Hence, let $\mathcal{C}$ denote the set populated with classes "non-deviant" and "deviant" defined according to the desirable outcome for a process execution. Let $\mathcal{E} = \mathcal{I} \times \mathcal{A} \times \mathcal{T} \times \mathcal{C}$ be the event universe for $\mathcal{P}$. An *event* $e \in \mathcal{E}$ is a quadruple $e = (i, a, t, c)$ to describe the occurrence of activity a in an execution i of a given business process $\mathcal{P}$ at timestamp t with outcome c. An event e is a *completion event* iff $a = \perp$; *ongoing event* otherwise. The outcome information c is a non-mandatory event information that is recorded in a completion event only; missing otherwise. Let us consider the projection functions: $\pi_{\mathcal{I}}: \mathcal{E} \mapsto \mathcal{I}$ so that $\pi_{\mathcal{I}}(e) = i$, $\pi_{\mathcal{A}}: \mathcal{E} \mapsto \mathcal{A}$ so that $\pi_{\mathcal{A}}(e) = a$, $\pi_{\mathcal{T}}: \mathcal{E} \mapsto \mathcal{T}$ so that $\pi_{\mathcal{T}}(e) = t$, and $\pi_{\mathcal{C}}: \mathcal{E} \mapsto \mathcal{C}$ so that $\pi_{\mathcal{C}}(e) = c$. A *trace* $\sigma \in \mathcal{E}^*$ is a non-empty sequence of events $\sigma = \langle e_1, e_2, \ldots, e_n \rangle$, sharing the same execution identifier and ordered by timestamp, so that: (1) $e_k \in \mathcal{E}$ for each $k = 1, 2, \ldots, n$, (2) $\pi_{\mathcal{I}}(e_h) = \pi_{\mathcal{I}}(e_k)$ for each $h = 1, 2, \ldots, n$ and $k = 1, 2, \ldots, n$, and (3) $\pi_{\mathcal{T}}(e_k) \leq \pi_{\mathcal{T}}(e_{k+1})$ for each $k = 1, 2, \ldots, n-1$. Let us consider the trace length function $len: \mathcal{E}^* \mapsto \mathbb{N}$ so that $len(\sigma)$ returns the number of events recorded in σ, the event projection function $\Pi: \mathcal{E}^* \times \mathbb{N}^+ \mapsto \mathcal{E}$ so that $\Pi(\sigma, k) = e_k$ with $1 \leq k \leq len(\sigma)$, and the trace head function $head: \mathcal{E}^* \times \mathbb{N}^+ \mapsto \mathcal{E}^*$ so that $head(\sigma, k) = \langle e_1, \ldots, e_k \rangle$ with $1 \leq k \leq len(\sigma)$. Notice that given a trace σ with $len(\sigma) = n$, function *head* may be used to extract the n *prefix event sequences* of σ with length varying between 1 and n (e.g., $head(\sigma, 1) = \langle e_1 \rangle$, $head(\sigma, 2) = \langle e_1, e_2 \rangle$). A trace σ is a *complete trace* if the last event recorded in the trace is a complete event, that is, $\pi_{\mathcal{A}}(\Pi(\sigma, len(\sigma)) = \perp$; an *ongoing trace* otherwise. No further event may be recorded into a complete trace after its completion. Given a complete trace σ, $n-1$ *labeled prefix event sequences* can be extracted from σ by concatenating each prefix event sequence, extracted from σ with length equal to k varying between 1 and $n-1$, and the completion event recorded in σ, that is, $\sigma^k = head(\sigma, k) \cdot \Pi(\sigma, len(\sigma))$ with $1 \leq k \leq n-1$ with $\cdot$ denoting the operator to concatenate two event sequences. An *event log* $\mathcal{L}$ is a set of traces $\mathcal{L} \subset \mathcal{E}^*$. A *complete event log* $\mathcal{L}^*$ is a set of complete traces. Let $\mathcal{L}^{+*}$ denote the complete event log populated with all labelled prefix event sequences extracted from all complete trace recorded in $\mathcal{L}^*$. An *event sequence encoder* is a function to transform an event sequence into a numeric feature vector. In this study, let us consider the *activity histogram encoder* that is an activity frequency-based encoder function $\varepsilon: \mathcal{E}^* \mapsto \mathbb{N}^m$ formulated with $m = |\mathcal{A}| - 1$, to transform every event sequence $\sigma \in \mathcal{E}^*$ into a numeric feature vector $\mathbf{x} \in \mathbb{N}^m$ so that each feature value $x_k \in \mathbf{x}$ measures the number of occurrences of the activity name $a_k \in \mathcal{A}^{-\perp}$ in the event sequence σ having $\mathcal{A}^{-\perp} = \mathcal{A} - \{\perp\}$.

Supervised Machine Learning in Ongoing PPM. Let us consider a complete event log $\mathcal{L}^*$ that records n complete traces of a business process $\mathcal{P}$. Let $\mathcal{L}^{+*}$ the complete event log populated with all N labeled prefix event sequences extracted from all n complete trace recorded in $\mathcal{L}^*$ with $N > n$. We denote: (a) $\mathbf{X} \in \mathbb{N}^{N \times m}$ – the matrix recording the encoded representation of all labeled prefix sequences recorded in $\mathcal{L}^{+*}$ so that each matrix row $\mathbf{x}_k \in \mathbf{X}$ is one-to-one associated with an event sequence $\sigma_k \in \mathcal{L}^{+*}$ with $\mathbf{x_k} = \varepsilon(\sigma_k)$; and (b) $\mathbf{Y} \in \mathcal{C}^N$ – the vector recording deviance labels of all event sequences recorded in $\mathcal{L}^{+*}$ so that each entry $y_k \in Y$ records whether the labeled prefix sequence $\sigma_k \in \mathcal{L}^{+*}$ is either "non-deviant" or "deviant" that is, $y_k = \pi_{\mathcal{C}}(\Pi_{\mathcal{E}}(\sigma_k, len(\sigma_k)))$. Any supervised machine learning algorithm can be used to learn a binary decision model $f\colon \mathbb{N}^m \mapsto \mathcal{C}$ with the supervision of information recorded in both $\mathbf{X}$ and $\mathbf{Y}$.

2.2 Counterfactual Explanations

Counterfactual methods provide explanations for decision model predictions by suggesting the minimal actionable alternative to reverse a decision [7]. In this study, we use the counterfactual explanation library DiCE [10] with the activity frequency features extracted through the activity histogram encoder. This library realizes several counterfactual explainers. In this study, we consider the model-agnostic method DiCE-Random that allows the generation of counterfactuals in a black-box scenario. In particular, it generates a set of counterfactual explanations of a sample by implementing an iterative process of random sampling from the input space [13]. In particular, it produces the counterfactuals of a feature vector by randomly perturbing some of the user-selected input features within the user-predefined bounds and querying the decision model to check if the model's decision is changed. Counterfactuals are obtained according to a combined function to achieve the trade-off between proximity (i.e., to identify the counterfactuals that are closer to the original sample in the input feature space), sparsity (i.e., to minimize the number of features changed) and diversity (i.e., to maximize the distance among counterfactuals). Since the DiCE-Random method does not use any knowledge about the internal structure of the decision model, it can be deployed with a decision model trained with any machine learning algorithm. DiCE-Random has a lower computational cost than gradient-based methods and approaches relying on expensive algorithms such as genetic algorithms or KDTree. Moreover, [13] showed that it offers a good balance between time efficiency and manifold closeness to the data innate structure.

3 FIREFOX Approach

FIREFOX approach comprises two phases: the offline phase to train a decision model for deviance detection on ongoing traces, and the ongoing phase to conduct

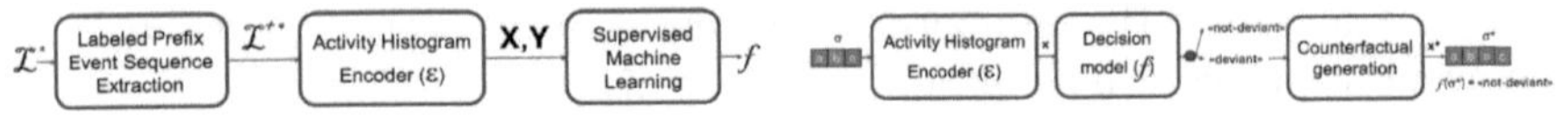

(a) Offline learning phase (b) Ongoing monitoring phase

Fig. 1. Schema of the FIREFOX approach

the predictive process monitoring of ongoing traces, detect risk of deviance and recommend near future actions (activities) to reverse deviance decisions.

Offline FIREFOX. In the offline phase, FIREFOX takes a complete event log $\mathcal{L}^*$ as input and uses a supervised machine learning method to train a decision model f for ongoing trace deviance detection by using the supervision of information recorded $\mathcal{L}^*$. The input event log was recorded by a PAIS that tracked historical, complete executions of a business process $\mathcal{P}$ for which the trace outcome was acquired with the completion event of each complete trace. A schematic view of the offline learning phase of FIREFOX is shown in Fig. 1a. It comprises the following steps:

1. **Labeled Prefix Event Sequence Extraction**: A new complete event log $\mathcal{L}^{+*}$ is obtained from $\mathcal{L}^*$ so that $\mathcal{L}^{+*}$ records all labelled prefix event sequences extracted from all complete traces recorded in $\mathcal{L}^*$. Prefix event sequences are extracted for simulating ongoing traces by tracking the progresses done in the logged process executions each a new event was recorded in the corresponding execution trace.
2. **Activity Histogram encoder**: $\mathcal{L}^{+*}$ is converted into the sample matrix $\mathbf{X}$ and the label vector $\mathbf{Y}$ with rows of matrix $\mathbf{X}$ recording the encoded representations of event sequences collected in $\mathcal{L}^{+*}$ and entries of vector $\mathbf{Y}$ recording the outcome of the source trace as it was filled in the corresponding completion event. The encoded representation of each event sequence is the feature vector of the activity frequencies computed with the activity histogram encoder ε.
3. **Supervised Machine Learning**: The decision model f is trained using any machine learning algorithm with supervision of feature vectors recorded in $\mathbf{X}$ and corresponding labels recorded in $\mathbf{Y}$. A grid search combined with a k-fold cross validation and Fscore-based evaluation can be used to identify the optimal parameter set-up of the wrapped-in machine learning algorithm.

Ongoing FIREFOX. In the ongoing phase, FIREFOX can be used for the predictive process monitoring of the deviance risk of any new ongoing trace. A schematic view of the ongoing phase of FIREFOX is shown in Fig. 1b. Each time a new event is recorded in the current ongoing trace σ (and until the trace is completed), the following steps are performed:

1. **Activity Histogram encoder**: The activity histogram encoder ε is used to transform the ongoing trace σ into the feature vector representation $\mathbf{x}$ of its activity histogram, with $\mathbf{x} = \varepsilon(\sigma)$.
2. **Decision model**: The decision model f is used to obtain a prediction of the deviance risk of σ accounting for information encoded in $\mathbf{x}$.

Table 1. Event log characteristics

Event Log	N.Activities	N.Traces	N.Events	Avg.TraceLength	%DeviantTraces
BPI11_1	193	1140	67480	59	20.21
BPI11_2	251	1140	149730	131	66.57
BPI11_3	190	1121	70546	63	10.72
BPI11_4	231	1140	93065	82	23.39
Production	26	220	2489	11	54.96
SP2020	13	23906	178078	7	67.40
RoadTraffic	10	129615	460556	4	52.00
Sepsis	15	782	12463	16	80.77

3. **Counterfactual generation**: If decision model f predicts the ongoing trace σ in class "deviant", then a counterfactual $\mathbf{x}^*$ is tentatively generated for its activity histogram $\mathbf{x}$ using DiCE-Random method. This counterfactual is produced as a what-if feature vector $\mathbf{x}^*$ so that each what-if k entry of $\mathbf{x}^*$ is either equal to the corresponding entry in $\mathbf{x}$ (i.e., $\mathbf{x}^*[k] = \mathbf{x}[k]$) or increased at most by an integer amount equal to p with $p \in \mathbb{N}^+$ (i.e., $\mathbf{x}^*[k] - \mathbf{x}[k] \leq p$). By default, the what-if step p is set equal to 1. The counterfactual that minimizes the number of what-if changes is preferred. Our expectation is that counterfactual $\mathbf{x}^*$ should recommend the minimum amount of repetition of each activity to perform in the near feature to bring the execution of the process back towards non-deviant behavior.
4. **Recommendations**: It is recommended to perform the activity (or activities) whose frequency is increased with the counterfactual.

4 Experimental Results

We evaluated the performance of FIREFOX by conducting a range of experiments on various event logs.

4.1 Event Logs, Experimental Setting and Metrics

We processed eight real-life event logs publicly available in the Business Process Intelligence (BPI) Challenges done in 2011,[1] Production repository,[2]the Customer Service repository[3] (SP2020), the Road Traffic Management repository[4] (RoadTraffic) and Sepsis Cases repository[5] (Sepsis). The BPI Challenge 2011 provided four event logs concerned the diagnosis and treatment activities

[1] https://data.4tu.nl/datasets/5ea5bb88-feaa-4e6f-a743-6460a755e05b/1.
[2] https://data.4tu.nl/datasets/67d71073-7ece-4455-9840-9d48ee480160/1.
[3] https://zenodo.org/records/3928487.
[4] https://data.4tu.nl/datasets/806acd1a-2bf2-4e39-be21-69b8cad10909/1.
[5] https://data.4tu.nl/datasets/33632f3c-5c48-40cf-8d8f-2db57f5a6ce7/1.

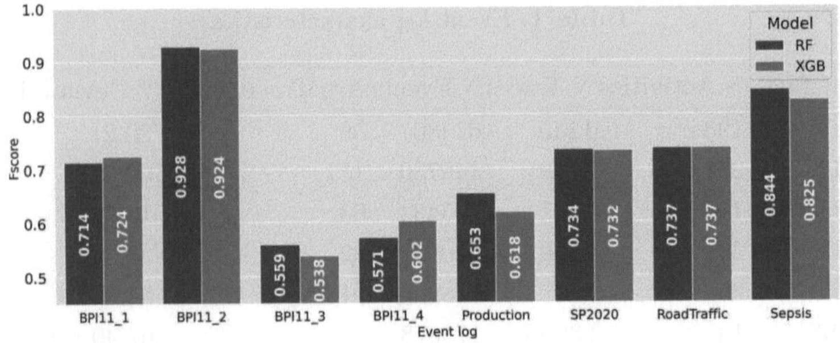

Fig. 2. Deviance risk accuracy analysis: **Fscore** of decision models trained with **Random Forest** and **XGBoost**, and used to predict the deviance risk of ongoing traces monitored in the testing phase

of cancer patients in a Gynecology department of a Dutch Academic Hospital. Production event log records data from a manufacturing process, with each trace capturing the activities, workers and/or machines involved in producing an item. SP2020 event log was recorded from a service process of a home appliances vendor for repairing faulty devices. RoadTraffic event log was obtained from an information system of a local police force in Italy managing road traffic fines. Finally, the Sepsis event log is a collection of traces involving patients affected by sepsis in a Dutch hospital. All selected event logs collected complete traces labelled for deviance detection. In particular, BPI 2011, Production, RoadTraffic and Sepsis event logs were used as preprocessed by [12]. Table 1 reports a summary of characteristics of considered event logs. In each event log, traces were sorted by the timestamp of the first event recorded in the traces. For the evaluation, we considered the first 66% of chronologically ordered traces for the offline learning phase, and the remaining 34% of chronologically ordered traces for the ongoing monitoring phase. In the offline learning phase, the decision model to monitor deviance risk in ongoing traces was trained with Random Forest and XGBoost. Both are machine learning algorithms often used for outcome-oriented PPM tasks [12]. In this evaluation study, they were used with learning parameters optimized using Fscore measured on 3-fold cross validation of training traces and learning parameters' search spaces set as described in [12]. Counterfactuals to reverse deviant predictions were generated with what-if step p set equal to 1. The Fscore, measured by considering class "deviant" as positive class, was analyzed to assess the accuracy of decision models. In addition, the Euclidean distance, measured between activity histograms of deviant predictions and corresponding counterfactuals, was analyzed to determine the average number of activities recommended with counterfactuals.

4.2 Results and Discussion

Figure 2 shows the Fscore measured with decision models developed in FIREFOX with Random Forest and XGBoost, to monitor the deviance risk of ongoing

Table 2. Counterfacutal analysis: Percentace of CounterFactuals (**%CF**) successfully produced to reverse deviant predictions of **Random Forest** and **XGBoost**, and average Euclidean Distance (**AvgEuclideanDis**) measured between activity histograms and corresponding counterfactual of "deviant" predictions

Event Log	Random Forest		XGBoost	
	%CF	AvgEuclideanDist	%CF	AvgEuclideanDist
BPI11_1	100	1.18	100	1.35
BPI11_2	98	2.84	100	2.87
BPI11_3	100	1.11	100	1.15
BPI11_4	100	1.09	100	1.25
Production	98	1.25	100	1.45
SP2020	85	1.34	87	1.28
RoadTraffic	100	1.00	100	1.00
Sepsis	99	1.31	100	1.31

traces. The results show that both machine learning algorithms are able to train decision models achieving good Fscore for deviance monitoring (Fscore greater than 70%) except for event logs (BPIC11_3, BPIC11_4 and Production), where the imbalance condition of class "deviant" is particularly critical for BPIC11_3, BPIC11_4 (since "non-deviant" traces greatly outnumber the "deviant" traces in the inference phase as reported in Table 1). In addition, Table 2 shows the amount of counterfactuals successfully produced to reverse "deviant" predictions and the average Euclidean distance measured between the activity histogram producing these predictions and their counterfactuals. These results show that counterfactuals were successfully generated in almost all cases, allowing us to commonly obtain recommendations of expected next-activities, to reverse the "deviant" predictions. In addition, except for BPI11_2, the average Euclidean distance is slightly greater than 1. Notably, this analysis of the Euclidean distance is aligned with the sparsity requirement formulated with counterfactual definition, (i.e., only a subset of the features should be changed with counterfactuals). Specifically, counterfactuals generated in this case study are commonly able to reverse the "deviant" predictions in one step by generally recommending a single next-activity. The considerations reported above are drawn independently of the machine learning algorithm used in the offline learning phase to develop the decision model used for monitoring the deviance risk. Finally, we examine an example of an ongoing trace of Sepsis event log, which was correctly recognized as labelled in the class "deviant", i.e., "Not Discharged" in Sepsis log (before its completion), and the next-activity recommended with the counterfactual for the same ongoing trace, to reverse the "deviant" prediction. In addition, Fig. 3 reports the evaluation of the recommendation obtained querying GPT-5 Mini with the following prompt:

"I am analyzing a counterfactual explanation for a sepsis case from the Sepsis Cases event log. I have the only activity data.

- *Case data (unordered activities): ER Registration (1), Leucocytes (2), CRP (2), ER Triage (1), ER Sepsis Triage (1), Admission NC (1);*
- *Label: Not Discharged;*
- *Model prediction: Not Discharged;*
- *Counterfactual explanation: Execute the activity Lactic Acid. With this additional activity, the model prediction changes to Discharged.*

Evaluate the quality of this counterfactual with a concise explanation."

The explanation provided by GPT-5 Mini can serve as a decision-support tool for including the stackholders (e.g., physicians) in the described counterfactual loop, so that they may validate and refine the generated counterfactual recommendations with their knowledge and experience. Notably, the generated counterfactual explanation is recognized as a plausible action by the medical staff with minimal impact (a single activity is suggested to reverse the decision on the clinical journey). The suggested activity "Measuring Lactic Acid" is considered a realistic intervention to change the patient's predicted outcome as this is a standard lab activity to assess the severity and suggest treatment adjustment based on elevated lactate.

Here's a concise evaluation of this counterfactual:

Quality assessment: Moderate

Reasoning:

1. **Feasibility / Actionability:**
   - Adding **Lactic Acid** is clinically actionable and plausible in sepsis cases, as measuring lactate is standard for assessing severity.
2. **Minimality:**
   - Only **one activity is added**, so the counterfactual is minimal.
3. **Realism / Clinical plausibility:**
   - Measuring Lactic Acid could influence clinical decisions and model predictions, making this a **realistic intervention**.
4. **Interpretability / Usefulness:**
   - The explanation is **clear and actionable**, highlighting a specific lab that might change the patient's predicted outcome.

Summary: This counterfactual is **actionable, minimal, and clinically relevant**, making it a **reasonable and useful explanation**. Its quality would improve further if it explicitly tied the Lactic Acid measurement to potential interventions (e.g., treatment adjustments based on elevated lactate).

Fig. 3. Prompt to evaluate the counterfactual explanation produced for the ongoing Sepsis trace with length equal to 8 (id=GG) in GPT-5 mini

5 Conclusion

This paper describes a PPM methodology that uses machine learning for predictive monitoring the deviance risk of ongoing traces of a business process, and counterfactuals to recommend next-activities to reverse "deviant" predictions. As future work we plan to explore the performance of methods specifically defined to generate counterfactual sequences accounting for sequence-level process aware characteristics [8], as well as possible multi-modal events [11]. We would explore how counterfactuals may be used in multi-perspective scenario considering resources and timestamps in addition to activities. Finally, we plan to investigate how counterfactuals can be used in the root cause analysis of trace deviance as an alternative to the declarative-based approach described in [6].

Acknowledgment. We acknowledge financial support under the National Recovery and Resilience Plan (NRRP), M4C2I1.1, funded by the European Union – NextGenerationEU– Project Title aRtificial intElligence for Process Analytics (REPA) - Grant Assignment Decree No. 2022CJWPNA (CUP Università degli Studi di Bari Aldo Moro H53C24000960006) by the Italian Ministry of University and Research (MUR).

References

1. van der Aalst, W.M.P., Carmona, J. (eds.): Process Mining Handbook, LNBIP, vol. 448. Springer, Cham (2022). https://doi.org/10.1007/978-3-031-08848-3
2. Ceravolo, P., Comuzzi, M., De Weerdt, J., Di Francescomarino, C., Maggi, F.M.: Predictive process monitoring: concepts, challenges, and future research directions. Process Sci. **1**(1), 2 (2024). https://doi.org/10.1007/s44311-024-00002-4
3. Cuzzocrea, A., Folino, F., Guarascio, M., Pontieri, L.: A robust and versatile multi-view learning framework for the detection of deviant business process instances. Int. J. Cooperative Inf. Syst. **25**(4), 1–56 (2016). https://doi.org/10.1142/S0218843017400032
4. Folino, F., Folino, G., Guarascio, M., Pontieri, L.: Combining active learning and fast DNN ensembles for process deviance discovery. In: ISMIS 2022. LNCS, vol. 13515, pp. 346–356. Springer, Cham (2022). https://doi.org/10.1007/978-3-031-16564-1_33
5. Folino, F., Folino, G., Guarascio, M., Pontieri, L.: The force of few: boosting deviance detection in data scarcity scenarios through self-supervised learning and pattern-based encoding. Soft. Comput. **29**(7), 3675–3690 (2025). https://doi.org/10.1007/S00500-025-10646-4
6. Francescomarino, C.D., Donadello, I., Ghidini, C., Maggi, F.M., Puura, J.: Business process deviance mining with sequential and declarative patterns. Bus. Inf. Syst. Eng. **67**(6), 877–894 (2025). https://doi.org/10.1007/S12599-024-00911-5
7. Guidotti, R.: Counterfactual explanations and how to find them: literature review and benchmarking. Data Min. Knowl. Discovery, 1–55 (2022). https://doi.org/10.1007/s10618-022-00831-6
8. Hundogan, O., Lu, X., Du, Y., Reijers, H.A.: Created: generating viable counterfactual sequences for predictive process analytics. In: CAISE 2023. pp. 541–557. Springer, Cham (2023). https://doi.org/10.1007/978-3-031-34560-9_32
9. Le, N.D., Padella, A., Vinci, F., de Leoni, M.: Leveraging counterfactuals for prescriptive process analytics. In: Responsible BPM Forum, Process Technology Forum, Educators Forum, pp. 200–215. Springer, Cham (2026). https://doi.org/10.1007/978-3-032-02936-2_15
10. Mothilal, R.K., Sharma, A., Tan, C.: Explaining machine learning classifiers through diverse counterfactual explanations. In: FAT 2020, pp. 607–617. ACM (2020). https://doi.org/10.1145/3351095.337285

11. Pasquadibisceglie, V., et al.: Multimodal predictive process monitoring and its application to explainable clinical pathways. Inf. Syst. **139**, 102698 (2026). https://doi.org/10.1016/j.is.2026.102698
12. Teinemaa, I., Dumas, M., Rosa, M.L., Maggi, F.M.: Outcome-oriented predictive process monitoring: Review and benchmark. ACM Trans. Knowl. Discov. Data **13**(2), 17:1–17:57 (2019). https://doi.org/10.1145/3301300
13. Yuan, Y., McAreavey, K., Li, S., Liu, W.: Multi-granular evaluation of diverse counterfactual explanations. In: ICAART 2024. vol. 2, pp. 186–197. SciTePress (2024). https://doi.org/10.5220/0012349900003636

Industry Session

How to Use Language Models for Vehicle Service Complaint Classification Under Industrial Constraints?

Adeel Zafar(✉), Sławomir Nowaczyk, Hamid Sarmadi, Saeed Gholami Shahbandi, and Nuwan Gunasekara

Center for Applied Intelligent Systems Research, Halmstad University, Halmstad, Sweden
{adeel.zafar,slawomir.nowaczyk,hamid.sarmadi,saeed.gholami.shahbandi, nuwan.gunasekara}@hh.se

Abstract. Vehicle service reports contain valuable information for diagnosing system-level faults, but their unstructured and domain-specific nature makes automated classification challenging. While language models (LMs) provide flexible adaptation strategies, their effectiveness across industrial data regimes remains unclear, particularly under data constraints. We present an empirical study of vehicle service complaint classification using the public NHTSA (https://www.nhtsa.gov/nhtsa-datasets-and-apis (Accessed: April 2026)) complaints dataset and a proprietary service dataset from a Swedish truck manufacturer. We evaluate prompt-based classification and supervised fine-tuning (SFT) across both datasets. On the NHTSA dataset, SFT substantially outperforms prompt-based approaches. In contrast, on the proprietary dataset, prompt-based classification achieves strong performance, while fine-tuning benefits significantly from transfer learning using a checkpoint trained on public data. Overall, our results highlight the role of data quality, domain alignment, and transferable supervision in selecting effective adaptation strategies for vehicle text classification.

1 Introduction

Transformer-based language models are increasingly adopted in automotive applications such as fault diagnostics, maintenance analysis, and customer support [8]. Modern vehicle ecosystems generate large volumes of textual data, including service reports, maintenance logs, and customer complaints, which contain valuable information about recurring issues, operational trends, and potential failures. Effectively analyzing this unstructured and domain-specific text is therefore an important practical problem in automotive service operations.

Despite the growing relevance of Natural Language Processing (NLP) in this domain, publicly available datasets containing detailed vehicle service reports remain scarce. Most existing resources focus on sensor measurements, fault codes, or owner-submitted complaints, rather than the rich technical descriptions

G. Andresini et al. (Eds.): ISMIS 2026, LNAI 16685, pp. 137–150, 2027.
https://doi.org/10.1007/978-3-032-32643-0_13

produced by service centers [12]. In industrial settings, such data is often proprietary, noisy, and multilingual, and labeling is costly and time-consuming [11]. These factors motivate alternative model adaptation strategies.

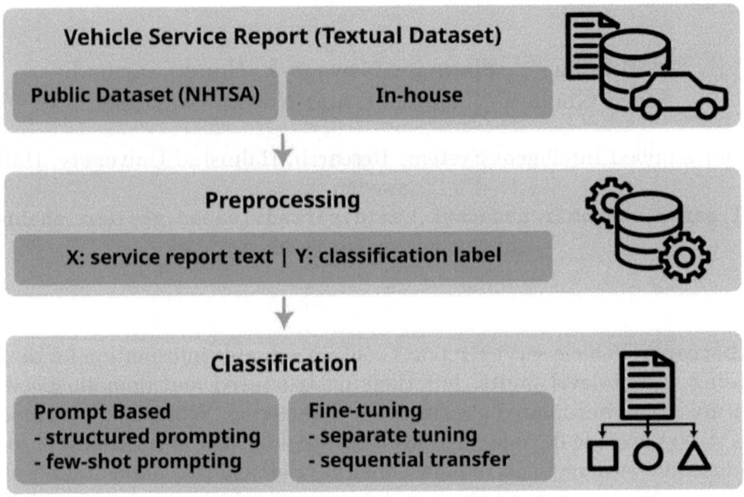

Fig. 1. Overview of the research flow

The goal of this paper is to empirically investigate how language models can be adapted for domain-specific text classification in the automotive sector under realistic industrial constraints. In industries like automotive, classifying service records or customer complaints into functional groups (Engine, Fuel system, and others) not only speeds up processing and enhances tracking, but also enables better prioritization, targeted resource allocation, and systematic trend analysis for quality improvement and strategic decisions. By categorizing issues, companies can quickly route records to the right teams, uncover systemic problems, and continuously improve service operations and customer satisfaction.

The classification task is defined as the mapping of unstructured vehicle service complaints into specialized diagnostic categories. Our methodology follows a three-stage pipeline: (1) **Semantic Discovery** via topic modeling to align raw data with manufacturer taxonomies, (2) **Adaptation** using two complementary strategies—SFT and prompt-based classification—and (3) **Industrial Stress-Testing** through ablation studies on metadata and data noise. Although these adaptation approaches are not mutually exclusive [18], we evaluate them separately to quantify their specific trade-offs with respect to data volume, compute efficiency, and domain-context requirements in industrial settings. This flow is depicted in Fig. 1. Based on this systematic evaluation, the paper makes the following key contributions:

Adaptation Strategy Analysis: We provide a systematic empirical comparison of prompt-based inference and SFT within the high-noise, technical domain of heavy-duty vehicle diagnostics.

Quantifying Metadata Criticality: We identify a performance "tipping point" for Small Language Models (SLMs); while 1B-parameter models struggle with raw text alone, the integration of structured industrial metadata enables them to achieve parity with fine-tuned experts.

Cross-Domain Transferability: We demonstrate that knowledge learned from public NHTSA can be successfully transferred to proprietary technician-written reports, offering a validated "cold-start" strategy for industrial NLP where labeled data is scarce.

2 Related Work

In order to align with the application domain and contribution of this work, this section organizes the related work according to the application domain, Language Model adaptation strategies for domain specific application and industrial constraints.

In [12], the authors utilized a BiLSTM combined with a CNN model to classify free-text reports. Similarly, traditional classifiers have shown limitations when processing NHTSA complaint data compared to LLMs [7].

LLMs like BERT [6] and GPT [1,4] have revolutionized domain-specific tasks. BERT enabled fine-tuning for specialized applications [6]. RoBERTa [13], an optimized version of BERT, demonstrated robust performance in such applications. Few-shot prompting with LLMs has been shown to reduce reliance on labeled data, though performance varies by domain [4]. However, fine-tuning was found to outperform prompting in code-related tasks, suggesting the efficacy of each method may depend on the task [17]. A hybrid "fine-tuning after prompting" method was proposed to improve interpretability [18]. Combining prompting and fine-tuning may offer balanced efficiency and accuracy. A hybrid pipeline was proposed to exploit the advantages of both methods [18]. However, open questions remain about scalability and the limitations of fine-tuning [17].

Prompt engineering leverages pre-trained domain knowledge without additional training. In a comparison of prompting and fine-tuning for taxonomy construction, prompting showed superior results in low-resource settings [5]. However, metadata-rich prompts (e.g., those leveraging in-house datasets) were found to achieve higher accuracy than prompts based on public datasets such as NHTSA, which typically provide less detailed metadata [7].

Topic modeling techniques like BERTopic [10] and Top2Vec [3] have outperformed traditional methods such as LDA and NMF in clustering vehicle complaints [10]. These approaches were shown to be effective on short, noisy text [9], and preprocessing was emphasized as crucial for maintaining topic coherence [14]. Real-world datasets often contain missing or multilingual entries. One approach addressed this via feature engineering [16], while another applied data-centric training using SmolLM2 to mitigate noise [2].

Prior work on text classification using prompt-based or fine-tuning approaches primarily targets public benchmarks and large language models. This often leads to overlooking industrial constraints such as proprietary data, domain-specific terminology, noisy multilingual text, limited annotation budgets, and high deployment costs. Under these data and deployment constraints, we evaluate BERT-based SFT alongside prompt-based methods using SLMs for vehicle service report classification. We hypothesize that competitive performance can be achieved while enabling cost-effective, low-latency industrial deployment [15].

3 Materials and Methods

3.1 Datasets

In this study we use two datasets, one is an in-house dataset sourced from a Swedish international manufacturer, and the is the NHTSA public dataset. Due to the sensitive nature and security restrictions of the proprietary data, we cannot provide an in-depth analysis, only high-level conclusions and findings – however, we believe that a study of the applicability of state-of-the-art methods to such a real-world case is of interest to the scientific community. To demonstrate the general applicability and in-depth details of our approach, we applied our prompt-based and fine-tuning classification methods to the NHTSA database.

The in-house dataset consisted of approximately 6,770 service records. Each service record contained fields including the original complaint text (often in various languages), the English translation of the complaint (when the original was non-English), the customer service response text, and additional metadata fields such as service category, timestamps, and record identifiers. These textual reports were used for a supervised multi-class classification task. The objective of the task was to automatically categorize each complaint into predefined classes related to vehicle components, such as engine, fuel systems, transmission, electrical systems, and other service-related categories.

To ensure consistency and quality in text analysis, the complaints were filtered to include only those in English. For each record, if the original complaint was in English, it was used directly; otherwise, the English translation was used. To ensure the inclusion of substantively informative service records, only entries containing at least 20 words were considered in the analysis. Records below this threshold frequently lacked sufficient semantic depth and contextual detail. Applying this criterion helped minimize noise arising from brief, incomplete, or minimally descriptive complaints, thereby improving the reliability and robustness of the classification model. The dataset was partitioned into training, and test sets using an 80/20 ratio with stratified sampling to ensure that technical categories were represented proportionally across all splits.

The NHTSA dataset is a comprehensive collection of 349,996 vehicle complaint reports spanning from 1995 to 2024, obtained from the National Highway Traffic Safety Administration. Each record contains consumer-submitted complaint narratives. These complaints are used for a supervised multi-class classification task, where each report was categorized into predefined vehicle system components (e.g., engine, fuel system, transmission, electrical system, braking system, and other related categories). The objective was to evaluate whether the proposed model could accurately identify and assign the correct component label based solely on the textual description of the complaint.

3.2 Topic Modeling

We performed topic modeling on both datasets to uncover emergent themes and qualitatively assess how well these natural groupings align with existing classification labels. In industrial settings, where taxonomies are often static or inherited from legacy systems, this step is crucial for Prompt Engineering. By identifying latent clusters that fall outside the standard taxonomy, we can refine the 'Expert System' instructions within our prompts to handle boundary cases (e.g., distinguishing between a 'General' fault and a 'Software' fault).

We compare four techniques: BERTopic and Top2Vec (embedding-based) against LDA and NMF (bag-of-words). BERTopic and Top2Vec were selected for their ability to capture the semantic nuances of technical service language, while LDA and NMF provided a baseline for word-level co-occurrence patterns.

BERTopic uses these embeddings to group complaints into coherent topics. It combines embedding similarity with class-based TF-IDF to extract interpretable topic representations. The next topic modeling technique we use is Top2Vec. This method learns document and topic vectors in a shared semantic space. Through hierarchical density-based clustering, Top2Vec produced dense clusters of similar complaints, uncovering subtle themes often missed by traditional methods.

In contrast, the traditional models LDA and NMF use bag-of-words representations generated through a CountVectorizer and stopword removal. LDA assumes documents are mixtures of latent topics, each represented as distributions over words, and infers topic-word and document-topic probabilities through a generative process. Equation 1 explains the process of LDA as it is a *Maximum Likelihood Estimate (MLE)* or empirical conditional probability of a word given a topic. It is used in *collapsed Gibbs sampling*, a common inference technique for LDA. It estimates given that in topic z_n, what the probability of seeing word w_n is:

$$p(w_n \mid z_n, \beta) = \frac{n(w_n, z_n)}{\sum_w n(w, z_n)} \tag{1}$$

NMF decomposes the document-term matrix into additive, non-negative components, capturing latent semantic structures. Both required the number of topics to be specified in advance and primarily relied on word co-occurrence patterns. The equation $V \approx WH$ represents a low-rank approximation of the non-negative matrix V, which is factorized into two lower-dimensional non-negative matrices W and H. Here, W captures the topics, and H contains the coefficients of the topics.

3.3 Prompt Driven Classification

In the prompt-based classification setting, we utilize SLMs to demonstrate that competitive performance can be attained without dependence on large language models, which incur significantly higher computational costs.

For our experiments, we utilize two SLMs, **SmolLM2-1.7B**[1] and **Llama-3.2-1B**[2], both of which are applied using structured prompts and few-shot strategies. A structured prompt organizes input information in a clear, formatted way helping the model understand context through explicit structure and instructions. In contrast, a few-shot prompt improves model performance by providing example input–output pairs before the actual task, allowing the model to learn the desired pattern or reasoning style from demonstrations.

The classification task required mapping service complaints into well-defined categories based on descriptions of symptoms and failures. The system was designed to assign exactly one label per complaint, chosen from a predefined taxonomy of functional groups. It is also important to note that the number of categories differs between the NHTSA and in-house datasets, requiring the formulation to be adjusted accordingly. Furthermore, the in-house dataset contains additional metadata, which we believe enriches the classification process. This hypothesis is supported by our results where using the dataset with this supplementary information significantly improves the performance.

3.4 Fine-Tuning for Classification

In the fine-tuning approach for classification, we fine-tune a pre-trained BERT-based transformer model (110M parameters[3]) on the multi-class text classification task. The fine-tuning process involved updating the weights of the pre-trained model using labeled complaint data related to automotive systems. The dataset is tokenized using a standard WordPiece tokenizer with appropriate padding and truncation. The model, based on bert-base-uncased, was fine-tuned using cross-entropy loss and the AdamW optimizer (batch size 16, learning rate 2e-5) for 4 epochs on the public dataset and 7 on the proprietary dataset. Training ran on a MacBook with Apple M3 (18 GB memory) using Metal Performance Shaders for GPU acceleration. Fine-tuning took 103 h for the NHTSA dataset and 45–50 min for the proprietary dataset.

We evaluate two fine-tuning adaptation strategies. The first strategy is to train the model on each dataset independently (separate tuning). The second strategy is to train the model on the NHTSA dataset followed by further training on the in-house dataset (sequential transfer).

[1] https://huggingface.co/HuggingFaceTB/SmolLM2-1.7B.
[2] https://huggingface.co/meta-llama/Llama-3.2-1B.
[3] https://huggingface.co/google-bert/bert-base-uncased.

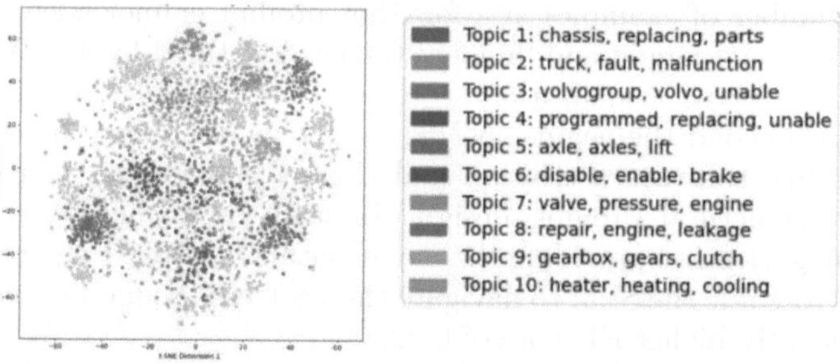

(a) In-house dataset embeddings.

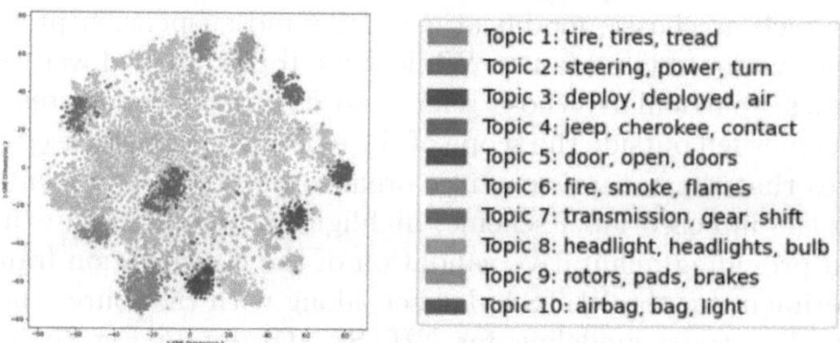

(b) NHTSA dataset embeddings.

Fig. 2. T-SNE visualization of complaint embeddings. The scattered distribution in (a) illustrates the complexity of industrial service data compared to public data (b).

4 Results and Discussion

4.1 Topic Modeling

We performed topic modeling as an exploratory pre-processing step to qualitatively assess semantic alignment with existing manufacturer taxonomies. It is important to note that topic modeling was used strictly for domain discovery and prompt engineering. Consequently, while the analysis was performed on the corpus to capture the full technical vocabulary, no label information or cluster assignments were leaked to the classification models during the supervised training phase. Visualization of the top topics from each model (Fig. 2a and Fig. 2b) highlighted clear distinctions in topic quality. BERTopic and Top2Vec generated more semantically rich representations, enabling a deeper understanding of the dataset's underlying structure. The semantic overlap and high similarity between the discovered topics are further visualized in the topic similarity graph provided in Appendix A, Fig. 4.

The scattered distribution revealed in the t-SNE visualizations (Fig. 2a) explains the performance gap observed in our classification tasks. Specifically, the broad variability and overlapping nature of these semantic clusters suggest why the Few-Shot Prompting approach struggled (0.55 F1 on In-house data);

the limited number of examples in a few-shot prompt cannot adequately cover the diverse technical jargon and 'hidden' themes identified by Top2Vec.

Furthermore, these visualizations revealed that the natural clusters in the data extended beyond the engine-specific taxonomy, including broader vehicle-level themes like software activation and chassis issues. This insight directly justified our 'Structural Prompt' design (Table 2): by explicitly defining these boundary categories and providing the model with a 'Quality Engineer' persona, we were able to guide the SLM to navigate this scattered semantic space, leading to the significantly higher F1 score of 0.92.

Topic modeling in Fig. 2a revealed that the latent structure of the complaint data extends beyond strictly engine-specific issues, uncovering broader vehicle-level themes such as chassis modifications, axle and suspension problems, and software or activation-related faults. While some topics aligned well with predefined categories—particularly those related to engine control systems—several prominent themes fell outside the scope of the existing engine-focused taxonomy. This indicates that the natural semantic organization of the complaints is more diverse than the imposed label scheme, highlighting potential gaps in category coverage and providing qualitative validation of the classification framework.

The experiment for the NHTSA dataset, along with the source code is available online[4]. The topic modeling for NHTSA dataset in Fig. 2b reveals several distinct clusters, each representing recurring patterns in vehicle issues. While these topics are meaningful and capture specific problems, they are often fine-grained, overlapping, and domain-specific, which makes the service reports challenging to classify.

4.2 Prompting vs. Finetuning

Table 1 summarizes the performance of prompt-based and fine-tuning approaches on both the in-house and NHTSA datasets. On the in-house dataset, prompt-based classification with SmolLM2-1.7B using a structured prompt achieves strong performance, reaching a weighted F1 score of 0.92 (the best performing prompt is mentioned in Appendix A, Listing 1). The few-shot prompt strategy was not useful for the in-house dataset and substantially underperformed for both SmolLM2 and Llama.

The strong performance of SmolLM2-1.7B using structural prompt can be attributed to its greater model capacity and its suitability for structured prompt-based classification, which enables clearer decision boundaries between functional groups. In contrast, the smaller Llama-3.2-1B model performs less consistently. Notably, Llama-3.2-1B failed to produce valid structured outputs under the same prompting strategy, frequently biasing predictions toward the first listed class—an issue commonly observed in smaller instruction-tuned models under zero-shot multi-class settings. Overall, these findings indicate that a moderately sized language model is sufficient for effective prompt-based classification, reducing the need for substantially larger models in this context.

[4] https://github.com/Adeelzafar/Adaptive-LMs.

Table 1. Comparison of model performance on the **NHTSA** and **In-house** datasets (the best result of each metric per dataset is marked in bold).

Models/Methods	Precision	Recall	F1-Score
NHTSA Dataset			
SmolLM2-1.7B-Instruct (Structural Prompt)	0.64	0.53	0.57
SmolLM2-1.7B-Instruct (Few-Shot Prompt)	0.55	0.55	0.43
Llama-3.2-1B (Few-Shot Prompt)	0.75	0.37	0.36
BERT (Fine-Tuned)	**0.86**	**0.86**	**0.86**
In-house Dataset			
SmolLM2-1.7B-Instruct (Structural Prompt with metadata)	**0.94**	0.91	**0.92**
SmolLM2-1.7B-Instruct (Structural Prompt without metadata)	0.52	0.42	0.40
SmolLM2-1.7B-Instruct (Few-shot Prompt with metadata)	0.87	0.78	0.80
Llama-3.2-1B (Few-Shot Prompt with metadata)	0.60	0.50	0.55
BERT (Fine-Tuned)	0.56	0.59	0.57
BERT (Fine-Tuned from NHTSA Checkpoint)	0.92	**0.92**	**0.92**

On the other hand, the BERT model trained directly on the in-house dataset achieved relatively low performance compared to the prompt-based approach, with an F1 score of 0.57. This substantial performance gap reflects the limited size and higher noise level of the proprietary dataset, where SFT from scratch struggles to generalize effectively. However, fine-tuning BERT from a checkpoint previously trained on the NHTSA dataset resulted in a significant improvement on the in-house data, achieving an F1 score of 0.92.

This F1 improvement (from 0.57 to 0.92) through sequential transfer learning represents a highly significant effect size. While computational constraints precluded multi-seed replication, the magnitude of this delta far exceeds the typical stochastic variance observed in BERT-based architectures (usually $\sigma \approx 0.01$–0.02). Furthermore, the convergence of both the Structured Prompting approach and the Sequential Transfer model on the same F1 score (0.92) provides independent methodological validation of the performance ceiling for this industrial task, suggesting the results are robust across different adaptation paradigms.

This finding highlights the value of transferable supervision: although the in-house dataset alone is insufficient to support robust fine-tuning, leveraging knowledge learned from a related large-scale public dataset enables performance comparable to prompt-based approaches.

In contrast, results on the NHTSA dataset present a different pattern. Using prompt-based classification as a baseline, the best-performing configuration—again SmolLM2-1.7B with a structured prompt—achieves a weighted F1 score of 0.57, with few-shot prompting showing inconsistent behavior across models. However, SFT of a BERT-based model yields the strongest overall performance on NHTSA, reaching an F1 score of 0.86.

This outcome aligns with the characteristics of the NHTSA dataset, which is substantially larger and more structured, providing sufficient labeled examples for effective supervised learning. These findings suggest that when labeled data is available at scale and label definitions are stable, SFT remains a reliable and robust strategy. In contrast, prompt-based methods appear more advantageous in low-resource or noisy proprietary settings, where transferable knowledge or strong metadata compensate for limited training data.

4.3 Ablation Study

Figure 3 further explores the robustness of the fine-tuning approach under conditions designed to more closely resemble those of the in-house dataset. Specifically, we reduced the size of the NHTSA training data to simulate a low-resource setting.

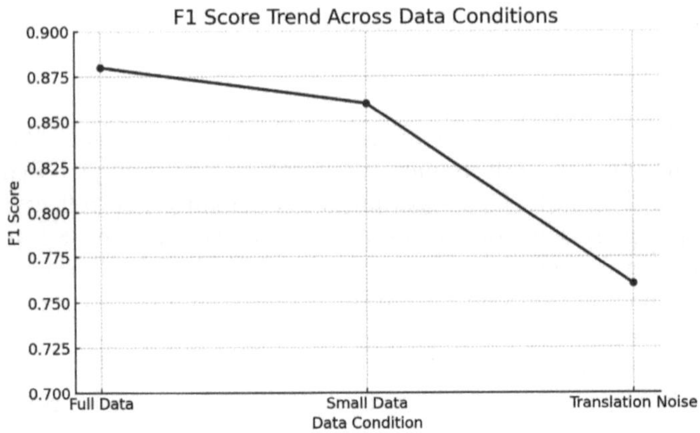

Fig. 3. F1 scores for fine-tuning on the NHTSA dataset under varying data sizes and translation noise settings, designed to approximate conditions observed in the in-house dataset.

The observed decrease in weighted F1 score is relatively modest, suggesting that the fine-tuned model maintains stable performance even with reduced training data, provided that the data quality remains high. An additional challenge arises from the multilingual nature of the proprietary service records, which introduces noise through translation and inconsistent phrasing. To approximate this condition, we introduced synthetic noise into the NHTSA dataset via back-translation, replacing original English complaints with translated-and-back-translated versions. In this setup, back-translated samples were used as replacements rather than as data augmentation. As shown in Fig. 3, this intervention leads to a notable degradation in performance.

We also assessed the impact of removing contextual metadata—such as severity, error codes, and summaries—from the prompts, to better align with the structure of the NHTSA dataset. Across the full dataset, the best-performing model, SmolLM2-1.7B-Instruct with structured prompting, achieved only modest F1score of 0.40 as shown in Table 1. The prompting method struggled to correctly classify complaints when metadata was excluded. These findings highlight that structured metadata provides critical contextual information for domain-specific classification of industrial service records.

4.4 Limitations

This study focuses on a representative set of SFT and prompt-based classification approaches and does not exhaustively explore the full space of prompting strategies, such as chain-of-thought reasoning or self-consistency. We also evaluate a limited set of model architectures and sizes, reflecting the paper's emphasis on understanding data characteristics under realistic constraints rather than comprehensive model stress testing.

5 Conclusion

This paper presents an empirical study of prompt-based and SFT strategies for vehicle service complaint classification under realistic industrial data constraints. SFT is an effective adaptation strategy when large amounts of high-quality labeled data with stable label definitions are available. However, independent fine-tuning on small and noisy datasets does not generalize well, as observed with the in-house dataset. Transfer learning can help mitigate that by leveraging supervision from a related large-scale public dataset (e.g., NHTSA) substantially improves adaptation performance on the in-house data. Prompt-based approaches demonstrate a positive correlation between the incorporation of metadata and classification performance. However, on noisy datasets, structured prompting becomes less effective when metadata is not utilized, as confirmed by the ablation study. Overall, our results indicate that the effectiveness of model adaptation strategies depends primarily on data quality and the availability of contextual information under resource constraints. Both prompting-based small language models and SFT remain viable approaches for automotive service classification.

Acknowledgement. The work was carried out with funding support from Sweden's innovation agency, Vinnova, through the Vehicle Strategic Research and Innovation Programme, FFI. (Reference Number: 2024-00763)

A Appendix

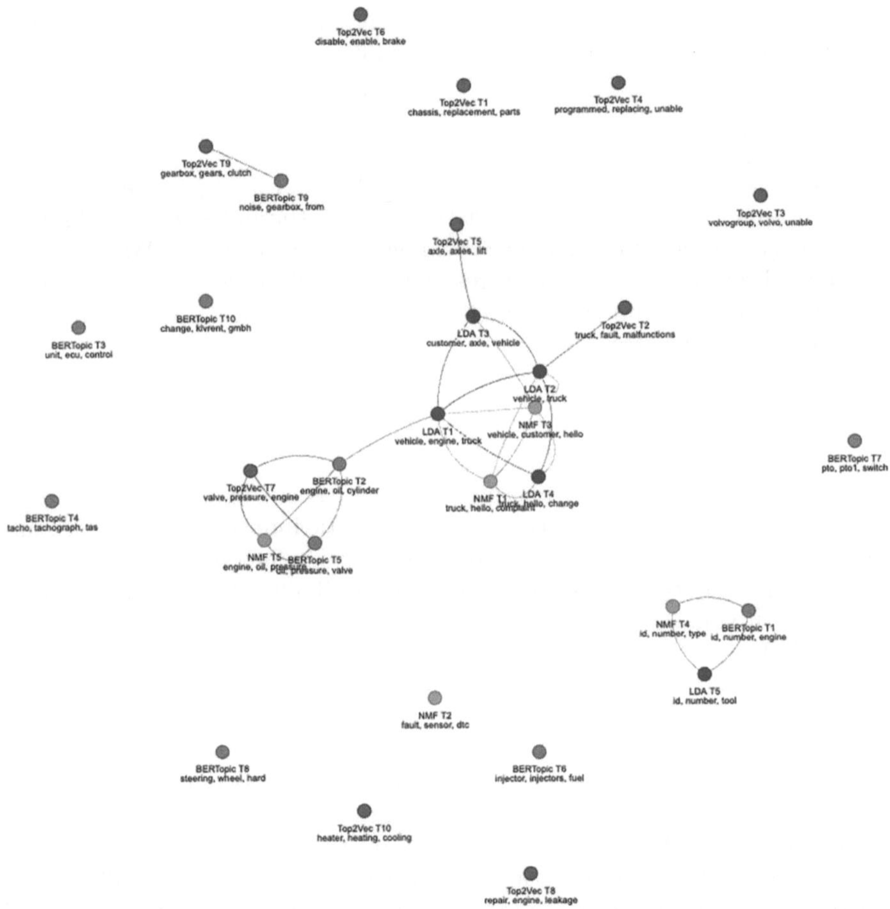

Fig. 4. Topic similarity graph for our in-house dataset across four topic modeling techniques. Each node represents a topic, labeled with the model name and top keywords. Edges indicate high semantic similarity between topics based on cosine similarity of sentence embeddings (threshold ≥ 0.6).

Listing 1. Best performing structural prompt for in-house dataset.

```
System:
You are an expert quality engineer who classifies truck
engine failures into specific categories based on detailed
descriptions of symptoms and failures.

User:
Analyze the following complaint and return only the
appropriate category label.
```

```
Complaint:
Severity: <Severity>
Service Open Date: <Service Open Date>
VIN: <VIN>
Error Code: <Error Code>
Summary of Complaint: <Summary>
Complaint: <Customer Complaint or Translation>
Response: <Service Response>
Remark: <Additional Remarks>

Choose only from these categories:

20. General - Broad or unclear issues.
21. Engine - Core engine
faults: knocking, failure to start, loss of power.
22. Lubricating
and oil system - Oil pressure, leaks, lubrication failure.
23. Pump
issues, contaminated fuel.
24. Fuel systems, gas operation - Natural
gas or LPG issues.
25. Intake and exhaust systems. Turbo - Air
intake, exhaust, turbocharger issues.
26. Cooling system -
Overheating, coolant leaks, radiator problems.
27. Engine / motor
controls - ECU, control units, electronic regulation issues.
28. Ignition and control systems - Spark/glow plugs, timing, ignition
modules.
29. Miscellaneous - Issues not fitting other categories but
relevant.

Return only the most relevant category label.
```

References

1. Achiam, J., et al.: Gpt-4 technical report. arXiv preprint arXiv:2303.08774 (2023)
2. Allal, L.B., et al.: Smollm2: When smol goes big-data-centric training of a small language model. arXiv preprint arXiv:2502.02737 (2025)
3. Angelov, D.: Top2vec: distributed representations of topics. arXiv preprint arXiv:2008.09470 (2020)
4. Brown, T., Mann, B., Ryder, N., Subbiah, M., Kaplan, J., Dhariwal, P., et al.: Language models are few-shot learners. Adv. Neural. Inf. Process. Syst. **33**, 1877–1901 (2020)
5. Chen, B., Yi, F., Varró, D.: Prompting or fine-tuning? A comparative study of large language models for taxonomy construction. In: 2023 ACM/IEEE International Conference on Model Driven Engineering Languages and Systems Companion (MODELS-C), pp. 588–596. IEEE (2023)
6. Devlin, J., Chang, M.W., Lee, K., Toutanova, K.: Bert: pre-training of deep bidirectional transformers for language understanding. In: Proceedings of NAACL-HLT pp, pp. 4171–4186 (2019)
7. Dhillon, A.S., Torresin, A.: Advancing vehicle diagnostic: exploring the application of large language models in the automotive industry (2024)
8. Dhillon, A., Torresin, A.: Advancing vehicle diagnostic: exploring the application of large language models in the automotive industry (2024)
9. Egger, R., Yu, J.: A topic modeling comparison between LDA, NMF, top2vec, and bertopic to demystify twitter posts. Front. Sociol. **7**, 886498 (2022)

10. Grootendorst, M.: Bertopic: neural topic modeling with a class-based tf-idf procedure. arXiv preprint arXiv:2203.05794 (2022)
11. Huyen, C.: AI Engineering: Building Applications with Foundation Models. O'Reilly (2025)
12. Khodadadi, A., Ghandiparsi, S., Chuah, C.N.: A natural language processing and deep learning based model for automated vehicle diagnostics using free-text customer service reports. Mach. Learn. Appl. **10**, 100424 (2022)
13. Liu, Y., Ott, M., Goyal, N., Du, J., Joshi, M., Chen, D.: Roberta: a robustly optimized bert pretraining approach. arXiv preprint arXiv:1907.11692 (2019)
14. Maier, D., et al.: Applying LDA topic modeling in communication research: toward a valid and reliable methodology. Commun. Methods Meas. **12**(2–3), 93–118 (2018)
15. Pham, N.T., Kieu, T., Nguyen, D.M., Xuan, S.H., Duong-Trung, N., Le-Phuoc, D.: Slm-bench: a comprehensive benchmark of small language models on environmental impacts. In: Findings of the Association for Computational Linguistics: EMNLP 2025, pp. 21369–21392 (2025)
16. Revanur, V., Ayibiowu, A.: Automatic generation of descriptive features for predicting vehicle faults (2020)
17. Shin, J., Tang, C., Mohati, T., Nayebi, M., Wang, S., Hemmati, H.: Prompt engineering or fine-tuning: an empirical assessment of llms for code. In: 2025 IEEE/ACM 22nd International Conference on Mining Software Repositories (MSR), pp. 490–502. IEEE (2025)
18. Wang, Z., et al.: Fine-tuning after prompting: an explainable way for classification. In: Proceedings of the 10th SIGHAN Workshop on Chinese Language Processing (SIGHAN-10), pp. 133–142 (2024)

Knowledge Extraction from Aviation Incident Reports via LLM Aspect-Based Summarization and Topic Modeling

Carl Hatoum[1(✉)], Catherine Combes[1], Virginie Burnaz-Fresse[1], Christophe Gravier[1], and Mathieu Orzalesi[2]

[1] Laboratoire Hubert Curien, UMR CNRS, Université Jean Monnet, 5516 Saint-Etienne, France
{carl.hatoum,catherine.combes,virginie.fresse, christophe.gravier}@univ-st-etienne.fr
[2] SEGULA Technologies, Courbevoie, France
mathieu.orzalesi@segula.fr

Abstract. Aviation safety organizations accumulate large repositories of incident reports whose operational knowledge remains difficult to extract systematically at scale. Standard topic modeling applied to raw documents surfaces distributional patterns anchored to surface form rather than the causal structures relevant to safety analysis, and industrial constraints further limit viable approaches. We propose a pipeline decoupling representation shaping from structure discovery: an open-weight LLM summarizes the cause of each incident before topic discovery on the resulting representations, with a weighted multi-dimensional quality filter acting as an automated safeguard against hallucination and aspect drift. Applied to a large corpus of NTSB incident reports, cause-focused representations outperform raw-document baselines in topic coherence, and alignment with expert taxonomy. These results establish representation shaping as the primary lever for aligning discovered topic structures with operational safety objectives, opening concrete deployment perspectives for aviation knowledge management.

Keywords: Topic modeling · Large Language Model · Aspect-based summarization · Aviation safety

1 Introduction

Aviation safety organizations maintain large repositories of incident reports whose operational knowledge remains difficult to extract systematically at scale. Incident reports are noisy documents: relevant information is embedded within lengthy narratives and diluted by procedural, descriptive content that may be irrelevant to target analysis. Topic modeling is a natural starting point for exploring large document corpora, yet it conflates two conceptually distinct operations: *representation shaping*, which determines what semantic content is surfaced, and *structure discovery*, which organizes that content into coherent groups. When

G. Andresini et al. (Eds.): ISMIS 2026, LNAI 16685, pp. 151–165, 2027.
https://doi.org/10.1007/978-3-032-32643-0_14

representations are noisy, clustering recovers the dominant vocabulary of the corpus, not the thematic structure relevant to a given user preference. Extracting the operationally relevant layer of information is therefore fundamentally a *representation problem*: Large Language Models (LLMs) offer a solution by acting as aspect-conditioned representation operators, reshaping each document into a targeted representation before topic discovery. However, industrial deployment introduces two hard constraints. Data sovereignty requirements mandate local processing on on-premise hardware, restricting viable models to open-weight alternatives. Moreover, the absence of a human validation loop at scale means hallucinations and aspect drift are *failure modes* that can corrupt topic structures.

We address both challenges through an end-to-end pipeline that prompts a locally deployable open-weight model to summarize each incident report through a target aspect before topic discovery. The pipeline embeds a weighted multi-dimensional filtering stage serving primarily as a reliability safeguard against hallucination and aspect drift, filtering summaries that fall below acceptable quality, preventing corrupted representations from propagating into topic structures. Applied to 3,427 NTSB aviation incident reports, this work makes four contributions: **(i)** a formal separation of representation shaping and structure discovery; **(ii)** an end-to-end industrial pipeline combining local aspect-based summarization, weighted filtering, and topic modeling; **(iii)** empirical evidence that representation is the primary driver of topic quality, with consistent gains over the raw-document baseline in coherence and diversity; and **(iv)** external alignment validation against expert taxonomy.

Section 2 surveys related work. Section 3–4 detail the pipeline and experimental protocol. Section 5 presents empirical findings. Section 6 provides deployment recommendations and Sect. 7 closes with limitations and future directions.

2 Related Work

Topic Modeling and Representation. Topic modeling has evolved from probabilistic generative models such as LDA [1] to neural representation-based frameworks, including BERTopic [5], which decouples representation from clustering via class-based TF-IDF over contextual embeddings. A parallel line explores LLMs as direct topic extractors [10], but prompted enumeration decouples topic scope from corpus statistics and cannot guarantee taxonomic coverage. More fundamentally, all these approaches treat raw-text embeddings as a fixed starting point, conflating representation shaping and structure discovery.

LLMs as Document Representation Operators. A complementary direction uses LLMs not as topic extractors but as representation operators [11], generating aspect-based summaries [4] that reshape document semantics. Decomposed chain-of-thought prompting [12] has shown particular utility in surfacing causal structure from complex narratives, including aviation incident reports [7]. However, this line of work has not been connected to topic modeling pipelines, and the downstream consequences of representation choice on topic quality and taxonomic alignment remain unstudied. Operating without a human validation loop further requires automated quality control over generated representations: multi-dimensional evaluation frameworks [13] and data-driven criterion weighting methods [3] offer complementary building blocks, yet neither has been deployed as a quality gate against hallucination and aspect drift in pipelines operating at scale without human review.

3 Proposed Methodology

The pipeline operationalizes the two-stage design introduced in Sect. 1, illustrated in Fig. 1, and proceeds in three stages: (1) aspect-conditioned summarization and quality evaluation (steps 1–3), (2) CRITIC-weighted filtering (steps 4–5), and (3) topic modeling with stability assessment and taxonomic validation (steps 6–8).

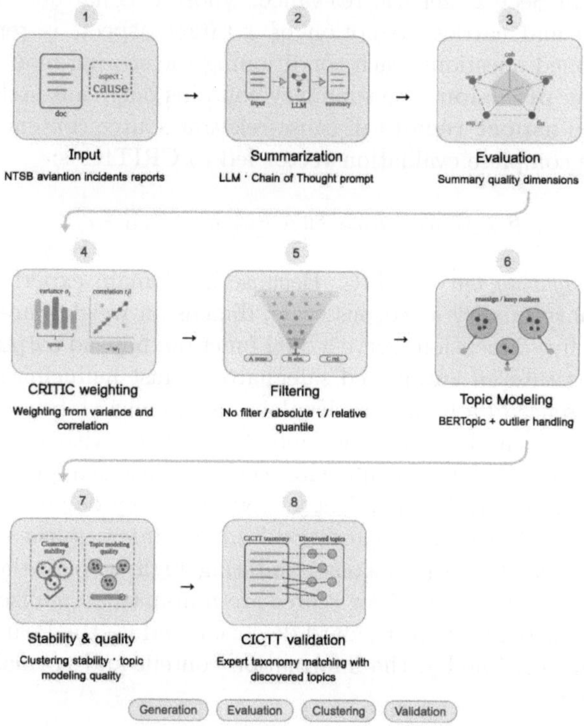

Fig. 1. Eight-step pipeline: (1–3) aspect-conditioned summarization and summaries scoring; (4–5) CRITIC-weighted filtering; (6–7) Topic modeling and assessment; (8) CICTT taxonomic matching.

Aspect-Conditioned Summarization: Each incident report is processed by Mistral 7B [6] via chain-of-thought prompting [7,12], conditioning generation on the causal dimension of the incident: the model identifies contributing factors and causal relationships, then synthesizes a cause-focused summary that suppresses procedural and descriptive content irrelevant to downstream topic discovery.

QA-Based Multi-Dimensional Filtering: To enforce quality constraints on generated summaries, we adapt UniEval [13], a T5-large model originally designed for generic summarization evaluation, which re-frames text evaluation as a unified Boolean QA task: each dimension i is operationalized as a natural-language question q_i, and the score s_i is derived from the model's conditional probability of a binary answer:

$$s_i = \frac{P(\text{Yes} \mid x, s, q_i)}{P(\text{Yes} \mid x, s, q_i) + P(\text{No} \mid x, s, q_i)}.$$

Evaluation Dimensions. UniEval's four task-invariant dimensions, consistency (source faithfulness), coherence (logical structure), fluency (linguistic well-formedness), and relevance (salience), are retained. To close the aspect-fidelity gap identified in Sect. 2, generic relevance, whose original question conditions on (x, s) alone and carries no notion of a target aspect, is replaced by two aspect-conditioned questions, each conditioning the scoring model on the triple (x, s, a): **aspect precision** (the summary contains only cause-relevant content, no leakage) and **aspect recall** (all cause-relevant source content is covered, no omission). The complete evaluation vector fed to CRITIC is:

$$\mathbf{s} = (s_{\text{cons}}, s_{\text{coh}}, s_{\text{flu}}, s_{\text{asp\_prec}}, s_{\text{asp\_rec}}).$$

Dimension Weighting via CRITIC. Because no domain expert is available to validate summary quality at corpus scale, dimension weights are derived automatically. The five dimensions serve a dual function: beyond corpus homogenization, they constitute an automated safeguard against hallucination and aspect drift, in the absence of a human review loop, a summary fabricating causal factors propagates unchecked into the embedding space without any observable signal. The CRITIC-weighted composite score Q provides a quality floor over all ingested representations, independently of whether any document is ultimately removed. CRITIC (*CRiteria Importance Through Intercriteria Correlation*) [3] assigns higher weight to dimensions exhibiting high score variability and low inter-dimensional correlation. Raw scores are min-max normalized to $[0, 1]$; letting σ_i denote the population standard deviation and r_{ij} the Pearson correlation between dimensions i and j, the information content and normalized weight of dimension i are:

$$C_i = \sigma_i \sum_{j=1}^{|\mathcal{M}|} (1 - r_{ij}), \qquad w_i = \frac{C_i}{\sum_{k=1}^{|\mathcal{M}|} C_k}.$$

Filtering Rule. A summary is retained only if $Q(s) = \sum_i w_i s_i$ exceeds a condition-specific threshold. We evaluate two regimes: *no-filter* (NF), retaining all summaries, and *relative* (REL), removing the bottom 20 % by composite score. An absolute threshold regime (ABS, $\tau = 0.50$) is also tested but proves inoperative on this corpus, as discussed in Sect. 5. Filtering operates on log-probabilities of binary decisions rather than free-form scores, reducing evaluation circularity with respect to the generation model.

Topic Modeling, Stability Assessment and External Validation: Validated summaries are embedded into a semantic space and clustered to reveal coherent thematic structures. We adopt the BERTopic [5] framework combining dimensionality reduction [9] and hierarchical density-based clustering (HDBSCAN) [8]. Cluster-level representations are derived using class-based TF-IDF to identify discriminative terms within each group. Two outlier handling strategies are evaluated: forced reassignment of unclustered documents to their nearest topic via cosine similarity (**OR**), and preservation of outliers as a separate class (**NO**). Intrinsic quality and structural stability 5.2 are then assessed to characterize each configuration. Finally, the discovered topics are externally validated by computing their semantic alignment with the categories of an expert taxonomy. To assess the validity of automated matching, the highest-similarity topic–taxonomy correspondences were further independently examined and validated by two human evaluators.

4 Experimental Protocol

We use a dataset of 3,427 aviation incident reports from the *National Transportation Safety Board*[1] (NTSB), covering 2008–2023, with an average length of 1318.32 characters. Aspect-conditioned summarization is applied with a = incident cause: each aspect-based summary is generated via the chain-of-thought strategy described in Sect. 3 [7,12]. All experiments were conducted on a single NVIDIA RTX 5000 Ada Generation GPU (16 GB), running Mistral 7B v0.3 [6]. Table 1 reports wall-clock latency per pipeline stage over the full 3,427-document corpus.

Table 1. Wall-clock latency per stage (RTX 5000 Ada, `float16`).

Stage	Total	Per doc.
Summarization (Mistral 7B CoT)	∼4 h 30 min	∼4.7 s
CRITIC filtering (UniEval scoring)	∼2 h 15 min	∼2.4 s
Topic modeling (BERTopic)	<4 min	<0.1 s

Topic modeling uses BERTopic with sentence embedding, UMAP (10 neighbors, 10 components, cosine metric, `min_dist=0.0`), and HDBSCAN (minimum

[1] https://www.ntsb.gov/safety/data/Pages/Data_Stats.aspx.

cluster size 15, 5 samples, Euclidean metric, EOM selection, $\varepsilon = 0.1$, soft-clustering enabled). The Euclidean metric operates on the UMAP-reduced space; soft-clustering is required for outlier reassignment.

5 Results

5.1 Qualitative Analysis and Representation Impact

Across all configurations, the choice of input representation is the dominant factor shaping discovered topic structure, consistently superseding algorithmic clustering choices. We examine this shift through two complementary lenses: label-level qualitative structure and hierarchical branching behaviour.

Overview. Tables 2a and 2b contrast the dominant thematic clusters. RAW topics are highly descriptive, situational, and often redundant—anchored to surface form (e.g. *tailwheel, float-equipped*) with low discriminant power for macro-safety analysis. SUM topics are analytical, causal, and normalized, reorganising the same corpus around cognitive failures, loss-of-control mechanisms, and systemic causal chains. This represents a fundamental transformation from raw factual inventory to actionable safety concepts.

Hierarchical Structure. We define *segmentation inertia* as the tendency of a hierarchical topic model to defer thematic resolution by propagating a large, heterogeneous cluster deeper into the tree rather than splitting it into semantically homogeneous sub-branches at higher levels. Both trees exhibit this phenomenon to markedly different degrees. In RAW (37 topics, max depth 12, mean 5.9), early branches at depth ≤ 3 are driven by surface lexical distinctiveness rather than thematic coherence, while the majority of splits (76%) occur late along taxonomic lines such as fuel-system variants or landing-gear subtypes. The SUM tree (50 topics, max depth 22, mean 11.3) retains a long unresolved spine, yet its early branches resolve into mechanistically interpretable classes: bird strike (T41) and turbulence encounter (T32) separate at the root, power loss (T48) at depth 1, and altitude-maintenance failure (T30) at depth 2. We interpret this as a measurable reduction in segmentation inertia induced by summarization: by normalising incident reports into causal predicate structures, the SUM representation increases inter-cluster discriminability at higher levels of the hierarchy, allowing the model to resolve mechanistically distinct accident classes earlier, even as the residual heterogeneity of the dominant class continues to suppress full resolution at depth. Table 3 summarizes the key structural differences.

Taken together, these observations confirm that aspect-conditioned summaries consistently yield more coherent and causally interpretable structures (+35% topic granularity), while RAW representations preserve fine-grained subsystem detail. Industrially, SUM topics are best suited to macro-level causal analysis, strategic safety reporting, taxonomy alignment, and investigator support tools, while RAW topics serve engineering investigation and component reliability studies; the choice of representation should therefore be driven by the primary analytical objective.

Table 2. Dominant thematic clusters in the RAW (a) and SUM (b) topic models (OR-NF configuration).

(a) RAW topic model

Thematic Category	Representative Topics
Fuel and powerplant	Carburetor icing; Magneto failure; Fuel pump malfunction; Fuel selector misuse; Oil starvation; Connecting rod failure
Aircraft configuration	Tailwheel ground loop; Trim system malfunction; Landing gear malfunction; Brake anomalies; Floatplane damage
Environmental	Crosswind landing; High-wind landing; In-flight icing; Severe turbulence
Operational phase	Bounced landing; Takeoff performance shortfall; Traffic pattern conflict; Precautionary diversion
External hazards	Bird strike; Powerline strike
Human physiology	Pilot medical incapacitation

(b) SUM topic model

Thematic Category	Representative Topics
Human factors	Pilot decision-making error; ATC communication breakdown; Non-instrument-rated pilot; Night spatial disorientation; Pilot impairment; Cardiac incapacitation
Loss-of-control	Aerodynamic stall; Low airspeed / angle-of-attack; Directional control loss; Crosswind excursion; Ground loop
Weather	Icing conditions; Severe turbulence; High density altitude; CFIT
Mechanical failures	Engine failure / power loss; Magneto-related power loss; Fuel starvation; Oil non-compliance
Runway events	Runway overrun; Fence collision; Hard landing; Braking degradation
Collision category	Midair / object collision

5.2 Topic Quality and Stability Analysis

We isolate the contribution of each pipeline component through a structured ablation crossing representation type, outlier-handling mode (OR / NO), and filtering regime (NF / REL). Table 4 summarizes the primary quality axes; Tables 6 and 7 detail filtering effects; Table 5 reports per-configuration intrinsic quality.

Intrinsic Quality Metrics. Three embedding-based metrics are computed over the top-k terms ($k = 10$) extracted per topic by class-based TF-IDF, using the same sentence-embedding model as the clustering backbone.

Contextual coherence (Eq. 1) measures the mean pairwise cosine similarity between the sentence-embedding encodings $\mathbf{e}(w_i)$ of the top-k terms of topic u. Higher values indicate that the topic's defining vocabulary is semantically tight in embedding space.

Table 3. Hierarchical topic-tree comparison (RAW vs. SUM): structural contrasts across depth, branching, and label semantics. *Bold* (SUM column only) = structurally superior property of the SUM representation.

Property	RAW	SUM
Topic count	37	**50** (+35%)
Max / mean depth	12 / 5.9	**22 / 11.3**
Topics at depth ≤ 3	9 / 37 (24%)	11 / 50 (22%)
Topics at depth ≤ 7	12 / 37 (32%)	17 / 50 (34%)
Early-split semantics	Peripheral / lexically isolated	**Mechanistically coherent**
Dominant spine length	12 levels	22 levels
Branching pattern	Surface-lexical splits	**Mechanism-driven early splits**

$$\mathrm{Coh}_{\mathrm{ctx}}(u) = \frac{2}{k(k-1)} \sum_{1 \leq i < j \leq k} \cos\big(\mathbf{e}(w_i), \mathbf{e}(w_j)\big) \tag{1}$$

Lexical diversity (Eq. 2) is the ratio of unique terms across all topic vocabularies (flat union $\mathcal{W}$) to total term slots. Low values signal vocabulary overlap between topics, indicative of semantic redundancy.

$$\mathrm{Div}_{\mathrm{lex}} = \frac{|\mathrm{unique}(\mathcal{W})|}{|\mathcal{W}|} \tag{2}$$

Contextualized diversity (Eq. 3) measures inter-topic separability in embedding space, computed as one minus the mean pairwise cosine similarity between topic keyword representations $\mathbf{e}(t_i)$, where t_i denotes the concatenation of the top-k c-TF-IDF terms of topic i.

$$\mathrm{Div}_{\mathrm{ctx}} = 1 - \frac{2}{T(T-1)} \sum_{1 \leq i < j \leq T} \cos\big(\mathbf{e}(t_i), \mathbf{e}(t_j)\big) \tag{3}$$

Intra-cluster CRITIC Score Statistics. The Gini coefficient $G(Q)$ measures the inequality of the CRITIC composite-score Q distribution within each cluster (0 = perfect equality, 1 = maximal concentration), averaged across all clusters. Shannon entropy $H(Q)$ is computed over a 20-bin histogram of per-document Q values within each cluster, measuring score spread in bits. A Kruskal–Wallis H-test assesses whether Q distributions differ significantly across clusters (non-parametric, no normality assumption). Spearman ρ then correlates per-cluster mean Q with per-cluster $\mathrm{Coh}_{\mathrm{ctx}}$, testing whether quality and coherence co-vary or constitute independent evaluation axes.

The ablation reveals a clear hierarchy of impact. **Representation shaping** is the principal gain: switching from RAW to SUM yields +0.012 coherence (OR-NF). **Filtering** acts as a moderate secondary gain, reducing topic count and stabilising clusters. Conversely, **CRITIC weighting** yields only marginal structural improvements: under REL filtering it upweights consistency (+0.059) and

Table 4. Ablation of representation choice and filtering regime (OR mode). Metrics: contextual coherence (Coh_{ctx}), lexical diversity, and ARI between RAW and SUM partitions. ABS ≡ NF throughout ($Q_{\min} = 0.512 > \tau = 0.50$). *Bold* = best value in each RAW/SUM pair; ↑ = SUM strictly better than RAW.

Repr.	Filter	#Topics	Coh_{ctx} ↑	Lex.Div. ↑	ARI(RAW↔SUM)
RAW	NF	37	0.315	**0.741**	0.379
SUM	NF	50	**0.327** ↑	0.718	
RAW	REL	33	0.311	0.767	0.372
SUM	REL	34	**0.320** ↑	**0.782** ↑	

aspect recall (+0.057) while downweighting aspect precision (−0.067), yet its aggregate impact on individual topics remains ≤ +0.41%. CRITIC's utility should be viewed as secondary compared to the gains provided by the representational shift.

Outlier Handling (OR vs. NO). Outlier reassignment (OR) eliminates the unclassified document rate entirely (0.0% vs. up to 29.1% in NO-NF RAW) by injecting marginal documents into their nearest cluster via cosine similarity. This improves corpus coverage but reduces lexical diversity (OR-NF SUM: 0.718 vs. NO-NF SUM: 0.952), as injected documents dilute cluster vocabulary. The ARI is substantially higher in NO configurations when outliers are excluded (NO-NF excluding outliers: 0.575 vs. OR-NF: 0.379; see Table 4), confirming that OR mode partially conflates cluster structure by absorbing heterogeneous documents. The choice between OR and NO depends on corpus completeness requirements: OR guarantees full assignment at the cost of semantic purity; NO preserves cluster integrity at the cost of leaving a share of the corpus unassigned.

CRITIC Filtering (NF vs. REL): Reliability at Scale. The fact that the absolute threshold (ABS, $\tau = 0.50$) is inoperative throughout should not be read as a null result. It is, in fact, the primary reliability finding: the corpus-wide quality floor $Q_{\min} = 0.512$ means that *every single LLM-generated summary* exceeds the absolute quality bar, without exception. In an industrial pipeline operating at scale without any human review loop, this is precisely the passive guarantee that prevents hallucinated or off-aspect representations from silently propagating into topic structures. Even when no document is explicitly removed (NF configuration), CRITIC monitors the composite quality of every ingested representation and would trigger removal the moment any summary fell below acceptable bounds. This transforms CRITIC from a simple filtering lever into a **reliability safeguard against hallucination and aspect drift at scale**, a function that remains active and valuable regardless of whether it visibly removes documents.

Table 5. Intrinsic topic-quality metrics for all effective configurations ($k = 10$, excluding outlier topic -1). *Bold* = best value in each RAW/SUM pair; ↑ = SUM better (higher-is-better); ↓ = SUM better (lower-is-better, outlier rate). †In NO-REL, SUM coherence (0.319) < RAW (0.328): the sole reversal.

Config.	#Topics	Coh_{ctx} ↑	Lex.Div. ↑	Ctx.Div. ↑	Outlier ↓
OR-NF (RAW)	37	0.315	**0.741**	**0.765**	0.0%
OR-NF (SUM)	50	**0.327** ↑	0.718	0.728	0.0%
OR-REL (RAW)	33	0.311	0.767	**0.769**	0.0%
OR-REL (SUM)	34	**0.320** ↑	**0.782** ↑	0.732	0.0%
NO-NF (RAW)	37	0.327	0.935	**0.811**	29.1%
NO-NF (SUM)	50	**0.330** ↑	**0.952** ↑	0.775	**24.3%** ↓
NO-REL (RAW)	33	**0.328**†	0.921	**0.805**	24.0%
NO-REL (SUM)	34	0.319	**0.944** ↑	0.758	**20.8%** ↓

On top of this passive floor, relative filtering (REL, bottom-20%) acts as an active homogenisation lever: it removes the bottom 20% by composite CRITIC score, reducing topic count (−11% for RAW, −32% for SUM), homogenising intra-cluster score distributions (Gini ≈ −38%, entropy ≈ +14%), and reducing the outlier rate by 3.5–5.1 pp in NO mode (RAW: 29.1% → 24.0%; SUM: 24.3% → 20.8%). Structural divergence between RAW and SUM partitions tightens markedly after filtering (JS divergence: 0.051 → 0.005 for OR, 0.057 → 0.008 for NO), confirming corpus homogenisation. Inter-cluster non-uniformity of CRITIC scores is highly significant in all configurations ($p < 10^{-9}$); however, the Spearman correlation between cluster mean quality and Coh_{ctx} is non-significant in seven of eight configurations, confirming that the two evaluation spaces are orthogonal and justify joint use as complementary dimensions.

These results confirm that CRITIC-weighted relative filtering reliably modifies topic structure as a secondary mechanism, while the quality floor it reveals ($Q_{\text{min}} = 0.512$) provides a passive safeguard against silent hallucination failures even in NF configurations. For industrial deployments operating without human review, OR-REL offers the best balance of corpus completeness and cluster homogeneity; the orthogonality of CRITIC scores and sentence-embedding coherence validates retaining both as independent quality signals rather than collapsing them into a single criterion.

Table 6. Experimental configurations and principal characteristics. OR = outlier reassignment; NO = outlier preservation. NF = no filter; REL = relative (bottom-20%). ABS ($Q \geq 0.50$) is omitted: it is inoperative throughout ($Q_{\min} = 0.512 > \tau$), yielding results identical to NF.

Outlier mode	Filter mode	#Docs	Outlier Rate		#Topics	
			RAW	SUM	RAW	SUM
OR	NF	3,427	0.0%	0.0%	37	50
OR	REL (bottom-20%)	2,741	0.0%	0.0%	33	34
NO	NF	3,427	29.1%	24.3%	37	50
NO	REL (bottom-20%)	2,741	24.0%	20.8%	33	34

Table 7. Intra-cluster statistics of CRITIC score Q averaged across all clusters. *Bold* rows = REL configuration (enhancement under REL relative to the matching NF baseline).

Config.	Dataset	$\bar{Q}$ ↑	Gini ↓	Entropy (bits) ↑
OR-NF	RAW	0.897	0.032	3.43
OR-NF	SUM	0.897	0.031	3.36
OR-REL	**RAW**	**0.914**	**0.020**	**3.92**
OR-REL	**SUM**	**0.914**	**0.020**	**3.89**
NO-NF	RAW	0.895	0.032	3.41
NO-NF	SUM	0.896	0.032	3.32
NO-REL	**RAW**	**0.914**	**0.020**	**3.86**
NO-REL	**SUM**	**0.914**	**0.020**	**3.79**

5.3 External Validation with the CICTT Taxonomy

Discovered topics are externally validated with the occurrence categories of the **Commercial Aviation Safety Team / ICAO Common Taxonomy Team** (CICTT v4.7 [2]). Each category is represented by embedding its full textual descriptor, code, name, and official definition using sentence embeddings, yielding a category embedding matrix $\mathbf{C} \in \mathbb{R}^{36 \times d}$. Topics are represented in two ways: (a) **centroid** embeddings, computed as the L2-normalized mean of the sentence-embedding vectors of all member documents, and (b) **keyword** embeddings, computed by embedding the concatenation of each topic's top-k c-TF-IDF terms. The full cosine-similarity matrix $\mathbf{S} \in \mathbb{R}^{T \times 36}$ is computed between topic and category embeddings; a topic–category pair is considered matched if $\max_c \mathbf{S}_{t,c} \geq 0.25$. From this matrix three alignment metrics are derived: **alignment strength** (mean best-match similarity across matched topics); **CICTT coverage** (fraction of the 36 categories matched by at least one topic); and **specificity** (mean number of topics per matched category). Keyword matching achieves higher taxonomic *coverage* than centroid matching across all configurations and is hence used throughout. To assess matching validity, two independent human evaluators reviewed the highest-similarity topic–CICTT correspondences.

Table 8. CICTT alignment metrics by configuration (keyword embeddings). *Bold* = best value in each RAW/SUM pair; ↑ = SUM strictly better than RAW.

Config.	Repr.	Align. Strength ↑	CICTT Cov. (%) ↑	Specificity (top. / cat.) ↑	Paired Topics
OR-NF	RAW kw	0.348	38.9%	2.07	29/37
OR-NF	SUM kw	**0.373** ↑	**50.0%** ↑	**2.56** ↑	46/50
NO-NF	RAW kw	0.336	38.9%	1.93	27/37
NO-NF	SUM kw	**0.378** ↑	**47.2%** ↑	**2.53** ↑	43/50
OR-REL	SUM kw	0.376	41.7%	2.13	32/34
NO-REL	SUM kw	0.370	44.4%	2.00	32/34

Alignment and Coverage. SUM representations drive consistent gains in both alignment strength and CICTT coverage across all configurations (Table 8): coverage climbs from 38.9% to 50.0% under OR-NF, with alignment strength increasing from 0.348 to 0.373. OR-NF SUM achieves the highest paired topic count (46/50) and the highest specificity ratio (2.56 topics per category), confirming that cause-focused representations are systematically more alignable with the CICTT taxonomy framework than surface-form embeddings.

Taxonomic Granularity. Table 9 reveals a granularity gradient corroborated by both human evaluators. Categories with strong terminological markers—ICE (0.664), MED (0.573), FUEL (0.565), MAC (0.520)—align robustly. T32 maps to MED (0.499) rather than TURB: *injuries sustained* and a second-best CABIN match (0.484) confirm the cluster captures turbulence incidents whose salient outcome is crew or passenger injury, correctly coded MED under CICTT. T49 (carburetor icing) is assigned to ICE (0.498); CICTTv4.7 formally codes carburetor icing as FUEL, but the ICE exclusion clause embeds the phrase verbatim, a concrete instance of the proposed automated matching limitation. Broad categories such as LOC-I or CFIT span multiple sub-topics and resist single-topic mapping; specificity values above 2.0 (Table 8) reflect this multi-topic coverage.

Table 9. Top-8 topic ↔ CICTT correspondences (OR-NF SUM, keyword embeddings), ranked by cosine similarity.

Topic	CICTT Category	Max Sim.	Representative topic terms
T25	ICE: Icing	0.664	icing conditions, decision fly, weather cond.
T05	MED: Medical	0.573	pilot impaired, pilot impairment, medical condition
T00	FUEL: Fuel Related	0.565	fuel tank, fuel selector, fuel starvation
T08	MAC: Mid-air Collision	0.520	mid air, air traffic, situational awareness
T32	MED: Medical	0.499	flight crew, turbulence encountered, injuries sustained
T49	ICE: Icing	0.498	carburetor icing, carburetor heat, glide power
T41	BIRD: Bird Strike	0.479	bird strike, incident collision, right wing
T38	LOC-I: Loss of Control–Inflight	0.445	loss control, test flight, pilot lack

Maximum coverage of 50.0% (18 of 36 categories) is distinct from the topic-level match rate of 92% (46/50). The 18 uncovered categories may reflect: low incident frequency in the corpus (GTOW, LOLI, EVAC, WILD, GCOL); lexical overlap with adjacent covered categories (CABIN with MED/TURB, UIMC with LOC-I, AMAN with TURB); and the multi-causal nature of residual categories (ATM, ADRM, NAV, OTHR, UNK).

6 Recommendations for Industrial Deployment

The empirical results expose a fundamental tension between corpus coverage and semantic purity; the following scenario-specific recommendations address it.

Regulatory Reporting and CICTT Pre-coding. Use **OR-NF + SUM**: maximises CICTT coverage (50.0%), guarantees zero outliers, and produces the highest paired topic count (46/50) and specificity ratio (2.56). Reduced lexical diversity (0.718) from marginal document injection is acceptable when completeness takes priority; the CRITIC floor ($Q_{\min} = 0.512$) provides a passive hallucination safeguard at no filtering cost.

Interpretable Topic Analysis and Investigator Support. Use **OR-REL + SUM**: REL filtering homogenises intra-cluster quality (Gini $\approx -38\%$) and reduces topic count to 34, while OR maintains zero outliers. CICTT coverage drops to 41.7%, but cleaner cluster semantics make topics easier to label, audit, and act on in analyst-facing interfaces.

Semantic Purity and Qualitative Research. Use **NO-NF + SUM**: preserves the highest lexical diversity (0.952) and cluster integrity (ARI 0.575), at a 24.3% outlier cost. Unclassified documents form an informative atypical-incident set meriting targeted review.

Fine-Grained Engineering Investigation. Use **RAW representation**: retains subsystem-level granularity (carburetor icing, magneto failure, tailwheel ground loops) suited to component reliability and maintenance analytics, complementing SUM's causal macro-framing as a parallel corpus for multi-view analysis.

RAG Integration and Incident Retrieval. Use **OR-NF + SUM**: topic-indexed clusters serve as structured retrieval units for few-shot CICTT coding, anomaly detection, or cross-fleet comparison; full document assignment and the CRITIC floor ensure passive consistency without per-query filtering overhead.

7 Conclusion, Perspectives and Limitations

This work shows that topic modeling quality is primarily representation-driven: the projection of documents into semantic space, determines the discovered thematic structure. By conceptualizing an LLM as an aspect-conditioned representation operator, we demonstrate that cause-focused representations of aviation incident reports yield topics that are more coherent, lexically diverse, and better aligned with the CICTT taxonomy than those derived from raw embeddings. CRITIC-weighted filtering acts as a complementary mechanism for corpus homogenization. The moderate ARI between RAW and SUM partitions confirms these are distinct semantic structures, each suited to different analytical goals: SUM topics support causal macro-analysis and taxonomy alignment, while RAW topics preserve technical micro-granularity for engineering investigation. Aspect conditioning, implemented here via chain-of-thought prompting with an LLM, thus offers a principled way to align topic structures with user-defined objectives, unlike standard pipelines with fixed surface-text representations. A direct extension perspective for this work is multi-aspect topic modeling: applying several aspect representations in parallel to obtain complementary views of the same corpus.

Limitations. (1) *Prompt dependency*: summary content is sensitive to prompt formulation; systematic ablations over prompt templates and chain-of-thought depth remain unexplored. (2) *Generation and model bias*: the LLM may introduce biases from pretraining data; sensitivity to summarization model and embedder choice has not been characterized. (3) *Pipeline stability*: topic structures depend on UMAP and HDBSCAN hyperparameter choices; a broader stability analysis has not been conducted. (4) *Computational cost*: generating aspect-based summaries at scale requires quantization or batch-optimized inference. (5) *Risk of taxonomic bias amplification*: improved CICTT alignment may partly reflect lexical memorization of taxonomy vocabulary rather than genuine semantic projection. (6) *Human validation scope*: taxonomic matching was reviewed by two evaluators; a broader expert panel with formal inter-annotator agreement computation is warranted. (7) *Quality weighting design choices*: the CRITIC aggregation scheme relies on statistical assumptions that may not generalize across corpora with different properties. Limitations (1)–(3) and (6) constitute the primary directions for future investigation.

References

1. Blei, D.M., Ng, A.Y., Jordan, M.I.: Latent dirichlet allocation. J. Mach. Learn. Res. **3**(null), 993–1022 (2003)
2. CAST/ICAO Common Taxonomy Team: Aviation Occurrence Categories: Definitions and Usage Notes. Technical report, International Civil Aviation Organization (2013), version 4.7. https://www.icao.int/safety/AIG/cictt
3. Diakoulaki, D., Mavrotas, G., Papayannakis, L.: Determining objective weights in multiple criteria problems: The CRITIC method. Comput. Oper. Res. **22**(7), 763–770 (1995)
4. Frermann, L., Klementiev, A.: Inducing document structure for aspect-based summarization. In: Korhonen, A., Traum, D., Màrquez, L. (eds.) Proceedings of the 57th Annual Meeting of the Association for Computational Linguistics, Association for Computational Linguistics, Florence, Italy (2019)
5. Grootendorst, M.: Bertopic: Neural topic modeling with a class-based tf-idf procedure (2022). https://doi.org/10.48550/arXiv.2203.05794

6. Jiang, A.Q., et al.: Mistral 7b (2023)
7. Liu, Q., Li, F., Ng, K.K.H., Han, J., Feng, S.: Accident investigation via llms reasoning: Hfacs-guided chain-of-thoughts enhance general aviation safety. Expert Syst. Appl. (2025). (in press)
8. McInnes, L., Healy, J., Astels, S.: hdbscan: Hierarchical density based clustering. J. Open Source Softw. **2** (2017). https://doi.org/10.21105/joss.00205
9. McInnes, L., Healy, J., Melville, J.: Umap: Uniform manifold approximation and projection for dimension reduction (2020). https://doi.org/10.21105/joss.00861
10. Pham, C.M., Hoyle, A., Sun, S., Resnik, P., Iyyer, M.: TopicGPT: A prompt-based topic modeling framework. In: Duh, K., Gomez, H., Bethard, S. (eds.) Proceedings of the 2024 Conference of the North American Chapter of the Association for Computational Linguistics: Human Language Technologies (Volume 1: Long Papers). Association for Computational Linguistics, Mexico City, Mexico (2024)
11. Takeshita, S., Green, T., Reinig, I., Eckert, K., Ponzetto, S.: ACLSum: A new dataset for aspect-based summarization of scientific publications. In: Duh, K., Gomez, H., Bethard, S. (eds.) Proceedings of the 2024 Conference of the North American Chapter of the Association for Computational Linguistics: Human Language Technologies (Volume 1: Long Papers). Association for Computational Linguistics, Mexico City, Mexico (2024)
12. Wei, J., et al.: Chain-of-thought prompting elicits reasoning in large language models. Adv. Neural Inf. Process. Syst. **35**, 24824–24837 (2022). https://doi.org/10.48550/arXiv.2201.11903
13. Zhong, M., et al.: Unieval: A unified metric for evaluating natural language generation. In: Proceedings of the 2022 Conference on Empirical Methods in Natural Language Processing, pp. 1336–1350. Association for Computational Linguistics (2022). https://doi.org/10.18653/v1/2022.emnlp-main.89

A Practical Evaluation Methodology for Generative AI in Maintenance Applications: Accuracy and Carbon Footprint

Najwa Er-rachidy(✉), Mounir Bechchi, and Dominique Chabot

Ocode, 322b Route du Puy Charpentreau, 85000 La Roche-sur-Yon, France
{najwa.errachidy,mounir,dominique}@o-code.co

Abstract. Ocode develops a digital maintenance log system based on a low-energy blockchain infrastructure, ensuring traceability and secure data sharing for assets such as vehicles, bicycles, housing, and high-value goods. With the emergence of generative AI, these logbooks are evolving into intelligent assistants capable of extracting relevant information, detecting inconsistencies, and supporting proactive asset management. The current implementation relies on cloud-based Large Language Models (LLMs) combined with Retrieval-Augmented Generation (RAG).

Although effective, this architecture raises concerns regarding data privacy and sovereignty, dependence on external providers, and the environmental cost of LLM inference. To address these challenges, we explore the use of Small Language Models (SLMs), which can be deployed in controlled environments, offering improved data governance and a lower carbon footprint while maintaining competitive performance.

However, the adoption of SLMs is hindered by the lack of standardized evaluation methodologies. This paper introduces a carbon-aware evaluation framework based on two key metrics: response accuracy and carbon footprint per request. The methodology supports informed industrial decision-making when choosing between local SLMs and external LLM services, and is validated using the IFEval benchmark to ensure reproducibility.

Our results highlight the trade-offs between performance and environmental impact, demonstrating that mid-sized models offer a strong balance between instruction-following capabilities and operational sustainability, paving the way for more frugal and trustworthy generative AI systems in industrial maintenance contexts.

Keywords: Industrial Maintenance · Generative AI · Small Language Models · Evaluation Methodology · Carbon Footprint · Data Sovereignty and Privacy

1 Introduction

The recent emergence of LLMs has significantly accelerated the adoption of generative AI across a wide range of industrial applications [1,2]. These models are

G. Andresini et al. (Eds.): ISMIS 2026, LNAI 16685, pp. 166–184, 2027.
https://doi.org/10.1007/978-3-032-32643-0_15

no longer limited to experimental settings and are now deployed in production systems, enabling new forms of automation and human–machine collaboration [3,4].

At Ocode [5], we have developed a digital maintenance log system for physical assets such as vehicles, bicycles, housing, and high-value goods applications [6,7]. Each asset is associated with a unique digital identity, implemented as a Non-Fungible Token (NFT) on a low-energy blockchain infrastructure. This system ensures the traceability, authenticity, and immutability of all documents and events throughout the asset lifecycle. The logbook is collaboratively maintained by various stakeholders (e.g., manufacturers, certified repairers, service providers, and end-users), creating a shared and trusted data environment.

LLMs open new opportunities to enhance this ecosystem. First, they streamline data contribution by stakeholders, making the logbook significantly easier to maintain. Instead of relying on manual entry, structured data formats, or complex APIs, documents such as maintenance invoices can be directly ingested and processed using RAG techniques to automatically classify them, associate them with the correct asset, and extract relevant information [8–10]. Second, LLMs enable a shift toward a user-centric intelligent assistant capable of providing actionable insights, such as maintenance reminders, detecting inconsistencies in records, and supporting end-users in proactively managing their assets [11].

In our current implementation, we rely on state-of-the-art LLMs available through SaaS APIs (e.g., OpenAI, Mistral). While effective in terms of performance, this architecture raises several critical issues. First, the reliance on external providers introduces major concerns regarding data privacy and sovereignty [12–15], as sensitive maintenance records and user interactions are processed outside Ocode's infrastructure. Second, it creates a strong technological and economic dependency on third-party providers, which can become unsustainable when scaling to large user bases. Third, the high computational requirements of these models lead to significant operational costs and a growing environmental footprint [16,17]. These limitations are particularly critical in industrial contexts, where data governance, cost predictability, and sustainability are key requirements.

To mitigate these issues, SLMs are emerging as a promising alternative [18–23]. By being deployed within controlled or local infrastructures, SLMs offer significant advantages in terms of data privacy, reduced operational costs, and a smaller environmental footprint. However, the adoption of SLM-based architectures remains limited by the lack of a clear and practical methodology to evaluate such systems. In particular, organizations lack practical tools to assess whether SLMs can effectively replace or complement LLMs under real-world constraints.

Adopting SLMs in place of LLMs requires a clear understanding of the trade-offs involved, particularly to assess whether these models can achieve comparable performance in terms of response quality while effectively minimizing their carbon impact.

Despite the growing interest in efficient and sustainable AI, existing evaluation approaches typically consider performance and environmental impact in isolation. This fragmentation limits their usefulness for industrial decision-making, where these dimensions must be jointly optimized.

In this paper, we propose an integrated and carbon-aware methodology for evaluating generative AI architectures, structured around two key metrics: accuracy and carbon footprint per generated tokens. A hybrid approach combining direct measurements and empirical extrapolation is adopted to reduce the footprint of the evaluation itself while preserving the ability to analyze scaling trends. Experimental evaluations are primarily conducted on SLMs, while a single intermediate-size model (20B parameters) is used as a reference LLM. Performance results for larger models are collected from public benchmark leaderboards, and their carbon footprint is estimated using empirical relationships between model size and energy consumption derived from our experiments.

The main contributions of this paper are as follows:

- We propose a carbon-aware evaluation methodology that jointly considers accuracy and environmental impact for generative AI systems.
- We introduce a stabilization-based evaluation protocol that reduces the computational cost of benchmarking while ensuring reliable performance estimation.
- We provide an empirical analysis of trade-offs between SLMs and LLMs using a controlled instruction-following benchmark, with implications for our industrial asset management assistant.
- We derive practical design guidelines for deploying efficient, trustworthy, and environmentally sustainable generative AI systems in industrial environments.

The methodology is validated on the IFEval benchmark [24], enabling reproducible and automated evaluation of instruction-following capabilities.

The remainder of this paper is organized as follows: Sect. 2 provides a review of related work on Large and Small Language Models, the carbon footprint associated with LLMs, and the need for improved evaluation frameworks for generative AI systems, especially in industrial contexts. Section 3 describes the evaluation methodology, covering the setup, evaluation metrics, benchmark selection, model selection strategy, and experimental protocol. Section 4 presents the experimental results obtained using the proposed methodology. Section 5 discusses the methodological choices underlying the evaluation protocol, interprets the main findings, and highlights the practical implications and limitations of the proposed approach. Finally, Sect. 6 concludes the paper and outlines future work.

2 Related Work

Large Language Models have demonstrated strong performance across a wide range of tasks, but this performance comes at a high cost. Their massive number of parameters requires substantial computational and energy resources [4], leading to significant operational expenses and carbon emissions. This raises major concerns regarding the sustainability of large-scale AI deployment [25,26].

These limitations are particularly critical in industrial contexts, where cost control, data governance, and environmental impact are key constraints.

Small Language Models and Efficient Architectures
The emergence of open-source models of moderate size—typically below 20 billion parameters—offers a viable alternative to proprietary solutions [27–30]. These SLMs benefit from advanced compression techniques, such as quantization, which reduce memory requirements and accelerate inference while maintaining competitive performance. Their ability to run in controlled environments makes them particularly suitable for industrial applications requiring data sovereignty and predictable costs.

Evaluation of Generative AI Systems
Despite these advances, evaluating LLM- and SLM-based systems remains a major challenge. Existing approaches primarily focus on accuracy, while environmental impact is often considered separately or overlooked [31]. In addition, many evaluation frameworks rely on LLM-based judges, introducing cost and reproducibility issues [32]. In industrial contexts, evaluation must also capture deterministic behavior and strict instruction-following, which are not always reflected in standard benchmarks.

Carbon Footprint and Green AI
The environmental impact of AI systems has gained increasing attention. Prior work has highlighted the significant carbon footprint of large-scale models and advocated for more efficient and transparent practices. However, most studies focus on training costs, while fewer address inference-time carbon footprint under controlled experimental conditions, which is critical for real-world deployment.

Positioning of This Work
This paper proposes a carbon-aware evaluation methodology that jointly considers accuracy and inference-time carbon footprint within a controlled and reproducible experimental setup. The proposed approach emphasizes low-cost evaluation through a stabilization-based protocol and targets practical decision-making in industrial deployment scenarios.

3 Evaluation and Experimental Design

To support the design of Ocode's generative AI–based system, we propose a controlled and reproducible evaluation methodology for comparing generative AI models under operational constraints. The objective is to assess different modeling strategies across two key dimensions: response accuracy and carbon footprint.

Given the challenges associated with measuring these metrics in production environments, our approach relies on controlled experimentation, combined with application-driven interpretation to ensure relevance to industrial use cases.

Importantly, the experimental protocol focuses exclusively on models that can be executed in a controlled local environment. This choice ensures accurate measurement of energy consumption and avoids the uncertainty associated with external infrastructures.

3.1 Motivation for a Controlled Experimental Setup

Evaluating generative AI systems in real-world conditions presents several challenges:

- variability in user inputs
- limited observability of system-level metrics in cloud environments
- difficulty in measuring energy consumption for API-based models

In particular, proprietary LLMs accessed through APIs do not provide direct access to hardware-level information, making precise measurement of energy usage and carbon footprint impractical. To address these limitations, we adopt a controlled experimental setup, where all measurements are performed locally. This approach provides:

- **full observability** of resource usage
- **accurate energy measurement**
- **reproducibility of results**
- **fair comparison across models**

3.2 Setup

All experiments were conducted on a controlled local environment to ensure reproducibility and accurate measurement of system-level metrics, in particular energy consumption.

The hardware configuration consists of a machine equipped with an 8-core 2.3 GHz Intel Core i9 processor, 16 GB of DDR4 RAM (2667 MHz), and both integrated and dedicated GPUs (Intel UHD Graphics 630 and AMD Radeon Pro 5500M with 4 GB of VRAM). In practice, all model inferences were executed on the CPU in order to maintain consistent and measurable energy consumption across experiments.

This choice is motivated by the need for reliable carbon estimation, as CPU-based execution provides more stable and interpretable energy measurements compared to heterogeneous GPU usage, where variability can be higher depending on drivers, memory transfers, and hardware scheduling. The implications of this choice are discussed in Sect. 5.

Only hardware characteristics that directly impact inference performance and energy consumption are reported. Other system details (e.g., operating system configuration or background processes) were kept stable throughout the experiments but are not expected to significantly influence the comparative results.

All models were executed in a local environment under identical conditions, ensuring that differences in performance and carbon footprint can be attributed to model characteristics rather than infrastructure variability.

3.3 Evaluation Metrics

While this setup does not fully capture real-world variability, it enables rigorous and reproducible analysis of fundamental trade-offs between performance and environmental impact. We define two complementary metrics to evaluate generative AI systems:

- **Accuracy**: measured as the proportion of tasks for which the model correctly follows the instruction, using deterministic evaluation criteria.
- **Carbon footprint**: estimated as the energy consumption per generated token, converted into carbon emissions using a region-specific carbon intensity factor (approximately $50gCO_2/kWh$ corresponding to the French electricity grid).

These metrics are jointly analyzed to capture trade-offs between performance and sustainability, which are critical in industrial deployment scenarios.

3.4 Benchmark Selection

We rely on the IFEval benchmark [24] as a reference framework for evaluation. This benchmark was selected for the following reasons:

- **Deterministic evaluation**
  Each task is evaluated using rule-based criteria, producing a binary outcome (success or failure), which avoids subjective interpretation.
- **No dependency on external evaluators**
  Unlike many recent benchmarks, IFEval does not require an additional language model to evaluate outputs, ensuring that the experimental cost remains controlled.
- **Automation and scalability**
  The benchmark allows systematic execution across a large number of tasks.
- **Relevance to our assistant**
  Instruction-following capabilities evaluated by IFEval are directly related to core functionalities of our assistant, such as structured document information extraction and response generation.

Although IFEval is not domain-specific, it provides a controlled and reproducible proxy for evaluating instruction-following behavior that is directly relevant to industrial document-centric applications. Table 1 illustrates how IFEval task categories map onto representative tasks encountered in the Ocode maintenance assistant system.

Table 1. Mapping between IFEval task types and real-world maintenance tasks at Ocode.

IFEval Task Type	Equivalent Task in Ocode System
Structured output generation	Extracting date, intervention type, and cost from a maintenance invoice into a predefined JSON format
Instruction following with constraints	Generating a structured intervention report complying with asset-specific templates
Length-constrained responses	Summarizing an asset's maintenance history within a fixed character limit
Format-constrained generation	Producing a maintenance reminder message following a standardized notification format

For instance, a typical maintenance task in the Ocode system requires the model to extract the date, type of intervention, and associated cost from an unstructured invoice and return them in a predefined JSON format. This is structurally equivalent to IFEval's structured output generation tasks, where the model must produce a response conforming to a specific format under explicit constraints. Similarly, generating a maintenance reminder or an intervention summary requires the model to follow length and formatting instructions—capabilities directly assessed by IFEval. This mapping justifies the use of IFEval as a meaningful proxy benchmark, even in the absence of a domain-specific evaluation dataset.

3.5 Model Selection Strategy

The experimental study focuses on small and medium-scale open source language models [33] that can be executed in a controlled local environment. This choice is driven by the need to obtain accurate and reproducible measurements of performance and energy consumption.

We consider models with fewer than approximately 20 billion parameters, which are compatible with on-premise or private infrastructures. These models can be instrumented with energy measurement tools and therefore enable precise estimation of their carbon footprint. In addition, they represent realistic alternatives to API-based large language models in industrial settings where data sovereignty, cost control, and environmental impact are critical concerns.

All selected models are evaluated through direct experimentation under identical controlled conditions to ensure fair comparison.

Large proprietary models accessed through APIs are not included in the experimental measurements. This limitation is primarily due to the lack of access to hardware-level information, which prevents reliable measurement of energy consumption. Furthermore, the variability introduced by remote infrastructures makes it difficult to ensure consistent and reproducible evaluation conditions.

However, rather than excluding these models entirely from the analysis, performance results for frontier proprietary models are obtained through two complementary approaches: GPT-4o is directly evaluated via its API on a fixed sample of IFEval tasks under a simplified protocol, while Mistral Large 2.1 is included as a publicly reported leaderboard reference. In both cases, their carbon footprint is estimated using empirical relationships between model size and energy consumption derived from our local experiments, as direct hardware-level measurement is not accessible for API-based models. This allows us to include frontier models as qualitative reference points in the discussion, without relying on direct measurements or unsupported quantitative assumptions. By focusing on measurable and reproducible settings while limiting unnecessary large-scale experimentation, this approach balances scientific rigor with environmental responsibility—in line with the core principles guiding this study.

Finally, frontier large language models are included in the discussion as reference points for performance and current industry practices, using a combination of direct API evaluation under a simplified protocol and publicly reported benchmark scores. This combined approach enables us to maintain experimental rigor while ensuring practical relevance for real-world system design.

3.6 Experimental Protocol

The experimental protocol is designed to ensure consistent, robust, and environmentally efficient evaluation across all considered models. In addition to reproducibility and fairness, the protocol explicitly aims to minimize the carbon footprint of the evaluation process itself. All experiments are conducted using the IFEval benchmark, from which tasks are incrementally sampled rather than exhaustively executed. For each task $t \in \tau$, a standardized prompt is provided to the model, which generates a response evaluated using a deterministic success/failure criterion. This evaluation produces a binary outcome:

$$S_t = \begin{cases} 1 & \text{if the instruction is correctly followed} \\ 0 & \text{otherwise} \end{cases} \quad (1)$$

The performance of a model is then estimated as the empirical mean over the sampled tasks:

$$\widehat{P_n} = \frac{1}{n} \sum_{t=1}^{n} s_t \quad (2)$$

where n is the number of evaluated tasks.

Instead of fixing the number of evaluated tasks in advance, tasks are processed incrementally and the performance estimate is monitored using a sliding window of size $W_P = 30$. After each new task, the coefficient of variation (CV), defined as the ratio of the standard deviation to the mean, is computed over the current window:

$$CV_P = \frac{\sigma(\widehat{P}_{n-W_{p+1}}, ..., \widehat{P}_n)}{\mu(\widehat{P}_{n-W_{p+1}}, ..., \widehat{P}_n)} \quad (3)$$

The stopping criterion is applied only after a minimum of $n_{min} = 50$ tasks have been evaluated. From that point, evaluation stops when $CV_P \leq 0.02$ holds over two consecutive windows, i.e., at step n and $n+1$, ensuring that convergence is not declared upon a transient drop. As for the upper bound, it is not imposed on the number of tasks, so evaluation continues until stabilization is genuinely reached. This approach yields a reliable performance estimate while avoiding unnecessary computations and reducing the overall carbon footprint.

In addition to performance evaluation, system-level metrics are collected during dedicated measurement phases for each inference, including token usage and energy consumption.

Energy is measured using *CodeCarbon* [34,35], which provides an estimate of the energy consumed during execution. Carbon emissions are then derived using a region-specific carbon intensity factor.

To estimate the carbon footprint, each task is executed multiple times in order to capture variability in runtime conditions. Let $E_{(t,i)}$ denote the energy consumed during the i-th execution of task t, and $N_{(t,i)}$ the number of generated tokens. The average energy per token is computed as:

$$\overline{e_t} = \frac{1}{k} \sum_{i=1}^{k} \frac{E_{t,i}}{N_{t,i}} \tag{4}$$

where k is the number of repetitions.

This number is not fixed in advance. Instead, after each new execution, the coefficient of variation is computed over a sliding window of size $W_C = 5$:

$$CV_C = \frac{\sigma(\overline{e}_{n-W_{C+1}}, \dots, \overline{e}_n)}{\mu(\overline{e}_{n-W_{C+1}}, \dots, \overline{e}_n)} \tag{5}$$

Repetitions stop when $CV_C \leq 0.02$ is satisfied over *two consecutive windows*, i.e., at steps k and $k+1$, subject to a minimum of $K_{min} = 5$ and a maximum of $K_{max} = 30$ repetitions. If stabilization is not reached by K_{max}, the estimate computed at that point is retained.

The final carbon footprint is expressed using normalized indicators, primarily **emissions per $10k$ generated tokens**, which provides a consistent basis for comparing models with different output lengths.

All experiments are conducted under controlled conditions to ensure fair comparison across models. The same prompts, generation parameters, and token limits are used throughout the evaluation, and all models are executed on the same hardware environment.

Overall, this protocol combines controlled benchmarking, statistical stabilization, and carbon-aware design. It provides a practical and reproducible framework for evaluating generative AI systems, while explicitly minimizing the environmental impact of the experimental process itself.

4 Results and Analysis

This section presents the experimental results obtained using the proposed evaluation methodology. We analyze model performance, carbon footprint, and the trade-offs between them, with a focus on implications for industrial deployment.

4.1 Performance Across Models

The evaluation results show that performance generally improves with model size, but this trend is neither strictly monotonic nor linear. (Fig. 1). Several small and medium-sized models (e.g., in the 2B–4B range) achieve performance levels comparable to significantly larger models. In particular, some models around 3B–4B parameters reach scores above 0.80, approaching the performance of larger models.

Conversely, certain larger models (e.g., 8B and above) do not consistently outperform smaller ones, highlighting variability in model efficiency across architectures and training strategies.

Additionally, the fitted trend line indicates a clear saturation effect, where performance gains become progressively smaller as model size increases. This suggests that beyond a certain scale, increasing model size yields limited improvements in instruction-following capability.

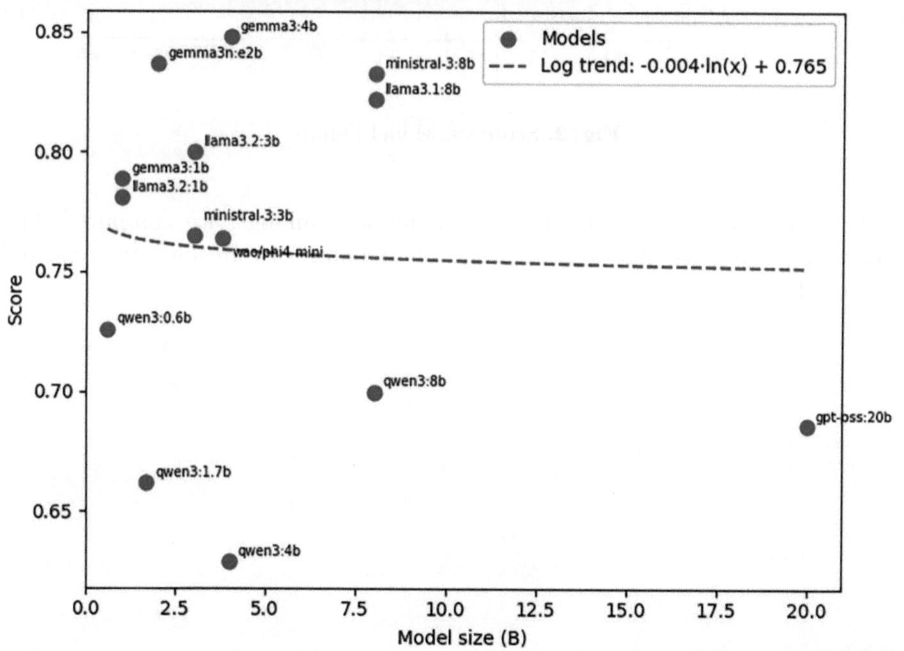

Fig. 1. Score vs. Model Size

Beyond model size, the results reveal significant differences across model families (Fig. 2). Models with similar parameter counts can exhibit noticeably different performance levels, reflecting the impact of architectural choices, training data, and optimization strategies. A striking example is the contrast between gemma3:4b (0.848) and qwen3:4b (0.629), two models of identical size whose performance differs by more than 0.21 points—a gap large enough to provide strong evidence of a statistically significant difference, as their confidence intervals (Table 2) do not overlap .

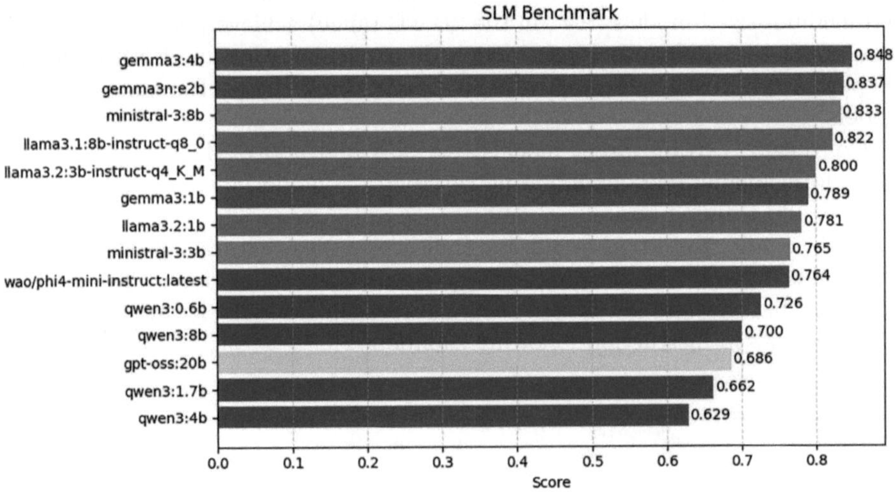

Fig. 2. Score vs. Model Family

To assess the statistical reliability of model rankings, we computed 95% bootstrap confidence intervals for all evaluated models. Results are reported in Table 2.

Table 2. Accuracy scores with 95% bootstrap confidence intervals

Model	n	Accuracy	95% CI
gemma3:4b	66	0.848	[0.758, 0.924]
gemma3n:e2b	43	0.837	[0.721, 0.930]
ministral-3:8b	54	0.833	[0.722, 0.926]
llama3.1:8b	45	0.822	[0.711, 0.933]
llama3.2:3b	75	0.800	[0.707, 0.880]
gemma3:1b	76	0.789	[0.697, 0.882]
llama3.2:1b	73	0.781	[0.685, 0.877]
ministral-3:3b	85	0.765	[0.671, 0.847]
wao/phi4-mini	72	0.764	[0.667, 0.861]
qwen3:0.6b	84	0.726	[0.631, 0.821]
qwen3:8b	100	0.700	[0.610, 0.790]
gpt-oss:20b	70	0.686	[0.571, 0.786]
qwen3:1.7b	74	0.662	[0.554, 0.770]
qwen3:4b	97	0.629	[0.536, 0.722]

The results suggest the presence of a high-performing cluster of models—gemma3:4b, gemma3n:e2b, ministral-3:8b, llama3.1:8b, and llama3.2:3b—with overlapping confidence intervals, indicating that within this group, performance differences are not statistically distinguishable.

This is itself a meaningful finding: within this cluster, model architecture and training strategy outweigh the effect of model size in determining performance. Notably, llama3.2:3b (3B parameters) is statistically indistinguishable from llama3.1:8b (8B parameters), despite being less than half the size.

A second observation concerns the qwen3 family, which exhibits unusually high variability across scales. qwen3:0.6b (0.726) outperforms both qwen3:1.7b (0.662) and qwen3:4b (0.629), with non-overlapping confidence intervals providing strong evidence of a statistically significant difference. This suggests that within this family, smaller models may have been more specifically optimized for instruction-following tasks.

The relatively small number of evaluated tasks per model (43–100) explains the width of the intervals. Larger sample sizes would yield narrower estimates, and this is acknowledged as a limitation of the current study.

4.2 Carbon Footprint Across Models

The analysis of energy consumption shows a clear and consistent increase in carbon emissions as model size grows (Fig. 3). Even within the range of locally executable models, the difference in carbon footprint between the smallest and largest models is substantial.

Smaller models exhibit very low emissions per generated token, while mid-sized models show moderate increases. Larger models, on the other hand, incur significantly higher carbon costs, reflecting their increased computational requirements.

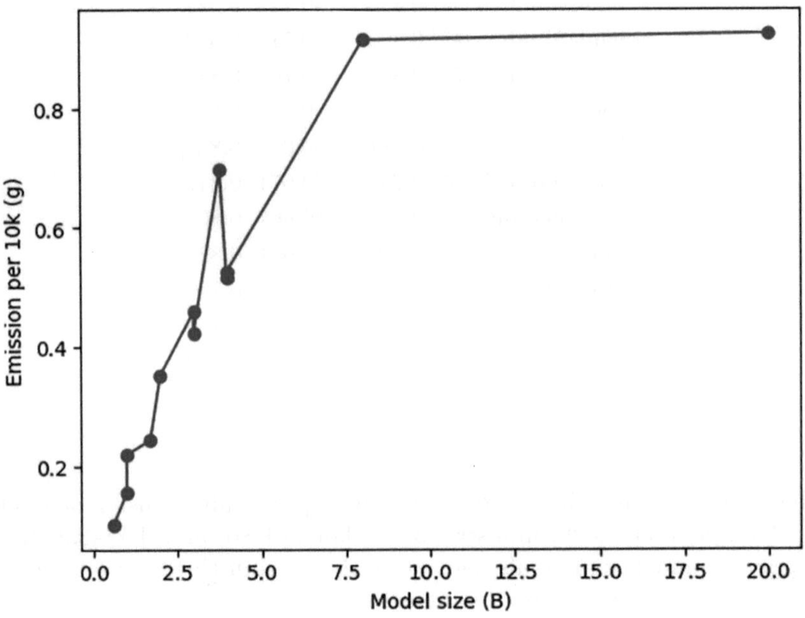

Fig. 3. Carbon Emission vs Model Size

Carbon footprint increases significantly with model size, leading to large disparities in environmental impact across evaluated models.

4.3 Performance–Carbon Trade-Off

When considering performance and carbon footprint jointly, a clear trade-off emerges. While larger models may provide marginal improvements in performance, these gains come at a disproportionately higher environmental cost.

Models in the mid-size range (approximately 2B–4B parameters) tend to offer the most favorable balance. They achieve high performance levels while maintaining moderate carbon emissions, making them particularly attractive for practical deployment. Importantly, since the top-performing models in this range are statistically indistinguishable in accuracy, the carbon footprint becomes the decisive criterion for selecting among them—favoring smaller models within the top cluster.

In contrast, the largest evaluated models provide limited additional performance despite significantly higher energy consumption. gpt-oss:20b (0.686) is a particularly illustrative case: despite being the largest locally evaluated model, its accuracy falls below that of several models with fewer than 4B parameters, with non-overlapping confidence intervals providing strong evidence of a genuine performance difference with the top cluster. Combined with its high carbon cost (0.924g CO_2 per 10k tokens—among the highest observed), this makes it one of the least efficient models evaluated across both dimensions jointly.

4.4 Implications for Larger Models

The observed scaling trend strongly suggests that larger models incur substantially higher environmental costs. Given the saturation effect observed in performance, this implies a growing imbalance between marginal performance gains and additional resource consumption.

To assess how frontier proprietary models compare under our protocol, we evaluated GPT-4o via its API on a fixed sample of 200 IFEval tasks. Running the full stabilization protocol on large API-based models was deliberately avoided, as it would contradict the environmental responsibility principles motivating this work; this estimate therefore carries higher uncertainty than our locally stabilized measurements. GPT-4o achieved 86.50% on this sample, compared to 84.8% for our best locally evaluated model (gemma3:4b). While this suggests a slight performance advantage for GPT-4o, the observed difference remains small relative to the uncertainty in our estimates and should therefore be interpreted with caution. In particular, the two results are not directly comparable from a statistical standpoint, as they rely on different evaluation protocols and sample sizes. Notably, this result differs from the 81.0% reported on OpenAI's official GPT-4.1 introduction blog [36], which likely reflects differences in evaluation setup, prompt formatting, or model version. This discrepancy itself illustrates why controlled and reproducible evaluation conditions matter—and further motivates the methodology proposed in this paper. As a complementary reference, the publicly reported IFEval score for Mistral Large 2.1 (Instruct-2411) is 84.01% [37].

These results confirm that the performance gap between top SLMs and frontier LLMs is narrow on structured instruction-following tasks. This marginal difference, however, is expected to come at a substantially higher environmental cost. While not directly measured in this study, larger models with tens or hundreds of billions of parameters generally require significantly greater computational resources for inference, and are therefore likely to exhibit markedly higher energy consumption than the mid-sized models evaluated here.

This reinforces the central argument of this paper: for a wide range of industrial tasks, the marginal performance gains offered by frontier LLMs do not justify their substantially higher environmental and operational costs. Locally deployable SLMs in the 2B–4B range represent a compelling alternative, combining near-frontier performance on instruction-following tasks with a fraction of the carbon footprint.

5 Discussion and Limitations

The proposed methodology provides a controlled and reproducible framework for evaluating generative AI systems with respect to both accuracy and carbon footprint. The results highlight the practical value of carbon-aware evaluation for industrial decision-making, particularly when comparing locally deployable SLMs with larger API-based LLMs. Importantly, the evaluation protocol was itself designed to limit its environmental impact: experiments were conducted without GPU acceleration, and frontier proprietary models such as GPT-4o and Mistral Large 2.1 were not subjected to extensive repeated testing. This choice reflects a deliberate effort to keep the evaluation process aligned with the carbon-aware principles of the study. However, several methodological choices and scope limitations should be considered when interpreting the results.

CPU-Only Execution. All experiments were conducted on CPU to ensure stable and interpretable energy measurements. This choice was also motivated by the objective of keeping the evaluation process itself lightweight and carbon-aware, by avoiding the additional energy overhead associated with GPU-based experimentation. This setup provides a reproducible baseline for comparing models under identical conditions, but it does not reflect the latency and throughput achievable in GPU-accelerated production environments, where absolute energy values per token would differ. We expect the relative ordering of models in terms of carbon footprint to remain broadly consistent across hardware configurations, as it is primarily driven by parameter count and number of generated tokens. Nevertheless, validating this assumption on GPU hardware remains an important direction for future work.

IFEval as a Proxy Benchmark. The evaluation relies on IFEval as a proxy for Ocode-specific tasks. While Table 1 establishes a structural mapping between IFEval task types and real-world maintenance operations, this mapping has not yet been empirically validated on actual Ocode data such as maintenance invoices, intervention reports, or asset histories. Additionally, findings such as the performance anomaly observed within the qwen3 family may reflect benchmark-specific behaviors that do not necessarily generalize to domain-specific maintenance tasks. Applying and validating the methodology on business-specific datasets is planned as a direct continuation of this work.

Carbon Measurement Scope. Energy consumption is measured using CodeCarbon, which relies on RAPL counters covering CPU power draw. This excludes contributions from DRAM, storage I/O, and cooling infrastructure, meaning that the absolute emission values reported here represent a lower bound on the true inference-time carbon footprint. However, comparisons across models remain meaningful under this setup, as all measurements are subject to the same scope limitations.

Region-Specific Carbon Intensity. Carbon emissions are derived using a region-specific carbon intensity factor corresponding to the French electricity grid, which is among the lowest in Europe at approximately 50 gCO_2/kWh

due to its high share of nuclear energy. Absolute emission values reported in this paper should therefore not be directly generalized to deployments in regions with higher carbon intensity grids. Practitioners should apply the methodology using the carbon intensity factor appropriate to their own infrastructure location.

Frontier Model Evaluation. GPT-4o was evaluated on a fixed sample of 200 IFEval tasks rather than under the full stabilization protocol, resulting in higher uncertainty for this estimate compared to locally stabilized measurements. Mistral Large 2.1 is included solely as a publicly reported reference point and was not directly evaluated. This limited evaluation of frontier models was a deliberate methodological choice to avoid the substantial computational and environmental cost associated with repeated API-based benchmarking. These figures should therefore be interpreted as indicative reference points rather than directly comparable experimental measurements.

Economic Considerations. Hardware capital expenditure and Total Cost of Ownership are outside the scope of this work. The proposed methodology deliberately focuses on accuracy and carbon footprint as two primary decision criteria for model selection in industrial contexts. Future work could extend this framework by integrating economic metrics, such as infrastructure costs, deployment constraints, and operational maintenance requirements.

6 Conclusion

In this paper, we addressed the practical challenge of selecting appropriate language models for industrial generative AI systems under real-world constraints. Motivated by the development of an industrial asset management assistant at Ocode, we proposed an evaluation methodology that jointly considers performance and carbon footprint.

To ensure reproducibility and limit the environmental cost of experimentation, we adopted a benchmark-driven approach based on IFEval, combined with statistical stabilization techniques for estimating both performance and carbon metrics. This methodology enables reliable comparison of locally deployable models while minimizing unnecessary computation.

Our experimental results highlight a clear trade-off between model size and efficiency. While performance generally improves with scale, the gains diminish beyond mid-sized models, whereas carbon footprint increases significantly. As a result, models in the 2B–4B range emerge as a particularly effective compromise under the experimental conditions described, offering strong performance with moderate environmental impact.

These findings have direct implications for industrial system design. They suggest that efficient and sustainable generative AI systems can be built by prioritizing appropriately sized models and adopting hybrid strategies, rather than systematically relying on the largest available models.

Finally, this work contributes to the broader perspective of Green AI, emphasizing the importance of integrating environmental considerations into the evaluation and deployment of machine learning systems.

Future work will focus on extending this evaluation framework to real-world datasets, as discussed in Sect. 5, particularly in the context of asset management and maintenance. Additionally, we plan to explore dynamic orchestration techniques, combining multiple SLMs to route tasks to the most appropriate model based on the specific need. This will enable a more efficient system, dynamically adapting model selection strategies based on task complexity and data type. Finally, adaptive model selection will be investigated to optimize routing decisions and improve the system's performance over time through real-time feedback in production environments.

References

1. Bommasani, R., Hudson, D.A., Adeli, E.: On the Opportunities and Risks of Foundation Models. arXiv preprint arXiv:2108.07258 (2022)
2. Cao, Y., et al.: A Comprehensive Survey of AI-Generated Content (AIGC): A History of Generative AI from GAN to ChatGPT. arXiv preprint arXiv:2303.04226 (2023)
3. Hadi, M.U., Al Tashi, Q., Qureshi, R., et al.: Large Language Models: A Comprehensive Survey of its Applications. Limitations, and Future Prospects. TechRxiv, Challenges (2025)
4. Minaee, S., et al.: Large Language Models: A Survey. arXiv preprint arXiv:2402.06196 (2025)
5. Ocode: Plateformes digitales et solutions de marquage et d'identification. https://www.ocode.fr/, Accessed 31 Mar 2026
6. O2feel, Douze Cycles, Moustache et Larrun choisissent Ocode pour le marquage des vélos. Transition Vélo. https://www.transitionvelo.com/velo-et-societe/o2feel-douze-cycles-moustache-et-larrun-choisissent-ocode-pour-le-marquage-des-velos/, Accessed 31 Mar 2026
7. Ocode et PHASIS lancent un poinçon numérique à l'échelle microscopique. Industrie Mag. https://www.industrie-mag.com/article35726.html, Accessed 31 Mar 2026
8. Gao, Y., et al.: Retrieval-Augmented Generation for Large Language Models: A Survey. arXiv preprint arXiv:2312.10997 (2024)
9. Zhao, P., et al.: Retrieval-Augmented Generation for AI-Generated Content: A Survey. arXiv preprint arXiv:2402.19473 (2024)
10. Zhao, S., Yang, Y., Wang, Z., He, Z., Qiu, L.K., Qiu, L.: Retrieval Augmented Generation (RAG) and Beyond: A Comprehensive Survey on How to Make your LLMs use External Data More Wisely. arXiv preprint arXiv:2409.14924 (2024)
11. Azeroual, O.: Streamlining research information management with large language models: automation, analysis, and user-centric solutions. In: 2025 10th International Conference on Big Data Analytics (ICBDA), pp. 281–287. IEEE, Singapore (2025). https://doi.org/10.1109/ICBDA65366.2025.11211236
12. Zhao, G., Song, E.: Privacy-Preserving Large Language Models: Mechanisms, Applications, and Future Directions. arXiv preprint arXiv:2412.06113 (2024)
13. Neel, S., Chang, P.: Privacy Issues in Large Language Models: A Survey. arXiv preprint arXiv:2312.06717 (2024)
14. Wu, F., Zhang, N., Jha, S., McDaniel, P., Xiao, C.: A New Era in LLM Security: Exploring Security Concerns in Real-World LLM-Based Systems. arXiv preprint arXiv:2402.18649 (2024)

15. Yao, Y., Duan, J., Xu, K., Cai, Y., Sun, Z., Zhang, Y.: A survey on large language model (LLM) security and privacy: the good, the bad, and the ugly. High-Confidence Comput. **4**(2), 100211 (2024). https://doi.org/10.1016/j.hcc.2024.100211
16. Amiri, S.M.H., Goswami, P., Islam, M.M., Hossen, M.S., Amiri, S.M.H., Akter, N.: The Carbon Cost of Conversation, Sustainability in the Age of Language Models. arXiv preprint arXiv:2507.20018 (2025)
17. Liu, V., Yin, Y.: Green AI: Exploring carbon footprints, mitigation strategies, and trade-offs in large language model training. Discover Artificial Intelligence **4**(1), 49 (2024). https://doi.org/10.1007/s44163-024-00149-w A Survey on Small Language Models
18. Nguyen, C.V., et al.: A Survey on Small Language Models. In: Angelova, G., Kunilovskaya, M., Escribe, M., Mitkov, R. (eds.) Proceedings of the 15th International Conference on Recent Advances in Natural Language Processing - Natural Language Processing in the Generative AI Era, pp. 807–821. INCOMA Ltd., Varna (2025). https://aclanthology.org/2025.ranlp-1.93/
19. Subramanian, S., Elango, V., Gungor, M.: Small Language Models (SLMs) Can Still Pack a Punch: A Survey. arXiv preprint arXiv:2501.05465 (2025)
20. Wang, F., et al.: A comprehensive survey of small language models in the era of large language models: techniques, enhancements, applications, collaboration with llms, and trustworthiness. ACM Trans. Intell. Syst. Technol. **16**(6), 1–87 (2025)
21. Sakib, T.H., Hosain, M.T., Morol, M.K.: Small Language Models: Architectures, Techniques, Evaluation, Problems and Future Adaptation. arXiv preprint arXiv:2505.19529 (2025)
22. Jain, H., Pandey, D., Vaidhyanathan, K.: CALM: A Self-Adaptive Orchestration Approach for QoS-Aware Routing in Small Language Model Based Systems. arXiv preprint arXiv:2602.03632 (2026)
23. Hassan, M.T.: Small Models, Large Impact: An SLM-Centric Playbook for Practical Agents. In: 2025 International Conference on Computer and Applications (ICCA), pp. 1–6. IEEE, Bahrain (2025). https://doi.org/10.1109/ICCA66035.2025.11430765
24. Zhou, J., et al.: Instruction-Following Evaluation for Large Language Models. arXiv preprint arXiv:2311.07911 (2023)
25. Strubell, E., Ganesh, A., McCallum, A.: Energy and policy considerations for deep learning in NLP. In: Korhonen, A., Traum, D., Màrquez, L. (eds.) Proceedings of the 57th Annual Meeting of the Association for Computational Linguistics, pp. 3645–3650. Association for Computational Linguistics, Florence (2019). https://doi.org/10.18653/v1/P19-1355
26. Kim, M.-K., Yoo, T.-A., Chung, J.-B.: Toward sustainable AI: a scoping review of carbon footprint and environmental impacts across training and inference stages. IEEE Access **14**, 18881–18896 (2026). https://doi.org/10.1109/access.2026.3659894
27. Touvron, H., Martin, L., Stone, K.: Llama 2: Open Foundation and Fine-Tuned Chat Models. arXiv preprint arXiv:2307.09288 (2023)
28. Gan, D., Li, J.: Small, open-source text-embedding models as substitutes to OpenAI models for gene analysis. Comput. Struct. Biotechnol. J. **27**, 3598–3608 (2025). https://doi.org/10.1016/j.csbj.2025.07.053
29. Zhang, P., Zeng, G., Wang, T., Lu, W.: TinyLlama: An Open-Source Small Language Model. arXiv preprint arXiv:2401.02385 (2024)
30. Zhou, Z., Li, L., Chen, X., Li, A.: Mini-Giants: "Small" Language Models and Open Source Win-Win. arXiv preprint arXiv:2307.08189 (2024)

31. Lu, Z., et al.: Small Language Models: Survey, Measurements, and Insights. arXiv preprint arXiv:2409.15790 (2025)
32. Li, H., et al.: LLMs-as-Judges: A Comprehensive Survey on LLM-Based Evaluation Methods. arXiv preprint arXiv:2412.05579 (2024)
33. Ollama Open source models page https://ollama.com/search, Accessed 31 Mar 2026
34. CodeCarbon Homepage. https://codecarbon.io, Accessed 31 Mar 2026
35. Lottick, K., Susai, S., Friedler, S.A., Wilson, J.P.: Energy Usage Reports: Environmental awareness as part of algorithmic accountability. arXiv preprint arXiv:1911.08354 (2019)
36. OpenAI: Introducing GPT-4.1 in the API (2025). https://openai.com/index/gpt-4-1/, Accessed 31 Mar 2026
37. Hugging Face: Open LLM Leaderboard Archived (2024). https://huggingface.co/spaces/open-llm-leaderboard/open_llm_leaderboard#/ Accessed 31 Mar 2026

Towards Personalized Oncology Rehabilitation: A Hybrid LLM–Knowledge Graph Recommendation Approach

Hiba Djebabria(✉), Yacine Sam, and Nizar Messai

LIFAT Laboratory, University of Tours, Tours, France
{hiba.djabrbia,yacine.sam,nizar.messai}@etu.univ-tours.fr

Abstract. Patients in oncology face challenges regarding their rehabilitation during and after the treatment. Development in the field of Clinical Decision Support Systems (CDSS) offer nowadays new opportunities to transform complex medical guidelines into personalized, and intuitive physical activity recommendations. In this paper, we present a hybrid neuro-symbolic approach that combines LLM-RAG with Knowledge Graph, to recommend adapted physical activity (APA) to patients in oncology. Our solution integrates a recommendation module that leverages a fine-tuned LLM algorithm for generating tailored APA recommendations using a Retrieval Augmented Generation (RAG) module, to ground the generation process in a clinical context, thereby mitigating the risk of LLM hallucination, and a Knowledge graph integrating the SNOMED-CT ontology to validate the LLM output. The framework is built in a modular way following Service Oriented Architectures (SOA) to allow multiple sources data integration, and was implemented in a mobile application prototype for validation. The recommendation process responds dynamically to patient data and context changes, demonstrating a workflow that continuously adapts to patient profiles, preferences, and other relevant information (This work is being carried out in the context of the regional project *SQVALD*: http://oncocentre.org/wp-content/uploads/4_SQVALD-08122022-Journ%C3%A9e-annuelle-Oncocentre-2022.pdf.).

Keywords: Large Language Models · Knowledge Graph · Oncology · Recommendation · Retrieval Augmented Generation

1 Introduction

Clinical Decision Support Systems (CDSS) are important tools in providing clinically grounded decisions to help both healthcare providers in making accurate choices, and patients in their supportive care journey, they operate on a foundation of medical knowledge, and patient data, aiming to bridge the gap between vast medical information and informed clinical decisions. Nowadays, CDSS are

G. Andresini et al. (Eds.): ISMIS 2026, LNAI 16685, pp. 185–199, 2027.
https://doi.org/10.1007/978-3-032-32643-0_16

increasingly leveraging the latest technologies, including AI technologies. Various AI-based platforms have attracted considerable attention from healthcare providers and patients, as they can offer the opportunity to implement patient-centered care within the healthcare systems, owing to a number of potential benefits that these technologies provide [1]. The literature indicates that AI systems have been successful in multiple medical use cases, such as detecting mitosis in breast cancer, classifying skin cancer with dermatologist-level accuracy, and predicting cardiovascular risk factors from retinal fundus photographs [2], which demonstrate the potential of AI systems to assist healthcare providers in improving diagnosis and prognosis. However, majority of AI-based solutions focus on the acute phase, leaving the post-treatment phase undeserved, a gap notably felt in oncology. Patients need supportive care including psychosocial therapy, nutritional assessment, and Adapted Physical Activities (APA), which has demonstrated significant progress in reducing treatment side effects, and enhancing the quality of life.

Nevertheless, when narrowing the scope to systems dedicated to supportive care and Adapted Physical Activities in oncology, significant limitations emerge, attributable to the intrinsic challenges of this domain as well as the constraints of currently deployed approaches. **First**, when delivering a clinical decision, there is a need of multi dimensional factors represented by different heterogeneous data sources to deliver accurate and precise recommendations, and integrating all these data sources into a unified framework is crucial, and also the capacity to ensure contextual awareness, enable fine-grained personalization [3], this challenge is amplified by the complexity of handling real-time data update and dynamicity produced by internal sources such patient medical information and personal context, and external sources such as available facilitates and medical guidelines updates. **Second**, personalization is a central requirement when delivering APA recommendations to oncology patients, as static and rule-based approaches fail to account for the multidimensional variability of individual profiles [4]. The precision and accuracy of such recommendations are essential, as the type, intensity, and duration of any recommended activity must dynamically adjust to any change in medical parameters or patient preferences [5]. This is of particular importance because patients themselves base their decision to engage in physical activity on their vital signs, such as heart rate and oxygen saturation, which have a direct bearing on both the safety and appropriateness of the recommended activity [6]. **Third**, a key limitation of existing deployed approaches lies in the inconsistent patient adherence they elicit, as individuals present highly heterogeneous profiles in terms of digital literacy, and technology acceptance. Deploying digital tools without accounting for this variability undermines their effectiveness and uptake [7,8]. **Last**, another challenge with AI-based approaches is that many AI algorithms, are so-called "black boxes," because the inner workings of the algorithm remain opaque to the user [9] when used alone or when the output depend fully on their intelligence, which decreases the credibility of the generated results.

These challenges appeal for innovative ways to take advantages of the recent advances in both generative and symbolic AI along with well established Service Oriented Architectures (SOA). This work is conducted within the regional multidisciplinary project *SQVALD*, in collaboration with the regional health agency *ARS* and the regional *OncoCenter*[1] referential. We propose in this paper a hybrid neuro-symbolic approach that combines LLM-RAG with Knowledge Graphs to build a recommendation pipeline in the context of oncology. The recommendation is built upon multiple sources integration following SOA. The contributions of this work are summarized as follows:

- Integrate multiple heterogeneous data sources including patient profiles and personal preferences, real world facility data preprocessed and hosted in dedicated APIs, into a unified SOA-based pipeline.
- Feed the LLM with relevant context drawn from those sources via RAG mechanism to mitigate hallucination.
- Employ a utility-based LLM algorithm in which a weighted function integrates two complementary sub-functions, one capturing personalization and one enforcing clinical alignment, with weights predefined and validated by domain oncologists. The approach applies a medical Knowledge Graph with integration of the medical ontology SNOMED-CT[2] for a validation and clinical implementation that comes after the generation of recommendations.
- Continuously adapt and respond to changes in patient's medical status, preferences and real-world constraints.

We note here that Data privacy and Security are beyond the scope of this paper and are being addressed in ongoing work.

The remainder of this article is structured as follows: Sect. 2 reviews related work in healthcare recommendation systems and positions our contributions within the existing literature. Section 3 details our proposed approach, focusing on the integration of multi-source data, the personalized utility-based scoring function, and KG-SNOMED validation. Section 4 reports the experimental results obtained from evaluations on a dataset of patient profiles and discusses the main findings. Finally, Sect. 5 concludes the paper and outlines future research directions.

2 Related Work

Building on the challenges outlined above, in addition to general health literature work presented already in Sect. 1 ([1]–[2]), we conduct hereafter a review of the literature in the context of oncology. This field is well-positioned to benefit from the incorporation of LLM technologies, especially given its emphasis on the synthesis of diverse data types such as clinical, imaging, laboratory and genomic reports integrated with the psychosocial elements of patient-centered

[1] https://oncocentre.org/.

[2] https://browser.ihtsdotools.org/?.

medicine [10]. GPT-4 has been evaluated for interpreting ASCO[3] and ESMO[4] guidelines in gastrointestinal cancers; it answered only 57% of statements correctly when not combined with an additional validation, illustrating the value of external evidence [11].

In [12], authors assume that existing methods, especially those depending only on deterministic KG, are quite limited when it comes to scaling and incorporating new data. This problem also remains in rule-based systems [13]. On the upside, autonomous LLMs perform well in processing unstructured text [14]. However, entertaining these two types of approaches separately still does not produce transparent reasoning capabilities, hence producing inconsistent outputs in key medical applications.

Delivering accurate and personalized recommendations further requires the coherent integration of heterogeneous data sources, including patient profiles, clinical guidelines, and real-world contextual data, into a unified pipeline. Service-Oriented Architecture (SOA) principles have been shown to support such integration by enabling interoperability across distributed, heterogeneous systems [3]. In oncology specifically, the inability to consolidate fragmented patient data across sources remains a key limitation of existing CDSS [15], and multi-source fusion has been identified as essential for fine-grained, context-aware personalization [16].

To the best of our knowledge, no existing work combines LLM, RAG, and KG with a utility-based scoring mechanism in a SOA architecture. In this context, our implemented solution introduces: (1) a hybrid architecture in which the LLM proposes APA recommendations and a grounded KG-SNOMED validates or corrects them; and (2) a dynamic tool where the generated recommendations respect the evolving patient data and context, so recommendations keep continually adapting over time.

3 Hybrid Recommendation Framework

In this section, we present our solution: a hybrid approach that combines Large Language Models (LLMs), Knowledge Graphs (KGs), Retrieval-Augmented Generation (RAG), and Service-Oriented-Architecture (SOA) for personalized APA recommendation in oncology. The framework integrates heterogeneous multi-source data into a unified pipeline, generates recommendation leveraging a utility-based algorithm with a RAG module, and validates its outputs through a SNOMED-CT-based Knowledge Graph. Together, these components are implemented in a end-to-end prototype that was tested with real patients. Figure 1 illustrates the general architecture of our proposed solution:

3.1 Multi-source Data Integration

Generating relevant and tailored APA recommendations for oncology patients requires the simultaneous consideration of multiple factors, captured through

[3] https://ascopubs.org/.
[4] https://www.esmo.org/.

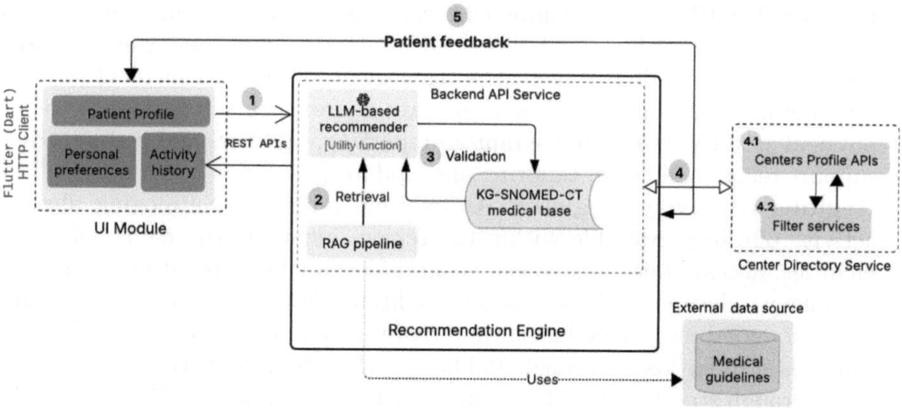

Fig. 1. System architecture of the proposed approach

heterogeneous data sources that differ in both source and format. As outlined in the first section, no single source is sufficient to fully characterize a patient's clinical situation, personal context, and environmental constraints. For this reason, the proposed framework begins with a structured multi-source data integration, taking advantage of the SOA solution, in which each source is independently preprocessed and normalized prior to being integrated into the pipeline. Figure 2 shows an overview of all data sources and their integration process:

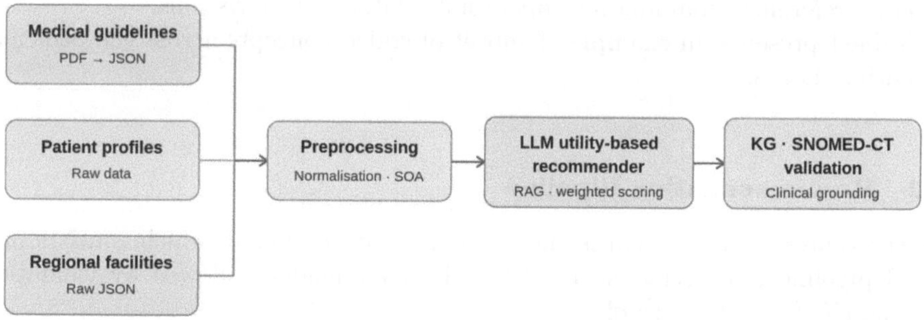

Fig. 2. Multi-source data integration process

- **Medical Guidelines.** A PDF document of evidence-based recommendations for supportive care and physical activity in oncology, provided by the regional oncology center. The document undergoes preprocessing, in order to enrich and standardize its knowledge representation, and is stored into a JSON file subsequently consumed by the utility-based LLM algorithm through the Retrieval Augmented Generation pipeline, detailed in the Subsect. 3.2.

- **Patient Profiles.** This component captures patient-specific information, including demographic attributes such as name, email, and age, alongside clinical data including cancer type, treatment stage, and medical parameters, notably vital signs such as heart rate and oxygen saturation, as well as physical activity level, daily symptom reporting, and personal preferences to support recommendation tailoring and updates.
- **Regional Activity Register.** An external repository cataloging physical activity offerings available within the region, including the names of public facilities, accessibility conditions, geographic location, operating hours, and pathology relevance. These records facilitate the alignment between clinically grounded recommendations and real-world activity provision. This data source is standardized, cleaned, and hosted via a dedicated API[5], made accessible through structured API calls in accordance with Service-Oriented Architecture (SOA) principles.
- **Knowledge Graph-SNOMED-CT.** A Knowledge Graph constructed from the medical guidelines and semantically enriched using the SNOMED-CT[6] ontology (2024-01 release). Each entity within the graph, including diseases, cancer stages, physical activities, etc., is annotated with a standardized SNOMED-CT concept identifier and its corresponding code. The built KG represents 18 cancer types (e.g., breast cancer: 254837009, lung cancer: 254637007), 15 clinical conditions (e.g., severe fatigue, neutropenia), 12 physical activities (e.g., walking: 229070002, yoga: 229294001), and 10 chemotherapy agents (e.g., doxorubicin: 372817009), all linked via typed edges encoding *recommends*, *contraindicates*, and *adapts* relationships. Each node carries both a SNOMED-CT URI(`http://snomed.info/id/{code}`) and an ICD-10 cross-reference, enabling interoperability with clinical systems.
  Table 1 presents an example of subset of coded concepts across the principal entity classes.

3.2 Recommendation Pipeline

At the center of the system is the recommendation engine, which consists of a RAG pipeline that feeds the LLM-based recommender, followed by validation via the KG-SNOMED graph.

RAG-Based Contextualization. One of the key limitations of LLMs is their tendency to hallucinate or rely on outdated knowledge. To mitigate this issue, we opted for RAG to integrate external, domain-specific content into the generation process [17].

The retrieval phase contextualizes and incorporates clinically validated information. This is achieved through semantic search over an indexed corpus of structured clinical guidelines and regionally available physical activity offerings.

[5] https://regionalcenters.onrender.com/.
[6] https://www.documentation-snds.health-data-hub.fr/standards/snomed-ct/.

Table 1. Sample of SNOMED-CT concepts used in the Knowledge Graph

Class	Concept	SNOMED-CT Code
Disease	Breast Cancer	254837009
	Lung Cancer	254637007
	Colorectal Cancer	363406005
	Prostate Cancer	399068003
Cancer Stage	Stage I	258215001
	Stage II	258219007
	Stage III	258224005
	Stage IV (Metastatic)	258228008
Drug	Doxorubicin	372817009
	Paclitaxel	387374002
	Pembrolizumab	716125002
	Tamoxifen	373345002
Physical Activity	Walking	129006008
	Yoga	229294001
	Breathing Exercise	304549008

The retrieved content is then embedded into the prompt sent to the LLM, ensuring that the generated recommendations are both context-aware and evidence-based [18].

The overall structure follows the standard RAG pipeline:

1. The multi-source data—including patient profile, personal preferences, and structured medical guidelines—are ingested by the RAG's loading component. This step filters the input to ensure contextual relevance and alignment with the patient's current clinical status.
2. Once loaded, the documents are segmented into coherent knowledge chunks.
3. Each segmented chunk is then transformed into a vector representation. Embeddings are aligned to a unified vector space that supports contextual retrieval via dense similarity matching, which significantly improves relevance over sparse keyword matching.
4. The embedded chunks are stored in a vector database that supports real-time similarity search, enabling the system to quickly fetch top-ranked content in response to a new query.

LLM-Recommender and Utility-Based Approach. To operationalize the recommendation, we implement a pipeline that combines RAG with utility-based filtering to ensure that the final recommendations are both contextually relevant and aligned with medical standards.

For each patient, a data sample aggregating medical parameters and personal preferences is constructed; relevant medical knowledge K is retrieved via semantic search over the retrieval corpus D, the indexed medical guidelines[7], and incorporated into a fixed prompt sent to the LLM-recommender, which generates a set S of candidate recommendations tailored to the patient's clinical and contextual attributes. Each candidate $s \in S$ is then scored using a utility function $M_C(s)$, where C represents the context including the patient profile and personal preferences, evaluating both clinical alignment and patient-specific relevance, not merely as a post-hoc filter, but as an implicit driver of retrieval and content selection during context construction.

The recommendation with the highest utility score is then selected. We propose the following sub-functions, following these steps:

1. Patient-Recommendation Similarity $f_1(S_{\text{patient}}, s)$:
   The patient profile S_{patient} and recommendation s are both embedded into a shared semantic vector space using a pretrained sentence embedding model. The similarity score f_1 is computed as the *cosine similarity* between the patient embedding vector and the recommendation embedding vector as shown in Eq. (1):
   $$f_1(S_{\text{patient}}, s) = \cos\left(\text{embed}(S_{\text{patient}}), \text{embed}(s)\right) \tag{1}$$
   This quantifies how closely the recommendation content matches patient-specific preferences, history, and context.
2. Clinical Alignment Score $f_2(S_{\text{ref}}, s)$:
   The recommendation s is compared against a reference set S_{ref} consisting of validated clinical guidelines and protocols. Each reference item and s are embedded in the same vector space. Equation (2) defines the maximum *cosine similarity* between the embeddings of the reference set and the recommendations:
   $$f_2(S_{\text{ref}}, s) = \max_{r \in S_{\text{ref}}} \cos\left(\text{embed}(r), \text{embed}(s)\right) \tag{2}$$
   This process ensures that the recommendations conform to established medical standards.
3. Weighted Combination:
   The final utility score is computed as a weighted sum as shown in the Eq. (3):
   $$M_C(s) = \epsilon_1 \cdot f_1(S_{\text{patient}}, s) + \epsilon_2 \cdot f_2(S_{\text{ref}}, s) \tag{3}$$
   where:
   - ϵ_1, ϵ_2 are weighting factors, they are tuned based on clinical expert validation to balance personalization, clinical correctness, and patient preferences [18].
   - f(1) and f(2) measure how well the recommendation matches the patient's profile, and the clinical guidelines respectively.

---
[7] Regional Medical Guidelines.

4. Ranking and Selection:
   Based on exhaustive computing of $M_C(s)$, we select the candidate s' with the highest score based on Eq. (4), and for small candidate sets ($|S| \leq 10$), $M(C, s)$ is computed exhaustively and the candidate with the highest score is selected:

$$s' = \arg\max_{s \in S} M_C(s) \tag{4}$$

   And for larger candidate sets, approximate ranking is performed by first filtering candidates using fast similarity heuristics (the top-k by f_1 and f_2), then re-ranking with the full weighted utility.

The recommendation process can be summarized formally in Algorithm 1:

Algorithm 1: Personalized Recommendation Generation with RAG and Utility-Based Function

Input: S_{patient}, S_{ref}, Retrieval corpus D
Output: Final personalized recommendation s'

Retrieval
$K \leftarrow$ `RAG_Retrieve`(S_{patient}, D)
$\mathcal{P} \leftarrow$ `FillPrompt`(S_{patient}, K)

Candidate Generation
$S \leftarrow$ `LLM_Generate`$(\mathcal{P})$

Utility Evaluation for $s \in S$ **do**
  $f_1 \leftarrow$ `Sim`(S_{patient}, s)
  $f_2 \leftarrow$ `Sim`(S_{ref}, s)
  $M_C(s) \leftarrow \varepsilon_1 \cdot f_1 + \varepsilon_2 \cdot f_2$

Selection
$s' \leftarrow \arg\max_{s \in S} M_C(s)$

return s'

Algorithm 1 operates in four steps: (1) **RAG_Retrieve** fetches the most relevant external knowledge K from corpus D based on the patient profile S_{patient}, which is then used by **FillPrompt** to construct the prompt $\mathcal{P}$; (2) **LLM_Generate** produces a set S of candidate recommendations from $\mathcal{P}$; (3) each candidate $s \in S$ is scored via the utility function $M_C(s) = \varepsilon_1 \cdot f_1 + \varepsilon_2 \cdot f_2$; and (4) the optimal recommendation s' is selected as $\arg\max_{s \in S} M_C(s)$.

KG-SNOMED Validation. Once the LLM-based recommender produces a list of physical activity candidates, each suggestion is passed through a safety layer implemented as a KG Validator module, whose rules are encoded in the SNOMED-CT–annotated Knowledge Graph. This validation step ensures that no activity reaches the patient interface without having been checked against structured medical knowledge.

For each candidate recommendation, the validator first derives the patient's active clinical conditions from their real-time parameters. It then applies a three-tier decision: (1) hard rejection, the activity is discarded if it is explicitly contraindicated; (2) parametric modification, the activity is retained but its duration and/or intensity are adjusted downward; (3) contextual annotation, disease-specific precautions are appended. Only activities that pass the hard-rejection test are forwarded, with any accumulated modifications and warnings surfaced as adaptations in the final response object.

The final score exposed to the mobile front-end is a combined utility score between the patient embedding and the activity embedding, and the KG validation weight (0–1 scale, derived from edge weights in the recommends graph). The top validated activities are returned alongside their SNOMED codes, evidence references, and geo-located sport-health facilities from the regional Sport-Santé Centre-Val de Loire directory. Algorithm 2 shows the steps we proposed to validate generated recommendations by the LLM-utility based process:

Algorithm 2: KG-SNOMED Validation

Input: Candidate set S, Patient profile S_{patient}, Knowledge Graph $\mathcal{G}$
Output: Ranked validated recommendations R^*

Step 1 – KG Profile Matching
Profiles $\leftarrow$ `KG.MatchProfiles`(S_{patient})
`KG_Recommended` $\leftarrow$ `KG.GetRecommended`(Profiles)
`KG_Contraindicated` $\leftarrow$ `KG.GetContraindications`(S_{patient})

Step 2 – KG Validation Score ; `// per candidate` $s \in S$

$$u(s) \leftarrow \begin{cases} 0.0 & \text{if } s \in \texttt{KG\_Contraindicated} \\ \text{weight}(s) & \text{if } s \in \texttt{KG\_Recommended} \\ 0.5 & \text{otherwise} \end{cases}$$

$U(s) \leftarrow \beta_1 \cdot u(s) + \beta_2 \cdot M_C(s), \quad \beta_1 = \beta_2 = 0.5$; `// validated by clincial expert`

Step 3 – Ranking & Safety Gate
$R^* \leftarrow$ `TopK`($\{s \mid U(s) > 0.3\}$, k=6)
for $s \in R^*$ **do**
  if hard constraint violated (ECOG, BP) **then** reject s
  else adjust duration/intensity

return R^*

Algorithm 2 details the KG-SNOMED validation phase applied to the recommendations produced by the LLM-recommender. Each candidate is first matched against KG profiles derived from the patient profile S_{patient} to determine whether it is clinically recommended, contraindicated, or neutral, yielding a validation score $u(s)$. This score is then combined with the semantic similarity score $M_C(s)$ into the final utility $U(s)$ with equal weights for both functions. Candidates are ranked and filtered by a threshold, before a hard safety gate enforces clinical constraints based on ECOG, and blood pressure levels, either rejecting or adapting the activity accordingly.

3.3 Feedback and Dynamic Adaptation

As illustrated in Step 5 of Fig. 1, the system involves a feedback loop in which the patient's outcome for the recommended activities, including his feedback introduced via the mobile application, and reported daily symptoms, is fed back into the system. This updated profile is then re-injected into the pipeline at the next interaction, triggering a new series of recommendations that take into consideration the patient's changing clinical condition and preferences. This ensures that recommendations remain continuously adapted throughout the patient's care journey.

4 Framework Implementation and Evaluation

4.1 Framework Implementation

We implemented our proposed approach as a mobile application prototype, whose technical architecture is illustrated in Fig. 3. The prototype follows a client-server architecture composed of two layers. The front-end is a cross-platform Flutter application exposing two modules: a *Patient Profile* interface for capturing clinical data and personal preferences, and a *Recommendation UI* for displaying results. Patient data is transmitted to the *FastAPI backend* via REST calls, which orchestrates two backend modules: the *LLM-based utility function*, responsible for generating and scoring candidate recommendations, using **GPT-4** (`gpt-4-0613`, OpenAI API), which scores clinical accuracy given the patient profile, with sentence embeddings that are computed using `all-MiniLM-L6-v2` (22M parameters, 384-dimensional output), and the *KG SNOMED validator*, which enforces clinical safety constraints. The system additionally queries the *Regional Centers API* uses a two-stage filter: first at data load time (only centers listing cancer in their pathology field are retained), then at matching time via discipline keyword lookup. The front-end makes a live REST query against the regional center directory, mapping each recommended activity to its French discipline name to provide suitable local facilities for patients.

4.2 Feasibility Study: Preliminary Results and Pilot Evaluation

As a preliminary feasibility study, we conducted a pilot evaluation with 10 real users presenting different clinical conditions to assess the system's initial viability across three dimensions, starting with these two clinical metrics:

QM1—Mean Recommendation Utility (MRU)

$$MRU = \frac{1}{k}\sum_{i=1}^{k} U_i, \quad U_i = \varepsilon_1 \cdot f_1 + \varepsilon_2 \cdot f_2, \quad (\varepsilon_1, \varepsilon_2) = (0.6,\, 0.4) \tag{5}$$

We adapted MRU to our utility score functions to measures the relevance of generated recommendations, and it's computed as the mean combined utility

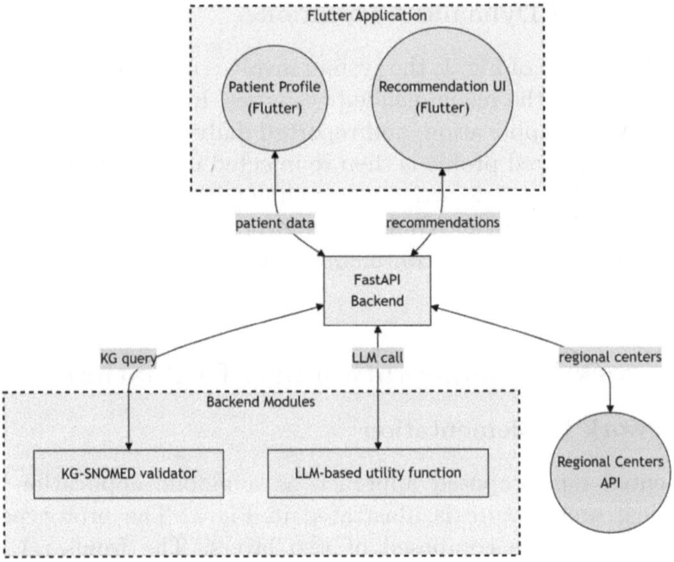

Fig. 3. Technical architecture of the implemented prototype

score over the top-$k = 6$ returned recommendations. The value of ε_1 and ε_2 were defined and validated in consultation with the oncologist.

QM2—KG Condition Coverage (KCC)

$$KCC = \frac{|\text{patient conditions mapped to KG nodes}|}{|\text{patient conditions extracted}|} \tag{6}$$

KCC quantifies how completely the Knowledge Graph represents the patient's clinical state. A low KCC means that the system is incomplete in terms of available profiles, which affects both safety and relevance [19]. Results are reported in Table 2. The MRU (mean = 0.783) is encouraging across all patients, suggesting that the system tends to retrieve medically relevant information regardless of diagnosis or severity. Regarding KCC (mean = 0.740), patients with higher fatigue scores and ECOG ≥ 2 (P02, P04) achieved perfect scores of 1.00, likely because their profiles matched multiple well-defined KG pathways, whereas patients with lower severity (ECOG 0, low fatigue) scored 0.60, as mild cases have fewer constrained clinical rules to match against.

Ablation Analysis. To quantify the contribution of each component, we evaluate two ablated variants of the system on the same patients: *RAG-only* (KG validation disabled) and *KG-only* (embedding similarity disabled). In each variant, the disabled component's score is fixed to 0.5, the non-informative neutrality of each function: the default score assigned by KG to activities for which no graph is available, and the median of the normalized cosine similarity representing semantic orthogonality. Results are reported in Table 3.

Table 2. Quality measure results.

Patient	Diagnosis	ECOG	Fatigue	MRU	KCC	KG Profiles Matched
P01	Breast cancer, St. II	1	0.40	0.79	0.80	Breast cancer, ECOG 0–1
P02	Breast cancer, St. III	2	0.75	0.83	1.00	Severe fatigue; Hypertension; Low immunity
P03	Colorectal cancer, St. I	0	0.18	0.70	0.60	—(preference-based)
P04	Lung cancer, St. II	2	0.60	0.80	1.00	Severe fatigue; Low immunity
P05	Breast cancer, St. I	0	0.12	0.81	0.60	Breast cancer, ECOG 0–1
P06	Prostate cancer, St. II	1	0.35	0.75	0.60	Cancer with hypertension
P07	Lymphoma	2	0.70	0.82	0.60	Severe fatigue; Low immunity
P08	Ovarian cancer, St. III	1	0.50	0.77	0.80	Cancer with low immunity
P09	Colorectal cancer, St. II	1	0.45	0.75	0.80	Cancer with hypertension
P10	Breast cancer, St. I	0	0.20	0.81	0.60	Breast cancer, ECOG 0–1
Mean	—	—	—	**0.783**	**0.740**	—

Table 3. Ablation results: mean MRU and KCC across all patients.

Variant	MRU (mean)	KCC (mean)
Full system (RAG + KG)	**0.780**	**0.740**
RAG-only (no KG)	0.701	0.000
KG-only (no RAG)	0.630	0.740

Removing the KG reduces MRU by 10.1% and eliminates all clinical condition coverage (KCC = 0), confirming the graph's role in safety filtering and profile-based guidance. In the other hand, removing the RAG reduces MRU by 19.2%, showing that semantic personalization contributes more to recommendation relevance. These results provide preliminary evidence that both components are necessary for the hybrid system to function effectively.

We also conducted a user evaluation via a LimeSurvey questionnaire[8], comprising three sections of three questions each, with results reported in Fig. 4.

Each line represents the distribution of 10 responses on a 5-point Likert scale – for example, A2 (*"The recommendations reflected my cancer type and treatment stage constraints"*). Overall, no negative responses were recorded, and all questions scored predominantly Agree or Strongly Agree across the three sections of questions. Additional details about the results, prototype screenshots, and demonstration video are provided with the source code in our public GitHub repository[9].

To go further, we are working on an evaluation involving Oncology Department of the regional hospital, and more real patients to provide the tool for 6 months period and measure its usefulness.

[8] https://hibadjbr.limesurvey.net/APACare_tool?lang=en&newtest=Y.
[9] Source code of the implemented Tool.

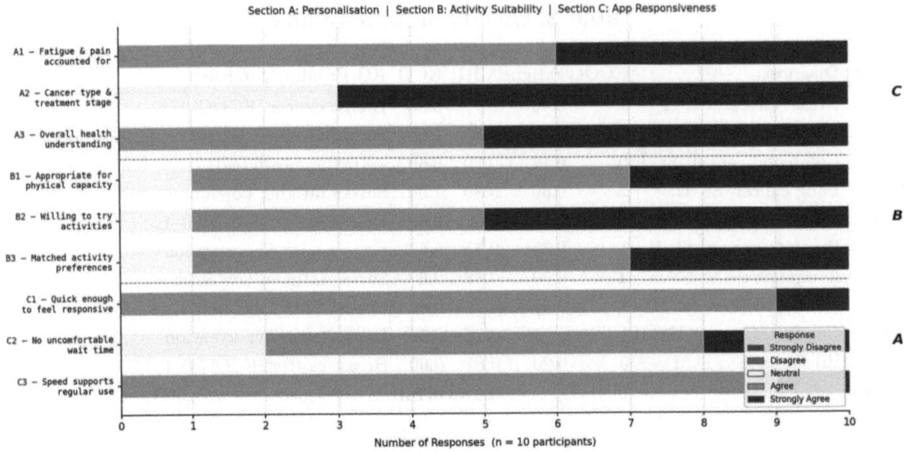

Fig. 4. Questionnaire results

5 Conclusion

In this paper, we presented a hybrid LLM–KG approach for generating personalized Adapted Physical Activity recommendations for oncology patients. The recommendation core system integrates a RAG pipeline for context-aware retrieval, a utility-based LLM recommender combining personalization and clinical alignment, and a SNOMED-CT knowledge graph for clinical validation. Evaluation across all patient profiles yielded a *Mean Recommendation Utility* of 0.783 and a mean *KG Condition Coverage* of 0.740. This work demonstrates the interest of our proposed approach.
The system processes sensitive oncology data, this data flows from the patient-facing interface to a local REST API, in-memory without persisting any records. However, the primary privacy risk lies in the exposure of sensitive clinical data, either through interception during API communication, or through leakage to external providers if a cloud-hosted model were substituted for the local one as already implemented in the current prototype. Full GDPR and HIPAA compliance, and data residency, is planned for the forthcoming phase.

References

1. Khosravi, M., Zare, Z., Mojtabaeian, S.M., et al.: Artificial intelligence and decision-making in healthcare: a thematic analysis of a systematic review of reviews. Health Serv. Res. Manag. Epidemiol. **11**, 23333928241234864 (2024)
2. Poplin, R., Varadarajan, A.V., Blumer, K., et al.: Prediction of cardiovascular risk factors from retinal fundus photographs via deep learning. Nat. Biomed. Eng. **2**(3), 158–164 (2018)
3. Xu, J., Wang, Y.: Enhancing healthcare recommendation systems with a multimodal LLMs-based MoE architecture. arXiv preprint arXiv:2412.11557 (2024)

4. Trestini, I., et al.: Physical activity guidelines in oncology: a systematic review of the current recommendations. Crit. Rev. Oncol. Hematol. **210**, 104700 (2025). https://doi.org/10.1016/j.critrevonc.2025.104700
5. Siddiqui, S.A., et al.: Personalized recommendations for physical activity e-coaching (OntoRecoModel): ontological modeling. JMIR Med. Inform. **10**(6), e33847 (2022). https://doi.org/10.2196/33847
6. McCormack, C., Kehoe, B., Cullivan, S., et al.: Exploration of physical activity knowledge, preferences and support needs among pulmonary hypertension patients. PLoS ONE **18**(1), e0277696 (2023). https://doi.org/10.1371/journal.pone.0277696
7. Grjan, V., et al.: Patients' perspectives on digital health tools: a narrative review of facilitators and barriers to uptake. Digit. Health **9**, 1–15 (2023). https://doi.org/10.1016/j.digitu.2023.100071
8. Park, Y.E., Tak, Y.W., Kim, I., et al.: User experience and extended technology acceptance model in commercial health care app usage among patients with cancer: mixed methods study. J. Med. Internet Res. **26**, e55176 (2024)
9. Kubben, P., Dumontier, M., Dekker, A. (eds.): Fundamentals of Clinical Data Science. Springer, Cham (2019). https://doi.org/10.1007/978-3-319-99713-1
10. Chen, D., et al.: Large language models in oncology: a review. BMJ Oncol. **4**(1), e000759 (2025)
11. Ferber, D., et al.: GPT-4 for information retrieval and comparison of medical oncology guidelines. NEJM AI **1**(6), AIcs2300235 (2024)
12. Sarabadani, A., Shamami, M.A., Sadeghsalehi, H., Asadi, B., Hesaraki, S.: DKG-LLM: a framework for medical diagnosis and personalized treatment recommendations via dynamic knowledge graph and large language model integration (2025). arXiv:2508.06186 arXiv preprint
13. Modaresnezhad, M., Vahdati, A., Nemati, H., Ardestani, A., Sadri, F.: A rule-based semantic approach for data integration, standardization and dimensionality reduction utilizing the UMLS: application to predicting bariatric surgery outcomes. Comput. Biol. Med. **106**, 84–90 (2019)
14. Naderi, H., Shojaei, A., Huang, L.: Foundation models for autonomous robots in unstructured environments. arXiv preprint arXiv:2407.14296 (2024)
15. Gao, Y., Li, R., Croxford, E., et al.: Leveraging medical knowledge graphs into large language models for diagnosis prediction: design and application study. JMIR AI **4**, e58670 (2025). https://doi.org/10.2196/58670
16. Kulkarni, C.: CancerKG.ORG - a web-scale, interactive, verifiable knowledge graph-LLM hybrid for assisting with optimal cancer treatment and care. In: Proceedings of the 33rd ACM International Conference on Information and Knowledge Management, pp. 1–10 (2024). https://doi.org/10.1145/3627673.3680094
17. Chen, J., Lin, H., Han, X.: Benchmarking large language models in retrieval-augmented generation. In: Proceedings of the AAAI Conference on Artificial Intelligence, pp. 17754–17762 (2024)
18. LIFAT - Scientific Report
19. Hogan, A., Blomqvist, E., Cochez, M.: Knowledge graphs. ACM Comput. Surv. (2021)

From Zero-Shot to Domain Precision: Synthetic Data Fine-Tuning for Robust NER in Low-Resource Domain-Specific Texts

Adeel Zafar(✉), Sławomir Nowaczyk, and Hamid Sarmadi

Center for Applied Intelligent Systems Research, Halmstad University, Halmstad, Sweden
{adeel.zafar,slawomir.nowaczyk,hamid.sarmadi}@hh.se

Abstract. Extracting fine-grained technical entities from unstructured automotive service reports is critical for data-driven fault diagnosis, yet remains challenging due to jargon-heavy language and limited labeled data. Zero-shot Named Entity Recognition (NER) models such as GLiNER enable rapid deployment without domain-specific training, but their effectiveness in specialized technical domains is unclear. We hypothesize that while zero-shot models perform well on broad-domain benchmarks, they fail in low-resource domain-specific settings where domain-adapted fine-tuning is required. To evaluate this, we compare zero-shot GLiNER with fine-tuned RoBERTa and WG-BERT. Models are evaluated on clean synthetic data, noisy synthetic data, and a gold set of manually annotated real-world service reports from a Swedish truck manufacturer. Results show that GLiNER enables fast prototyping but achieves substantially lower F1-scores, while WG-BERT fine-tuned on synthetic data consistently outperforms RoBERTa and general-purpose zero-shot models. To the best of our knowledge, no publicly available NER model is currently tailored to fine-grained automotive technical entities. Consequently, we release our datasets and source code to facilitate further research in this domain(Project code and datasets are available at https://github.com/Adeelzafar/From-Zero-Shot-to-Domain-Precision.).

1 Introduction

Extracting structured, fine-grained information from automotive service reports and free-text customer complaints is beneficial for effective fault diagnosis, maintenance planning, and product improvement within the automotive industry. These texts, however, are highly unstructured and domain-specific, characterized by specialized terminology and complex expressions related to equipment, device parameters, fault phenomena, detection tools, and maintenance methods [13]. Named Entity Recognition (NER) [26] plays a vital role in transforming this vast and heterogeneous unstructured data, including service records, diagnostic

G. Andresini et al. (Eds.): ISMIS 2026, LNAI 16685, pp. 200–212, 2027.
https://doi.org/10.1007/978-3-032-32643-0_17

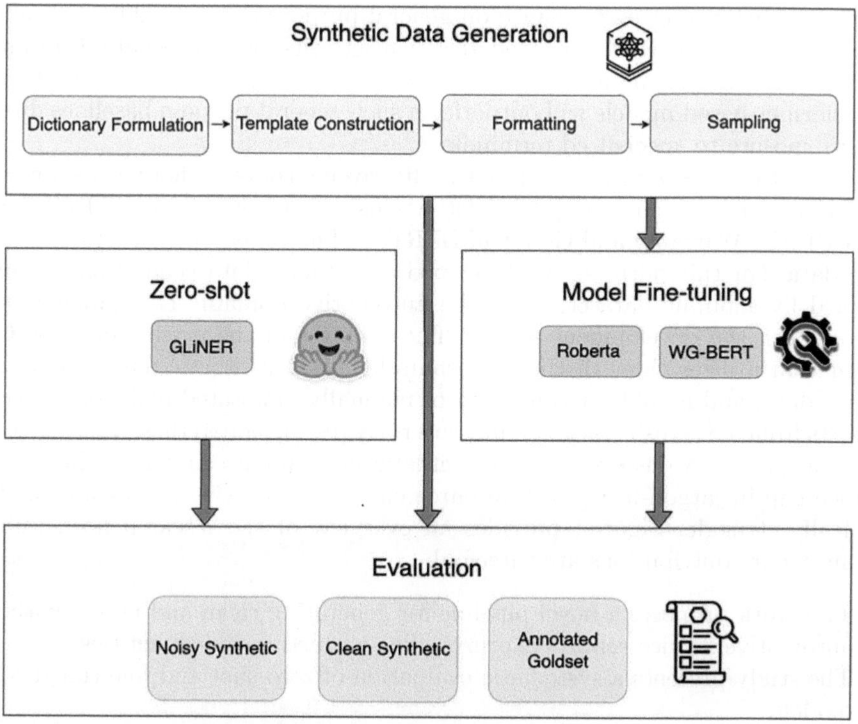

Fig. 1. Overview of the Proposed Approach

logs, customer feedback, and sensor information, into structured and actionable knowledge. By accurately identifying and categorizing key entities such as fault codes, vehicle components, symptoms, and maintenance activities, NER enables more precise analysis and supports data-driven decision-making processes including predictive maintenance, operational planning, and product enhancements. Most existing NER models are tailored specifically for the Chinese automotive sector, as noted in [18], and there is a notable absence of well-developed NER schemas for English-language automotive service reports.

Low-resource setting where annotated datasets are not available, often due to high cost of annotation, is challenge in effective deployment of conventional NER requiring supervised learning. Recent advances in zero-shot [29] and prompt-based NER [1] leveraging large language models (LLMs) offer promising annotation-free alternatives. However, their effectiveness on noisy, jargon-rich and highly technical automotive texts is not well explored [6,21]. Additionally, synthetic data generation [14] emerges as a practical strategy to augment limited labeled data, enabling fine-tuning and domain adaptation of NER models even in annotation-poor conditions.

In industrial settings, zero-shot models are often preferred for rapid deployment and minimal labeling costs. While zero-shot models such as GLiNER have demonstrated strong performance on general-purpose datasets [29], their effectiveness in extracting fine-grained technical entities from specialized automotive service texts remains unclear [23]. We hypothesize that domain-adapted transformer-based models will outperform such general-purpose baselines due to their exposure to specialized terminology.

To address this gap, we evaluate the effectiveness of zero-shot versus domain-adapted models by comparing GLiNER against two models—RoBERTa [19] and WG-BERT (Warranty and Goodwill BERT)[1]—fine-tuned on synthetic automotive data. For this purpose, we developed a synthetic data generation pipeline, primed by a public dataset, to fit the automotive domain. This pipeline generates both the development sets for fine-tuning and the evaluation sets. Our evaluation utilizes three distinct benchmarks: clean synthetic data, noisy synthetic data, and a gold set consisting of manually annotated real-world service reports from a Swedish truck manufacturer. By testing across these varying levels of data quality, we assess whether synthetic fine-tuning can bridge the performance gap in jargon-heavy, low-resource environments where zero-shot models typically struggle. Figure 1 provides an overview of the research flow. Subsequently, our contributions are threefold:

- This work proposes a novel pipeline for generating clean and noisy synthetic automotive service reports capturing fine-grained technical entities.
- The study presents a systematic evaluation of zero-shot and fine-tuned NER models.
- We publicly released the synthetic datasets, trained models, and source code are, offering a reproducible benchmark.

2 Literature Review

The field of NER has undergone substantial development and transformation since its inception in 1996 [3], with techniques evolving across rule-based, machine learning, and deep learning paradigms over the past three decades [22]. NER has undergone significant evolution with various methodologies being applied for different domains and data settings. Traditional models such as conditional random fields (CRF) [17] and their modern extensions like LSTM-CRF [11] remain relevant, especially in scenarios with limited training data or domain-specific terminology. These models leverage probabilistic graphical modeling and recurrent neural networks, respectively, to capture context and label dependencies, achieving competitive results in specialized domains [16]. The transition to Transformer-based architectures, pioneered by BERT [7], further advanced the field by enabling the fine-tuning of pre-trained models on specific downstream tasks like NER.

There have also been studies that apply NER for specific domains, including biomedical [9], social networks [5], and the automotive industry [25]. In auto-

[1] https://huggingface.co/lukasweber/WG_BERT.

motive industry, a hybrid NER approach [25] was proposed that combined rule-based techniques with Hidden Markov Models, outperforming pure HMM methods on accuracy and efficiency for entity recognition. However, general-purpose models often struggle with the technical jargon found in this sector. Gururangan et al. [8] demonstrated that domain-adaptive pretraining is essential for improving performance in such specialized, low-resource settings. Additionally, term frequency mapping was used to identify and track new automotive technologies by linking extracted entities to temporal data. Keraghel et al. [15] proposed a domain-specific NER schema with thirteen classes such as segment, motor, and car type. They employed a supervised learning approach combining rule-based patterns and machine learning classifiers to accurately identify and categorize automotive entities. Hyun et al. [12] developed large-scale English and Korean datasets for aspect-level sentiment analysis in the automotive field. Their method involved crowdsourcing annotations focused on customer opinion aspects, leveraging both linguistic features and domain knowledge to facilitate fine-grained sentiment detection, though not designed specifically for NER tasks.

To address the scarcity of labeled data in these niche domains, alternative supervision strategies have emerged. Ratner et al. [24] introduced weak supervision through Snorkel, which utilizes noisy heuristics instead of manual labels to train models. For specialized NER, Dai et al. [4] and Yaseen et al. [28] explored data augmentation and synthetic generation as a means to build robust models in low-resource environments. More recently, the focus has shifted toward LLMs for data curation; for example, ProgGen [10] uses LLMs to generate entire training datasets, while NuNER [2] leverages LLM-annotated data to pre-train specialized NER encoders. Our work builds upon these synthetic strategies by utilizing an expert-designed template approach to ensure the logical consistency required for automotive diagnostics.

3 Materials and Methods

This section explains the synthetic data generation pipeline, evaluation sets, and model selection.

3.1 Synthetic Data Generation

To enable robust NER training in the automotive diagnostic domain, we generate a synthetic dataset using structured information from vehicle fault logs. Our approach relied on controlled template-based synthesis based on domain driven dictionaries, combined with randomized entity insertion. This yields diverse sentences with automatically aligned entity annotations. Furthermore, we integrate a noise perturbation component to mimic the noise of real-world data.

A domain-specific NER schema is essential for capturing the technical granularity of automotive diagnostics, ensuring that nuanced terminology is accurately categorized. The NER schema was carefully designed with the help of domain experts to reflect the key components present in typical vehicle service reports. The comprehensive schema ensures the dataset captures both technical diagnostics and operational context, enabling models to learn rich semantic representations. We focus on ten automotive entity types relevant for fault diagnosis and service analytics. Table 1 presents the full descriptions of entities, which is the backbone of the NER-schema.

Dictionary Formulation. A critical step in generating realistic synthetic data is creating high-quality dictionaries (entity pools) for each schema category. These dictionaries were curated from multiple authoritative and domain-specific sources to maximize coverage and authenticity. The National Highway Traffic Safety Administration (NHTSA)[2] complaint database was a primary source for extracting real-world terms related to vehicle parts, fault descriptions, and failure modes. By analyzing complaint texts and metadata, we identified common equipment names, fault types, and other entities frequently cited by consumers. This ensured that the dictionary reflected practical and diverse vocabulary actually used in the field. Official Diagnostic Trouble Codes (DTCs) code lists and their descriptions were incorporated to populate the fault code entity pool, enabling accurate representation of fault identification in vehicle diagnostics.

As such, curated dictionaries used for entity sampling encompass a broad and realistic vocabulary that enhances the representativeness and utility of the generated data.

Template-Based Construction. Template-based construction utilizes predefined sentence skeletons with placeholders to systematically generate diverse training data. Templates were repeatedly instantiated with fault-related values, yielding thousands of synthetic samples with text aligned to entity labels. DTCs forms the backbone of template-based construction, where each DTC encodes a specific fault type, component location, and often a corresponding symptom. In constructing the dataset, we maintained these logical links so that generated samples consistently paired codes with their true descriptions, components, and associated symptoms. This careful alignment ensured plausibility and prevented unrealistic pairings, such as linking a brake system code to an engine-related symptom.

Once entity values were inserted into templates, we generated coherent sentences that simulate natural technical descriptions. To introduce linguistic variability and avoid repetitive patterns, we reordered clauses, substituted synonyms and alternative phrasings (e.g. "reported fault code", "observed measurement", "time duration"), and added filler expressions such as "approximately" or "observed" to better reflect real-world reporting styles.

Each entity was then automatically labeled according to its source column, ensuring exact alignment between the generated text and the entity annotations required for NER training. This method of template construction provides a reliable foundation for developing robust NER models adapted to the terminology and structure of automotive service contexts.

[2] https://www.nhtsa.gov.

Table 1. A list of named entities derived from automotive domain, along with their descriptions and examples. These entities are used in our proposed data synthesis pipeline and NER experiment setup.

Entity	Description	Example
`CustomerReportedSymptom`	Observed issues reported by the vehicle owner	dashboard warning, engine stalling
`DeviceProperties`	Observable or measurable conditions related to equipment behavior	voltage fluctuation, temperature spike
`EquipmentName`	Specific automotive part or module involved	brake caliper, oxygen sensor
`FaultCode`	Standardized diagnostic trouble codes (DTCs) referenced in vehicle diagnostics	P0171
`FaultType`	Description of the type of failure or malfunction	seized, clogged
`MaintenanceMethod`	Service action taken to address the fault	replaced unit, cleaned and reinstalled
`MeasurementValue`	Quantitative readings indicating system status	12.6V, 150 PSI
`TimeDuration`	Temporal context relevant to fault occurrence or maintenance	during startup, after 500 miles
`VehicleComponentLocation`	Physical location of the equipment within the vehicle	engine bay, rear suspension
`VehicleMakeModel`	Specific vehicle identifiers	Tesla Model 3, Ford F-150

Formatting and Sampling. For formatting and sampling, we first transformed the annotated dataset into the CoNLL format, which represents each token-label pair on a single line and separates sentences with blank lines. Each token is paired with its corresponding BIO-formatted label, making the data suitable for token classification tasks. Following conversion, we performed a stratified sampling procedure to split the dataset into training and testing subsets. Stratification was performed to ensure a representative distribution of entity types across both splits, which is essential for fair evaluation in NER tasks.

The training sets from this distribution are used for fine-tuning RoBERTa and WG-BERT and the testset is used for evaluation of GLiNER.

3.2 Evaluation Sets

For evaluation, we evaluated our models on diverse datasets. First, a synthetic dataset was generated using the same data creation pipeline to enable controlled evaluation of GLiNER.

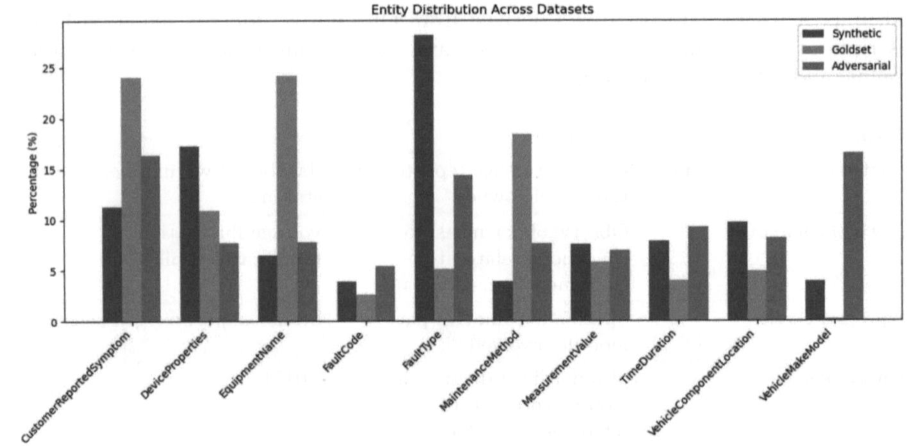

Fig. 2. Normalized entity distribution across the Synthetic, Gold and Noise evaluation datasets.

Second, a noise-perturbed dataset was developed to evaluate model robustness under noisy conditions. This dataset introduces controlled surface-level noise, including typographical perturbations (random adjacent character swaps applied probabilistically at the token level) and lexical variation through synonym substitution of selected high-frequency terms. The perturbations are applied stochastically, resulting in varying noise intensity across samples rather than uniform corruption. No syntactic restructuring is performed, allowing isolation of robustness to lexical and character-level noise. Entity annotations were derived after perturbation using exact string matching, which naturally introduces label noise and reflects the imperfect annotation conditions typical of user-generated technical logs. Noise perturbations are designed to reflect realistic user-generated logging errors rather than worst-case adversarial attacks.

Finally, an in-house gold dataset, drawn from proprietary service reports from a Swedish truck manufacturer and annotated by automotive domain experts, provides a realistic benchmark for real-world performance. Together, these three datasets enable a comprehensive evaluation across clean synthetic data, noise perturbations, and real-world in-domain examples. To better understand the distributional characteristics of the three evaluation datasets, we analyzed the relative frequencies of entity categories in each dataset. Since the absolute number of annotated entities differs significantly across the datasets (approximately 20k for the synthetic and noise, and 4k for the gold dataset), we normalized the entity counts into percentages. Figure 2 presents a grouped bar chart of the normalized entity distributions.

Table 2. Entity-wise F1-score comparison across models and evaluation sets.

Entity	Synthetic	Goldset			Synthetic with Noise		
	GLiNER	GLiNER	RoBERTa	WG-BERT	GLiNER	RoBERTa	WG-BERT
CustomerReportedSymptom	0.03	0.00	0.25	0.37	0.00	0.28	0.55
DeviceProperties	0.03	0.00	0.01	0.15	0.00	0.00	0.11
EquipmentName	0.17	0.17	0.10	0.16	0.19	0.11	0.42
FaultCode	0.64	0.21	0.39	0.56	0.04	0.66	0.91
FaultType	0.56	0.27	0.08	0.14	0.35	0.03	0.06
MaintenanceMethod	0.17	0.09	0.03	0.09	0.64	0.00	0.19
MeasurementValue	0.15	0.46	0.64	0.47	0.68	0.85	0.76
TimeDuration	0.16	0.14	0.05	0.08	0.69	0.85	0.84
VehicleComponentLocation	0.17	0.11	0.28	0.24	0.44	0.65	0.74
VehicleMakeModel	0.00	0.00	0.21	0.50	0.81	0.00	0.17
F1 score	0.21	0.14	0.60	**0.62**	0.39	0.59	**0.70**

3.3 Model Selection

For our experiments, we compared zero-shot and fine-tuned approaches to NER in the automotive domain. Model selection was guided by two criteria: (i) inclusion of a state-of-the-art zero-shot model for direct NER without domain adaptation, and (ii) evaluation of fine-tuned transformer models encompassing both general-purpose and domain-specific architectures. General-purpose LLMs were excluded from this study, as they demonstrate strong semantic understanding and extensive knowledge but struggle with token-level NER due to hallucination—confidently labeling non-entity words as entities—and incur high training and computational costs [27]. Based on these criteria, we selected three models: GLiNER [29] for zero-shot evaluation, RoBERTa-base as a strong general transformer baseline to be fine-tuned, and WG-BERT as a domain-specialized model also for fine-tuning. WG-BERT is a pretrained encoder designed specifically for analyzing automotive entities in technical texts. It is obtained by continually pretraining the BERT-base-uncased architecture on a large corpus of 1.8 million automotive workshop feedback reports ($\sim$ 4 million sentences) using the masked language modeling objective. WG-BERT's advantage stems from its vocabulary and pretraining exposure to automotive and mechanical terminology, which improves representation of domain-specific entities.

4 Results and Discussion

4.1 In-Domain Evaluation on Automotive Service Reports

Table 2 shows the evaluation results of all three models. GLiNER exhibits consistently low performance across all sets, confirming the necessity of domain-specific fine-tuning. The fine-tuned model WG-BERT performs better on both goldset and noise synthetic set in comparison to the RoBERTa fine-tuned model.

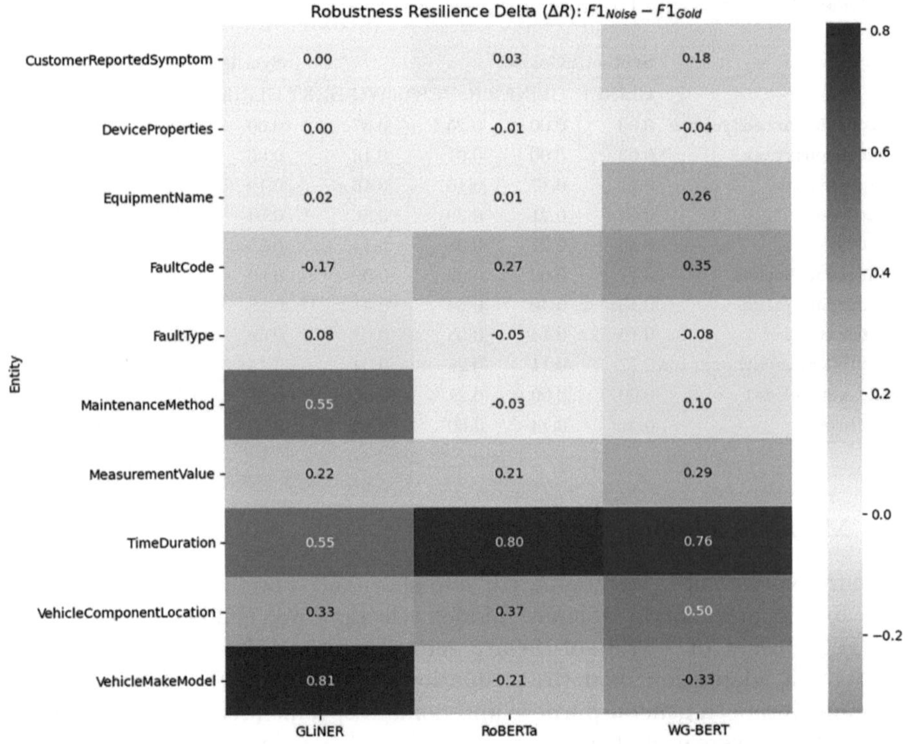

Fig. 3. Comparative analysis of model stability using the Robustness Resilience Delta.

To quantify model stability against distribution shifts, we define the *Robustness Resilience Delta* (ΔR) as the absolute performance shift between the adversarial and baseline environments:

$$\Delta R = F1_{\text{Noise}} - F1_{\text{Gold}} \tag{1}$$

where $F1_{\text{Noise}}$ represents the F1-score achieved on the noisy dataset containing synthetic character-level perturbations, and $F1_{\text{Gold}}$ denotes the baseline performance on the clean gold dataset. This metric serves as a measure of *performance retention*; a ΔR value approaching zero indicates high model invariance, while a large negative ΔR signifies a lack of structural robustness. As illustrated in Fig. 3, the results reveal a divergent landscape of architectural resilience. **WG-BERT** demonstrates the most consistent general robustness, maintaining a positive ΔR across 80% of entity categories, with a notable peak in `FaultCode` ($\Delta R = +0.35$). This suggest that its bidirectional transformer architecture, combined with domain-specific pre-training, is highly effective at regularizing against the character-level perturbations present in the adversarial set.

Table 3. NER performance on the NCBI Disease test set.

Model	Precision	Recall	F1-score
GLiNER	0.70	0.52	0.60
BioBERT Fine-tuned	0.86	0.91	0.89

In contrast, **RoBERTa** exhibits significant volatility; while it achieves high stability in alphanumeric entities like `MeasurementValue` ($\Delta R = +0.21$), it suffers from catastrophic degradation in `VehicleMakeModel` ($\Delta R = -0.21$), indicating a reliance on fragile contextual cues that are easily disrupted by synthetic noise. Furthermore, **GLiNER** shows a unique "noise-affinity" pattern, where its zero-shot mechanism appears to leverage the structured nature of the synthetic noise to improve detection in categories where it previously failed on gold data (e.g., `VehicleMakeModel`, $\Delta R = +0.81$). Collectively, these results suggest that while **WG-BERT** provides the most reliable semantic extraction for complex automotive text, **RoBERTa**'s robustness is highly dependent on entity-specific templates rather than generalized linguistic understanding.

4.2 External Evaluation on Specialized Domains

To further assess the generalization of domain-adapted NER models, we evaluate their performance on highly specialized, low-resource datasets outside the automotive domain. We evaluate GLiNER on the NCBI Disease dataset[3], a biomedical corpus with sparse disease entity annotations. Unlike the original GLiNER evaluation using span-level exact matches, we use the Hugging Face token-level test set, requiring span reconstruction that can reduce recall in this sparse, single-class task. As shown in Table 3, GLiNER achieves low metric score in comparison with BioBERT fine-tuned demonstrating the substantial improvement gained from domain-specific training.

Additional evidence from biomedical information extraction challenges, such as the GUTBRAINIE benchmark [20], supports the conclusion that prompt-based and zero-shot LLM approaches underperform compared to fine-tuned, domain-specific models. These results underscore the importance of domain adaptation for specialized NER tasks and demonstrate that our approach of fine-tuning transformer-based models on synthetic, domain-specific datasets can effectively generalize to diverse low-resource technical domains, not limited to automotive service texts.

4.3 Limitations

While our results highlight the comparative effectiveness of WG-BERT, this study is subject to several limitations. First, our evaluation does not exhaustively explore the entire landscape of transformer-based architectures. While we

[3] https://huggingface.co/datasets/ncbi/ncbi_disease.

selected representative models like RoBERTa and GLiNER, further fine-tuning of other general-purpose encoders (e.g., DeBERTa or ELECTRA) or utilizing larger parameter scales might impact the baseline performance and the resulting Robustness Resilience Delta (ΔR).

Second, our adversarial analysis relies on specific synthetic noise templates designed to simulate character-level perturbations and technical inconsistencies. While these provide a controlled environment for stress-testing, they may not fully encompass the linguistic complexity and stochastic nature of real-world "in-the-wild" automotive reports. Finally, the hyperparameters used for fine-tuning were standardized across models to ensure a fair baseline; however, model-specific optimization could potentially narrow the performance gaps observed in specific entity categories.

5 Conclusion

We present a study on fine-grained named entity recognition in unstructured automotive service texts, addressing the challenges posed by domain-specific terminology. Through evaluation of manually annotated gold data sourced from a Swedish truck manufacturer and carefully curated synthetic data, we demonstrate that WG-BERT, a domain-adapted model, consistently outperforms the general-purpose RoBERTa and the zero-shot GLiNER baseline. These findings highlight the importance of domain-specific adaptation for reliable and robust entity extraction in specialized technical domains, where general-purpose and zero-shot approaches fail to generalize under realistic conditions. While large general-purpose language models have shown promise across many NLP tasks, they are often impractical for production-grade NER due to high inference latency, computational cost, and limited controllability for structured prediction.

Furthermore, this work shows that synthetic data generation provides a practical and scalable solution to the data annotation bottleneck, enabling the training of high-performing NER models in low-resource industrial environments. These results establish synthetic data–driven, domain-specific fine-tuning as a practical foundation for accurate and deployable industrial NER systems.

Acknowledgements. The work was carried out with funding support from Sweden's innovation agency, Vinnova, through the Vehicle Strategic Research and Innovation Programme, FFI. (Reference Number: 2024-00763)

References

1. Ashok, D., Lipton, Z.C.: PromptNER: Prompting For Named Entity Recognition (2023). https://doi.org/10.48550/arXiv.2305.15444, arXiv:2305.15444 [cs]
2. Bogdanov, S., Constantin, A., Bernard, T., Crabbé, B., Bernard, E.P.: Nuner: Entity recognition encoder pre-training via LLM-annotated data. In: Proceedings of the 2024 Conference on Empirical Methods in Natural Language Processing, pp. 11829–11841 (2024)

3. Chinchor, N.: Appendix c: Named entity task definition (v2.1). In: Proceedings of the Sixth Message Understanding Conference (MUC-6). Columbia, Maryland (1995). https://aclanthology.org/M95-1024/
4. Dai, X., Adel, H.: An analysis of simple data augmentation for named entity recognition. In: Proceedings of the 28th International Conference on Computational Linguistics, pp. 3861–3867 (2020)
5. Derczynski, L., Nichols, E., Van Erp, M., Limsopatham, N.: Results of the wnut2017 shared task on novel and emerging entity recognition. In: Proceedings of the 3rd Workshop on Noisy User-generated Text, pp. 140–147 (2017)
6. Deußer, T., et al.: A comparative study of large language models for named entity recognition in the legal domain. In: 2024 IEEE International Conference on Big Data (BigData), pp. 4737–4742. IEEE (2024)
7. Devlin, J., Chang, M.W., Lee, K., Toutanova, K.: Bert: Pre-training of deep bidirectional transformers for language understanding. In: Proceedings of the 2019 Conference of the North American Chapter of the Association for Computational Linguistics: Human Language Technologies, volume 1 (long and short papers), pp. 4171–4186 (2019)
8. Gururangan, S., et al.: Don't stop pretraining: Adapt language models to domains and tasks. In: Proceedings of the 58th Annual Meeting of the Association for Computational Linguistics, pp. 8342–8360 (2020)
9. Hakala, K., Pyysalo, S.: Biomedical named entity recognition with multilingual bert. In: Proceedings of the 5th Workshop on BioNLP Open Shared Tasks, pp. 56–61 (2019)
10. Heng, Y., et al.: Proggen: Generating named entity recognition datasets step-by-step with self-reflexive large language models. In: Findings of the Association for Computational Linguistics: ACL 2024. pp. 15992–16030 (2024)
11. Huang, Z., Xu, W., Yu, K.: Bidirectional LSTM-CRF Models for Sequence Tagging (2015). https://doi.org/10.48550/arXiv.1508.01991, arXiv:1508.01991 [cs]
12. Hyun, D., Cho, J., Yu, H.: Building large-scale English and Korean datasets for aspect-level sentiment analysis in automotive domain. In: Proceedings of the 28th International Conference on Computational Linguistics, pp. 961–966 (2020)
13. Jie, H.: Information Extraction for Test Identification in Repair Reports in the Automotive Domain (2023). https://urn.kb.se/resolve?urn=urn:nbn:se:uu:diva-505634
14. Kamath, G., Vajjala, S.: Does Synthetic Data Help Named Entity Recognition for Low-Resource Languages? (2025). https://doi.org/10.48550/arXiv.2505.16814, arXiv:2505.16814 [cs]
15. Keraghel, A., Benabdeslem, K., Canitia, B.: Data augmentation process to improve deep learning-based ner task in the automotive industry field. In: 2020 International Joint Conference on Neural Networks (IJCNN), pp. 1–8. IEEE (2020)
16. Keraghel, I., Morbieu, S., Nadif, M.: Recent Advances in Named Entity Recognition: A Comprehensive Survey and Comparative Study (2024). https://doi.org/10.48550/arXiv.2401.10825, arXiv:2401.10825 [cs] version: 3
17. Lafferty, J.D., McCallum, A., Pereira, F.C.N.: Conditional random fields: probabilistic models for segmenting and labeling sequence data. In: Proceedings of the Eighteenth International Conference on Machine Learning. pp. 282–289. ICML '01, Morgan Kaufmann Publishers Inc., San Francisco, CA, USA (2001)

18. Li, C., Zhao, Y., Tang, F.: named entity recognition for automotive fault domain based on adaptive transformer. In: Proceedings of the 2025 International Conference on Big Data, Communication Technology and Computer Applications, pp. 55–59. BDCTA '25, Association for Computing Machinery, New York, NY, USA (2025). https://doi.org/10.1145/3727505.3727514, https://dl.acm.org/doi/10.1145/3727505.3727514
19. Liu, Y., et al.: Roberta: A robustly optimized bert pretraining approach. arXiv preprint arXiv:1907.11692 (2019)
20. Martinelli, M., et al.: A domain-specific curated benchmark for entity and document-level relation extraction. In: Proceedings of the 18th Conference of the European Chapter of the Association for Computational Linguistics (EACL). Association for Computational Linguistics, TBD (2026)
21. del Moral-González, R., Gómez-Adorno, H., Ramos-Flores, O.: Comparative analysis of generative LLMs for labeling entities in clinical notes. Genomics Inf **23**(1), 3 (2025). https://doi.org/10.1186/s44342-024-00036-x
22. Munnangi, M.: A brief history of named entity recognition. arXiv preprint arXiv:2411.05057 (2024)
23. Nayak, A., Timmapathini, H.P.: Wiki to Automotive: Understanding the Distribution Shift and its impact on Named Entity Recognition (2021). https://doi.org/10.48550/arXiv.2112.00283, arXiv:2112.00283 [cs]
24. Ratner, A., Bach, S.H., Ehrenberg, H., Fries, J., Wu, S., Ré, C.: Snorkel: Rapid training data creation with weak supervision. In: Proceedings of the VLDB endowment. International Conference on Very Large Data Bases, vol. 11, p. 269 (2017)
25. Sivaraman, N.K., Koduri, R., Manalikandy, M.: A hybrid method for automotive entity recognition. Tech. rep, SAE Technical Paper (2021)
26. Ventirozos, F., Nteka, I., Nandy, T., Baca, J., Appleby, P., Shardlow, M.: Shifting ner into high gear: The auto-adver approach. arXiv preprint arXiv:2412.05655 (2024)
27. Xu, W., Dang, R., Huang, S.: Llm's weakness in ner doesn't stop it from enhancing a stronger slm. In: Proceedings of the Second Workshop on Ancient Language Processing, pp. 170–175 (2025)
28. Yaseen, U., Langer, S.: Data augmentation for low-resource named entity recognition using backtranslation. In: Proceedings of the 18th International Conference on Natural Language Processing (ICON), pp. 352–358 (2021)
29. Zaratiana, U., Tomeh, N., Holat, P., Charnois, T.: GLiNER: Generalist Model for Named Entity Recognition using Bidirectional Transformer (2023). https://doi.org/10.48550/arXiv.2311.08526, arXiv:2311.08526 [cs]

Time Series and Stream Data

Similarity-Guided Forecasting of Multiple Sequences from Mechanical Testing Data of Additively Manufactured Components

Antonio Pellicani[1,2], Gianvito Pio[1,2(✉)], Donato Malerba[1,2], and Michelangelo Ceci[1,2,3]

[1] Department of Computer Science, University of Bari, Bari, Italy
{antonio.pellicani,gianvito.pio,donato.malerba, michelangelo.ceci}@uniba.it

[2] Data Science Laboratory, National Interuniversity Consortium for Informatics, Rome, Italy

[3] Department of Knowledge Technologies, Jožef Stefan Institute, Ljubljana, Slovenia

Abstract. Additive manufacturing processes can generate heterogeneous mechanical testing data, which can be precious to characterize and predict material performance. In this work, we propose a similarity-guided forecasting method to analyze multivariate time series acquired during mechanical testing of additively manufactured components. The proposed method first clusters test trajectories via Dynamic Time Warping similarity measure, computed on force response signals, then trains cluster-specific LSTM-based models for multi-step multivariate forecasting. We evaluate the proposed approach on a public dataset comprising bending and compression tests, systematically analyzing the effect of different DTW windowing strategies and of the number of clusters. The obtained results show that computing DTW similarity on the entire time series, combined with a relatively small number of clusters, yields the best forecasting performance, with substantial improvements over a baseline model trained on full unclustered data.

Keywords: Additive manufacturing · Time series analysis · Multi-step forecasting · Temporal Clustering

1 Introduction

Additive Manufacturing (AM) has emerged as a transformative technology in modern industrial production, enabling rapid prototyping, mass customization, and reduced lead times [18]. However, the layer-wise deposition process introduces inherent variability, including porosity and inter-layer bonding imperfections, that can significantly affect mechanical performance [13]. To ensure quality and reliability, manufacturers continuously monitor printed components

G. Andresini et al. (Eds.): ISMIS 2026, LNAI 16685, pp. 215–224, 2027.
https://doi.org/10.1007/978-3-032-32643-0_18

through standardized mechanical tests, such as three-point bending and compression, generating multivariate time-series data that capture the evolving force-displacement response under load. Analyzing these signals to characterize material behavior and predict potential damages is increasingly gaining attention for data-driven quality assurance.

A key challenge in modeling mechanical testing data lies in the heterogeneity of response trajectories. Even components produced under identical conditions may exhibit distinct temporal dynamics due to material variability, printing-induced defects, or measurement noise. The need for an accurate forecast of the evolution of mechanical signals during testing motivates the adoption of advanced techniques accounting for such a heterogeneity, including machine learning-based forecasting methods [9]. Nevertheless, traditional machine learning approaches for time-series forecasting in this domain typically rely on global models trained across all available tests, implicitly assuming a homogeneous underlying process. While such methods may benefit from larger training sets, they risk blurring distinct behavioral regimes and producing predictions that inadequately capture the diversity of mechanical responses [8]. Existing strategies based on metadata stratification (e.g., grouping by material or process parameters) only partially address this issue, as they do not account for latent variability that emerges within nominally identical conditions [2].

Recent work in multivariate time-series forecasting has demonstrated the effectiveness of similarity-guided pipelines that cluster correlated sequences prior to learning predictive models. The rationale behind these approaches is that heterogeneous collections of time series often contain latent subgroups with distinct dynamics. By identifying such groups and training specialized models for each of them, the forecasting accuracy can be improved compared to global models, as shown in diverse domains, including financial forecasting [15,16], energy consumption prediction [3,11,12], and epidemiological modeling [1,4].

In this paper, we propose a similarity-guided forecasting method for mechanical testing of additively manufactured components. Our approach *i)* clusters test trajectories which appear similar in terms of force response signals, and *ii)* trains cluster-specific predictive models for multivariate forecasting, i.e., for the prediction of multiple characteristics simultaneously. Such characteristics are predicted for multiple future time steps [5,6], making the proposed approach a multivariate multi-step forecasting solution able to provide a more comprehensive view of what is going to happen on the component under test in the near future.

In our experiments, we systematically evaluate the effects of different clustering parameters, comparing the obtained results with those achieved by a baseline model trained on the whole unclustered dataset.

2 The Proposed Method

The proposed method addresses the forecasting of multivariate mechanical testing time series using a two-stage approach. The first stage clusters the trajectories of mechanical tests exhibiting similar temporal dynamics, using a similarity measure suitable for time series with potential temporal misalignments. The second stage trains cluster-specific models for multi-step multivariate forecasting of the mechanical response signals. This partitioning enables the training of specialized models for each group, rather than a single global model that would need to accommodate heterogeneous response patterns. In Fig. 1 we show a graphical representation of the method, while in the following subsections we describe each stage of the method in detail.

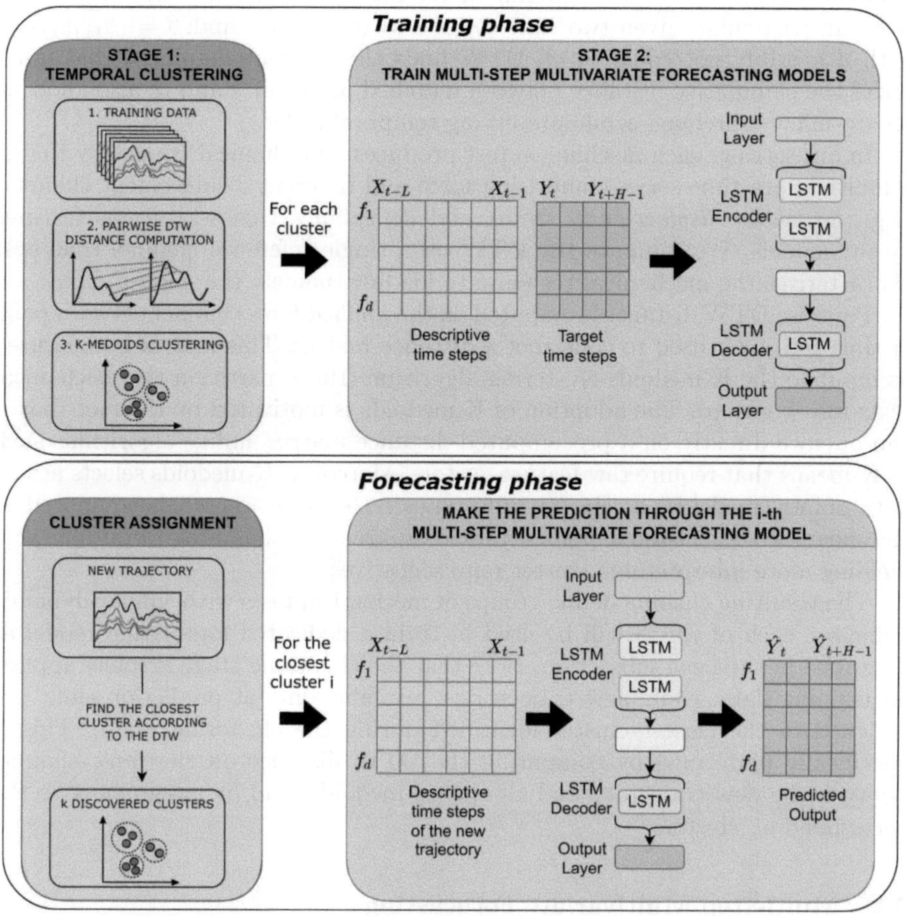

Fig. 1. Graphical representation of the proposed method.

2.1 Temporal Clustering

Mechanical tests, even if performed under nominally identical conditions, may exhibit heterogeneous response patterns due to material variability, printing defects, or measurement noise [2]. To manage this variability, we identify tests exhibiting similar response patterns, by resorting to a temporal clustering strategy that groups test trajectories according to their temporal similarity.

Methodologically, we start by calculating the Dynamic Time Warping (DTW) distance [17] between all pairs of mechanical test trajectories. We adopt DTW since, unlike other common distance measures like the Euclidean distance or the Manhattan distance, it can align time series that exhibit similar shapes but differ in phase or local timing, thus making it well-suited for mechanical response signals where the beginning or the rate of deformation may vary across tests. In particular, given two time series $\alpha = \langle \alpha_1, ..., \alpha_n \rangle$ and $\beta = \langle \beta_1, ..., \beta_m \rangle$, with n possibly not equal to m, DTW finds the optimal alignment that minimizes the cumulative distance between matched points in α and β, also allowing one-to-many matchings while preserving temporal order.

In our setting, each mechanical test produces a mechanical trajectory that is a multivariate time series comprising force and different displacement channels (e.g., *crosshead displacement*, *strain*, and *deflection*), that will act as features in our models. We compute the DTW on a single reference channel that best characterizes the mechanical response to loading, namely the *applied force*.

Pairwise DTW distances computed on the *applied force* channel between pairs of time series are used to construct a distance matrix. This matrix is then used as input to the K-medoids clustering algorithm [10] to partition the mechanical tests into k groups. The adoption of K-medoids is motivated by the fact that it can operate directly on a precomputed distance matrix, unlike algorithms such as K-means that require raw feature vectors. Moreover, K-medoids selects actual data points (medoids) as cluster prototypes rather than centroids computed as the mean of the clustered points, providing greater robustness to outliers and yielding more interpretable cluster representatives.

The resulting clusters define groups of mechanical tests with similar dynamic behavior, each of which will be used to train a dedicated forecasting model as described in the next subsection. Note that the clustering stage is solely applied on training data, while new trajectories, available only at prediction time, are assigned to the closest cluster identified during the clustering phase. This is specifically performed by computing the DTW distance on the *force* channel between the new trajectory and all cluster medoids, and by assigning it to the corresponding cluster.

2.2 Multi-step Multivariate Forecasting

Once the mechanical tests are partitioned, we train a dedicated forecasting model for each cluster. The goal is to predict multiple future time steps of all response channels (*force* and *displacements*) given a sequence of past observations.

To formulate the supervised learning task, we apply a sliding window approach to transform each time series into a set of input-output pairs. Specifically, given a multivariate time series consisting of T time steps and d channels, we define a lookback window of length L and a prediction horizon of length H.

Starting from the time step $t = L$, we define examples by sliding the window with a stride equal to 1. For each time step t, we have an input matrix $X_t \in \mathbb{R}^{d \times L}$ containing the observations from time step $t - L$ to $t - 1$, and an output matrix $Y_t \in \mathbb{R}^{d \times H}$ containing the observations from time step t to $t + H - 1$.

Accordingly, X and Y represent, respectively, the values of all the d variables for L descriptive (past) time steps and the H target (future) time steps for all the examples. This formulation allows the model to learn temporal dynamics within the lookback window of size L and predict how the mechanical response will evolve in the next H time steps. The sliding window is applied to each time series in the cluster, forming cluster-specific training sets.

To learn the forecasting model, we adopt a sequence-to-sequence architecture based on Long Short-Term Memory (LSTM) networks. LSTMs are a type of recurrent neural network specifically designed to capture long-range dependencies in sequential data, addressing the vanishing gradient problem that affects standard recurrent networks [14]. This makes them particularly well-suited for time series forecasting tasks where patterns may span extended temporal intervals.

The LSTM architecture consists of an encoder and a decoder. The encoder processes X sequentially, updating its hidden state at each time step through stacked LSTM layers. At the end of the input sequence, the encoder produces a fixed-dimensional latent representation that summarizes the temporal dynamics observed in the lookback window. Formally, the encoder computes:

$$h_t, c_t = LSTM_{enc}(X_t, h_{t-1}, c_{t-1}) \tag{1}$$

where X_t is the input at time step t, and h_t and c_t are the hidden state and cell state, respectively. After processing all T-L+1 time steps, the final hidden state serves as the encoded representation of the input sequence. The decoder takes this encoded representation and generates the output sequence $\hat{Y}_t$ of length H. The decoder is initialized with the final hidden state of the encoder and produces one output at each time step through its own LSTM layers, followed by a fully-connected output layer that maps the hidden state to the dimension d, namely:

$$h'_t, c'_t = LSTM_{dec}(\hat{Y}_{t-1}, h'_{t-1}, c'_{t-1}) \qquad \hat{Y}_t = W_{out} \times h'_t + b_{out} \tag{2}$$

where $\hat{Y}_t$ is the predicted output at time step t, and W_{out} and b_{out} are the weights and bias of the output layer.

In our method, for the encoder, we adopt two stacked LSTM layers with 64 units each, followed by a dropout layer with rate 0.4. For the decoder, we include a single LSTM layer with 64 units and two fully connected layers (one layer with 64 units with ReLU activation function and one linear output layer).

At inference time, the prediction process mirrors the training procedure. Once a new trajectory is assigned to a cluster, we extract input windows using the same sliding window parameters (lookback length L, horizon H, and stride 1) adopted during training. Each input window is then fed to the corresponding cluster-specific encoder-decoder model, which generates predictions for the next H time steps across all mechanical response channels.

3 Experiments

In this section, we present the experimental evaluation of the proposed method. We first describe the dataset used in our experiments. Then we detail the experimental setting, and finally discuss the obtained results.

3.1 The Considered Dataset

The dataset used in this study is publicly available on the Harvard Dataverse [7] and contains data about 359 mechanical tests performed through the Zwick/Roell Z250 testing machine on additively manufactured polymer components. Two standardized mechanical testing procedures were carried out in order to characterize the structural response of the printed components under different loading conditions: three-point bending tests, performed according to ISO 178:2019, and compression tests, conducted following ISO 604:2002.

Data of each test is stored as a multivariate time series, where measurements are roughly performed every 100ms. In particular, in bending tests, the recorded channels comprise *time*, *deflection*, *standard displacement*, *crosshead displacement*, and *applied force*, whereas compression tests include *time*, *test time*, *crosshead displacement*, *standard displacement*, *compression strain*, *nominal compression*, and *applied force*.

Notably, due to differences in material response and test termination conditions, the resulting time series exhibit variable lengths. This characteristic reflects the intrinsic nature of mechanical testing procedures and motivates the adoption of the DTW measure for clustering, as discussed in Sect. 2.1.

3.2 Experimental Setting

Prior to clustering and forecasting, continuous features were standardized, while categorical variables, such as *material type*, were encoded using one-hot encoding. Experiments were performed through a 80%-20% training-testing split, performed at the level of time series, namely, each time series entirely falls either into the training set or into the testing set.

The clustering phase was performed on the training set by evaluating different configurations for the DTW computation and of the number of clusters k. In particular, two DTW windowing strategies were considered: *full-series similarity*, computed over the entire time series, and *late-phase similarity*, computed over the last half of each series. The latter focuses on the portion of the test where material-specific behaviors, such as yielding or failure onset, are more pronounced. Combining these two strategies with three values of clusters k, namely, $k \in \{3, 5, 7\}$, yields six experimental configurations, denoted as **L3**, **L5**, **L7** (late-phase) and **F3**, **F5**, **F7** (full-series).

As hyperparameters, we set the lookback length $L = 32$ and the prediction horizon $H = 4$. The LSTM model was trained using the Adam optimizer (learning rate $= 0.001$) and a batch size of 64. The maximum number of epochs was set to 200, with an early stopping patience of 20 epochs to mitigate overfitting.

The predictive performance was assessed using the Mean Absolute Error (MAE) measure. To perform a detailed analysis of the results, MAE was collected separately for each predicted variable and for each timestep of the prediction horizon, considering bending and compression tests separately.

As a baseline competitor, we considered a single LSTM model trained on all mechanical tests of a given type (bending or compression) without clustering, using the same LSTM architecture and training configuration of our approach. This baseline allows to assess the possible contribution provided by the partitioning of time series through clustering, as performed by our approach.

3.3 Results and Discussion

Figure 2 shows the MAE results for each configuration for bending (on the top) and compression (in the bottom) tests. Each subplot shows the MAE for a predicted variable along the four time steps of the prediction horizon (t_1 to t_4).

For bending tests, full-series DTW configurations consistently outperform the late-phase ones across all predicted variables. Among them, **F3** achieves the lowest MAE in most cases, particularly for displacement-related channels (*deflection*, *standard displacement*, and *crosshead displacement*). The advantage of **F3** over the baseline is substantial, with relative improvements ranging from approximately 30% to 45% depending on the variable and time step. The only exception is at t_4 for the variable *force_N*, where performances are comparable with those of the baseline. Configurations **F5** and **F7** also outperform the baseline, although with smaller margins. In contrast, the late-phase configurations show mixed results: **L5** and **L7** are generally comparable to the baseline, while **L3** often performs worse. The *force* channel exhibits higher MAE values across all configurations, suggesting that *force* prediction is inherently more challenging than displacement prediction in bending tests.

For compression tests, the gap among configurations is narrower. Full-series configurations again tend to outperform late-phase ones, although the difference is less pronounced than in bending tests. **F5** emerges as the best configuration overall, achieving the lowest MAE on *crosshead displacement* and *compression strain*. **F3** performs comparably on several variables, while **F7** shows more oscillating results. Among late-phase configurations, **L3** appears competitive on some channels, particularly *nominal compression* and *force*.

For both test types, the results indicate that full-series DTW similarity is more effective than late-phase similarity for grouping tests. This suggests that considering the complete temporal trajectory is needed to provide the necessary information for properly capturing similarity patterns through the DTW. On the contrary, the lower performances exhibited by the late-phase approach may be due to the focus on the final portion of the test, which may be very specific of the tests at hand, preventing the identification of more general patterns.

Regarding the number of clusters, smaller values of k (3 or 5) generally yield better results, possibly because larger values fragment the training data in too small clusters, with insufficient samples for effective model specialization.

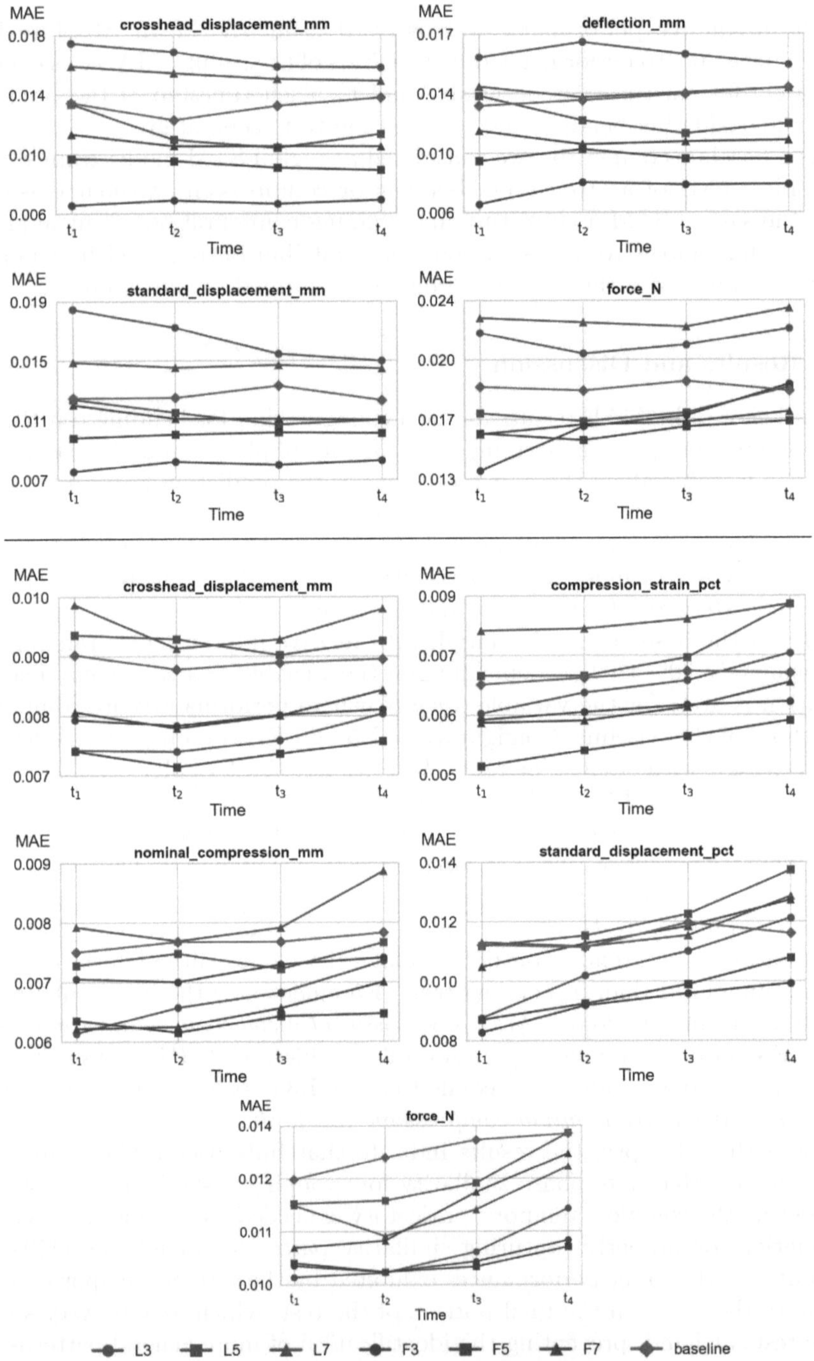

Fig. 2. MAE results for bending (on the top) and compression (in the bottom) tests for all the predicted variables. Lk and Fk denote late-phase and full-series DTW, respectively, with $k \in \{3, 5, 7\}$. The baseline is a single LSTM trained without clustering.

4 Conclusion

In this paper, we proposed a similarity-guided multi-step forecasting method for multivariate time series from mechanical testing of additively manufactured components. The proposed method clusters test trajectories based on DTW similarity computed on force signals, then trains cluster-specific LSTM encoder-decoder models for multi-step multivariate forecasting.

Our experimental evaluation on a public dataset comprising bending and compression tests demonstrated the effectiveness of the proposed approach. In particular, the results showed that cluster-specific models learned from clusters identified through full-series DTW similarity consistently outperforms those achieved through late-phase similarity. In general, cluster-specific models leads to up to 45% improvement over a baseline LSTM model learned from unclustered tests. These findings suggest that the cluster-then-forecast approach, previously applied in other domains, such as energy and financial forecasting, transfers effectively to mechanical testing data. By partitioning tests into homogeneous groups before model training, each forecaster specializes on trajectories with similar dynamics, leading to more accurate predictions.

Future work could explore alternative clustering strategies, also based on multi-channel DTW or learned representations. We will also perform a deep sensitivity analysis of the method's hyperparameters, including the lookback length L and the horizon H. Finally, we will investigate the integration of the proposed approach into a more comprehensive monitoring system for real-time quality assessment during additive manufacturing processes.

Acknowledgments. This research was supported by the Italian MUR, through the project "MAD – La metamorfosi Additiva del Design", Grant No. ARS01_00717 (MAD – The Additive Metamorphosis of Design) for the activities of WP3 & WP5.

Disclosure of Interests. The authors have no competing interests to declare that are relevant to the content of this article.

References

1. Alahakoon, P., McCaw, J.M., Taylor, P.G.: Use of clustering to improve estimation of epidemic model parameters under a Bayesian hierarchical framework. medRxiv, pp. 2022–12 (2022)
2. Becker, C., et al.: Experimental quantification of the variability of mechanical properties in 3d printed continuous fiber composites. Appl. Sci. **11**(23), 11315 (2021)
3. Corizzo, R., Pio, G., Ceci, M., Malerba, D.: DENCAST: distributed density-based clustering for multi-target regression. J. Big Data **6**(1), 43 (2019)
4. Corradin, R., Danese, L., KhudaBukhsh, W.R., Ongaro, A.: Model-based clustering of time-dependent observations with common structural changes. Stat. Comput. **36**(1), 1–15 (2026)
5. D'Aversa, A., Pio, G., Ceci, M.: Modeling spatio-temporal locality in multi-step forecasting of geo-referenced time series. Mach. Learn. **114**(10), 231 (2025)

6. D'Aversa, A., Pio, G., Ceci, M.: Leveraging spatio-temporal locality in linear model trees for multi-step time series forecasting. In: 2024 IEEE International Conference on Big Data (BigData), pp. 1282–1287 (2024)
7. Frohn-Sörensen, P., Geueke, M., Löffler, B., Bickendorf, P., Asimi, A.: Measurements of mechanical material properties under compressive and bending load of additive manufactured polymers (2022). https://doi.org/10.7910/DVN/1ARRM2
8. Godahewa, R., Bandara, K., Webb, G.I., Smyl, S., Bergmeir, C.: Ensembles of localised models for time series forecasting. Knowl.-Based Syst. **233**, 107518 (2021)
9. Inayathullah, S., Buddala, R.: Review of machine learning applications in additive manufacturing. Results Eng. **25**, 103676 (2025)
10. Kaufman, L., Rousseeuw, P.J.R.: Partitioning Around Medoids (Program PAM), chap. 2, pp. 68–125. Wiley (1990)
11. Kim, H., Park, S., Kim, S.: Time-series clustering and forecasting household electricity demand using smart meter data. Energy Rep. **9**, 4111–4121 (2023)
12. Kubheka, S., Zyl, T.V., Wang, H.: Clustered bootstrap similarity learning framework: time series forecasting. IEEE Access **13**, 207733–207748 (2025)
13. Mao, Y., et al.: Origin of deposition errors and layer-wise control strategies during laser additive manufacturing. Virtual Phys. Prototyp. **18**(1), e2173615 (2023)
14. Pascanu, R., Mikolov, T., Bengio, Y.: On the difficulty of training recurrent neural networks. In: International Conference on Machine Learning, pp. 1310–1318. PMLR (2013)
15. Pellicani, A., Pio, G., Ceci, M.: CARROT: simultaneous prediction of anomalies from groups of correlated cryptocurrency trends. Expert Syst. Appl. **260**, 125457 (2025)
16. Pellicani, A., Pio, G., Džeroski, S., Ceci, M.: Real-time anomaly prediction from cryptocurrency time series. In: Meo, R., Silvestri, F. (eds.) ECML PKDD 2023. CCIS, vol. 2135, pp. 553–561. Springer, Cham (2025). https://doi.org/10.1007/978-3-031-74633-8_42
17. Vintsyuk, T.K.: Speech discrimination by dynamic programming. Cybernetics **4**(1), 52–57 (1968)
18. Zhou, L., et al.: Additive manufacturing: a comprehensive review. Sensors **24**(9), 2668 (2024)

Leveraging Foundational Time-Series Models for Zero-Shot Appliance-Level Load Forecasting

Angelo Impedovo(✉)

NSA Italia srl, piazza Aldo Moro 33A, 70125 Bari, Italy
a.impedovo@nesea.it

Abstract. Foundational time-series models, that is potentially large and pre-trained architectures trained on diverse temporal data, offer a promising new paradigm for building energy management systems (BEMS), where accurate load forecasting is essential yet often constrained by limited appliance-level data. This study investigates the zero-shot forecasting capabilities of several state-of-the-art foundational models when applied to appliance-level load forecasting across heterogeneous appliances and buildings. Without any task-specific fine-tuning, these models are evaluated on their ability to generalize to unseen appliances, varying consumption patterns, and diverse operational contexts. The analysis spans multiple building types and device categories, reflecting realistic BEMS deployment scenarios. Results highlight the extent to which broad temporal priors embedded in foundational models can substitute for traditional, data-hungry forecasting pipelines. The findings reveal both the strengths and current limitations of zero-shot approaches, offering insights into their practical viability and outlining pathways for integrating foundational models into next-generation energy management systems.

Keywords: Machine Learning · Time Series · Load Forecasting · Foundational Models

1 Introduction

Building Energy Management Systems (BEMS) play a central role in modern energy-efficient buildings by coordinating sensing, control, and analytics to optimize energy use at both the whole-building and appliance levels. Through continuous monitoring of electrical loads, occupancy patterns, and environmental conditions, BEMS enable intelligent decision-making that reduces operational costs, enhances comfort, and supports grid-responsive behavior. Their effectiveness, however, relies heavily on accurate forecasting models capable of anticipating the energy demand across diverse devices and buildings.

In particular, load forecasting in BEMS involves predicting future electricity demand over horizons ranging from minutes to months. Accurate forecasts

G. Andresini et al. (Eds.): ISMIS 2026, LNAI 16685, pp. 225–235, 2027.
https://doi.org/10.1007/978-3-032-32643-0_19

are essential because nearly every operational decision, from real-time appliance scheduling to long-term planning, depends on anticipating future demand. In BEMS, both short-term and long-term predictions are needed: short-term ones enable rapid control actions, such as adjusting HVAC or responding to sudden occupancy changes, while long-term forecasts support storage planning, tariff-aware scheduling, and coordination with distributed resources. Likewise, fine-grained predictions at the appliance or zone level allow the BEMS to optimize specific loads and detect localized anomalies, whereas coarse, building-level forecasts are needed for global energy budgeting and peak-demand management. Since these requirements vary across buildings and over time, and cannot be anticipated at BEMS-development time, a general BEMS must flexibly handle heterogeneous forecasting horizons and granularities rather than relying on a single, fixed setup.

However, training load forecasting models that can operate across different buildings and appliance types is particularly challenging because reliable, high-quality data are often scarce or inconsistent. In a truly general BEMS the model must be able to generalize across an essentially open-ended set of scenarios. This is difficult to achieve in practice: each building exhibits its own usage patterns, sensor configurations, and operational constraints, while appliances differ in dynamics, intermittency, and sensitivity to contextual factors. These factors make it hard to train models that remain accurate and stable across heterogeneous environments and changing conditions. Models trained under such constraints struggle when applied to new buildings, unseen appliance categories, or forecasting tasks that differ from those observed during training, thus limiting the generalization ability of a given BEMS to different scenarios.

Pre-trained models for time-series tasks offer a compelling way to overcome these data limitations because they encode broad temporal patterns learned from large and diverse datasets, far beyond what is typically available in individual buildings. By leveraging these rich priors, foundational models can provide strong initial representations of temporal dynamics, enabling them to perform meaningful load forecasts even in zero-shot settings where no task-specific training is possible. This approach bypasses the need to collect extensive appliance-level histories or retrain models from scratch for every new building or every new appliance type, making forecasting more scalable and accessible. As a result, pre-trained time-series models present a promising pathway toward robust, data-efficient load-forecasting solutions suitable for real-world BEMS deployments. Foundational time-series models exhibit the kind of broad temporal understanding that makes them naturally suited for handling the variability found in building-level energy data. Their ability to internalize generic structures—such as periodicity, seasonality, and short-term temporal dependencies—allows them to recognize and extrapolate similar patterns in load-consumption signals, even when encountering new buildings or unfamiliar appliances. For this reason, we argue that zero-shot load forecasting is not only feasible but a promising direction when leveraging pretrained foundational models. In our view, these models provide a strong basis for scalable, data-efficient forecasting pipelines capable of delivering meaningful predictions without requiring any local training effort.

2 Related Works

Recent research on load forecasting within BEMS has increasingly focused on leveraging machine learning techniques to improve prediction accuracy at both whole-building and appliance granularity. Several studies investigate building-level consumption forecasting as a core component of BEMS optimization. For instance, [4] explores deep learning approaches for forecasting electricity consumption in modern BEMS, highlighting the importance of accurate predictions for real-time control and energy-efficiency strategies. At a finer level of granularity, appliance-level load forecasting has gained significant attention due to its relevance for demand-side management and smart home applications. [5] propose an LSTM-based model for forecasting the load of individual household appliances, demonstrating improved performance over traditional baselines. Similarly, [6] employs a sequence-to-sequence architecture to capture appliance-specific temporal patterns, comparing it against multiple competitors.

Foundational models for time-series forecasting represent a shift toward large, pre-trained architectures that learn general-purpose temporal representations from broad and heterogeneous datasets. By decoupling training from downstream tasks, they aim to deliver universal forecasting capabilities, enabling zero-shot or few-shot inference much like foundational models in natural language processing. For instance, Chronos-2, introduced by [1], is a 120M-parameter encoder-only model, supporting univariate, multivariate, and covariate-aware forecasting. Through in-context learning and group-attention mechanisms, Chronos-2 efficiently processes related time series and produces multi-step probabilistic forecasts, achieving strong zero-shot performance across diverse benchmarks. Additionally, Google's TimesFM [3] follows a similar philosophy, leveraging large-scale pre-training on extensive temporal datasets to provide broadly generalizable forecasts across domains such as economics, energy, and retail. Its emphasis on scalability and ease of deployment further illustrates the growing maturity of foundational approaches. Together, Chronos-2 and TimesFM highlight the movement toward universal, task-agnostic forecasting engines.

This work positions itself at the intersection of BEMS research, load forecasting methodologies, and the emerging field of foundational time-series models. Together, these developments highlight both the rapid progress in foundational time-series modeling and the growing emphasis on appliance and building-level load forecasting within next-generation BEMS. Across these areas, a consistent theme emerges: the need to cope with heterogeneous device behaviors and the persistent scarcity of representative training data for each of them. Despite the promise of recent foundational models such as Chronos-2, a systematic assessment of their performance across multiple buildings and diverse appliance types has not yet been reported, leaving an important gap in understanding their practical applicability to real-world energy-management scenarios. By bringing these threads together, foundational time-series models offer a promising and scalable path forward, capable of addressing long-standing challenges in load forecasting without relying on conventional, data-intensive training pipelines.

3 Background

The goal of appliance-level load forecasting is to predict future power consumption values for individual devices based on past observations. From a supervised learning perspective, appliance-level load forecasting can be formulated as a sequence-to-sequence prediction problem. Given a univariate power consumption signal $(x_1, x_2, \ldots, x_T) \in \mathbb{R}^T$ for a single appliance, we construct a dataset of labeled forecasting instances by sliding a window of length $w \in \mathbb{N}$ over the series. Each instance consists of an input window $\mathbf{x}_{t,w} = (x_t, x_{t+1}, \ldots, x_{t+w-1})$ paired with its corresponding future target window $\mathbf{y}_{t+w:h} = (x_{t+w}, x_{t+w+1} \ldots, x_{t+h-1})$ for a forecasting horizon $h \in \mathbb{N}$. The resulting supervised dataset is

$$\mathcal{D} = \{(\mathbf{x}_{t,w}, \mathbf{y}_{t+w,h})\}_{t=1}^{T-w-h}$$

To respect temporal ordering, $\mathcal{D}$ is typically partitioned chronologically into a training set $\mathcal{D}_{\text{train}}$ and a test set $\mathcal{D}_{\text{test}}$. The goal is to learn a forecasting function $f : \mathbb{R}^w \to \mathbb{R}^h$. Model parameters are optimized on $\mathcal{D}_{\text{train}}$ using an appropriate loss function, and performance is evaluated on $\mathcal{D}_{\text{test}}$ to assess generalization to unseen time windows. Learning such a function from scratch is challenging due to (i) *data scarcity*, as many appliances exhibit short or irregular usage histories; (ii) *heterogeneity*, since different devices follow distinct temporal patterns; and (iii) *behavioral variability*, where human-driven usage introduces strong non-stationarity. Traditional supervised approaches therefore struggle, as they require substantial labeled data for each appliance or building, limiting scalability in real-world BEMS deployments. This motivates forecasting frameworks that do not rely on device-specific training data. In a zero-shot setting, the forecasting function f is assumed to be pretrained on large, diverse time-series corpora and then applied directly to new appliances without further fine-tuning.

4 Foundational Time-Series Models

We propose addressing the load forecasting problem using two state-of-the-art foundational time-series models: Chronos-2 and TimesFM. Both models are pretrained on large and diverse collections of temporal data, enabling them to generalize across domains without appliance or building-specific training. By leveraging their inference-only forecasting capabilities, we investigate whether these foundational architectures can accurately predict appliance-level and building-level power consumption in settings where historical data are scarce or unavailable, thereby offering a scalable alternative to traditional, data-intensive forecasting pipelines.

4.1 Chronos-2

Chronos-2 is a foundational time-series model designed to provide universal forecasting capabilities across diverse temporal domains. It adopts an encoder-only Transformer architecture inspired by T5, equipped with group attention to jointly process related series and with tokenization schemes tailored to continuous-valued time-series data. The model is pretrained at scale on large and heterogeneous collections of temporal signals, enabling it to internalize general temporal structures such as seasonality, periodicity, and both short- and long-term dependencies. A central property of Chronos-2 is that it operates in an inference-only, zero-shot mode. Rather than being trained from scratch on each new dataset, the model leverages its pretrained representations and performs forecasting through in-context learning: given a short window of recent observations, the encoder produces multi-step probabilistic forecasts directly. This makes Chronos-2 particularly suitable for settings where historical data are scarce or where maintaining separate models for each appliance or building is impractical. The architecture supports both univariate and multivariate inputs, allowing the inclusion of auxiliary covariates when available. Within the supervised formulation of appliance-level load forecasting, learning a forecasting function from scratch is difficult due to limited training data, strong heterogeneity across appliances, and high variability induced by human behavior. Chronos-2 directly addresses these challenges by providing a pretrained, domain-general forecasting mechanism that can be applied without appliance-specific training. Chronos-2 effectively supplies the function f in a zero-shot manner: the model parameters are fixed after pre-training, and the same encoder is applied directly to appliance-level power signals. This enables forecasting even for newly installed devices or buildings with minimal monitoring history and forms the basis of our investigation into zero-shot load forecasting for appliance and building power signals.

4.2 TimesFM

TimesFM is a foundational time-series model developed by Google to provide broadly applicable forecasting capabilities across diverse temporal domains. The model is built on a decoder-only Transformer architecture, similar in spirit to large language models, and operates on tokenized representations of continuous-valued time series. Its architecture includes multi-head self-attention layers, causal masking for autoregressive forecasting, and feed-forward blocks designed to capture both short- and long-term temporal dependencies. TimesFM is pretrained at scale on extensive collections of heterogeneous time-series datasets, enabling it to internalize general temporal patterns such as seasonality, regime shifts, and irregular dynamics. A defining characteristic of TimesFM is its zero-shot inference mode. Rather than being trained from scratch on each new dataset, the model leverages its pretrained autoregressive structure to generate multi-step forecasts directly from a short conditioning window. This makes TimesFM particularly suitable for scenarios where appliance-level data are scarce or where maintaining separate models for each device or building is impractical. The architecture supports univariate and multivariate inputs, allowing the inclusion of exogenous covariates when available. Within the supervised formulation of appliance-level load forecasting, learning a forecasting function from scratch is hindered by limited training data, strong heterogeneity across appliances, and high behavioral variability. TimesFM addresses these challenges by providing a pretrained, domain-general forecasting mechanism that can be applied without appliance-specific training. TimesFM supplies the function f in a zero-shot manner: the model is used as-is after pre-training and applied directly to appliance-level power signals. This enables forecasting even for newly installed devices or buildings with minimal historical data and motivates our investigation into zero-shot load forecasting using foundational time-series models.

5 Validation

This section empirically evaluates the performance of foundational time-series models for appliance-level load forecasting. The central claim is that pretrained models such as Chronos-2 and TimesFM can serve as universal forecasting functions, offering competitive accuracy and superior generalization compared to costly conventional models, trained on appliance-specific signals, in drifting scenarios (e.g. different appliances, eventually from different buildings). To test this hypothesis, experiments have been designed around three core research questions:

1. **RQ1:** Do foundational models generalize better than ad-hoc models to previously unseen appliances from the same building?
2. **RQ2:** Do foundational models generalize better than ad-hoc models to previously unseen appliances from different buildings
3. **RQ3:** Do foundational models generalize better than ad-hoc models for different w and h?

These questions are addressed by comparing the predictive performance of both ad-hoc supervised models and foundational models. Specifically, every ad-hoc model we consider (LSTM and GRU as neural baselines) is trained on the power signal observed for a given appliance from a fixed building, then we test them on power signals from both seen and unseen power signals, possibly from other appliances eventually recorded in different buildings. Complementarily, foundational models are only tested on both seen and unseen power signals, possibly from other appliances from different buildings, without retraining or fine-tuning them. When not directly specified, the values for w and h have been fixed to 256 and 25, respectively.

Experiments have been performed on a PC running Windows 11 and equipped with 32 GB RAM and an i7-14700hx (2.10GHz). The training pipeline has been developed with Python 3.11 (using scikit-learn, pandas, and the Darts[1]

[1] https://unit8co.github.io/darts/.

framework specifically designed for time series analytics tasks. In particular, multiple univariate time series have been considered, each recording 48 h of power consumption (mW) per minute from appliances across different buildings in the REDD benchmark dataset for appliance-level forecasting and disaggregation tasks. REDD provides appliance-level and whole-home electricity measurements from several residential buildings. It includes high-frequency power signals for common household devices. The dataset has been i) downloaded in h5 format from zenodo[2], and ii) loaded and manipulated leveraging data loaders from the *Nilmtk*[3] [2], thus constructing a representation compatible with Sect. 3 by sliding two adjacent time windows of size w and h over the resulting time series. In particular, 3 appliance types (light, fridge, dish washer) from 3 different buildings (bld.1, bld.2, bld.3) have been considered, and no data preparation, scaling, or outlier removal has been performed. Finally, the predictive accuracy of zero-shot Chronos-2 and TimeGPT against that of traditional LSTM and GRU trained on purpose was measured on the latest 20% of examples. Furthermore, LSTM and GRU have been trained on the initial 80% of examples over 100 epochs, while using their default RNN implementations available in Darts (using the Adam optimizer with learning rate set to 0.001, default dropout rate to 0, hidden_dim to 25, and n_rnn_layers to 1). Training code cannot be disclosed as it contains intellectual property.

5.1 RQ1: Load Forecasting Accuracy over Unseen Appliances Within the Same Building.

Table 1. load forecasting accuracy (avg mae, mW, lowest wins) of foundational and ad-hoc models over unseen appliances from the same building.

train	test	avg mae (mW)			
		LSTM	GRU	Chronos2	TimesFM
light (bld. 1)	light (bld. 1)	52.39	52.63	**0.408**	<u>0.455</u>
light (bld. 1)	fridge (bld. 1)	13.8	0.278	**0.034**	<u>0.042</u>
light (bld. 1)	dish-washer (bld. 1)	0.491	0.397	**0.255**	<u>0.291</u>
fridge (bld. 1)	light (bld. 1)	70.76	68.06	**0.408**	<u>0.455</u>
fridge (bld. 1)	fridge (bld. 1)	1.671	1.997	**0.034**	<u>0.042</u>
fridge (bld. 1)	dish-washer (bld. 1)	6.952	13.41	**0.255**	<u>0.291</u>
dish-washer (bld. 1)	light (bld. 1)	50.81	53.04	**0.408**	<u>0.455</u>
dish-washer (bld. 1)	fridge (bld. 1)	23.57	21.15	**0.034**	<u>0.042</u>
dish-washer (bld. 1)	dish-washer (bld. 1)	19.71	5.781	**0.153**	**0.153**

[2] https://zenodo.org/records/13917372.
[3] https://nilmtk.github.io/.

Addressing RQ1 means to evaluate whether zero-shot pretrained foundational time-series models can act as universal forecasting functions for appliance-level load prediction *within* a given building. The analysis compared the forecasting average MAE of both zero-shot models and conventional supervised baselines when i) the training data originated from appliances within same building, and ii) the test data originated from other appliances from the same building. This setup allowed us to quantify the extent to which pretrained models provide reliable zero-shot forecasts under potentially *within-building* drifting conditions: that is, training (only for LSTM and GRU) on a given appliance type and testing (all models) over unseen ones within the same building.

The results in Table 1 reveal a clear and consistent pattern: Chronos-2 and TimesFM, outperform the ad-hoc neural baselines (LSTM and GRU) across all train-test combinations. When trained on one appliance type and evaluated on another from the same type within the same building, LSTM and GRU exhibit large errors, confirming their inability to generalize beyond the specific device they were trained on. In contrast, both Chronos-2 and TimesFM achieve sub-milliwatt MAE in every scenario, demonstrating strong zero-shot transfer even when the target appliance differs substantially from the source. This gap is also observed in cross-appliance settings (e.g., training on *light* and testing on *fridge* or *dish-washer*), where LSTM and GRU degrade, while the foundational models maintain stable accuracy. The near-identical performance of Chronos-2 and TimesFM across all rows further suggests that large-scale pre-training on heterogeneous time-series corpora yields robust, appliance-agnostic temporal representations.

5.2 RQ2: Load Forecasting Accuracy over Unseen Appliances from Different Buildings.

Table 2. Load forecasting accuracy (avg mae, mW, lowest wins) of foundational and ad-hoc models over unseen appliances from different buildings.

train	test	avg mae (mW)			
		LSTM	GRU	Chronos2	TimesFM
light (bld. 1)	light (bld. 1)	52.39	52.63	**0.408**	0.455
light (bld. 1)	light (bld. 2)	13.82	0.412	**0.123**	0.438
light (bld. 1)	light (bld. 3)	0.429	0.292	**0.046**	0.1
fridge (bld. 1)	fridge (bld. 1)	1.671	1.997	**0.034**	0.042
fridge (bld. 1)	fridge (bld. 2)	153	150.5	**2.222**	2.329
fridge (bld. 1)	fridge (bld. 3)	**9.213**	14.92	18.08	11.14
dish-washer (bld. 1)	dish-washer (bld. 1)	0.378	1.352	**0.255**	0.29
dish-washer (bld. 1)	dish-washer (bld. 2)	5.06	0.34	0.089	**0.061**
dish-washer (bld. 1)	dish-washer (bld. 3)	19.71	5.78	**0.153**	**0.153**

Similarly, addressing RQ2 involves evaluating whether zero-shot pretrained foundational time-series models can serve as universal forecasting functions in a more challenging scenario, namely, for *cross-building* appliance-level load prediction, rather than the *within-building* one. Specifically, the analysis compared the forecasting average MAE of both zero-shot models and conventional supervised baselines when i) the training data originated from an appliance type from a building, and ii) the test data originated from the same appliance type in different buildings. This setup allowed us to quantify the extent to which pretrained models provide reliable zero-shot forecasts under potentially *cross-building* drifting conditions: that is, training (only for LSTM and GRU) on a given appliance type and testing (all models) over the same appliance type from unseen buildings.

The results in Table 2 show that cross-building load forecasting is substantially more challenging than within-building prediction, yet the foundational models maintain a clear advantage over the ad-hoc baselines. Chronos-2 and TimesFM remain consistently accurate across all building pairs. Even when the target building exhibits markedly different consumption profiles, both foundational models achieve sub-milliwatt MAE, demonstrating strong zero-shot generalization. Overall, the table highlights the limitations of ad-hoc supervised models in cross-building forecasting and underscores the value of pretrained foundational models as universal forecasting functions. Their ability to generalize across appliances and buildings without retraining makes them well suited for scalable BEMS deployments where device-level historical data are scarce or unavailable.

5.3 RQ3: Load Forecasting Accuracy When Varying w and h

Table 3. load forecasting accuracy (avg mae, mW, lowest wins) of foundational and ad-hoc models trained and tested on dish washer (bld. 1) for different w and h.

	avg mae (mW) @ w, $h = 25$					avg mae (mW) @ h, $w = 256$				
	50	150	250	350	450	5	15	25	35	45
LSTM	2.372	0.567	6.887	0.132	0.144	0.321	0.901	0.378	2.659	0.248
GRU	13.27	8.396	7.032	0.257	4.307	0.283	0.305	1.352	1.565	8.165
Chronos-2	**0.235**	**0.316**	**0.263**	**0.033**	**0.016**	**0.235**	**0.248**	**0.255**	**0.252**	**0.241**
TimesFM	0.334	0.401	0.297	0.078	0.041	0.253	0.279	0.29	0.296	0.298

Finally, addressing RQ3 involves evaluating whether zero-shot pretrained foundational time-series models can serve as universal forecasting functions under different predictive window sizes (w) and prediction horizons (h). For simplicity, the analysis compared the forecasting average MAE of both zero-shot models and conventional baselines over the dish-washer consumption in *within-building* (bld. 1) scenario by: i) fixing h and gradually increasing w, and ii) fixing w and gradually increasing h.

The results in Table 3 show a clear contrast between foundational models and traditional ones when the input window w and forecasting horizon h are varied. Chronos-2 and TimesFM remain consistently accurate across all configurations, with only minor fluctuations, indicating strong robustness to changes in temporal context. In contrast, LSTM and GRU models behave unpredictably: their errors vary widely and sometimes spike dramatically, revealing a limited generalization. Overall, the table suggests that foundational models provide stable, reliable performance across heterogeneous forecasting setups, whereas ad-hoc models struggle to maintain accuracy outside narrow, well-tuned configurations. In the considered scenario, that is dish-washer in within-building mode, pretrained foundational models are capable of providing short-term and long-term load forecasts under reduced and expanded window sizes and predictive horizons. Despite this, a more complete analysis is needed, in particular by considering alternative appliance types and buildings.

6 Conclusions

This study shows that foundational time-series models can serve as a practical and scalable option for appliance-level load forecasting, offering strong performance without requiring device-specific training data. Our evaluation of Chronos-2 and TimesFM across multiple appliances and buildings suggests that pretrained models can generalize well to new devices and environments, easing the reliance on extensive historical datasets and reducing the need to maintain separate models for each setting. Their zero-shot capabilities point toward more flexible and deployable solutions for real-world energy-management systems, and their role is likely to grow as foundational modeling continues to advance.

Looking ahead, several directions merit further exploration. Broadening the analysis to more diverse datasets—spanning different building types, climates, and appliance categories—would help clarify how these models behave across varied operational contexts. Equally important is evaluating them within live BEMS deployments, where researchers can assess not only forecasting accuracy but also system-level impacts, integration considerations, and the practical value of zero-shot forecasting in everyday energy-management scenarios.

References

1. Ansari, A.F., et al.: Chronos-2: from univariate to universal forecasting. CoRR abs/2510.15821 (2025). https://doi.org/10.48550/ARXIV.2510.15821
2. Batra, N., et al.: NILMTK: an open source toolkit for non-intrusive load monitoring. In: Crowcroft, J., Penty, R.V., Boudex, J.L., Shenoy, P.J. (eds.) The Fifth International Conference on Future Energy Systems, e-Energy 2014, Cambridge, United Kingdom, 11–13 June 2014, pp. 265–276. ACM (2014). https://doi.org/10.1145/2602044.2602051
3. Das, A., Kong, W., Sen, R., Zhou, Y.: A decoder-only foundation model for time-series forecasting. In: Proceedings of the 41st International Conference on Machine Learning, ICML 2024. JMLR.org (2024)

4. Qureshi, M., Arbab, M.A., Rehman, S.U.: Deep learning-based forecasting of electricity consumption. Sci. Rep. **14**(1), 6489 (2024)
5. Razghandi, M., Turgut, D.: Residential appliance-level load forecasting with deep learning. In: IEEE Global Communications Conference, GLOBECOM 2020, Virtual Event, Taiwan, 7–11 December 2020, pp. 1–6. IEEE (2020). https://doi.org/10.1109/GLOBECOM42002.2020.9348197
6. Razghandi, M., Zhou, H., Erol-Kantarci, M., Turgut, D.: Short-term load forecasting for smart home appliances with sequence to sequence learning. In: ICC 2021 - IEEE International Conference on Communications, Montreal, QC, Canada, 14–23 June 2021, pp. 1–6. IEEE (2021). https://doi.org/10.1109/ICC42927.2021.9500767

Predictive Process Monitoring Through the Lens of Deep Online Learning

Vincenzo Pasquadibisceglie(✉), Simone Capone, Annalisa Appice, and Donato Malerba

University of Bari Aldo Moro, Bari, Italy
{vincenzo.pasquadibisceglie,annalisa.appice,donato.malerba}@uniba.it, s.capone7@studenti.uniba.it

Abstract. Predictive Process Monitoring (PPM) leverages historical event data recorded during historical business process executions, to forecast future scenarios of new ongoing process executions. Traditional PPM methods assume that business processes remain in a steady state over time. However, this is often not the real-world case due to concept drifts. This paper presents a PPM method, named ATLAS, which uses an online learning strategy coupled with a LLM, to develop a LSTM model for predicting the next-activity of ongoing process executions (running cases). It keeps the PPM model continuously updated each time a new event is observed. The evaluation assesses the performance the proposed approach in terms of accuracy and computation time also compared to several related online PPM approaches.

Keywords: PPM · Next-activity prediction · Online learning · Drift explanation

1 Introduction

Process-Aware Information Systems (PAISs) play a crucial role in modern organizations recording big volumes of events generated during the execution of business processes. Recorded events concern executed activities and timestamps of activities' execution. Predictive Process Monitoring (PPM) is a branch of Process Mining that aims to use Artificial Intelligence (AI), to process historical events recorded with PAISs to predict the future progression (e.g., next-activity, outcome) of ongoing process executions [4]. PPM services can be of crucial importance during decision-making to improve operational performances of business processes. For example, the allocation of resources or the intervention into a process execution can be decided according to knowledge disclosed with PPM. In this paper, we focus on a deep PPM model trained for next-activity prediction.

The majority of PPM methods use AI techniques, and are designed for static scenarios, assuming that logged processes remain in a steady state over time. Instead, due to the evolving nature of business processes, monitoring concept drifts (i.e., changes) in event streams is crucial to maintaining the accuracy of

G. Andresini et al. (Eds.): ISMIS 2026, LNAI 16685, pp. 236–246, 2027.
https://doi.org/10.1007/978-3-032-32643-0_20

PPM models over time. Hence, recent PPM literature has begun to explore strategies for detecting and handling concept drifts in event streams. For example, [14] compares re-training and fine-tuning as learning strategies for maintaining an up-to-date MLP trained for next-activity prediction. The model update is done accounting for the newest windowed events as any concept drift has been detected. [3] uses a window-based approach to detect concept drifts related to shifted or novel activities. Upon the concept drift detection, [3] incrementally updates an LSTM model for the next-activity prediction, to the newest events in combination with augmented samples and replay buffer process executions. Both [14] and [3] use a fixed-length window (e.g., 1 month) for concept drift analysis and PPM model updating. Instead, [10] describes a PPM method that leverages the adaptive window mechanism of ADWIN [1], to detect concept drifts for next-activity prediction tasks using windows with adaptive sizes. It uses a Word2Vec model, which is trained to derive feature vector representations of process executions and to feed an LSTM model for next-activity prediction. Both Word2Vec and LSTM models are fine-tuned on the newest windowed event data saved by ADWIN as concept drifts have been detected in an event streaming. Finally, [9] evaluates an online tree-based learner, e.g., the Hoeffding Adaptive Tree, where a tree-based PPM model is continuously updated with each new stream sample, inherently handling concept drift during learning, and addresses an outcome prediction task.

With the goal of advancing the exploration of PPM for next-activity prediction through the lens of deep online learning, we propose ATLAS (next-AcTivity prediction through the Lens of a streAm learning Scenario): an online learning method to develop a LSTM model for the next-activity prediction and keep this PPM model continuously updated each time a new event is observed. To this aim, we use a story telling approach to obtain the textual story of any incoming process execution [12], and we consider a pretrained foundation LLM, namely GPT-2, to encode each story. This bases on recent achievements described in [11], which outline that a foundation LLM can provide the encoding of a process execution story by handling the appearance of unseen activities without the need of any specific encoder adaptation. The output of the GPT-2 is then used to learn online a LSTM for next-activity prediction. Unlike [10], that fine-tunes the LSTM model as a concept drift is detected, ATLAS uses the online learning approach defined in [8] to update the LSTM as any new event is recorded in any process execution. To better fit the LSTM to concept drifts by definitely forgetting up-of-date process executions, ATLAS is equipped with the concept drift detector of ADWIN, so that a new LSTM is initialized with events windowed by ADWIN in correspondence of each concept drift detection.

In the following, Sect. 2 describes the background and Sect. 3 illustrates the approach. Section 4 presents experiments and Sect. 5 sketches future work.

Fig. 1. An example of an event stream Σ illustrating a running case c_1 composed of events e_1, e_2, and e_4, its prefix $\mathit{prefix}(c_1) = \langle e_1, e_3 \rangle$, and the corresponding next-activity $\mathit{next}(\mathit{prefix}(c_1)) =$ *Take in charge ticket.*

2 Background

Let us consider a business process. A case describes the life-cycle of a process execution in terms of the sequence of activities executed. According to this definition of a case, an event refers to an activity executed within a case at a specific time. Formally, let $\mathcal{C}$, $\mathcal{A}$, and $\mathcal{T}$ denote the sets of case identifiers, activity names, and timestamps. Let $\mathcal{E} = \mathcal{C} \times \mathcal{A} \times \mathcal{T}$ be the event universe. Let $\perp$ denote the activity corresponding to the completion of a case execution.[1] An event e is a triple $e = (c, a, t) \in \mathcal{C} \times \mathcal{A} \times \mathcal{T}$ that represents the occurrence of activity a in case c at timestamp t. Let us introduce projection functions $\pi_{\mathcal{C}} : \mathcal{E} \mapsto \mathcal{C}$ so that $\pi_{\mathcal{C}}(e) = c$; $\pi_{\mathcal{A}} : \mathcal{E} \mapsto \mathcal{A}$ so that $\pi_{\mathcal{A}}(e) = a$; $\pi_{\mathcal{T}} : \mathcal{E} \mapsto \mathcal{T}$ so that $\pi_{\mathcal{T}}(e) = t$. An event stream Σ is an unbounded sequence of events $e_1, e_2, \ldots, e_i, \ldots$ so that, for all $j \geq 1$, $e_j \in \mathcal{E}$ and $\pi_{\mathcal{T}}(e_j) \leq \pi_{\mathcal{T}}(e_{j+1})$. A case c is an event sequence $c = \langle e_1, \ldots, e_n \rangle$ such that: (1) $c[j] \in \Sigma$ with $j = 1, \ldots, n$, (2) $\pi_{\mathcal{C}}(c[j]) = c$ with $j = 1, \ldots, n$, and (3) $\pi_{\mathcal{T}}(c[j]) \leq \pi_{\mathcal{T}}(c[j+1])$ with $j = 1, \ldots, n-1$. Let j be a positive number, $c[j]$ denotes the j-th event recorded in c, with $1 \leq j \leq n$. A case c is a *full case* if $\pi_{\mathcal{A}}(c[n]) = \perp$, and a *running case* otherwise, with n equal to the length of c. In addition, let $prefix(c)$ denote the event prefix of c consisting of the first $n-1$ events recorded in c, i.e., $prefix(c) = \langle e_1, e_2, \ldots, e_{n-1} \rangle$. $\pi_{\mathcal{A}}(c[n])$ is the next-activity of $prefix(c)$, i.e., $\mathit{next}(prefix(c)) = \pi_{\mathcal{A}}(c[n])$. For the remainder of this paper, we represent a case c and its $prefix(c)$ through their activity sequences: $\langle \pi_{\mathcal{A}}(e_1), \pi_{\mathcal{A}}(e_2), \ldots, \pi_{\mathcal{A}}(e_n) \rangle$ and $\langle \pi_{\mathcal{A}}(e_1), \pi_{\mathcal{A}}(e_2), \ldots, \pi_{\mathcal{A}}(e_{n-1}) \rangle$,respectively. Accordingly, the activity story telling of c is the text "$\pi_{\mathcal{A}}(e_1)$" + "$\rightarrow$" + ... + "$\rightarrow$" + "$\pi_{\mathcal{A}}(e_n)$", where + is the string concatenation operator. Similarly, the activity story telling of $prefix(c)$ is the text "$\pi_{\mathcal{A}}(e_1)$" + "$\rightarrow$" + ... + "$\rightarrow$" + "$\pi_{\mathcal{A}}(e_{n-1})$". For example, let us consider the event stream Σ in Fig. 1, the running case c_1 is the sequence of events: e_1, e_3 and e_4, while $prefix(c_1)$ is the sequence of the events: e_1 and e_3. The activity story telling of case c_1 is "Assign seriousness $\rightarrow$ Wait $\rightarrow$ Take in charge ticket", while the activity story telling of $prefix(c_1)$ is "Assign seriousness $\rightarrow$ Wait". The next-activity of $prefix(c_1)$ is activity "Take in charge ticket" recorded in e_4. The activity story telling of $prefix(c_1)$ labeled with $\mathit{next}(prefix(c_1))$ is used in the online update on a PPM model for next-activity prediction. This PPM model is used to predict $\mathit{next}(c_1)$, while the accuracy of this prediction will be established as a new event will be recorded for case c_1 in Σ.

[1] The completion is commonly declared in several business processes, such as ticket resolution or hospitalization processes.

Algorithm 1: ATLAS pseudo-code

```
   Data: Σ (Event stream)
   Result: Eval (PPM evaluation)
1  begin
2      encoder ← load_pretrained_LLM()
3      detector ← ADWIN
4      Eval ← []
5      model ← LSTM
6      D, Â ← {}, {}
7      for e ∈ Σ do
8          c ← π_C(e), A ← π_A(e)
9          D[c] ← D[c] • ⟨A⟩          ▷ with • denoting the concatenation operator
10         if there exists Â[c] then
11             Eval.append(CE(A, Â[c]))
12             drift ← detector.update(encoder(story(prefix(D[c]))),A, Â[c])
13             if drift = True then
14                 model ← LSTM
15                 model.learn_many(detector.WINDOW))
16             else
17                 model.learn_one(encoder(story(prefix(D[c]))), A)
18         if A = ⊥ then
19             Delete c from D and Â
20         else
21             Â[c] ← model.predict_one(encoder(story(D[c])))
22     return Eval
```

3 ATLAS approach

In this section, we describe ATLAS – a PPM method formulated for next-activity prediction in event streams. It combines: the pretrained foundation LLM GPT-2 [15] to extract a smart representation of process cases, the online deep learning strategy described in [8] to learn and update a LSTM model in an event stream setting, and the concept drift detector ADWIN [1], to monitor concept drifts and re-initialize the LSTM model in presence of concept drifts. The pseudo-code of ATLAS is reported in Algorithm 1. It takes an event stream Σ as input and returns the stream *Eval* of misclassification errors made on the next-activity predictions produced for any new update of the ongoing cases as output.

In the *initialization phase* (Algorithm 1, lns. 2–6) ATLAS loads the foundational LLM GPT-2, initializes the adaptive window of ADWIN, the empty stream of classification evaluation *Eval*, as well as the LSTM model fo the next-activity prediction, and creates two empty dictionary data structures, namely, $\mathbf{D}$ to record the activity sequences of the ongoing cases acquired in Σ, and $\hat{\mathbf{A}}$ to record the last next-activity predictions yielded for the running cases. The LSTM model is trained on a feature vector representation of the activity story telling of each prefix case obtained with GPT-2 and labeled with the activity recorded in the last event of the case considered for the prefix extraction. This information is processed through an LSTM layer and forwarded to an MLP layer. Both layers have hidden size equal to 768. The final prediction is obtained through a classification head that produces classification logits using cross-entropy loss.

In the *online phase* (Algorithm 1, lns. 7–21), ATLAS processes each new event e recorded in Σ to update the LSTM model. Let c be the running case for which a new event e has been just recorded in Σ. Let A be the activity executed in e. A is concatenated to the sequence of activities already observed for c in Σ and currently recorded in the dictionary entry $\mathbf{D}[c]$. If a next-activity prediction has been already produced for c and recorded in $\hat{\mathbf{A}}[c]$, then *Eval* is fueled with the misclassification error $CE(A, \hat{\mathbf{A}}[c]) = 0$ if $A = \hat{\mathbf{A}}[c]$, 1 otherwise. In addition, the ADWIN detector is updated with the sample composed of the encoder of the activity story telling of $\mathbf{D}[c]$, the next-activity A associated with this prefix and the prediction $\hat{\mathbf{A}}[c]$ done in the past for this next-activity. This information is used by ADWIN to monitor misclassification errors through an adaptive window. This window also records the prefix information with the observed next-activity, which will be subsequently used to re-initialize the LSTM model in presence of concept drift alerts. As any new misclassification error is added to the detector, ADWIN compares error distributions in all possible pairs of sliding sub-windows within the current adaptive window. If significant differences are found, then it alerts a concept drift and discards the oldest prefix samples with their labels from the window. Upon the detection of a concept drift, a new LSTM model is initialized from the labeled prefix samples kept in the adaptive window of ADWIN. Otherwise, the current LSTM model is updated as described in [8] to fit it to the prefix of current c labeled with activity A. Finally, if A denotes the completion activity, then c is declared a full case and removed from both $\mathbf{D}$ and $\hat{\mathbf{A}}$. Otherwise, the current LSTM model, as it has been updated until now, is used to predict the next-activity of c and record this prediction in $\hat{\mathbf{A}}$. The evaluation *Eval*, finally, returns the stream of misclassification errors checked at the time the ground truth of a next-activity prediction has been recorded in Σ.

4 Experimental Results

We evaluated the performance of ATLAS by conducting a range of experiments on the event streams obtained from benchmark event logs.

4.1 Event Logs, Experimental Setting and Metrics

We considered six real-life event logs to generate the event streams of the evaluation. Specifically, BPIC18G, BPIC18P, BPIC20R and Helpdesk are available on the 4TU Centre for Research[2], while CDLS and MIMICEL are available on Physionet repository[3]. BPIC18G includes cases related to geo-parcel document applications for EU direct payments to German farmers, funded by the European Agricultural Guarantee Fund and recorded after 2007. BPIC18P covers cases for parcels that had subsidy requests before 2007. BPIC20R includes cases related to Requests for Payment, which occasionally involved travels. Helpdesk relates to the cases of

---

[2] https://data.4tu.nl/portal.

[3] https://physionet.org/.

Table 1. Event log description: number of activities, events, cases, and case-variants, the number of cases per activity variant, the average case length (in days) and the total stream duration (in days)

Event stream	Act.	Cases	Events	Vars	Cases/Vars	$\text{Case}_{\text{AVG}_\text{d}}$	$\text{Case}_{\text{AVG}_\text{T}}$	Duration
BPIC18G	23	29059	569209	9372	19.58	20	143.5	576
BPIC18P	10	14750	132963	3615	9.01	9	196	976
BPIC20R	19	6886	36796	89	77.37	5	8.2	941
Helpdesk	14	4580	21348	226	20.26	5	40.9	1451
CDLS	10	4040	265245	3918	1.03	66	11.1	428
MIMICEL	6	12485	99941	2428	5.14	8	0.3	1827

the ticket management process of a private Italian software company. CDSL [16] records cases regarding the hospitalization of COVID-19 patients in the Spanish "HM Hospitales" between December 26, 2019, and February 13, 2021. MIMICEL [17] documents cases regarding stays of patients in an Emergency Department as they were extracted from the MIMIC-IV-ED dataset. Table 1 illustrates the main characteristics of the selected event logs. Both MIMICEL and CDSL are provided by the PhysioNet Project [5].

The compared methods of the evaluation include: ATLAS (the online deep PPM method proposed in this study); Deep-river [8] (the baseline of ATLAS that keeps away the concept drift detection performed with ADWIN); DARWIN [10] (the online deep PPM competing method that fine-tunes a LSTM model on concept drift samples selected with ADWIN); AHT [2] (the stream learning method that learns incrementally a Hoeffding tree by guaranteeing the Hoeffding bound and building alternate trees whenever changes are alerted with ADWIN); ARF [6] (the stream learning method that adapts Random Forest of Hoeffding trees to streaming scenarios); and SRP [7] (the stream ensemble method based on Streaming Random Patches to cope with evolving streaming scenarios). Selected methods were run to handle the study event streams updating an online PPM model for next-activity prediction. In particular, ATLAS, Deep-river and DARWIN are online deep learning method that train and update a LSTM model, while AHT, ARF and SRP are state-of-the-art stream learning methods that train and update a tree-based or tree ensemble-based model. In this study, all compared methods were run on NVIDIA GeForce RTX 4090 24 GB, 32 CPU Intel(R) Core(TM) i9-14900K, 64 GB Ram Memory, Ubuntu 24.04.1 LTS.

The comparison was performed with the Prequential Evaluation strategy that is commonly used for assessing the accuracy of online predictive methods in data streams. According to this strategy, we predicted the next-activity of running cases, and continuously measured the PPM model's accuracy by comparing predictions with corresponding ground truths once the true labels for predictions were available in event streams. For each method, we measured the **Fscore** on next-activity predictions made from the time 10% of events were processed in the considered event streams. In the computation of the **Fscore**, we gave equal

Table 2. Comparative performance analysis: **macroFscore** and **Time** (in seconds) of ATLAS, Deep-river, DARWIN, AHT, ARF and SRP. For each event stream, the best results are in bold.

Metric	Methods	BPIC18G	BPIC18P	BPIC20R	Helpdesk	CDLS	MIMICEL
macroF	ATLAS	**0.440**	**0.356**	0.339	**0.313**	**0.269**	**0.620**
	Deep-river	0.432	0.352	0.328	0.301	0.257	0.616
	DARWIN	0.362	0.348	0.334	0.308	0.266	0.551
	AHT	0.361	0.304	0.353	0.285	0.228	0.552
	ARF	0.402	0.341	0.351	0.306	0.263	0.605
	SRP	0.390	0.336	**0.360**	0.299	0.248	0.521
Time	ATLAS	21549.22	4370.10	829.17	629.48	6401.91	3608.16
	Deep-river	15908.86	2907.32	794.60	424.11	6646.95	3176.34
	DARWIN	53934.60	6230.80	2709.17	1819.20	11440.04	4319.80
	AHT	**9746.56**	**612.04**	**33.86**	**13.77**	**38.90**	**7.72**
	ARF	14453.67	855.52	81.65	32.93	215.69	66.65
	SRP	14567.99	1043.50	134.01	69.70	1074.22	350.02

weights to each activity type (computing the **macroFscore**), to avoid that our evaluation offsets the possible impact of imbalanced data learning. Finally, we also measured the total **Time** spent in seconds processing event streams.

4.2 Results and Discussion

We start illustrating the results of the accuracy and computation time performance analysis. Table 2 reports the **macroFscore** and **Time** of both ATLAS and the competing methods. Regarding the online deep learning methods (i.e., ATLAS, Deep-river and DARWIN), ATLAS achieves higher **macroFscore** than Deep-river that uses the same online learning strategy of ATLAS to update the LSTM model as any new event is recorded in the event stream, but keeps away the use of ADWIN to monitor concept drifts and initialize a new LSTM model in correspondence of concept drift alerts. On the other hand, ATLAS also achieves higher **macroFscore** than DARWIN that uses ADWIN for concept drift monitoring, but updates an LSTM model through fine-tuning in correspondence of concept drift alerts only. The use of ADWIN makes ATLAS slightly more time consuming than Deep-river, while the use of the online learning strategy, originally introduced in [8], allows ATLAS and Deep-river to complete the stream processing spending less computation time than in DARWIN. Regarding the stream learning methods of this evaluation (i.e., AHT, ARF and SRP), ATLAS achieves higher **macroFscore** than AHT, ARF and SRP on five out of the six considered event streams. The only exception is observed with BPIC20R that is also the event stream of this study with the higher number of cases per activity variants, as well as the lower number of distinct activity case variants observed in the

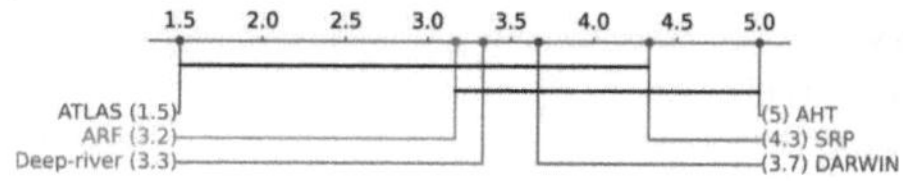

Fig. 2. Comparison between ATLAS and the related methods in terms of **macroFscore** with the Friedman-Nemenyi test. Groups of methods that are not significantly different (at $p \leq 0.05$) are connected.

stream (see Table 1). This suggests that tree- and ensemble tree-based models may perform better than deep neural models in presence of business processes whose executions follow the Pareto's principle (i.e., about 80% of the behavior in the event data is described by about 20% of the activity case variants). In addition, ATLAS is more time consuming than AHT, ARF and SRP due to the higher complexity in keeping updated a deep neural model than tree- and tree ensemble-based models. However, if we account for the entire duration of all considered event streams, then the total time spent by ATLAS, to process each entire event stream, is significantly lower than the real duration of processed streams (see Table 1). To complete this performance analysis, we also performed the Friedman's test to compare the **macroFscore** of all multiple methods across multiple event streams. In this test, the null hypothesis states that all methods are equivalent. Under this hypothesis, the ranks of the compared methods should be equal. In the evaluation, we rejected the null hypothesis with a *p-value* ≤ 0.05, hence, we conducted the post-hoc Nemenyi test for pairwise comparisons. The results of the Nemenyi test, reported in Fig. 2, show that ATLAS achieves the highest **macroFscore** of this comparative evaluation, with ARF as the runner-up.

Finally, we used LLM-generated explanations to examine concept drifts detected with ATLAS. To this purpose, we employed the LLM GPT-5, to analyze detected concept drifts by comparing samples contained in the alert ADWIN window with samples taken from the background ADWIN window associated with the preceding concept drift (or the window of samples recorded in the beginning of the stream). As an example, let us consider the first concept drift detected in Helpdesk using the first 10% of events recorded in the event stream as background window for the concept drift explanation. Figure 3 reports the explanation obtained querying GPT-5 Mini with the following prompt coupled with the list of activity story telling of prefix cases saved in both the current window and the background window:

"You are an expert in process mining. I will show you the variations (top-10 variants) in a ticket management process relating to two different points in time (Initialization and Drift - 1) where the concept drift detector has noticed a change. What can you tell me about this?"

The explanation of GPT-5 outlines that the helpdesk process maintained a stable structure at Drift-1 time, although a drift in performance was detected. In

Concise summary

- The **process structure is stable**: the main flow *Assign seriousness → Take in charge → Resolve → Closed* remains unchanged.
- The detected drift is **not structural**, but **distributional/performance-based**.
- **Fewer cases progress to resolution and closure** in Drift-1; longer variants lose relatively more weight, indicating **reduced throughput**.
- **Waiting and rework patterns** (repeated seriousness assignment, wait loops) persist, becoming **relatively more prominent**, suggesting **capacity or prioritization issues**.
- Ticket intake (`Insert ticket`) appears **better integrated** in Drift-1, hinting at improved logging or tighter coupling with handling.
- Overall, this is a **gradual performance degradation drift**: the process works the same way, but **completes fewer tickets and stalls earlier**.

Fig. 3. Explanation formulated by in GPT-5 mini for the first concept drift detected in the event stream Helpdesk

particular, during the Drift-1 period, the number of cases reaching resolution and closure decreases with a reduction in the longest paths. This may be considered a sign of lower throughput. Wait times and rework (e.g., severity reassignment) persist and become more frequent than in the past, suggesting emerging capacity or priority issues. This drift explanation, which triggered a restart of the deep neural model in ATLAS, can support managers in understanding the helpdesk process and improving KPIs.

5 Conclusion

The paper introduces an online deep PPM method that couples a LSTM with a foundation LLM and the concept drift detector ADWIN, to handle the problem of the next-activity prediction in a dynamic process environment. As future work, we plan to investigate the effect of different foundation LLMs and concept drift detectors on the performance of the proposed method. In addition, we plan to explore the management of multimodal event streams as in [13], to handle modalities that go beyond the activity storytelling of process executions.

Ethical Statement and Acknowledgment. This study was conducted for scientific purposes using the CDLS and MIMICEL datasets under the PhysioNet Credential Health Data Use Agreement 1.5.0, with access restricted to personnel who completed the training program in human research subject protections and HIPAA regulations. We acknowledge financial support under the National Recovery and Resilience Plan (NRRP), M4C2I1.1, funded by the European Union – NextGenerationEU– Project Title aRtificial intElligence for Process Analytics (REPA) - Grant Assignment Decree No. 2022CJWPNA (CUP Università degli Studi di Bari Aldo Moro H53C24000960006) by the Italian Ministry of University and Research (MUR).

References

1. Bifet, A., Gavaldà, R.: Learning from time-changing data with adaptive windowing. In: Proceedings of the Seventh SIAM International Conference on Data Mining, ICDM 2007, pp. 443–448. SIAM (2007). https://doi.org/10.1137/1.9781611972771.42
2. Bifet, A., Gavaldà, R.: Adaptive learning from evolving data streams. In: Adams, N.M., Robardet, C., Siebes, A., Boulicaut, J.-F. (eds.) IDA 2009. LNCS, vol. 5772, pp. 249–260. Springer, Heidelberg (2009). https://doi.org/10.1007/978-3-642-03915-7_22
3. Chen, Q., Rinderle-Ma, S.: Class incremental learning with drift detection and data augmentation for dynamic processes. In: 7th International Conference on Process Mining, ICPM 2025, pp. 1–8 (2025). https://doi.org/10.1109/ICPM66919.2025.11220682
4. Di Francescomarino, C., Ghidini, C.: Predictive process monitoring. In: van der Aalst, W.M.P., Carmona, J. (eds.) Process Mining Handbook. LNBIP, vol. 448, pp. 320–346. Springer, Cham (2022). https://doi.org/10.1007/978-3-031-08848-3_10
5. Goldberger, A., et al.: PhysioBank, PhysioToolkit, and PhysioNet: components of a new research resource for complex physiologic signals. Circulation **101**(23), E215–220 (2000). https://doi.org/10.1161/01.cir.101.23.e215
6. Gomes, H.M., et al.: Adaptive random forests for evolving data stream classification. Mach. Learn. **106**(9–10), 1469–1495 (2017). https://doi.org/10.1007/s10994-017-5642-8
7. Gomes, H.M., Read, J., Bifet, A., Durrant, R.J.: Learning from evolving data streams through ensembles of random patches. Knowl. Inf. Syst. **63**(7), 1597–1625 (2021). https://doi.org/10.1007/s10115-021-01579-z
8. Kulbach, C., Cazzonelli, L., Ngo, H.A., Halford, M., Mastelini, S.M.: DeepRiver: a deep learning library for data streams. J. Open Source Softw. **10**(105), 7226 (2025). https://doi.org/10.21105/joss.07226
9. Maisenbacher, M., Weidlich, M.: Handling concept drift in predictive process monitoring. In: IEEE International Conference on Services Computing, SCC 2027, pp. 1–8 (2017). https://doi.org/10.1109/SCC.2017.10
10. Pasquadibisceglie, V., Appice, A., Castellano, G., Malerba, D.: Darwin: an online deep learning approach to handle concept drifts in predictive process monitoring. Eng. Appl. Artif. Intell. **123**, 106461 (2023). https://doi.org/10.1016/j.engappai.2023.106461
11. Pasquadibisceglie, V., Appice, A., Discanno, G., Malerba, D.: Leveraging a foundation deep neural embedding in process discovery under not-pareto distribution. In: 7th International Conference on Process Mining, ICPM 2025, pp. 1–8. IEEE (2025). https://doi.org/10.1109/ICPM66919.2025.11220731
12. Pasquadibisceglie, V., Appice, A., Malerba, D., Fiameni, G.: Leveraging a large language model (LLM) to predict hospital admissions of emergency department patients. Expert Syst. Appl. **287**, 128224 (2025). https://doi.org/10.1016/J.ESWA.2025.128224
13. Pasquadibisceglie, V., et al.: Multimodal predictive process monitoring and its application to explainable clinical pathways. Inf. Syst. **139**, 102698 (2026). https://doi.org/10.1016/j.is.2026.102698
14. Pauwels, S., Calders, T.: Incremental predictive process monitoring: the next activity case. In: Polyvyanyy, A., Wynn, M.T., Van Looy, A., Reichert, M. (eds.) BPM 2021. LNCS, vol. 12875, pp. 123–140. Springer, Cham (2021). https://doi.org/10.1007/978-3-030-85469-0_10

15. Radford, A., Wu, J., Child, R., Luan, D., Amodei, D., Sutskever, I.: Language models are unsupervised multitask learners. OpenAI (2019)
16. Ritoré, Á., Oprescu, A.M., Estirado Bronchalo, A., Armengol de la Hoz, M.Á.: COVID data for shared learning (CDSL): a comprehensive, multimodal COVID-19 dataset from HM hospitales (2024). https://doi.org/10.13026/1176-6c44
17. Wei, J., He, Z., Ouyang, C., Moreira, C.: MIMICEL: MIMIC-IV event log for emergency department. PhysioNet (2023). https://doi.org/10.13026/c9yj-1t90

Predicting Quality of Life Deterioration in Cancer Immunotherapy Using Multi-timepoint Data Aggregation

Rihab Ayed[1,3](✉), Yanis Bouallouche[3], Mehdi Hennequin[3], Mohand-Said Hacid[3], and Juba Agoun[2]

[1] LyRIDS, Ecole Centrale d'Electronique, Lyon, France
[2] Université Lumière Lyon 2, Université Claude Bernard Lyon 1, ERIC, 69007 Lyon, France
juba.agoun1@univ-lyon2.fr
[3] LIRIS, Université Claude Bernard Lyon 1, Lyon, France
rayed@ece.fr, {mehdi.hennequin,mohand-said.hacid}@univ-lyon1.fr

Abstract. Cancer patients undergoing immunotherapy experience diverse and evolving Quality of Life (QoL) trajectories that can significantly impact treatment outcomes. This study presents a machine learning framework for predicting QoL deterioration by integrating patient clustering with symptom classification over an 18-month follow-up period. We analyzed longitudinal data from the QUALITOP real-world cohort, comprising cancer patients from two European hospital partners. Our methodology introduces several key innovations: a temporal aggregation approach consolidating variable-length trajectories into predictive features; direct analysis of patient-reported FACT-G item responses rather than composite scores, enhancing model explainability while maintaining high accuracy performances; dual-perspective analysis clustering patients into distinct QoL trajectories while identifying symptom patterns simultaneously; and empirical validation through ensemble comparison of multiple clustering algorithms and classification methods. Our findings demonstrate that patient-centric, temporal-aggregation-based analysis of QoL data can effectively support clinical decision-making in oncology.

Keywords: Quality of life · Cancer immunotherapy · Machine learning · Patient clustering · FACT-G · Temporal aggregation

1 Introduction

Immunotherapies have transformed cancer treatment, with Immune Checkpoint Inhibitors (ICI) and CAR-T therapy demonstrating substantial clinical efficacy across multiple cancer types [13,19]. However, immune-related adverse events (irAEs) significantly impact patient quality of life (QoL) [26], and predicting QoL deterioration is essential for timely clinical intervention [11]. Despite growing

G. Andresini et al. (Eds.): ISMIS 2026, LNAI 16685, pp. 247–257, 2027.
https://doi.org/10.1007/978-3-032-32643-0_21

recognition of QoL's importance [4,20,21,30], predicting deterioration remains challenging: clinical trial data often fail to reflect real-world complexity [29]; composite QoL scores obscure interpretable symptom-level patterns [15]; and significant discordance exists between clinician- and patient-reported outcomes [7]. This work addresses these gaps through a temporal aggregation approach consolidating 18-month patient-reported QoL trajectories into predictive features. Rather than relying on composite scores, we analyse individual FACT-G item responses – collected with clinical staff assistance at two European hospitals [10] – to identify symptoms driving QoL deterioration, and validate prediction models across multiple clustering and classification algorithms.

Contributions: (1) a temporal aggregation methodology for variable-length trajectories with missing follow-ups; (2) direct use of patient-reported FACT-G items over composite scores, enhancing explainability; (3) dual-perspective patient clustering and symptom classification; (4) ensemble validation across seven clustering and six classification algorithms on cross-hospital real-world data.

The remainder is organised as follows: Sect. 2 reviews related work; Sect. 3 describes datasets and methodology; Sect. 4 presents results; Sect. 5 discusses findings and limitations.

2 Background and Related Work

We adopt the WHO definition of QoL as an individual's perception of their position in life [12], encompassing four HRQoL dimensions [11]: physical, mental, social, and functional health.

2.1 QoL Assessment in Oncology

QoL instruments range from generic (EORTC QLQ-C30), global composite (FACT-G, EORTC QLQ-C30 Global Health Status) [6], profile (SF-36), disease-targeted (FACT-B) [14], to patient-reported outcomes such as PROMIS [17,25]. EORTC QLQ and FACT are the most prevalent tools in oncology; our study uses FACT-G collected with clinical staff assistance at partner hospitals.

2.2 Symptom and Patient Clustering

Cancer symptoms frequently co-occur as clusters [2]. Al-Qadire et al. [2] applied EFA to breast cancer patients with combined therapies, identifying five clusters (*psychological, treatment side-effects, nausea/vomiting, pain, fatigue*), with psychological, nausea/vomiting, and pain as strongest QoL predictors via linear regression. So et al. [28] confirmed three recurring clusters across breast cancer treatment phases (*psychological, pain/fatigue/sleep, gastrointestinal*), with the psychological cluster most persistent. Lee et al. [18] applied Latent Class Profile Analysis across seven cancer types, confirming a common *fatigue–sleep–depression* subgroup and showing sociodemographic factors (e.g., younger age) amplify QoL deterioration. A recurring finding is clinician–patient outcome discordance, with clinicians consistently underreporting symptom severity and number [3,22].

For patient subgroup identification, McDowell et al. [22] distinguished high- and low-functioning oropharyngeal cancer subgroups; Mohamed et al. [24] linked high unmet-needs clusters to worse QoL and greater psychological burden; Bergsneider et al. [5] identified six subgroups via Random Walk clustering with QoL profiles ranging from minimal symptoms to high burden. Temporally, Zhang et al. [31] used Growth Mixture Modeling on seven-timepoint colorectal cancer trajectories; Cuzzocrea et al. [8] combined temporal frequency streams with k-means to detect hidden physical well-being patterns in immunotherapy patients. Savander et al. [27] and D'Amico et al. [9] demonstrated that UMAP combined with clustering effectively separates clinically meaningful patient or genomic subgroups, with QoL summary score emerging as the most discriminative clustering feature in radiotherapy patients.

2.3 Research Gaps

Four critical limitations emerge. First, most studies use composite HRQoL scores [2,28], obscuring symptom-level interpretability. Second, temporal approaches [8,31] focus on specific health dimensions rather than comprehensive patient-reported attributes. Third, in most studies, symptom correlations and patient clustering are examined in isolation [5,22]. Fourth, clinician–patient discordance [3,22] highlights the need for frameworks centred on patient-reported item responses collected in formal clinical settings. Our work addresses all four gaps simultaneously and tries to consolidate the literature findings, as well.

3 Methodology

3.1 Cross-Hospital Datasets

Two Qualitop project cohorts [10] were analysed: IPOL (49 lymphoma patients, 483 attributes, 16 domains) and HCB (55 melanoma patients, 459 attributes, 14 domains). Both achieved high baseline completion ($\geq$60%). Patient retention differed substantially: IPOL showed substantial loss to follow-up (49 to 15 patients at month 18), while HCB maintained higher consistency (51 to 28). HCB served as the reference for attribute harmonisation.

3.2 Temporal Aggregation

Datasets were restructured from domain-specific matrices to patient-level observations by treating time as an aggregation dimension rather than a stratification variable. Baseline and follow-up attributes were mapped to enable cross-timepoint synthesis[1]. Six features were derived as patient-level temporal

[1] Code and additional details are available at: https://github.com/rayed19/QoL_temporalaggregation_baseline.

means: (i) disease status post-immunotherapy, (ii) post-other therapies, (iii) total medication count, (iv) immunotherapy count, (v) other therapy count, and (vi) immunotherapy dosing interval. Formally, for patient p, attribute a, and valid timepoints T_p:

$$\bar{X}_{p,a} = \frac{1}{|T_p|} \sum_{t \in T_p} X_{p,a,t} \tag{1}$$

Three target variables were aggregated: patient-reported QoL contentment, clinician-assessed disease status, and AE drug relationship. Attributes with >60% missing values were removed. Final merged dataset: 210 observations (68 unique patients) across 53 attributes (IPOL: 58 observations, 16 patients; HCB: 152 observations, 52 patients). These observations are considered patient feelings correlated with their aggregated features.

3.3 Patient Clustering

To improve clustering efficiency, we applied UMAP (Uniform Manifold Approximation and Projection) [23] reduced the 210 × 51 observation matrix; dimensions 2, 3, 6, 8, 10, 12, and 14 were evaluated. Seven clustering algorithms were applied: Birch, K-means, Gaussian Mixture (GM), Robust K-means, Agglomerative, K-Medoids, and Mini-Batch K-means, building upon the methodology of Agoun et al. [1] optimized for QoL data. The Six-dimensional UMAP reduction yielded the lowest cluster count variance (0.24) with consistent identification of six clusters across all seven algorithms, and was selected as the optimal configuration. Cluster interpretation used the feature extraction algorithm of Khoie et al. [16].

3.4 Symptom Classification

Six classifiers were implemented via scikit-learn: Random Forest, SVM, Logistic Regression, GBM, Gaussian Process, and MLP. Preprocessing: StandardScaler normalisation and KNN imputation ($k = 3$). Feature selection used Random Forest importance scores (top-10 per target). Model performance was evaluated using 10-fold cross-validation.

4 Results

We present in the following consensual results over clustering algorithms, followed by symptom classification and correlations.

4.1 Clustering Results

Table 1 summarizes the six consensus clusters identified by all seven algorithms. The last column highlights the most important non-consensual refinements added by the algorithms. For better understanding of results, we do not report

Table 1. Consensus clusters and algorithm-specific refinements. (+) high, (–) low. **Bold** = aggregated features.

ID	Label	Key attributes	Algorithm refinements
C1	Cannabis melanoma, no children	Melanoma+, Children–, Cannabis+, Anxiety+, Cheerful–, **QoL cont.**+, Reflux meds+	Average therapy number +, Past fatigue – (Birch)
C2	Lymphoma/ psychological burden	Lymphoma+, Past sadness+, Past stress+, Past fatigue impact+, past sleep disorders+, **QoL cont.**–, **Avg number of immuno.**–, **Avg. days interval of immuno.**–	AE related to drugs +, Other-therapy response – (K-Medoids)
C3	Melanoma with children	Melanoma+, Children+, Cheerful+, Anxiety –, Past pain/reflux meds–	**QoL cont.**+ (GM, Robust, Agglomerative)
C4	Acute post-immunotherapy	Nausea+, Pain+, Trouble family needs+, Cheerful–, Enjoying Things–, Laugh –, Past fatigue–, Past stress–	Disease status(DS) immuno–, DS other-therapies +, AE related to drugs – (GM, Robust)
C5	Young resilient lymphoma	Lymphoma+, Young+, Cheerful+, Past fatigue impact+, **Disease Status**+, **Avg number of immuno**–, **Avg. days interval of immuno.**–	Physical activity+ (4 algos)
C6	Cannabis melanoma, high meds	Melanoma+, Children-, Cannabis+, Anxiety+, Cheerful–, Past fatigue meds+, Past stress/anxiety meds+, **Avg number of immuno**+, **Avg. days interval of immuno.**+	Past reflux medications + (GM, Robust)
C4'	Old, nausea	Birth date–, Nausea+, Lack of energy+, Cheerful–, Past meds+, **AE-drugs**+, **DS immuno**–	Contradiction: high past meds yet low reported past fatigue/stress (GM, Robust)
C3'	Social-support melanoma	Melanoma+, Children+, Health discussion with partner–, **QoL cont.**+, **AE-drugs**+	Novel social-support factor (K-Medoids, Mini-Batch)

Fact-G items as-is (e.g. Physical Activity low value corresponds to high physical activity).

C1 and **C6** (see Table 1) share a profile of cannabis-consuming melanoma patients without children, with high anxiety and low cheerfulness, but they are averagely content of their QoL, differing in medication history: C1 shows high reflux medications, refined by Birch algorithm with low past fatigue and high number of therapies; C6 shows high past fatigue and psychological administrated medications. They received a high number of immunotherapies, and a low number of doses of immunotherapies. **C2** captures lymphoma patients with heavy past psychological burden (sadness, stress, anxiety), past sleep disorders, past fatigue and low QoL contentment. They received a low number of immunotherapies and a high number of doses of immunotherapies. Refined by K-Medoids, their Adverse Events (AE) are related to administrated drugs and they averagely did not respond well to other therapies (chemo/radiotherapies). **C3** identifies melanoma patients with children with low past pain and reflux medications, expressing happiness and low anxiety. Refined by GM, Robust k-means and Agglomerative, with high QoL contentment. **C4** Both lymphoma and melanoma patients with nausea, pain after immunotherapies, low past fatigue and psychological issues, low happiness (laughing, enjoying things, cheerful), and trouble meeting family needs despite low past fatigue and stress. Refined by GM and Robust k-means as badly responded to immunotherapy and well responded to other therapies and with AE not related to drugs.

C5 describes young lymphoma patients with positive affect (cheerful), high past fatigue impact. They received a low number of immunotherapies and high number of doses of immunotherapies. They averagely responded well to therapies. Refined by GM, Robust k-means Agglomerative, and K-Medoids as practicing physical activity.

Mini-Batch is the most individual algorithm generating 3 clusters out of 6 different from the other algorithms. It correlates the 3 target aggregated features in two clusters (C2' similar to C2, and C3' similar to C3). Mini-Batch further reveal social-support behaviors (health discussions with partner) in extra clusters C3' (similar to C3) and C2" (similar to C2). GM and Robust k-means reveals a noteworthy contradiction in C4' (similar to C4): old patients with high past medication use, yet with low reported past fatigue and psychological distress.

QoL contentment is the most stable aggregated feature, cited across all algorithms in 3 out of 6 clusters. **AE-drug relationship** and **disease status** appear less consistently, likely reflecting limited clinician-reported data in the cohort. The aggregated number of therapies is present in 4 out of 6 clusters across all algorithms. Among unaggregated attributes, cheerfulness and past fatigue are the most cross-cutting features, each appearing in 5 out of 6 clusters. Anxiety appearing in 3 out of 6 clusters.

4.2 Classification Results

GBM achieves best overall performance (Table 2): QoL Contentment 81.8%, AE-Drug Relationship 88.6%, and Disease Status 89.5%.

Table 2. Classification accuracy (mean ± std, 10-fold CV)

Algorithm	QoL Cont.	AE-Drug	Dis. Status
Random Forest	0.736 ± 0.080	0.881 ± 0.041	**0.895** ± 0.038
SVM	0.631 ± 0.047	0.819 ± 0.068	0.767 ± 0.014
Log. Regression	0.593 ± 0.016	0.810 ± 0.059	0.800 ± 0.023
GBM	**0.818** ± 0.049	**0.886** ± 0.031	**0.895** ± 0.018
Gaussian Process	0.569 ± 0.065	0.829 ± 0.065	0.719 ± 0.007
MLP Network	0.593 ± 0.025	0.857 ± 0.031	0.871 ± 0.020

Random Forest matches GBM for Disease Status but underperforms on QoL Contentment. First, Disease Status is the most predictable target across all algorithms. Second, QoL Contentment is the hardest target to predict, reflecting its subjective and multidimensional nature. Third, AE-Drug Relationship yields consistently high accuracy across most algorithms, indicating that drug-related adverse events follow relatively stable patterns learnable from patient-reported and few clinical features. Finally, the high variance observed for some algorithms on QoL Contentment (e.g., Random Forest ± 0.080) suggests sensitivity to data splits, reinforcing the value of ensemble methods such as GBM for this target.

Table 3. Top-10 predictive features per target using GBM

<table>
<tr><th>Rank</th><th>QoL Contentment</th><th>AE-Drug</th><th>Disease Status</th></tr>
<tr><td>1</td><td>Avg # medications</td><td>Birth date</td><td>DS Immuno</td></tr>
<tr><td>2</td><td>Birth date</td><td>DS other therapies</td><td>Birth date</td></tr>
<tr><td>3</td><td colspan="3">Avg days interval of immuno</td></tr>
<tr><td>4</td><td>Bothering side effects</td><td colspan="2">Avg # medications</td></tr>
<tr><td>5</td><td>Past sadness/depression</td><td>DS Immuno</td><td>Avg # therapies</td></tr>
<tr><td>6</td><td>Family needs</td><td>Past stress/anxiety meds</td><td>DS other therapies</td></tr>
<tr><td>7</td><td>Enjoying things</td><td>Worrying thoughts</td><td>Cancer Type</td></tr>
<tr><td>8</td><td>Laugh</td><td>Education level</td><td>Hospital</td></tr>
<tr><td>9</td><td>Nausea</td><td>Enjoying Things</td><td>Past stress/anxiety</td></tr>
<tr><td>10</td><td>DS other therapies</td><td>Avg # therapies</td><td>Education level</td></tr>
</table>

4.3 Top Predictive Features

Table 3 lists the top-10 features per target using GBM. Birth date (age), average number of medications, and the average number of doses of immunotherapies (Avg days interval) rank among the top predictors for all three targets. Anxiety-related symptoms (worrying thoughts, past stress/anxiety), level of education, and average number of therapies appear across two targets (AE-relationship to drug and Disease Status). Aggregated disease status predictors (DS Immuno, DS other therapies) rank prominently, supporting our temporal aggregation approach: past treatment response predicts future outcomes.

5 Discussion

5.1 Clinical Implications

The six stable clusters reveal QoL heterogeneity that composite scores would mask. The 89.5% accuracy for disease status confirms that longitudinal treatment history (DS Immuno, DS other therapies) carries strong prognostic value for early patient therapy response identification. Age and education consistently rank among top predictors across all three targets, supporting stratified interventions. The social-support feature (health discussions with partner) suggests its incorporation into QoL monitoring. A prediction model trained on the studied data can output clinical indicators: low *QoL contentment* with good response to therapy (Disease status), and negative AE-related to drugs signals the potential need for psychological/social support; disease progression (Disease status) with high *QoL contentment* and negative AE-related to drugs can orient to therapy re-evaluation.

5.2 Methodological Contributions and Limitations

Temporal aggregation (Eq. 1) handles irregular follow-up patterns while preserving all patient information. The dual-perspective clustering and seven-algorithm ensemble provide robustness against algorithm-specific biases. Despite UMAP's stochastic nature, patients with similar feature profiles were consistently grouped together across most clustering algorithms, supporting the robustness of the identified structures. Limitations include the small combined sample (68 unique patients), the cancer-type/hospital confound (one cancer per hospital), and IPOL's substantial loss to follow-up (49 to 15 patients at month 18), which may introduce survivorship bias toward healthier patients. Temporal aggregation via feature *averaging* provides a simple yet informative baseline for identifying patient groups and symptoms associated with QoL. The resulting analysis offers a preliminary characterization of QoL deterioration factors, which can be further consolidated through additional analysis, evaluation metrics, and datasets.

6 Conclusion

We presented a temporal aggregation approach for predicting QoL deterioration in cancer immunotherapy patients achieving high accuracy with clinical interpretability. By directly analyzing patient-reported FACT-G item responses and integrating dual-perspective clustering with supervised classification, our work addresses key limitations and consolidation of existing QoL studies in oncology.

The psychological triad and treatment history emerge as consistent cross-cluster QoL determinants, providing caregivers with interpretable indicators for early identification of at-risk patients and supporting personalized cancer care.

Acknowledgments. This work was supported by the European Union's Horizon 2020 research and innovation programme under grant agreement No. 875171 (QUALITOP).

Disclosure of Interests. The authors declare no competing interests that are relevant to the content of this article.

References

1. Agoun, J., Bouallouche, Y., Hacid, M.S.: OptiClust4Rec: Unsupervised data-driven methodology for quality of life recommendations during a medical therapy. In: CoopIS (Demos), pp. 6–10 (2023)
2. Al Qadire, M., et al.: Symptom clusters predictive of quality of life among Jordanian women with breast cancer. In: Seminars in Oncology Nursing, vol. 37, p. 151144. Elsevier (2021)
3. Annakib, S., et al.: Patient versus clinician reported symptoms agreement in advanced metastatic bladder cancer patients. Cancer Med. (2025). https://doi.org/10.1002/cam4.70896
4. Belzer, A., Pach, J.J., Valido, K., Leventhal, J.S.: The impact of dermatologic adverse events on the quality of life of oncology patients: a review of the literature. Am. J. Clin. Dermatol. **25**(3), 435–445 (2024)
5. Bergsneider, B.H., et al.: Symptom network analysis and unsupervised clustering of oncology patients identifies drivers of symptom burden and patient subgroups with distinct symptom patterns. Cancer Med. **13**(19), e70278 (2024). https://doi.org/10.1002/cam4.70278
6. Bottomley, A., et al.: Adjuvant pembrolizumab versus placebo in resected stage III melanoma (EORTC 1325-mg/keynote-054): health-related quality-of-life results from a double-blind, randomised, controlled, phase 3 trial. Lancet Oncol. **22**(5), 655–664 (2021)
7. Chen, Y., Sun, Z., Wan, L., Chen, H., Xi, T., Jiang, Y.: Tumor microenvironment characterization for assessment of recurrence and survival outcome in gastric cancer to predict chemotherapy and immunotherapy response. Front. Immunol. **13**, 890922 (2022)
8. Cuzzocrea, A., De Bock, G.H., Maas, W.J., Soufargi, S.: F-TBDA: a frequency-based temporal big data analytics technique for mining and analyzing quality-of-life indicators of cancer patients. In: 2023 IEEE International Conference on Big Data (BigData), pp. 5197–5205. IEEE (2023)
9. D'Amico, S., et al.: Mosaic: an artificial intelligence–based framework for multimodal analysis, classification, and personalized prognostic assessment in rare cancers. JCO Clin. Cancer Inform. (8), e2400008 (2024). https://doi.org/10.1200/CCI.24.00008, https://ascopubs.org/doi/abs/10.1200/CCI.24.00008. pMID: 38875514
10. European Cancer Patient Coalition: QUALITOP Project (2024). https://cancerpatientseurope.org/qualitop/. Accessed 27 Feb 2026
11. Gour, N., Chaudhary, M.: The quality of life in cancer patients. In: Supportive and Palliative Care and Quality of Life in Oncology. IntechOpen (2023)

12. Haraldstad, K., et al.: A systematic review of quality of life research in medicine and health sciences. Qual. Life Res. **28**, 2641–2650 (2019)
13. Hosseinkhani, N., et al.: Immune checkpoints and CAR-T cells: the pioneers in future cancer therapies? Int. J. Mol. Sci. **21**(21), 8305 (2020)
14. Kaplan, R.M., Hays, R.D.: Health-related quality of life measurement in public health. Annu. Rev. Public Health **43**, 355–373 (2022)
15. Kara, P., Valentin, J.B., Mainz, J., Johnsen, S.P.: Composite measures of quality of health care: evidence mapping of methodology and reporting. PLoS ONE **17**(5), e0268320 (2022)
16. Khoie, M.R., Tabrizi, T., Khorasani, E., Marhamati, N.: A hospital recommendation system based on patient satisfaction survey. Appl. Sci. **7**, 966 (2017). https://doi.org/10.3390/app7100966
17. Kuspinar, A., Mate, K.K., Lafontaine, A.L., Mayo, N.: Validation of an individualized measure of quality of life, patient generated index, for use with people with Parkinson's disease. Neurol. Res. Int. **2020** (2020)
18. Lee, L.J., Han, C.J., Saligan, L., Wallen, G.R.: Comparing symptom clusters in cancer survivors by cancer diagnosis: a latent class profile analysis. Support. Care Cancer **32**, 308 (2024). https://doi.org/10.1007/s00520-024-08489-0
19. Liu, C., Yang, M., Zhang, D., Chen, M., Zhu, D.: Clinical cancer immunotherapy: current progress and prospects. Front. Immunol. **13**, 961805 (2022)
20. Lustberg, M.B., Kuderer, N.M., Desai, A., Bergerot, C., Lyman, G.H.: Mitigating long-term and delayed adverse events associated with cancer treatment: implications for survivorship. Nat. Rev. Clin. Oncol. **20**(8), 527–542 (2023)
21. Marzorati, C., et al.: Psychosocial factors associated with quality of life in cancer patients undergoing treatment: an umbrella review. Health Qual. Life Outcomes **23**(1), 31 (2025)
22. McDowell, L., et al.: Symptom burden, quality of life, functioning and emotional distress in survivors of human papillomavirus associated oropharyngeal cancer: an Australian cohort. Oral Oncol. **122**, 105560 (2021)
23. McInnes, L., Healy, J., Melville, J.: UMAP: uniform manifold approximation and projection for dimension reduction. arXiv preprint arXiv:1802.03426 (2018)
24. Mohamed, N.E., Leung, T.M., Kata, H.E., Shah, Q.N., Lee, C.T., Quale, D.: Identifying distinct high unmet-need phenotypes and their associated bladder cancer patient demographic, clinical, psychosocial, and functional characteristics: results of two clustering methods. In: Seminars in Oncology Nursing, vol. 37, p. 151112. Elsevier (2021)
25. Pai, S., et al.: Defining current gaps in quality measures for cancer immunotherapy: consensus report from the society for immunotherapy of cancer (SITC) 2019 quality summit. J. Immunother. Cancer **8**(1) (2020)
26. Pozzessere, C., et al.: Immune-related adverse events induced by immune checkpoint inhibitors and CAR-T cell therapy: a comprehensive imaging-based review. Cancers **16**(14), 2585 (2024)
27. Savander, J.: Clustering of radiotherapy patients based on the usage patterns in the Kaiku health application and electronic patient-reported outcomes (2023)
28. So, W.K., et al.: Symptom clusters experienced by breast cancer patients at various treatment stages: a systematic review. Cancer Med. **10**(8), 2531–2565 (2021)
29. Vinke, P.C., et al.: Protocol: monitoring multidimensional aspects of quality of life after cancer immunotherapy: protocol for the international multicentre, observational qualitop cohort study. BMJ Open **13**(4) (2023)

30. Wenzel, L., et al.: Quality of life and adverse events: prognostic relationships in long-term ovarian cancer survival. JNCI: J. Natl. Cancer Inst. **113**(10), 1369–1378 (2021)
31. Zhang, J., et al.: Clustering on longitudinal quality-of-life measurements using growth mixture models for clinical prognosis: implementation on CCTG/AGITG CO. 20 trial. Cancer Med. **12**(5), 6117–6128 (2023)

AI for Urban and Environmental Systems

Improving Indoor Cellular Coverage Mapping Using a Mobile Robot

Fatma Ltaief(✉), Adam Gouguet, Guillaume Lozenguez, and Luc Fabresse

Center for Digital Systems, Institut Mines-Télécom (IMT) Nord Europe, 59653 Villeneuve d'Ascq Cedex, France
{fatma.ltaief,adam.gouguet,guillaume.lozenguez, luc.fabresse}@imt-nord-europe.fr
http://www.imt-nord-europe.fr

Abstract. Accurate indoor radio coverage mapping is essential for coordinating multi-agent robotic systems, like MARS (Multi-Agent Robotic Systems), and ensuring reliable wireless communication in complex environments. This paper presents a method to validate and improve cellular signal coverage maps predicted via physics-based ray tracing using robot-collected measurements. A mobile robot performs Simultaneous Localization and Mapping (SLAM) while recording signal metrics such as Received Signal Strength Indicator (RSSI) and Signal-to-Interference-plus-Noise Ratio (SINR). An initial coverage map is generated using a differentiable ray tracing simulator (Sionna RT), and residuals are defined as the difference between measured signals and simulated predictions. We observe that these residuals correlate with simple geometric features. Therefore, we propose a lightweight, structure-aware model that predicts the residuals based on wall count and distance, and integrates them into the ray-tracing output to obtain a corrected map. Experiments conducted in multiple indoor environments using a 5G small-cell transmitter demonstrate that the proposed approach significantly improves prediction accuracy compared to ray tracing alone.

Keywords: Mobile Robotics · Coverage map · Residual Model

1 Introduction

Reliable wireless communication is essential for modern robotic systems, especially fleets of robots operating in complex indoor environments where maintaining connectivity is challenging [18]. Knowledge of the spatial distribution of signal strength (a *radio map*) enables robots to plan communication-aware trajectories [20], deploy as communication relays [5], or adapt multi-robot coordination strategies to network conditions [3]. However, predicting radio signal coverage in cluttered, occlusion-rich environments is difficult due to complex interactions of radio waves with walls, floors, and objects. In extreme cases like

G. Andresini et al. (Eds.): ISMIS 2026, LNAI 16685, pp. 261–271, 2027.
https://doi.org/10.1007/978-3-032-32643-0_22

underground settings, wireless signals suffer severe attenuation and multipath effects, making accurate mapping critical yet hard to achieve.

Traditional approaches to model radio propagation range from empirical models (e.g., log-distance pathloss models with wall attenuation factors [14]) to site-specific deterministic simulation. Deterministic ray-tracing simulators can capture detailed geometry effects and have long been used for indoor coverage prediction [1,19]. Recently, high fidelity differentiable ray tracers like Sionna RT have emerged, enabling integration of propagation simulation into learning frameworks [8]. These simulators form the backbone of wireless digital twins that mirrors real RF environments in simulation. In practice, however, purely physics based predictions are often slightly different from reality simplified geometry, unknown material parameters, or propagation effects that are difficult to model precisely. This motivates techniques to calibrate or correct simulations using real measurements [15,17]. A promising direction, inspired by residual physics modeling in robotics [13], is to learn a data driven residual to compensate for the simulation's systematic errors while retaining its generalization capacity.

To address these limitations, we propose a hybrid approach that combines ray-tracing simulation with robot-collected measurements. A mobile robot equipped with a 5G modem performs using LiDAR-based SLAM [7]while recording signal metrics such as RSSI and SINR across the environment. Using the reconstructed map, a geometric model is generated and used to simulate radio propagation with the Sionna RT simulator [8]. We then compute the residual between simulated and measured signals and learn a lightweight correction model based on structural features extracted from the environment, including transmitter–receiver distance and the number of intervening walls. This residual model is used to correct the ray-tracing predictions and produce improved coverage maps. Experiments conducted in multiple indoor environments and under different transmitter placements demonstrate that the proposed approach significantly improves prediction accuracy compared to ray tracing alone, while preserving the physical interpretability of the simulation model.

2 Related Works

Ray-Tracing and Wireless Simulation. Physics-based ray tracing has long been used for site specific channel modeling. Methods based on geometric optics and uniform theory of diffraction compute propagation by tracing rays interacting with the environment. When the scene geometry is accurately defined, ray tracing simulators can produce radio maps that closely math real world measurments. Modern simulators (Wireless InSite [21], QuaDriGa [11], SIonna RT [9]) support 3D CAD models, multiple reflections/diffractions, and high-frequency (mmWave/sub-THz) channels [12] More recently, differentiable and GPU-accelerated ray-tracing frameworks have been introduced. In particular, Sionna RT enables high-fidelity wireless propagation simulations that can be integrated into learning pipelines and digital twin environments. While these simulators capture many important propagation phenomena, their accuracy depends strongly on the quality of the environment model and the correctness of material parameters. In practice, simplified geometry, unknown wall materials, and unmodeled propagation effects often lead to systematic discrepancies between simulated and measured signals. Several recent works therefore investigate learning-based corrections to physics-based propagation models. For example, neural channel models such as WiNeRT attempt to approximate ray tracing using neural networks. In contrast, our approach does not replace the physical simulator but instead learns a residual correction that compensates for systematic errors while preserving the physical structure of the ray-tracing prediction.

Radio Mapping in Robotics: The problem of constructing radio signal maps using mobile robots has been studied in the robotics community for nearly two decades. Early work by Hsieh et al. [10] presented one of the first systems for constructing signal strength maps with a team of robots, formulating it as an exploration problem given a known floorplan. Fink and Kumar [6] later proposed online techniques for radio mapping with a single robot, where measurements are used to update a probabilistic model of signal strength during exploration. Others extended to multi-robot scenarios and communication maintenance: e.g., Banfi et al. [3] and Penumarthi et al. [16] studied exploration strategies where robots build a communication map while remaining connected, often using simplified disk or exponential models for connectivity. There is also extensive literature on planning robot positions for maintaining network topology [18,20] and deploying robotic relays [5], which typically assume some prior knowledge of the RF environment or use online measurements to infer it [2].

In contrast to these approaches, which primarily focus on using signal maps for planning and coordination, our work focuses on improving the accuracy of the radio map itself. We leverage a mobile robot to densely collect wireless measurements and combine these data with a physics-based propagation model. By learning a residual correction that depends on simple geometric features extracted from the environment, our approach improves the accuracy of ray-tracing coverage predictions while maintaining their interpretability.

3 Methodology

An overview of our approach is given on Fig. 1. It involves three main components: (1) environment mapping and ray tracing simulation, (2) collection of ground-truth signal measurements and computation of residuals, and (3) learning a residual correction model that is a function of environment features. The corrected coverage map is then obtained by summing the ray tracing prediction and the learned residual term.

3.1 Environment Mapping and Ray Tracing

To perform site-specific signal prediction, we first obtain a geometric model of the environment. A LiDAR-based SLAM system is used to produce a 2D occupancy grid of the indoor environment. In our implementation, we exploit SLAM

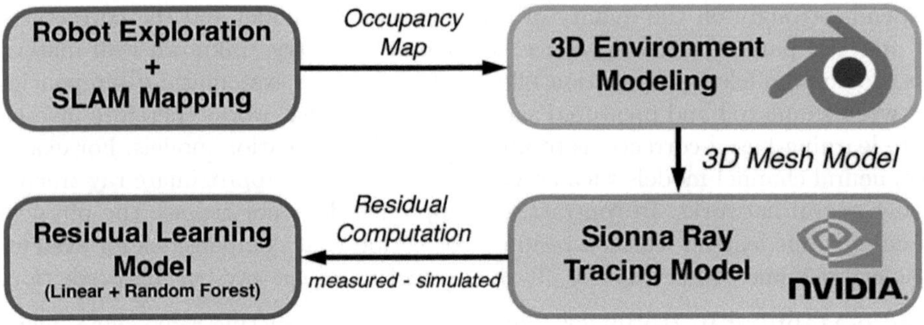

Fig. 1. Hybrid coverage mapping pipeline. A mobile robot collects wireless measurements while performing SLAM to reconstruct the environment map. The map is converted into a 3D mesh used by the Sionna RT simulator, and regression models learn residuals between simulated and measured signals to correct the coverage prediction.

techniques [4] that allow us to simultaneously build a map of the environment and localize the robot while collecting wireless measurements.

The resulting 2D occupancy map is then converted into a simple 3D geometric model. The transmitter (a 5G small-cell base station) is placed in the mesh at the known deployment location with a specified antenna pattern and transmit power. We use *Sionna RT* [9] to simulate the propagation of a downlink reference signal across the environment, computing the received power and SINR at receiver locations sampled on a regular grid. Sionna RT performs full 3D ray tracing with reflections. The output is a predicted coverage map $\hat{y}_{RT}(\mathbf{x})$ (expressed in dBm for RSSI or in dB for SINR) defined over the area of interest. This prediction serves as the baseline model of signal strength. We note that the accuracy of $\hat{y}_{RT}(\mathbf{x})$ depends on the quality of the mesh and the correctness of the material parameters used in the simulation. The mesh derived from the occupancy grid is a simplified representation of the environment: walls may be slightly misplaced, small obstacles and furniture are ignored, and all walls are assumed to share the same generic material properties. These simplifications introduce some error in the ray tracing results. Nonetheless, the main propagation phenomena, such as distance-dependent path loss and shadowing caused by walls, are qualitatively captured by $\hat{y}_{RT}(\mathbf{x})$.

3.2 Robot Data Collection

A mobile robot equipped with a 5G router and a LiDAR (Fig. 2a) is used to collect actual signal measurements (Fig. 2b). The robot is driven around the indoor environment (an office floor with several rooms and corridors) to sample a wide range of locations and wall configurations relative to the transmitter. The 5G router records metrics such as RSSI and SINR. Meanwhile, the LiDAR SLAM provides the robot's pose and map.

Each measurement y_i is tagged with the robot's 2D coordinates (x_i, y_i) in the map frame. After the run, we have a dataset of N measurements

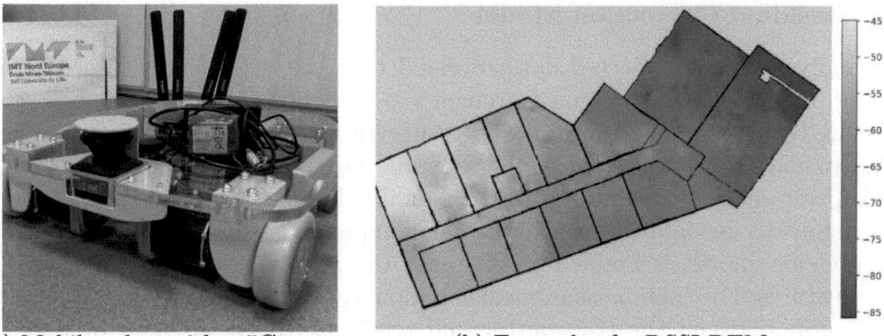

(a) Mobile robot with a 5G router. (b) Example of a RSSI REM map.

Fig. 2. Robot-based measurement setup and resulting radio environment map.

$(x_i, y_i), , y(x_i, y_i)_{i=1}^{N}$. These are then converted to world coordinates in the mesh and aligned with the ray tracing outputs. For each measurement location x_i, we compute the residual which is then defined as :

$$r(x_i) = y(x_i) - \hat{y}_{RT}(x_i), \tag{1}$$

where $y(x_i)$ denotes the measured signal value and $\hat{y}_{RT}(x_i)$ the corresponding ray-tracing prediction. Figure 3 shows the distribution of RSSI residuals as a function of the number of walls between the transmitter and receiver. The interval of the residual variation becomes larger according to the number of walls, a residual between -30 and -10 (0 wall) compared to -30 and 20 (15 walls). This observation shows that even in line-of-sight open areas, the residuals exhibit a consistent negative bias, indicating that the ray-tracing simulation tends to overestimate signal strength in these conditions.

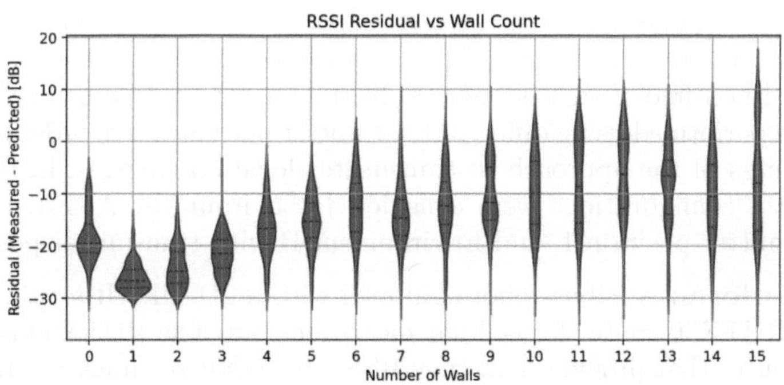

Fig. 3. Distribution of RSSI residuals as a function of the number of walls.

3.3 Residual Correction Model

The analysis of the collected data revealed that the discrepancy between ray-tracing predictions and real measurements is not purely random, but is instead correlated with simple structural and geometric properties of the environment. In particular, the number of walls between the transmitter and receiver, the transmitter–receiver distance, and the signal value predicted by the ray tracer were found to be informative features for explaining the residual magnitude. A regression model is trained to estimate the residual $\hat{r}(x)$ from a vector of three features. For each measurement location x_i, we compute: (i) the Euclidean distance d_i between the transmitter and receiver, (ii) the number of walls w_i intersected by the line segment between the transmitter and receiver line on the occupancy map, and (iii) the ray-tracing prediction $\hat{y}_{RT}(x_i)$ at that location. Thus, the vector feature is defined as: $(d_i, w_i, \hat{y}_{RT}(x_i))$. In this work, we evaluate three alternatives: linear regression, Random Forest regression, and a hybrid model combining both. Linear regression provides a simple interpretable baseline that captures global trends, while Random Forest can represent nonlinear dependencies and interactions between features. The hybrid model aims to benefit from both properties. The final corrected signal prediction is obtained by adding the predicted residual to the ray-tracing estimate:

$$\hat{y}(x) = \hat{y}_{RT}(x) + \hat{r}(x). \tag{2}$$

This formulation allows the ray-tracing simulator to retain the main propagation physics, while the learned residual compensates for systematic errors caused by simplified geometry, imperfect material assumptions, or missing environmental details.

4 Experimental Setup and Results

Environment: Experiments were conducted in two indoor environments located in an academic building. These environments consist of corridors, offices, and open areas, providing a variety of propagation conditions including both line-of-sight and non-line-of-sight scenarios. In the second environment, two experiments were performed using different transmitter placements in order to evaluate the robustness of the approach to transmitter location changes. In total, three experimental configurations were considered: Environment A, Environment B with transmitter position 1, and Environment B with transmitter position 2.

Robot Platform: A Bibus robot equipped with a 2D LiDAR for SLAM and a Teltonika RUTX50 router for cellular measurements. The RUTX50 is a CAT20 LTE/5G router that provides real-time RSSI and SINR readings via its API. We logged these metrics at 1 Hz while teleoperating the robot. During the teleoperating, the robot traversed corridors and entered several rooms, collecting around $N \approx 6000$ data points on average for each scenario. The robot's pose and the SLAM map were recorded; after each run, we post-processed the SLAM map to obtain a consistent global occupancy map.

Simulation: The 2D occupancy map (with resolution 0.05 m) was converted to a 3D model using Blender: each wall pixel became a vertical rectangle spanning floor to walls. The transmitter was placed in the mesh at the measured height. We used Sionna RT [8] with 5 reflections allowed, and a receiver grid spacing of 0.5 m. Diffraction and diffuse scattering were disabled to reduce simulation time; we rely on reflections to capture non-line-of-sight propagation. The material of walls was set to generic "brick" with dielectric constant $\epsilon_r = 3.91$ and conductivity $\sigma = 0.0326\,\text{S/m}$ (since Sionna did not have a specific drywall material, we chose a moderately lossy material). As for the floor, we opted for generic "concrete" with dielectric constant $\epsilon_r = 5.3$ and conductivity $\sigma = 0.029\text{S/m}$. The simulation produced a map of path loss, RSSI and SINR.

Residual Model: To account for the systematic offset between measurements and simulation, we first estimated the mean residual on the training set and used it as a constant bias-correction baseline. The residual learning models were then trained on the debiased residual values. We evaluated three correction strategies: linear regression, Random Forest regression, and a weighted ensemble combining both models, where the final prediction is computed as $0.7\,y_{LR} + 0.3\,y_{RF}$. These weights were selected empirically based on validation performance on the training environment, providing a balance between the stability of the linear model and the flexibility of the Random Forest.

Evaluation: The evaluation was carried out in two settings. In the first setting, the model was trained on environment A, and tested on the same environment, but with different antenna position in order to assess robustness to a transmitter-location change. In the second setting, the model was trained on a different environment in order to assess cross-environment generalization. Performance was evaluated by comparing the corrected predictions against the measured values using the mean absolute error (MAE), root mean square error (RMSE), and bias, for both RSSI and SINR. Figure 4 shows that Sionna RT has a clear negative bias (≈ -18 dB), indicating systematic signal overestimation. Bias correction reduces this shift but residuals remain broad and still negative (≈ -12 dB for RSSI, ≈ -14 dB for SINR). This behavior is explained by the fact that the bias is not constant across configurations. The linear model recenters the residuals closer to zero, but with a slight positive bias ($+4-5$ dB for RSSI, $\approx +2$ dB for SINR). The RF model is more balanced but remains negatively shifted (≈ -4 dB for RSSI, ≈ -6 dB for SINR). Overall, the hybrid RF+Linear model provides the best compromise, with RSSI residuals close to zero ($\approx +1$ dB) and SINR stays near zero although with a slightly bimodal distribution.

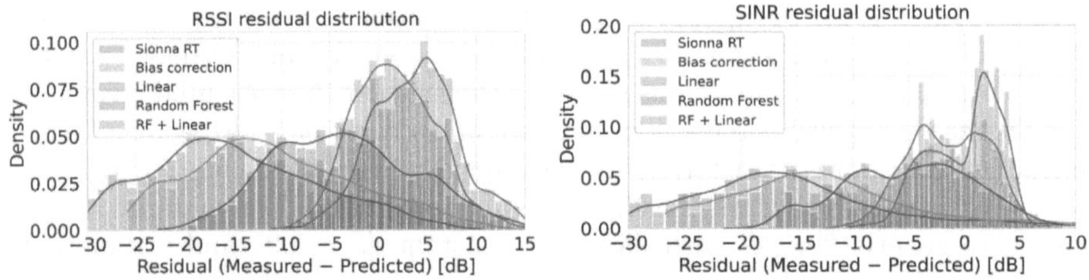

Fig. 4. Residual distributions on the test environment A position 2 for the Sionna RT baseline and the different correction strategies.

The quantitative evaluation results are summarized in Table 1. For RSSI, the hybrid RF+Linear model achieves the best performance, reducing the RMSE by more than 60% compared to the baseline ray-tracing simulation. For SINR, the linear regression model provides the most consistent improvement across environments. These results suggest that simple structure-aware features can effectively capture systematic modeling errors in ray-tracing predictions.

Table 1. Test-set RMSE (dB) for the retained environments.

- Environment A -

Method	RSSI	SINR
Sionna RT	16.98	17.94
Bias correction	13.58	15.13
Linear	6.16	**3.24**
Random Forest	8.10	7.62
RF + Linear	**4.72**	3.82

- Environment B -

Method	RSSI	SINR
Sionna RT	21.59	24.57
Bias correction	21.15	24.71
Linear	9.38	6.52
Random Forest	17.07	17.75
RF + Linear	**6.84**	**6.46**

The qualitative evaluation is plotted through the Fig. 5 shows the spatial distribution of the corrected residuals obtained with the RF+ Linear model in the two evaluation environments. The results indicate that most large errors observed in the origin l ray-tracing predictions are significantly reduced after applying the residual correction.

Overall, the proposed RF+Linear model substantially improves the accuracy of the Sionna RT predictions, reducing the test RMSE by 68.31% for RSSI and 73.71% for SINR compared with the raw simulated outputs.

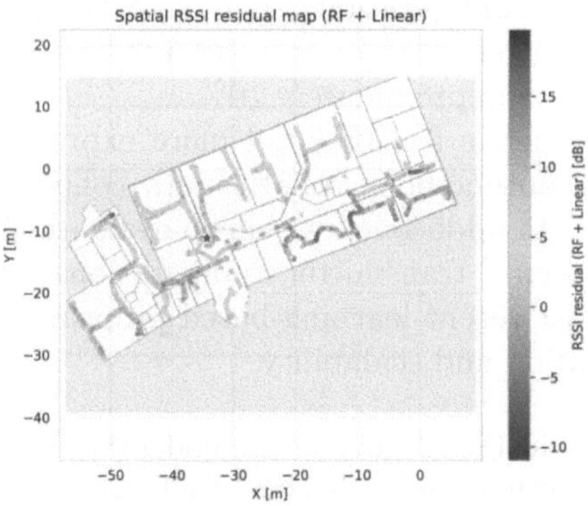

(a) Environnement A – RSSI

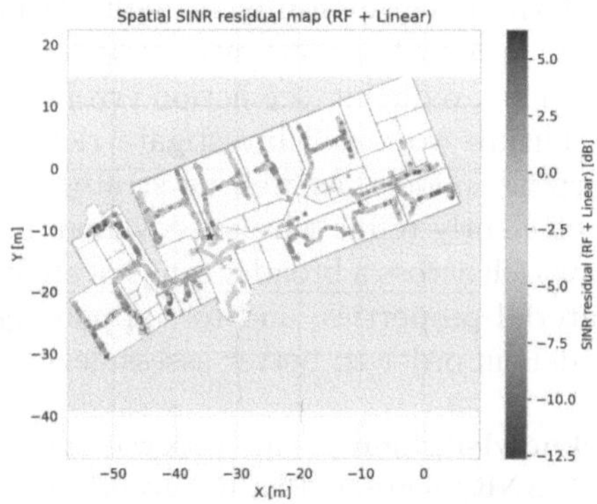

(b) Environnement A – SINR

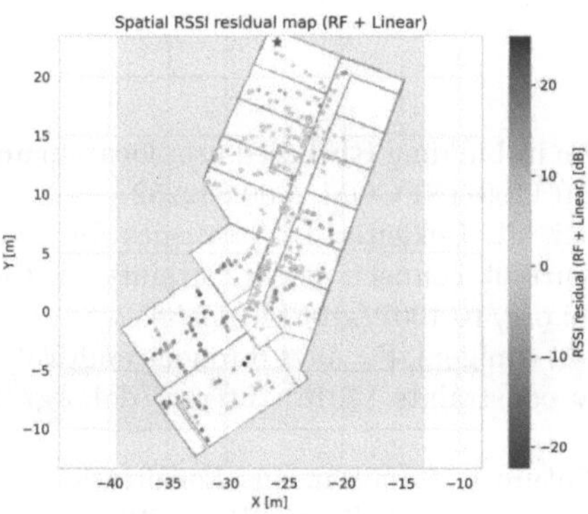

(c) Environnement B – RSSI

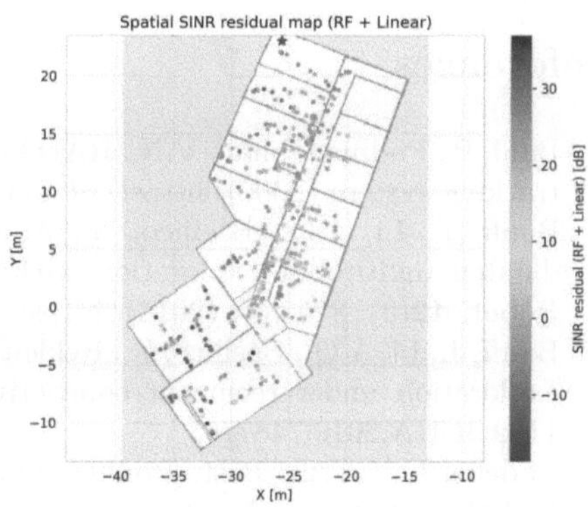

(d) Environnement B – SINR

Fig. 5. Spatial distribution of corrected residuals using the RF + Linear hybrid model in the two evaluation environments.

5 Conclusion

This paper presented a hybrid approach for improving indoor cellular coverage maps by combining physics-based ray tracing with robot-collected signal measurements. A mobile robot equipped with a 5G modem was used to collect RSSI and SINR measurements while building a map of the environment through SLAM. Using this map, a geometric model was generated and used to simulate radio propagation with the Sionna RT framework.

To compensate for discrepancies between simulated and measured signals, we introduced a residual learning model based on simple structural features, including transmitter–receiver distance and the number of intervening walls. The learned residual is added to the ray-tracing prediction to produce a corrected coverage map.

Experimental results in multiple indoor configurations show that the proposed approach significantly improves prediction accuracy compared to ray tracing alone, reducing prediction errors by up to approximately 70%.

Future work will investigate richer geometric features and more expressive learning models, as well as strategies for autonomous robotic data collection to efficiently refine wireless coverage maps. In addition, we plan to evaluate the approach across a broader range of environments, transmitter configurations, and material properties, and to compare against recent learning-based propagation models in order to better assess generalization and scalability.

Acknowledgment. This work was funded by the French government under the France 2030 ANR program "PEPR Networks of the Future" (ref. ANR-22-PEFT-0007).

References

1. Bahl, P., Padmanabhan, V.N.: RADAR: an in-building RF-based user location and tracking system (2000). https://doi.org/10.1109/INFCOM.2000.832252
2. Banfi, J., Li, A.Q., Basilico, N., Amigoni, F., Rekleitis, I.: Strategies for coordinated multirobot exploration with recurrent connectivity constraints. Auton. Robot. **42**(4), 875–894 (2018). https://doi.org/10.1007/s10514-017-9652-y
3. Banfi, J., Li, A.Q., Basilico, N., Rekleitis, I., Amigoni, F.: Asynchronous multirobot exploration under recurrent connectivity constraints (2016). https://doi.org/10.1109/ICRA.2016.7487763
4. Cadena, C., et al.: Past, Present, and Future of Simultaneous Localization and Mapping: Towards the Robust-Perception Age. IEEE Trans. Rob. **32**(6), 1309–1332 (2016). https://doi.org/10.1109/TRO.2016.2624754
5. Dixon, C., Frew, E.W.: Maintaining optimal communication chains in robotic sensor networks using mobility control (2009). https://doi.org/10.1109/ROBOT.2009.5152770
6. Fink, J., Kumar, V.: Online methods for radio signal mapping with mobile robots (2010). https://doi.org/10.1109/ROBOT.2010.5509607
7. Hess, W., Kohler, D., Rapp, H., Andor, D.: Real-time loop closure in 2D lidar slam (2016). https://doi.org/10.1109/ICRA.2016.7487258
8. Hoydis, J., et al.: Sionna: an open-source library for next-generation physical layer research. arXiv preprint arXiv:2203.11854 (2023), version 2, Mar 2023
9. Hoydis, J., Cammerer, S., Dörner, S., Ait Aoudia, F.: Sionna RT: Differentiable Ray Tracing for Radio Propagation Modeling (2023)
10. Hsieh, M.A., Kumar, V., Taylor, C.J.: Constructing radio signal strength maps with multiple robots (2004). https://doi.org/10.1109/ROBOT.2004.1308854
11. Jaeckel, S., Raschkowski, L., Börner, K., Thiele, L.: QuaDRiGa: a 3-D multi-cell channel model with time evolution for enabling virtual field trials. IEEE Trans. Antennas Propag. **62**(6), 3242–3256 (2014)
12. Ltaief, F., Lozenguez, G., Savard, A., Fabresse, L.: Toward robot-based validation of simulated 5G coverage maps in an industrial context (2025)
13. Miyagusuku, R., Yamashita, A., Asama, H.: Improving gaussian processes-based mapping of wireless signals using path loss models (2016). https://doi.org/10.1109/IROS.2016.7759625

14. Motley, A.J., Keenan, J.M.: Personal communication radio coverage in buildings at 900 mhz and 1700 mhz. Electron. Lett. **24**(12), 763–764 (1988). https://doi.org/10.1049/el:19880505
15. Orekondy, T., Kumar, P., Kadambi, S., Ye, H., Soriaga, J.B., Behboodi, A.: WiNeRT: towards neural ray tracing for wireless channel modelling and differentiable simulations (2023). https://openreview.net/forum?id=tPKKXeW33YU
16. Penumarthi, P.K., et al.: Multirobot exploration for building communication maps with prior from communication models (2017). https://doi.org/10.1109/MRS.2017.8250936
17. Ruah, N., Eldar, Y.C.: Federated learning for 6G robotics networks. IEEE J. Sel. Areas Commun. (2024, to appear)
18. Sabattini, L., Chopra, N., Secchi, C.: Decentralized connectivity maintenance for cooperative control of mobile robotic systems. Int. J. Robot. Res. **32**(12), 1411–1423 (2013). https://doi.org/10.1177/0278364913498912
19. Shin, H.J., Lee, C.E., Cho, Y.J.: Radio mapping scheme using collective intelligent robots for teleoperation in unstructured environments (2014). https://doi.org/10.1109/ROMAN.2014.6926356
20. Tekdas, O., Yang, Y.W., Isler, V.: Robotic routers: algorithms and implementation. Int. J. Robot. Res. **29**(1), 110–126 (2010). https://doi.org/10.1177/0278364909105053
21. Wireless InSite: Wireless InSite, 3D Wireless Prediction Software. https://www.remcom.com/wireless-insite-em-propagation-software

Cognitive Digital Twins for Smart Cities: Adaptive Agent-Based Urban Simulation with Online Learning

Elio Masciari and Enea Vincenzo Napolitano(✉)

University of Naples Federico II, Naples, Italy
{elio.masciari,eneavincenzo.napolitano}@unina.it

Abstract. Digital Twins are increasingly adopted in Smart Cities to simulate complex urban systems such as mobility and energy infrastructures. However, most existing approaches focus on physical dynamics while neglecting adaptive and goal-driven behavior of urban actors, limiting realistic policy evaluation. This paper introduces the Cognitive Digital Twin (CDT), an extension of the Digital Twin paradigm integrating adaptive agents endowed with goals, memory, and online decision-making capabilities. Urban entities are modeled as autonomous agents using contextual bandit learning to enable scalable and interpretable behavioral adaptation. We propose a formal CDT model, an agentic layered architecture, and a reproducible Python-based simulation framework. The approach is evaluated through mobility–energy simulations under baseline, policy, and stress scenarios involving 500 agents and multi-seed experiments. Results show that adaptive behavior produces emergent trade-offs between travel efficiency, energy consumption, and user utility, enabling behavior-aware policy analysis. The proposed CDT bridges physical simulation and adaptive multi-agent learning, providing a scalable decision-support framework for Smart City governance.

Keywords: Cognitive Digital Twin · Smart Cities · Agent-Based Simulation

1 Introduction

Digital Twins have emerged as a key enabling technology for Smart Cities, supporting monitoring, simulation, and optimization of complex urban systems such as transportation, energy, and infrastructure. Most existing Digital Twin implementations, however, focus primarily on the physical and operational layers of cities, modeling traffic flows, energy consumption, or resource utilization through deterministic, statistical, or rule-based approaches. While effective for descriptive analysis and short-term forecasting, these models often abstract away the intentions, goals, and adaptive decision-making processes of urban actors.

In real cities, urban dynamics are strongly shaped by the behavior of heterogeneous agents: citizens, institutions, and service providers, who continuously

G. Andresini et al. (Eds.): ISMIS 2026, LNAI 16685, pp. 272–281, 2027.
https://doi.org/10.1007/978-3-032-32643-0_23

adapt their actions in response to policies, incentives, congestion, and external events. Ignoring this cognitive and behavioral dimension limits the ability of traditional Digital Twins to support realistic policy evaluation, stress testing, and what-if analysis, especially in the presence of non-linear feedback loops and emergent collective phenomena.

To address this limitation, we introduce the concept of the *Cognitive Digital Twin* (CDT) [8], an extension of the Digital Twin paradigm that explicitly incorporates agent-level cognition, learning, and adaptation. In a CDT, urban entities are modeled as autonomous agents provided with goals, memory, and adaptive decision policies. System-level behavior then emerges endogenously from the interaction of many individual learning agents within a shared environment, rather than being imposed through fixed rules or equilibrium assumptions.

Unlike recent LLM-centered agentic approaches, CDT adopts lightweight learning agents to ensure interpretability and scalability.

In this work, we propose an agentic CDT framework for Smart Cities and demonstrate its feasibility through a simulation-based case study focused on urban mobility and energy dynamics. The framework combines a formal definition of CDT components, a layered agentic architecture, and a reproducible experimental pipeline supporting baseline, policy, and stress scenarios. Through systematic parameter sweeps and scenario analysis, we illustrate how adaptive agent behavior gives rise to meaningful and policy-relevant system-level patterns.

Unlike traditional agent-based models, CDT embeds learning policies as persistent components of a Digital Twin architecture, enabling continuous co-evolution between governance policies and agent behavior. This shifts Digital Twins from predictive replicas toward adaptive experimentation environments.

Contributions:

- Formal definition of Cognitive Digital Twins for urban systems.
- Agentic architecture integrating contextual-bandit learning agents.
- Reproducible simulation framework for policy and stress scenario analysis.

2 Related Work

Our work lies at the intersection of Urban Digital Twins for Smart Cities, multi-agent urban simulation, and adaptive decision-making through lightweight online learning. Unlike many existing Smart City Digital Twins that primarily replicate physical and infrastructural processes, we focus on a *Cognitive Digital Twin* (CDT) in which adaptive agents continuously update their decision policies, producing emergent system-level dynamics.

Urban Digital Twins for Smart Cities. Urban Digital Twins (UDTs) have emerged as a key paradigm for monitoring, simulation, and decision support in Smart Cities. Recent surveys highlight rapid growth in this area while identifying persistent challenges related to interoperability, data integration, and standardization, as well as the limited representation of human behavior within current models [5]. Studies comparing conceptual visions and real-world implementations further show significant variability in maturity levels and integration strategies across existing city-scale twins [4]. The notion of *Digital Twin City* extends this paradigm toward urban governance by combining IoT infrastructures, simulation, and AI-driven analytics [3], with applications supporting citizen participation and policy decision processes [7]. Nevertheless, planning-oriented perspectives emphasize that many digital twins still operate at aggregate levels, leaving behavior-aware and agent-centric modeling as an open challenge [1].

Multi-agent Urban Simulation. Agent-based modeling (ABM) and multi-agent simulation provide established tools for representing heterogeneous urban actors and decentralized interactions. Prior work demonstrates the effectiveness of ABM in modeling diverse urban phenomena, including mobility, land use, and infrastructure dynamics [2]. However, most existing models rely on predefined behavioral rules or offline calibration, limiting their ability to capture adaptive responses to policies, incentives, or unexpected disruptions. This constraint reduces their suitability for realistic policy evaluation and stress testing in dynamic urban environments.

Adaptive Decision-Making with Online Learning. Lightweight online learning methods offer a promising direction for improving behavioral realism while preserving scalability and interpretability. Contextual bandits, in particular, have been applied to adaptive decision-making problems in Smart City domains involving dynamic contexts and multi-objective optimization [6]. Despite these advances, online learning mechanisms are rarely embedded as *native decision policies* within city-scale digital twins.

Positioning of the Cognitive Digital Twin. The proposed CDT addresses this gap by integrating contextual-bandit learning directly at the agent level, enabling decentralized adaptation and emergent collective behavior within a digital twin environment. By bridging Digital Twin modeling, agent-based simulation, and online learning, the CDT supports behavior-aware scenario analysis and policy evaluation beyond static or rule-based urban simulations.

To better position the proposed Cognitive Digital Twin (CDT) with respect to existing approaches, Table 1 summarizes the main differences between Urban Digital Twins, Agent-Based Models, and learning-based urban simulation frameworks.

3 Cognitive Digital Twin: Concept and Formalization

We formalize the Cognitive Digital Twin (CDT) as an extension of the traditional Digital Twin paradigm in which adaptive, goal-driven agents explicitly model behavioral dynamics within an urban system.

Table 1. Comparison between existing urban modeling approaches and the proposed Cognitive Digital Twin (CDT).

Approach	Physical Modeling	Agents	Online Learning	Policy Evaluation
Urban Digital Twins	✓	–	–	Limited
Agent-Based Models (ABM)	Partial	✓	–	Partial
RL Urban Simulation	Partial	✓	✓	Limited scalability
CDT (ours)	✓	✓	✓	✓

3.1 CDT Model

A Cognitive Digital Twin is a discrete-time, agent-based representation of an urban environment where entities learn and adapt through interaction with both the environment and governance mechanisms. Unlike conventional Digital Twins, which mainly reproduce physical or infrastructural processes, the CDT embeds cognitive decision-making at the agent level.

Formally, a CDT is defined as the tuple

$$\langle \mathcal{S}, \mathcal{A}, \mathcal{O}, \Pi, f \rangle,$$

where $\mathcal{S}$ is the environment state space, $\mathcal{A}$ the set of agents, $\mathcal{O}$ the observation space, Π the set of agent policies, and f the system transition function.

The environment evolves in discrete time with state $s_t \in \mathcal{S}$ representing aggregate urban indicators such as congestion, energy consumption, and policy signals. State transitions depend on collective agent actions and external perturbations, enabling both endogenous dynamics and exogenous shocks.

Each agent $i \in \mathcal{A}$ operates under partial observability and is characterized by a local observation o_t^i, an internal memory state m_t^i, a set of goals g^i, and a policy π^i mapping perceived context and internal state to actions. This separation between global state and local perception reflects realistic information constraints in urban systems.

3.2 Adaptive Policies and Learning

Agent policies are implemented as adaptive decision mechanisms based on online contextual bandits. In the current instantiation, each policy π^i follows a LinUCB strategy that selects actions from a context vector derived from observations and memory. After each interaction, agents receive individual rewards and update policy parameters online, allowing behavior to evolve continuously in response to environmental and policy changes.

Contextual bandits are adopted to balance adaptivity, interpretability, and computational scalability in large agent populations.

Consequently, decision policies are not predefined rules but learned behaviors emerging from repeated interaction with the environment and other agents.

3.3 System Dynamics and Emergence

Let $a_t = \{a_t^i\}_{i \in \mathcal{A}}$ denote the set of actions selected at timestep t. The system evolves according to

$$s_{t+1} = f(s_t, a_t, \xi_t),$$

where ξ_t represents stochastic disturbances such as demand fluctuations or infrastructure disruptions.

The key distinction of the CDT lies in the continuous adaptation of agent policies. Macro-level patterns, e.g., congestion levels, modal split, or energy demand, emerge endogenously from decentralized learning processes rather than being explicitly encoded. This coupling between micro-level adaptation and system-level evolution enables behavior-aware scenario analysis and policy evaluation within complex urban environments.

4 Agentic Architecture

This section describes the agentic architecture of the proposed Cognitive Digital Twin (CDT), designed to transform urban observations into adaptive decisions and to generate emergent system-level dynamics through decentralized agent interaction.

4.1 Architecture Overview

The CDT follows a layered perception–decision–action architecture composed of four functional components: perception, cognitive core, institutional layer, and environment interaction. Together, these components enable agents to operate under partial observability while continuously adapting their behavior.

Perception Layer. Each agent observes a local representation of the urban environment through a compact context vector $\mathbf{x}_{i,t}$. The perceived context includes time-dependent features (e.g., normalized time of day), congestion indicators derived from demand–capacity relations, and policy signals such as mobility restrictions or incentives. This representation transforms heterogeneous urban information into features usable by the decision mechanism.

Cognitive core. The cognitive core implements goal-directed behavior and adaptive decision-making. Each agent maintains a short-term memory $m_{i,t}$ encoding recent outcomes and a set of goals g_i defining individual preferences. Decisions are produced through a contextual bandit policy based on LinUCB, balancing exploration and exploitation while updating parameters online from observed rewards. Memory introduces behavioral persistence and switching costs, preventing unrealistic volatility while preserving adaptability.

Institutional Layer. Governance mechanisms are represented by an authority agent that observes aggregate indicators and sets continuous policy variables (e.g., mobility restrictions or incentives). These policies modify agent rewards and feasible actions, enabling controlled policy experimentation and what-if analysis.

Environment Interaction. Agents operate within a shared environment where collective actions determine macro-level outcomes such as congestion and energy consumption. Updated system states feed back into agent observations and rewards, forming a closed perception–decision–feedback loop that drives adaptive dynamics.

4.2 Agent Types

The CDT models three interacting entity types: citizens, an authority, and infrastructure constraints.

CitizenAgent. A citizen agent represents an individual traveler selecting a mobility mode at each timestep from

$$\mathcal{A} = \{\texttt{car, transit, bike, telework}\}.$$

Given context $\mathbf{x}_{i,t}$, the agent selects an action $a_{i,t}$ using a LinUCB policy and receives a reward reflecting a generalized cost–utility trade-off:

$$r_{i,t} = -\alpha T_{i,t}(a_{i,t}) - \beta C_{i,t}(a_{i,t}) + \gamma I_t(a_{i,t}),$$

where travel time $T_{i,t}$, cost $C_{i,t}$, and policy incentives I_t are weighted by non-negative parameters α, β, γ. Rewards are used to update policies online, enabling continuous behavioral adaptation.

AuthorityAgent. The authority agent represents institutional decision-making by setting policy levels that influence system dynamics, such as restrictions on private car usage or incentives for sustainable mobility. This component allows simulation of governance interventions under baseline and stress scenarios.

Infrastructure. Infrastructure encodes capacity and structural constraints of the urban system, including transportation throughput and resource limits. These parameters influence congestion formation and reward realization and may vary under stress scenarios.

4.3 Architectural Properties

The CDT architecture exhibits three defining properties:

- **Autonomy:** agents act locally using partial observations and individual objectives;

- **Adaptation:** policies evolve online through contextual-bandit learning;
- **Emergence:** system-level patterns arise from decentralized interactions rather than predefined rules.

Overall, this architecture provides a modular foundation for behavior-aware digital twins, enabling scalable simulation of policy interventions and adaptive urban dynamics.

5 Experimental Design and Implementation

This section describes the experimental framework used to evaluate the proposed Cognitive Digital Twin (CDT), integrating simulation design, implementation details, and experimental protocol within a unified setup.

5.1 Simulation Framework

The CDT is implemented as a modular Python-based simulation environment integrating adaptive agents, an urban environment model, and a scenario-driven experimental controller. Citizen agents, the authority agent, and infrastructure constraints interact through a shared environment that aggregates individual actions, updates global indicators (e.g., congestion and energy demand), and returns rewards and observations at each timestep.

The simulation evolves in discrete time following a perception–decision–feedback loop. At each timestep, agents observe local contextual features, select mobility actions using LinUCB policies, and update their internal parameters based on received rewards. Aggregate outcomes modify the global system state, creating a closed feedback loop between micro-level learning and macro-level dynamics.

5.2 Experimental Design

Experiments are conducted through a systematic parameter sweep exploring heterogeneous urban conditions. The main parameters include:

- **Forced car fraction:** proportion of agents constrained to use private cars;
- **Forced telework fraction:** proportion of agents required to telework;
- **Extra demand:** additional agents injected during stress scenarios.

Each configuration is evaluated under three canonical scenarios:

- **Baseline:** no policy intervention or external perturbation;
- **Policy:** introduction of mobility restrictions or incentives;
- **Stress:** exogenous shocks such as increased demand or reduced capacity.

5.3 Experimental Protocol

Each simulation run includes 500 citizen agents and a horizon of 100 timesteps, allowing learning dynamics to stabilize. To account for stochastic variability, every configuration is executed across multiple random seeds and aggregate metrics are computed by averaging results.

System performance is evaluated using mean travel time, energy consumption, average reward, and modal split indicators. These metrics enable analysis of trade-offs induced by adaptive behavior, policy interventions, and environmental stressors.

All experiments are fully reproducible through an open-source implementation.

6 Results

Results are presented for both individual runs and aggregate statistics, with the aim of highlighting how adaptive agent behavior and policy interventions shape system-level performance.

6.1 Baseline Results and Scenario Comparison

Table 2 reports detailed simulation outputs for different random seeds under the default parameter configuration (no forced modes and no extra demand). For each seed, we report mean travel time, mean energy consumption, mean reward, and the fraction of agents using private cars, across the three scenarios.

Table 2. Simulation results for different seeds and scenarios (default parameters: Forced Car = 0, Forced Telework = 0, Extra Demand = 0)

Seed	Scenario	Mean Travel Time	Mean Energy	Mean Reward	Car Frac
0	baseline	0.5620	0.4055	−0.5929	0.01
0	policy	0.8999	0.2996	−0.4180	0.01
0	stress	0.5694	0.4065	−0.6051	0.012
1	baseline	0.5620	0.4055	−0.5926	0.01
1	policy	0.9068	0.2961	−0.4181	0.01
1	stress	0.5694	0.4065	−0.6047	0.012
2	baseline	0.5620	0.4056	−0.5937	0.01
2	policy	0.8912	0.3040	−0.4260	0.01
2	stress	0.5694	0.4065	−0.6057	0.012

Across seeds, the baseline scenario exhibits stable behavior with low car usage and moderate travel time and energy consumption. The policy scenario systematically reduces mean energy consumption and improves average reward, at the expense of increased travel time, reflecting the trade-offs induced by mobility restrictions. The stress scenario shows a slight increase in travel time and a degradation in reward, indicating reduced system efficiency under adverse conditions.

To provide a clearer comparison, Table 3 aggregates results across seeds for the default configuration.

Table 3. Aggregate metrics (3 seeds) by scenario, default parameters

Scenario	Mean Travel Time	Mean Energy	Mean Reward	Mean Car Fraction
baseline	0.5620	0.4055	−0.5929	0.01
policy	0.8999	0.2996	−0.4180	0.01
stress	0.5694	0.4065	−0.5930	0.01

These results confirm that policy interventions can significantly alter system-level outcomes even when individual agents adapt autonomously through learning. In particular, the policy scenario achieves lower energy consumption and higher average reward, demonstrating the CDT's ability to capture policy-driven behavioral shifts.

Beyond the default configuration, we analyze system sensitivity to key behavioral and environmental parameters. Varying the forced car fraction, forced telework fraction, and extra demand produces distinct and interpretable patterns.

Increasing the forced car fraction leads to higher congestion and travel time, particularly under stress conditions, as a larger share of agents is constrained to use high-impact mobility modes. Conversely, forced telework reduces overall demand and mitigates congestion effects. The introduction of extra demand amplifies congestion and energy consumption, and in combination with stress scenarios can push the system toward degraded performance regimes.

The results demonstrate that the CDT captures meaningful interactions, the observed patterns are consistent with intuitive expectations while emerging endogenously from the learning-based decision process, supporting the validity of the proposed agentic framework.

7 Discussion and Conclusion

This work introduced the Cognitive Digital Twin (CDT) as an extension of the Digital Twin paradigm for Smart Cities, explicitly incorporating adaptive, goal-driven decision-making at the agent level. By modeling citizens, institutions, and infrastructure as learning agents, the CDT enables urban dynamics to emerge from decentralized adaptation rather than predefined behavioral rules.

Experimental results demonstrate that adaptive agents respond coherently to policy interventions and external stressors, producing interpretable system-level patterns. In particular, the framework captures trade-offs between travel efficiency, energy consumption, and user utility, highlighting how governance strategies reshape collective outcomes through individual adaptation. Sensitivity analyses further show that policy effectiveness depends on population constraints and demand conditions, emphasizing the importance of behavior-aware modeling for realistic scenario analysis.

While the current evaluation is simulation-based, the framework is designed to support integration with real urban datasets in future deployments.

From a methodological perspective, the CDT bridges Digital Twin simulation, agent-based modeling, and lightweight online learning within a unified and reproducible framework. The proposed architecture enables scalable experimentation while preserving interpretability, making it suitable for policy evaluation and stress testing in complex urban environments.

The current implementation adopts linear contextual bandits (LinUCB), which provide stability and transparency but limit policy expressiveness. Additionally, the simulated environment is intentionally stylized to ensure experimental control, which may restrict direct real-world applicability. Future work will investigate richer learning models, data-driven calibration, and adaptive policy agents operating in more realistic urban settings.

References

1. Batty, M.: Digital twins in city planning. Nat. Comput. Sci. **4**(3), 192–199 (2024). https://doi.org/10.1038/s43588-024-00606-7
2. Crooks, A.T., Heppenstall, A., Malleson, N., Manley, E.: Agent-based modeling and the city: a gallery of applications. In: Urban Informatics, pp. 885–910. The Urban Book Series. Springer, Cham (2021). https://doi.org/10.1007/978-981-15-8983-6_46
3. Deng, T., Zhang, K., Shen, Z.J.M.: A systematic review of a digital twin city: a new pattern of urban governance toward smart cities. J. Manage. Sci. Eng. **6**(2), 125–134 (2021). https://doi.org/10.1016/j.jmse.2021.03.003
4. Jeddoub, I., Nys, G.A., Hajji, R., Billen, R.: Digital twins for cities: analyzing the gap between concepts and current implementations with a specific focus on data integration. Int. J. Appl. Earth Obs. Geoinf. **122**, 103440 (2023). https://doi.org/10.1016/j.jag.2023.103440
5. Mazzetto, S.: A review of urban digital twins integration, challenges, and future directions in smart city development. Sustainability **16**(19), 8337 (2024). https://doi.org/10.3390/su16198337
6. Qassimi, S., Rakrak, S.: Multi-objective contextual bandits in recommendation systems for smart tourism. Sci. Rep. **15**, 13669 (2025). https://doi.org/10.1038/s41598-025-89920-2
7. White, G., Zink, A., Codecá, L., Clarke, S.: A digital twin smart city for citizen feedback. Cities **110**, 103064 (2021). https://doi.org/10.1016/j.cities.2020.103064
8. Zheng, X., Lu, J., Kiritsis, D.: The emergence of cognitive digital twin: vision, challenges and opportunities. Int. J. Prod. Res. **60**(24), 7610–7632 (2022)

A Hybrid CNN-BiLSTM Approach for Whale Monitoring Using Distributed Acoustic Sensing System

Michel Dione[1(✉)], Jerry Lonlac[1], Helene Louis[1], Stephane Lecoeuche[2], and Anthony Fleury[1]

[1] IMT Nord Europe, Institut Mines-Telecom, Univ. Lille, Centre for Digital Systems Lille, Villeneuve-d'Ascq Cedex, France
michel.dione@imt-nord-europe.fr
[2] IMT Mines Ales, Institut Mines-Telecom, Ales, France

Abstract. Distributed Acoustic Sensing (DAS) technology has emerged as a powerful tool for large-scale acoustic monitoring, transforming standard fiber optic cables into dense arrays of virtual microphones. When combined with artificial intelligence, particularly deep learning, DAS enables scalable and automated detection of acoustic events, making it a promising solution for whale monitoring across vast marine environments. In the field of marine bioacoustics, DAS provides significant advantages in terms of spatial coverage and robustness compared to traditional hydrophone arrays. This paper presents a novel deep learning-based approach to detect whale vocalizations from DAS data. The proposed method leverages a hybrid architecture combining Convolutional Neural Networks (CNN) and Bidirectional Long Short-Term Memory (BiLSTM) networks to extract both spatial and temporal features from waterfall diagrams derived from DAS recordings. A multi-stage preprocessing pipeline including frequency filtering and frequency-wavenumber (f-k) filtering is applied to enhance signal quality and isolate whale calls from background noise. Each DAS recording is treated as a spatio-temporal matrix, and sequences of such matrices are sequentially analyzed capturing temporal dependencies. Experimental evaluations on a public dataset from the Ocean Observatories Initiative (OOI) RCA North Cable demonstrate that the CNN-BiLSTM model outperforms CNN and CNN-LSTM baselines, achieving a F1-score of 96% and an accuracy of 94%.

Keywords: Distributed Acoustic Sensing · Conventional Neural Network · Bidirectional Long Short-Term Memory · Ocean Wildlife Monitoring

1 Introduction

Distributed Acoustic Sensing (DAS) is an emerging technology capable of providing dense acoustic measurements over long distances by transforming optical

G. Andresini et al. (Eds.): ISMIS 2026, LNAI 16685, pp. 282–293, 2027.
https://doi.org/10.1007/978-3-032-32643-0_24

fibers into arrays of virtual sensors [6]. Its ability to capture vibration information (amplitude, frequency, phase) along tens of kilometers makes it highly attractive for applications such as infrastructure monitoring, geophysics, and transportation systems [2]. More recently, DAS has also been explored for wildlife monitoring, particularly in marine environments [3]. Despite its potential, DAS generates massive and noisy datasets, often reaching several terabytes, making data processing and analysis particularly challenging. Deep learning has emerged as a powerful solution to address these issues by enabling scalable and automated feature extraction from complex data [1,14,21].

In this work, we propose a deep learning approach for whale vocalization detection based on a hybrid CNN-BiLSTM architecture. CNNs are used to extract spatial features from DAS waterfall diagrams, while BiLSTMs capture temporal dependencies across sequential recordings. By modeling both spatial and temporal patterns, the proposed approach improves the detection of acoustic events in noisy DAS data. The core principle of our approach is to transform the acoustic detection problem into a visual recognition task, enabling the use of deep learning techniques for analyzing spatio-temporal patterns in DAS recordings. Thus, we proposed a hybrid deep learning model composed of a convolutional neural network (CNN) and a bidirectional long short-term memory (BiLSTM). The remaining of this paper is structured as follows. Section 2 reviews the related work relevant to our study. Section 3 details the methodology, including the configuration of the DAS system, the data structure, and our proposed hybrid CNN-BiLSTM approach. Section 4 presents the experimental results obtained using the OOI dataset which is described in [23], and discusses the key findings. Finally, Sect. 5 concludes with a summary of the main contributions and outlines directions for future research.

2 Related Work

Distributed Acoustic Sensing (DAS) has emerged as a powerful technology for large-scale monitoring in domains such as infrastructure surveillance, geotechnical engineering, and underwater sensing [2,9]. Its integration with artificial intelligence, particularly deep learning, has significantly improved event detection and classification capabilities [1]. Early works demonstrated the effectiveness of DAS combined with deep learning for applications such as railway monitoring, achieving high accuracy [7]. However, these approaches generally rely on single-recording analysis and limited temporal modeling, restricting their applicability to dynamic scenarios such as marine bioacoustics. In parallel, DAS has been successfully applied to whale monitoring using physics-based methods such as TDOA [3], though these approaches lack scalability and automation. In Passive Acoustic Monitoring (PAM), deep learning models such as CNNs have shown strong performance for whale call detection [4,5]. Nevertheless, these methods are designed for 1D hydrophone signals and do not generalize to DAS data, which are inherently spatio-temporal.

Unlike traditional acoustic signals, DAS recordings are structured as 2D spatio-temporal matrices, requiring models capable of jointly capturing spatial propagation patterns and temporal dynamics. Existing approaches remain limited: some flatten the data into 1D vectors [19], leading to high dimensionality and inefficiency, while others convert signals into images for CNN-based classification [14], without modeling temporal dependencies across recordings. Overall, current methods struggle to handle the high dimensionality, noise, and complex spatio-temporal structure of DAS data, particularly in challenging environments such as marine ecosystems [2]. This highlights the need for dedicated architectures tailored to DAS-based bioacoustic monitoring.

To address these limitations, we propose a hybrid CNN-BiLSTM model designed to process 2D DAS waterfall diagrams while capturing both spatial features within recordings and temporal dependencies across sequences. This approach enables scalable and accurate detection of whale vocalizations over large spatial extents.hnology. The details of our methodology are presented in the next section.

3 Methodology

In this section, we first introduce the general structure of DAS data, which partly motivates our proposed approach detailed in the final part of this section. Next, we provide an overview of the waterfall diagram, a key tool for visualizing spatio-temporal patterns in DAS recordings. Finally, we detail our proposed deep learning-based approach for detecting acoustic events, specifically applied to whale monitoring through their vocalizations.

3.1 Distributed Acoustic Sensing (DAS) System

DAS utilizes Rayleigh backscattering to measure sound or vibrations along an optical fiber over ultra-long distances [18]. The operation of the DAS system is based on the propagation of light pulses within the optical fiber. Sensitive to acoustic signals generated by various vibratory sources along the fiber [15], the optical fiber undergoes deformations caused by these acoustic signals. These deformations, which induce changes in the Rayleigh back-scattering, are measured at specific points called *channels* (virtual sensors) distributed along the fiber. The measurements depend on the DAS configuration set at the interrogator. The main configuration parameters are as follows:

- **Sampling frequency** (fs): Rate of strain measurements; in Hertz (Hz).
- **Spatial resolution** (dx): Distance between virtual sensors (measurement points); in meters (m).
- **Fiber length** (fl): Total fiber length used; in meters (m).
- **Number of channels** (nx): Total number of measurement points.
- **Gauge length** (gl): Size of each virtual sensor; in meters (m).

The operating principle of the *DAS* technology is illustrated in Fig. 1.

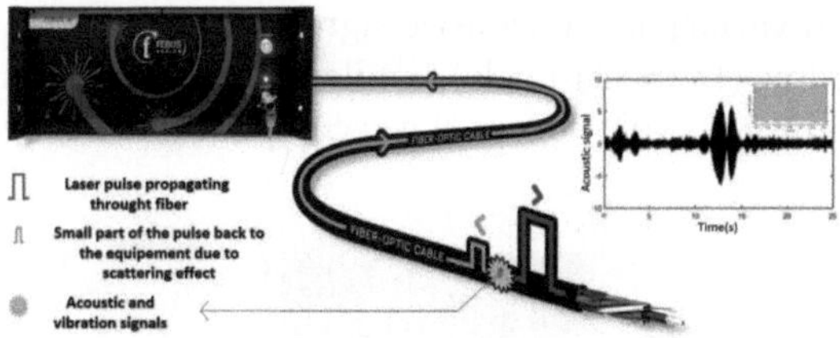

Fig. 1. Distributed Acoustic Sensing Principle [24]

3.2 Spatio-Temporal Representation in DAS

A DAS recording is structured as spatio-temporal data, represented as follows:

$$\mathbf{X} = \begin{bmatrix} X_{1,1} & X_{1,2} & \cdots & X_{1,n} \\ X_{2,1} & X_{2,2} & \cdots & X_{2,n} \\ \vdots & \vdots & \ddots & \vdots \\ X_{m,1} & X_{m,2} & \cdots & X_{m,n} \end{bmatrix} \tag{1}$$

This X matrix provides a detailed overview of the data structure recorded by the DAS system in its configured state. Each row corresponds to a sampling instant t_i, and each column represents a measurement point along the optical fiber. For $i \in [1, m]$ and $j \in [1, n]$, where $m = fs \times T$ (T recording duration) and $n = nx$ (see Table 1), $X_{i,j}$, expressed in microstrain ($\mu\xi$) units, denotes the phase strain measurement of Rayleigh backscattered light at position j along the fiber at sampling instant t_i.

Table 1. Configuration of the DAS system on the OOI RCA North Cable [11].

Parameters	Values
Sampling frequency (Hz)	200
Spatial resolution (m)	2.04
Fiber length (Km)	66.6
Number of channels	32,600
Gauge length (m)	51.04

With this configuration detailed in Table 1, DAS recordings are continuously acquired, each recording having a duration of 60 s. As shown in the matrix X, each recording is a two-dimensional, precisely spatio-temporal data structure consisting of 12,000 rows (temporal dimension) and 32,600 columns (spatial dimension). This structure represents the phase strain measurements over time for all channels along the optical fiber.

Figure 2 presents an example of a waterfall diagram generated from a DAS recording (filtered data) acquired by the OOI RCA North Cable. It visualizes the spatio-temporal variations of acoustic signals. The horizontal axis represents the spatial dimension (DAS channels), while the vertical axis represents time, illustrating the temporal evolution of the recorded acoustic signals.

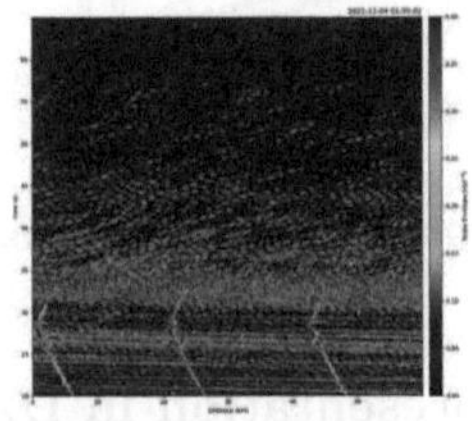

Fig. 2. Waterfall diagram from a DAS recording on the OOI RCA North Cable.

3.3 Proposed Approach

Processing DAS data presents numerous challenges due to its:

- Massive data volume: Each 60-second OOI DAS recording generates approximately 570 MB, accumulating to terabytes of data over extended periods, making storage and processing highly demanding.
- High noise levels: Submarine acoustic data acquisition captures diverse signals from various sources, including passing ships, submarine earthquakes, whale calls, etc. Effectively isolating whale calls from background noise remains a significant challenge.
- Complex feature extraction: The spatio-temporal nature of DAS data introduces dependencies both within individual recordings and across successive recordings. Extracting meaningful features while preserving these dependencies is particularly challenging, especially for OOI DAS data.

To address these challenges and achieve efficient acoustic event detection, particularly for whale calls, we propose an approach consisting of two main stages detailed below:

1. **Data pre-processing:**
   DAS data often contain various noise types that degrade the signal-to-noise ratio, potentially obscuring signals of interest. To enhance data quality, targeted denoising techniques are applied. Given that whale vocalizations have known frequency characteristics, appropriate filtering methods are used to suppress background noise and improve detection accuracy (Fig. 3).
   As shown in Figure **(a)**, the raw DAS data is visually saturated with background noise, preventing any meaningful identification of acoustic events such as whale vocalizations. To enhance the visibility of the acoustic signals of interest, we apply a band-pass filter between 10 and 30 Hz. According to [11], the vocalization frequency of fin whales is estimated at approximately 20 Hz.

By applying this filter to the raw data, we obtain the enhanced result illustrated in Figure **(b)**. In **(b)**, whale calls appear clearly over several kilometers along the fiber, forming a characteristic "V" shape [11]. While the acoustic signals are significantly enhanced compared to Figure **(a)**, persistent background noise remains in certain areas. To better isolate whale vocalizations, we apply an additional frequency-wavenumber (f,k) filtering step [22]. Using a 2D Fourier transform, the data is projected into the (f,k) domain, where specific filtering techniques are applied to extract fin whale calls. We utilize a band-pass filter (1480–3400 m/s) and a notch filter (1400–3500 m/s) to suppress unwanted noise while preserving relevant acoustic signals. Applying this filter to the raw data illustrated in **(b)**, we obtain the more enhanced result illustrated in Figure **(c)**. By applying this pre-processing pipeline to the entire dataset, we significantly enhance data quality, making it easier to distinguish whale vocalizations. This improvement is crucial to effectively detect whale calls using deep learning techniques. From the filtered data, we generate waterfall diagrams, which provide a visual representation of the spatio-temporal evolution of acoustic signals captured by the DAS system. These diagrams are then processed as time-series images by a deep learning model, designed to recognize specific patterns, such as the characteristic "V" shape associated with whale calls.

2. **CNN-BiLSTM Model**

Our objective is to develop a deep learning model capable of processing spatio-temporal 2D data structures derived from DAS recordings for acoustic event detection. Each DAS recording is inherently structured as a 2D matrix, as described in Table 1. However, since these recordings are acquired sequentially over time, the detection task requires processing not just individual 2D DAS matrices but an entire sequence of these recordings to capture potential temporal correlations. To achieve robust event detection, the deep learning model must take into account two key dependencies:

(a) **Spatial dependencies** within each recording, where neighboring fiber [1.] channels may exhibit correlated strain responses due to a propagating acoustic wave.

(b) **Temporal dependencies** across successive DAS recordings, where acoustic events may persist or evolve over multiple time windows, necessitating a model that can track such patterns over time.

A suitable deep learning approach must therefore be able to efficiently extract spatial correlations (fiber positions) within each recording while simultaneously learning temporal relationships across consecutive DAS recordings to improve event detection accuracy. To address these challenges, we propose a hybrid deep learning model, named **CNN-BiLSTM**, for detecting acoustic events, such as whale calls. The model consists of two key components:

– **Feature Extraction with CNN**: the input to the model is a grayscale image (128 × 128 pixels) representing a waterfall diagram of a DAS recording. The convolutional block begins with a 2D convolutional layer with 32 filters and a kernel size of (3 × 3), using ReLU activation, followed by

a max-pooling layer (2×2) to reduce spatial resolution. A second convolutional layer with 64 filters and the same activation and pooling operations follows. These layers progressively extract spatial features relevant to acoustic patterns, particularly the "V"-shaped structures associated with whale vocalizations. The resulting feature maps are then flattened and reshaped into a format suitable for temporal modeling.
- **Temporal Analysis with BiLSTM**: The reshaped feature sequence is fed into a Bidirectional Long Short-Term Memory (BiLSTM) layer with 32 hidden units. This layer analyzes the input in both forward and backward temporal directions, allowing the model to capture past and future dependencies, which is particularly useful for detecting events spanning multiple consecutive images. The output is passed through a fully connected dense layer of 128 units using ReLU activation, followed by a dropout layer (rate = 0.4) to prevent overfitting. Finally, a sigmoid-activated output neuron performs binary classification to indicate the presence or absence of a whale vocalization.

The model is trained using a binary cross-entropy loss function and optimized with the Adam optimizer (learning rate = 0.001). The training process uses a batch size of 16 over 100 epochs. This architecture, fine-tuned through hyperparameter optimization, achieved a test accuracy of **94%**, demonstrating strong robustness in detecting acoustic events in DAS data particularly for the recognition of whale vocalizations.

Figure 4 illustrates Overview of the proposed DAS-based whale call detection pipeline using a hybrid CNN-BiLSTM model.

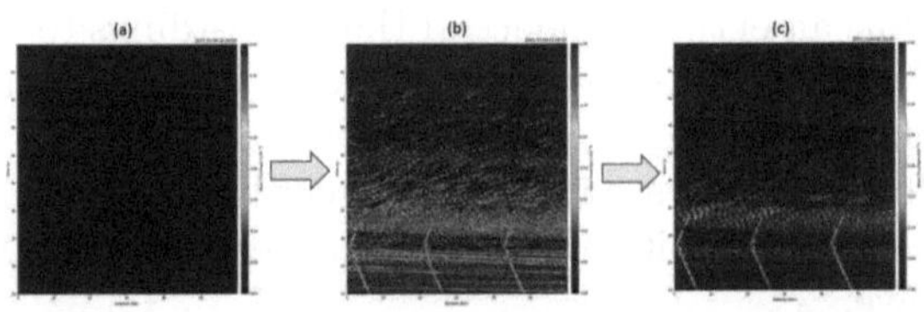

Fig. 3. Progressive Denoising of DAS Waterfall Diagrams: (a) Raw Data, (b) Pass-Band Frequency Filtering, (c) Wave Propagation Speed Filtering.

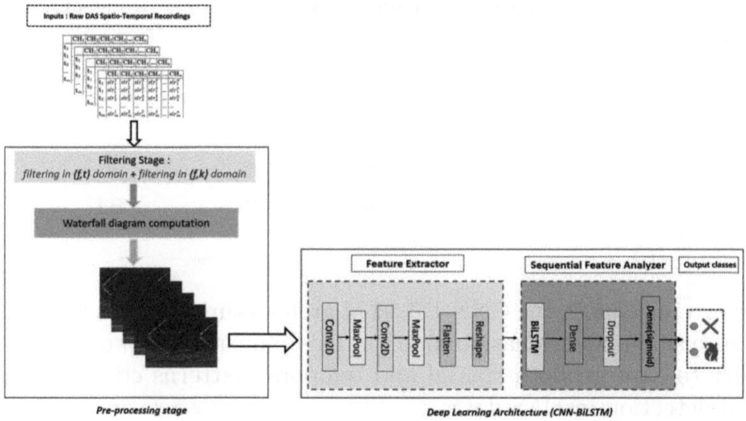

Fig. 4. Overview of the proposed whale call detection pipeline using DAS data and a hybrid CNN-BiLSTM model. The process includes spatio-temporal filtering, waterfall diagram generation, and classification via a CNN-BiLSTM model.

4 Results and Discussions

The dataset used in this study is a subset of the OOI RCA North Cable DAS recordings, which are publicly accessible online[1]. Each recording lasts 60 s and is structured as a spatio-temporal matrix, capturing the strain measurements across thousands of fiber channels over time. This dataset is divided for model development as follows: 80% of the dataset is allocated for training and validation, while the remaining 20% is reserved for testing. Within the training set, the data is further split into two subsets: one for model training (80%) and the other for validation.

4.1 Performance Evaluation

We evaluated the performance of our proposed CNN-BiLSTM model for DAS-based whale call detection using four standard classification metrics: accuracy, precision, recall, and F1-score. Table 2 compares the performance of three deep learning architectures CNN, CNN-LSTM, and our proposed CNN-BiLSTM trained and evaluated on the same DAS-based whale vocalization dataset. These architectures are inspired by existing models from the literature [7,14], and have been adapted to address the challenges of continuous marine mammal monitoring using DAS technology.

[1] http://piweb.ooirsn.uw.edu/das/data/Optasense/NorthCable/TransmitFiber/North-C1-LR-P1kHz-GL50m-Sp2m-FS200Hz_2021-11-03T15_06_51-0700/.

Table 2. Performance Comparison of Different Deep Learning Models for DAS-based Whale Monitoring

Model	Precision (%)	Recall (%)	F1-score (%)	Accuracy (%)
CNN [14]	82,35	98	89,50	83,21
CNN-LSTM [7]	93	92	93	90
CNN-BiLSTM (ours)	**97**	**94**	**96**	**94**

As shown in Table 2, the CNN-BiLSTM architecture achieves the best overall performance across all evaluation metrics. This confirms its robustness and superior ability to capture both spatial and temporal patterns critical for accurate whale call detection in DAS data.

To further illustrate model behavior, Fig. 5 presents the confusion matrices corresponding to each model. The CNN model achieves a high recall rate but generates a larger number of false positives, resulting in lower precision and revealing a limited ability to distinguish whale vocalizations from background noise. The CNN-LSTM model introduces temporal modeling, leading to more balanced predictions and improved reliability. Our proposed CNN-BiLSTM model further enhances performance by significantly reducing both false positives and false negatives, delivering the most consistent and accurate detection results.

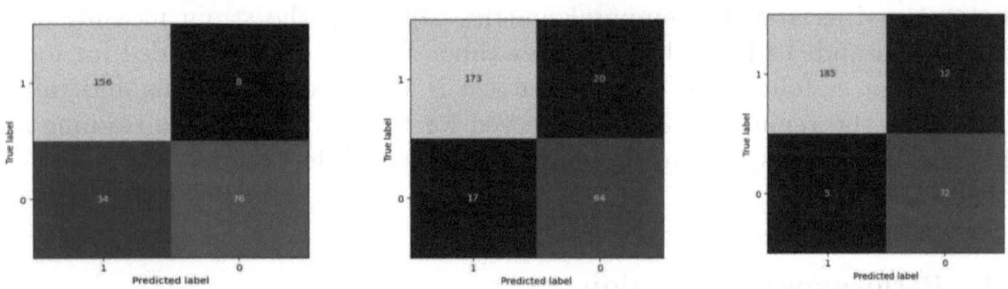

(a) CNN (b) CNN-LSTM (c) CNN-BiLSTM

Fig. 5. Confusion matrices for CNN, CNN-LSTM, and CNN-BiLSTM models.

4.2 Discussion

The results in Table 2 highlight the importance of jointly modeling spatial and temporal information for DAS-based whale call detection. The CNN baseline [14] achieves high recall (98%) but lower precision (82.35%), indicating a tendency to generate false positives due to its inability to capture temporal dependencies in noisy spatio-temporal data.

Introducing temporal modeling with CNN-LSTM significantly improves performance, with both precision and recall exceeding 90%. This confirms that sequential modeling helps better discriminate whale calls from background noise. However, the unidirectional nature of LSTM limits its ability to fully exploit temporal context.

The proposed CNN-BiLSTM model achieves the best performance (97% precision, 94% recall, 94% accuracy), demonstrating the benefit of bidirectional temporal modeling. By capturing both past and future dependencies, it provides a more robust and balanced detection, reducing both false positives and false negatives.

Overall, these results emphasize the necessity of combining spatial feature extraction with advanced temporal modeling for DAS data. Future improvements could include attention mechanisms to focus on informative regions and optimization for real-time deployment in large-scale marine monitoring systems.

5 Conclusion

To the best of our knowledge, this study presents the first application of a deep learning approach for whale monitoring using Distributed Acoustic Sensing (DAS) system. The proposed CNN-BiLSTM model achieves strong performance in detecting whale vocalizations, with 94% accuracy, 97% precision, 94% recall, and a 96% F1-score. These results highlight the model's ability to learn both spatial features (across fiber channels) and temporal patterns (across successive recordings). A key aspect of this work lies in the preprocessing pipeline, which includes band-pass filtering to isolate the frequency band of whale calls (around 20 Hz), followed by frequency-wavenumber (f-k) filtering to eliminate background noise and irrelevant wave modes. This process enhances the signal-to-noise ratio and improves the visibility of whale vocalizations in the resulting waterfall diagrams. While the results are promising, future work may focus on optimizing computational efficiency, expanding the dataset for better generalization, and incorporating attention mechanisms. This approach could also be extended to multi-label classification of marine acoustic events, including species-specific vocalizations, vessel detection, or seismic activity. Detecting abnormal call patterns could provide insights into whale health and environmental conditions.

References

1. Rahman, J., Taheri, H., Dababneh, F., Karganroudi, S.S., Arhamnamazi, S.: A review of distributed acoustic sensing applications for railroad condition monitoring. Philos. Trans. R. Soc. Lond. **208**, 110983 (2024)
2. Ghazali, M.F., et al.: State-of-the-art application and challenges of optical fibre distributed acoustic sensing in civil engineering. Opt. Fiber Technol. **87**, 103911 (2024)
3. Bouffaut, L., et al.: Eavesdropping at the speed of light: distributed acoustic sensing of baleen whales in the Arctic. Front. Mar. Sci. **9**, 901348 (2022)

4. Kirsebom, O.S., Frazao, F., Simard, Y., Roy, N., Matwin, S., Giard, S.: Performance of a deep neural network at detecting North Atlantic right whale upcalls. J. Acoust. Soc. Am. (2020)
5. Sagredo, B., Español-Jiménez, S., Tobar, F.: Detection of blue whale vocalisations using a temporal-domain convolutional neural network. In: 2021 IEEE Latin American Conference on Computational Intelligence (LA-CCI), pp. 1–5. IEEE (2021)
6. He, Z., Liu, Q.: Optical fiber distributed acoustic sensors: a review. J. Lightwave Technol. (2021)
7. Rahman, M.A., Jamal, S., Taheri, H.: Remote condition monitoring of rail tracks using distributed acoustic sensing (DAS): a deep CNN-LSTM-SW based model. Green Energy Intell. Transp. (2024)
8. Belghith, E.H., Rioult, F., Bouzidi, M.: Acoustic diversity classifier for automated marine big data analysis. In: Proceedings of the 2018 IEEE 30th International Conference on Tools with Artificial Intelligence (ICTAI), pp. 130–136. IEEE (2018)
9. Lior, I., et al.: On the detection capabilities of underwater distributed acoustic sensing. J. Geophys. Res.: Solid Earth (2021)
10. Rahman, M.A., Kim, J., Dababneh, F., Taheri, H.: Railroad condition monitoring with distributed acoustic sensing: an investigation of deep learning methods for condition detection. J. Appl. Remote Sens. (2024)
11. Wilcock, W.S.D., Abadi, S., Lipovsky, B.P.: Distributed acoustic sensing recordings of low-frequency whale calls and ship noise offshore Central Oregon. JASA Express Lett. (2023)
12. Wen, L., Zhou, K., Yang, S., Lu, X.: Optimal load dispatch of community microgrid with deep learning based solar power and load forecasting. Energy **171**, 1053–1065 (2019)
13. Zhou, Y., Chang, F.-J., Chang, L.-C., Kao, I.-F., Wang, Y.-S.: Explore a deep learning multi-output neural network for regional multi-step-ahead air quality forecasts. J. Clean. Prod. (2019)
14. Bublin, M.: Event detection for distributed acoustic sensing: combining knowledge-based, classical machine learning, and deep learning approaches. Sensors **21**, 7527 (2021)
15. Jiang, F., Li, H., Zhang, Z., Zhang, X.: An event recognition method for fiber distributed acoustic sensing systems based on the combination of MFCC and CNN. In: International Conference on Optical Instruments and Technology: Advanced Optical Sensors and Applications, SPIE (2018)
16. Arpison, G.: Nouvelle stratégie de mesure d'ondes acoustiques par capteur à fibre optique distribuée. Ph.D. thesis, Université Grenoble Alpes (2021)
17. Shatalin, S., Parker, T., Farhadiroushan, M.: High definition seismic and microseismic data acquisition using distributed and engineered fiber optic acoustic sensors. In: Distributed Acoustic Sensing in Geophysics: Methods and Applications, pp. 1–32. Wiley Online Library (2021)
18. Xie, Y., Wang, M., Zhong, Y., Deng, L., Zhang, J.: Label-free anomaly detection using distributed optical fiber acoustic sensing. Sensors **23**, 4094 (2023)
19. Alam, A., Das, A., Tasjid, M.S., Marouf, A.A.: Leveraging sensor fusion and sensor-body position for activity recognition for wearable mobile technologies. Int. J. Interact. Mob. Technol. (2021)
20. Yang, L., Fomel, S., Wang, S., Chen, X., Chen, Y.: Denoising distributed acoustic sensing data using unsupervised deep learning. Geophysics (2023)
21. Dumont, V., Tribaldos, V.R., Ajo-Franklin, J., Wu, K.: Deep learning for surface wave identification in distributed acoustic sensing data. In: IEEE International Conference on Big Data (Big Data), pp. 1293–1300 (2020)

22. Zhou, H.-W.: Practical Seismic Data Analysis. Cambridge University Press (2014)
23. Ocean Observatories Initiative (OOI): OOI RCA DAS Dataset – Processed Data (2021). http://piweb.ooirsn.uw.edu/das/processed/metadata/readme.pdf
24. Jestin, C., Hibert: integration of machine learning on distributed acoustic sensing surveys. Copernicus Meetings (2020)

Author Index

G. Andresini et al. (Eds.): ISMIS 2026, LNAI 16685, pp. 295–296, 2027.
https://doi.org/10.1007/978-3-032-32643-0

MIX
Papier aus verantwortungsvollen Quellen
Paper from responsible sources
FSC® C105338
FSC
www.fsc.org

If you have any concerns about our products,
you can contact us on
ProductSafety@springernature.com

In case Publisher is established outside the EU,
the EU authorized representative is:
Springer Nature Customer Service Center GmbH
Europaplatz 3, 69115 Heidelberg, Germany

Printed by Libri Plureos GmbH
in Hamburg, Germany